ANNUAL ED

American History
Volume II
Reconstruction through the Present

16th Edition

EDITOR

Robert James Maddox
Pennsylvania State University
University Park

Robert James Maddox, distinguished historian and professor of American history at Pennsylvania State University, received a B.S. from Fairleigh Dickinson University in 1957, an M.S. from the University of Wisconsin in 1958, and a Ph.D. from Rutgers in 1964. Dr. Maddox has written, reviewed, and lectured extensively, and he is widely respected for his interpretations of presidential character and policy.

McGraw-Hill/Dushkin
530 Old Whitfield Street, Guilford, Connecticut 06437

Visit us on the Internet
http://www.dushkin.com

Credits

1. Reconstruction and the Gilded Age
Unit photo—Courtesy of the National Archives.
2. The Emergence of Modern America
Unit photo—Courtesy of the National Archives.
3. From Progressivism to the 1920s
Unit photo—Courtesy of the Collections of Henry Ford Museum and Greenfield Village.
4. From the Great Depression to World War II
Unit photo—Courtesy of Library of Congress.
5. From the Cold War to 2000
Unit photo—Associated Press.
6. New Directions for American History
Unit photo—Courtesy New York State Department of Commerce.

Copyright

Cataloging in Publication Data
Main entry under title: Annual Editions: American History, Vol. Two: Reconstruction through the Present. 16/E.
  1. United States—History—periodicals. 2. United States—Historiography—Periodicals. 3. United States—Civilization—Periodicals. I. Maddox, Robert James, comp. II. Title: American history, vol. two: Reconstruction through the present.
ISBN 0–07–242582–2   973'.05   75–20755   ISSN 0733-3560

© 2001 by McGraw-Hill/Dushkin, Guilford, CT 06437, A Division of The McGraw-Hill Companies.

Copyright law prohibits the reproduction, storage, or transmission in any form by any means of any portion of this publication without the express written permission of McGraw-Hill/Dushkin, and of the copyright holder (if different) of the part of the publication to be reproduced. The Guidelines for Classroom Copying endorsed by Congress explicitly state that unauthorized copying may not be used to create, to replace, or to substitute for anthologies, compilations, or collective works.

Annual Editions® is a Registered Trademark of McGraw-Hill/Dushkin, A Division of The McGraw-Hill Companies.

Sixteenth Edition

Cover image © 2001 PhotoDisc, Inc.

Printed in the United States of America   4567890BAHBAH54321   Printed on Recycled Paper

Members of the Advisory Board are instrumental in the final selection of articles for each edition of ANNUAL EDITIONS. Their review of articles for content, level, currentness, and appropriateness provides critical direction to the editor and staff. We think that you will find their careful consideration well reflected in this volume.

EDITOR

Robert James Maddox
Pennsylvania State University
University Park

ADVISORY BOARD

Arthur H. Auten
University of Hartford

Neal A. Brooks
Community College of
Baltimore County, Essex

Nancy Gentile-Ford
Bloomsburg University

Celia Hall-Thur
Wenatchee Valley College

Melvin G. Holli
University of Illinois

Harry Russell Huebel
Texas A & M University

Wilma King
University of Missouri
Columbia

Carl E. Kramer
Indiana University
Southeast

Larry Madaras
Howard Community College

Ronald McCoy
Emporia State University

Rameth Owens
Clemson University

Robert C. Pierce
Foothill College

John Snetsinger
California Polytechnic University

Irvin D. Solomon
Florida Gulf Coast University

James R. Sweeney
Old Dominion University

EDITORIAL STAFF

Ian A. Nielsen, Publisher
Roberta Monaco, Senior Developmental Editor
Dorothy Fink, Associate Developmental Editor
Addie Raucci, Senior Administrative Editor
Cheryl Greenleaf, Permissions Editor
Joseph Offredi, Permissions/Editorial Assistant
Diane Barker, Proofreader
Lisa Holmes-Doebrick, Senior Program Coordinator

TECHNOLOGY STAFF

Richard Tietjen, Senior Publishing Technologist
Jonathan Stowe, Director of Technology
Janice Ward, Technology Editorial Assistant

PRODUCTION STAFF

Brenda S. Filley, Director of Production
Charles Vitelli, Designer
Laura Levine, Graphics
Mike Campbell, Graphics
Tom Goddard, Graphics
Eldis Lima, Graphics
Nancy Norton, Graphics
Juliana Arbo, Typesetting Supervisor
Marie Lazauskas, Typesetter
Karen Roberts, Typesetter
Larry Killian, Copier Coordinator

To the Reader

In publishing ANNUAL EDITIONS we recognize the enormous role played by the magazines, newspapers, and journals of the public press in providing current, first-rate educational information in a broad spectrum of interest areas. Many of these articles are appropriate for students, researchers, and professionals seeking accurate, current material to help bridge the gap between principles and theories and the real world. These articles, however, become more useful for study when those of lasting value are carefully collected, organized, indexed, and reproduced in a low-cost format, which provides easy and permanent access when the material is needed. That is the role played by ANNUAL EDITIONS.

New to ANNUAL EDITIONS is the inclusion of related World Wide Web sites. These sites have been selected by our editorial staff to represent some of the best resources found on the World Wide Web today. Through our carefully developed topic guide, we have linked these Web resources to the articles covered in this ANNUAL EDITIONS reader. We think that you will find this volume useful, and we hope that you will take a moment to visit us on the Web at *http://www.dushkin.com* to tell us what you think.

Some scholars have pointed out how much the "velocity of history" has speeded up. If one were to go back in the past to the year 1800, conditions would not have changed all that much from what they had been 100 or 150 years earlier. People wore much of the same clothing, ate the same foods cooked in the same way, traveled overland on foot or horseback, and relied on the same remedies for illnesses. In the 140 years since the end of the Civil War, however, revolutionary changes have taken place in virtually all areas. Following the development of automobiles, people were able to travel in just hours distances that would have taken days. Airplanes have put any place on the globe within reach. Radio, television, and computers have vastly changed the transmission of knowledge, earlier restricted to word of mouth or the printed page. Still, many of the issues we confront today have echoes in the past: race relations, gender roles, domestic terrorism, and environmental problems, to name just a few. We can all profit from studying history, not to get "answers" to our problems but perhaps to discover in the past some guidelines for our own time.

The study of history has changed over the years. Early scholars mostly wrote about "chaps," usually prominent white men of achievement. Now virtually everything that has happened is considered fair game. Books and articles tell us about the lives of ordinary people, about groups previously ignored or mentioned only in passing, and about subjects previously considered too trivial or commonplace to warrant examination. History "from the bottom up," once considered innovative, has become commonplace.

New approaches to the study of history complement, but do not replace, the more traditional emphasis upon people who made large differences as *individuals.* Presidents such as Woodrow Wilson and Franklin D. Roosevelt had to make decisions that affected tens of thousands if not millions of lives. The Reverend Martin Luther King Jr. provided inspiration through his oratory and presence that people of lesser gifts could not have hoped to achieve. Margaret Sanger and Eleanor Roosevelt, though never holding official positions of power, nonetheless exercised influence over the ways that people perceived a number of issues.

This sixteenth edition of *Annual Editions: American History, Volume II,* constitutes an effort to provide a balanced collection of articles that deal with great leaders and great decisions as well as with ordinary people at work, at leisure, and at war. Practically everyone who uses the volume will think of one or more articles that he or she thinks would have been preferable to the ones included. Some readers will wish more attention had been paid to one or another subject; others will regret the attention devoted to matters that seem marginal to themselves. That is why we encourage teachers and students to let us know what they believe to be the strengths and weaknesses of this edition.

Annual Editions: American History, Volume II contains a number of features designed to make the volume "user friendly." These include the *table of contents,* which summarizes each article with key concepts in boldface; a *topic guide* to help locate articles on specific individuals or subjects; *World Wide Web* sites that can be used to further explore the topics (these sites are cross-referenced by number in the *topic guide*); and a comprehensive *index.*

Articles are organized into six units. Each unit is preceded by an overview that provides background for informed reading of the articles, briefly introduces each one, and presents key points to consider. World Wide Web sites are also listed to match the unit's theme. Please let us know if you have any suggestions for improving the format.

There will be a new edition of *Annual Editions: American History, Volume II* in 2 years, with approximately half the readings being replaced by new ones. By completing and mailing the postpaid *article rating form* included in the back of the book, you will help us judge which articles should be retained and which should be dropped. You can also help to improve the next edition by recommending (or better yet, sending along a copy of) articles that you think should be included. A number of essays included in this edition have come to our attention in this way.

Robert James Maddox
Robert James Maddox
Editor

Contents

To the Reader iv
Topic Guide 2
○ Selected World Wide Web Sites 4
Overview 6

1. **The New View of Reconstruction,** Eric Foner, *American Heritage*, October/November 1983. 8
   Prior to the 1960s, according to Eric Foner, **Reconstruction** was portrayed in history books as "just about the darkest page in the American saga." This article presents a balanced view of the era and suggests that, even though Reconstruction failed to achieve its objectives, its "animating vision" still has relevance.

2. **A Road They Did Not Know,** Larry McMurtry, *American Heritage*, February/March 1999. 15
   When gold was discovered in the Black Hills of South Dakota, the United States government prepared to take back the land it had given to the Sioux in 1868. Indian leaders knew that their way of life was coming to an end. They could either go along or fight until they were destroyed. Larry McMurtry discusses the **events** that **led** to the **Battle of Little Big Horn.**

3. **Buffalo Soldiers,** T. J. Stiles, *Smithsonian*, December 1998. 21
   Many writers have depicted **Afro-American soldiers in the post–Civil War era** as a footnote to history. "In fact," Stiles writes, "black regulars took center stage in the Army's great Western drama, shouldering combat responsibilities far out of proportion to their numbers." These "buffalo soldiers," as the Indians called them, perservered in spite of poor food and equipment and the local prejudices that they found where they were stationed.

4. **Undermining the Molly Maguires,** Joseph H. Bloom, *American History*, August 1999. 27
   Mine workers in Pennsylvania faced the threats of explosions and cave-ins and put in long hours of back-breaking labor for wages that were barely sufficient for existence. Some miners joined **secret organizations** known as the **"Molly Maguires"** in order to improve conditions. These groups were alleged to have been responsible for murders and beatings over the years, and, in 1876, a number of men who were accused of being Mollys were tried. Twenty were found **guilty of murder,** 10 of whom were hanged on June 21, 1877.

UNIT 1

Reconstruction and the Gilded Age

Six unit articles examine the development of the United States after the Civil War. Society was changed enormously by western expansion and technology.

The concepts in bold italics are developed in the article. For further expansion please refer to the Topic Guide and the Index.

5. **'The Chinese Must Go,'** Bernard A. Weisberger, *American Heritage*, February/March 1993.   33
San Francisco in 1877 was in the grip of depression, with unemployment running around 20 percent. The Chinese population provided a convenient scapegoat for frustrations. **Anti-Chinese sentiment** grew in California and then nationally as prominent Americans pronounced the Chinese "ignorant of civilized life." Congress in 1882 **banned all Chinese immigration** for 10 years.

6. **The Nickel & Dime Empire,** Joseph Gustaitis, *American History*, March 1998.   35
When **F. W. Woolworth** opened his first stores in 1879, all merchandise sold for a nickel or less. In order to sell higher quality goods, he soon raised the top price to a dime. His **five-and-ten-cent stores** offered customers an unprecedented choice of goods at affordable prices. The idea caught on and his chain spread across the country.

UNIT 2
The Emergence of Modern America

In this section, six articles review the beginnings of modern America. Key issues of this period are examined, including terrorism, turn-of-the century lifestyles, politics, and military conflicts.

Overview   40

7. **Captain Pratt's School,** Mary Kay Morel, *American History*, May/June 1997.   42
From the time it opened in 1879 until 1918, the Carlisle Indian Industrial School totally immersed **Indian children** in the white man's culture: language, hair, and dress. Mary Kay Morel examines this well-intentioned effort to "help" Native Americans, and concludes that it produced young people who were culturally neither white nor Indian.

8. **"Hang 'em First, Try 'em Later,"** Bruce Watson, *Smithsonian*, June 1998.   50
Between 1882 and 1902, **Judge Roy Bean** presided over the small town of Langtry, Texas. This legendary "hanging judge" has been the subject of books, movies, and television shows. Bruce Watson tries to separate the facts from the fiction of this colorful figure.

9. **"If You Men Don't Withdraw, We Will Mow Every One of You Down,"** William C. Kashatus, *American History*, April 2000.   57
On July 6, 1892, the Pinkerton National Detective Agency sent 300 armed men to the mill town of Homestead, Pennsylvania. Labor trouble had arisen there because wages had been lowered by mill owner Andrew Carnegie. Soon after the Pinkertons arrived, shots were fired and the **"Homestead massacre"** began. Carnegie had left the country before the violence began, but he had told his plant manager to break the union and said in advance that he would approve "anything you do" to bring this about.

10. **Electing the President, 1896,** Edward Ranson, *History Today*, October 1996.   63
The **election of 1896** was an emotional one, with both Democrats and Republicans predicting dire consequences if the other side won. Depression hung over the land, relations between labor and capital approached industrial warfare, and sectional antagonisms ran high. Democratic candidate **William Jennings Bryan** lost because he "was the champion of old America in the vain struggle against an emerging twentieth-century new America."

The concepts in bold italics are developed in the article. For further expansion please refer to the Topic Guide and the Index.

11. **Our First Southeast Asian War,** David R. Kohler and James W. Wensyel, *American History,* January/February 1990.
In 1898, the United States fought a short, victorious **war with Spain.** When President William McKinley decided to acquire the Philippine Islands from Spain, however, a bloody insurrection began that lasted for years. David Kohler and James Wensyel claim that this struggle should have provided lessons about Vietnam for American policymakers 60 years later.

69

12. **The American Century, 1900–1910: How It Felt When Everything Seemed Possible,** Henry Allen, *Washington Post National Weekly Edition,* October 4, 1999.
A retired baseball player, Davy Jones, remembered that, "Back at the turn of the century, you know, we didn't have the mass communication and mass transportation that exist nowadays. As a result," he said, "people were more unique then, more unusual, more different from each other." Henry Allen takes an impressionistic journey through **the first decade of the twentieth century.**

77

Overview

80

13. **Blacks and the Progressive Movement: Emergence of a New Synthesis,** Jimmie Franklin, *OAH Magazine of History,* Spring 1999.
Historians of the Progressive movement traditionally have treated it as a white, middle-class movement. "Much like white reformers," Jimmie Franklin writes, **"black Progressives** wanted to achieve a greater sense of community and order, the preservation of moral values, and the perfection of social institutions." He stresses the roles played by black churches and black women.

82

14. **The Ambiguous Legacies of Women's Progressivism,** Robyn Muncy, *OAH Magazine of History,* Spring 1999.
Hundreds of thousands of women threw themselves into Progressive reform, the legacies of which are with us today. Most students assume that such activism and power must have tended unambiguously to liberate women. Robyn Muncy points out that truth is not that simple, and that **female Progressive activism** left a complicated legacy.

86

15. **Woodrow Wilson, Politician,** Robert Dallek, *The Wilson Quarterly,* Autumn 1991.
Unfortunately best remembered for his failure to bring the United States into the **League of Nations, Woodrow Wilson** was a "brilliant Democratic politician" who was elected on a wave of Progressive reform sentiment. Robert Dallek argues that Wilson's first presidential term marks one of the "three notable periods of domestic reform in twentieth-century America."

91

UNIT 3

From Progressivism to the 1920s

Seven essays in this section examine American culture in the early twentieth century. The economy began to reap the benefits of technology, women gained the right to vote, and Henry Ford ushered in mass production.

The concepts in bold italics are developed in the article. For further expansion please refer to the Topic Guide and the Index.

16. **Margaret Sanger,** Gloria Steinem, *Time,* April 13, 1998.   97

In 1914 **Margaret Sanger** launched *The Woman Rebel,* a feminist newspaper that advocated birth control. She was arrested for inciting violence and promoting obscenity. Two years later she opened the first **family-planning clinic** in the United States, for which she was arrested again. Gloria Steinem discusses the career of one of the most important forerunners of **women's liberation.**

17. **Unearthing a Riot,** Brent Staples, *New York Times Magazine,* December 19, 1999.   99

Tulsa, Oklahoma, grew explosively between 1910 and 1920, largely as the result of a booming oil business. In 1921 the city exploded into **race riots** that resulted in hundreds of people being shot, burned alive, or dragged to death tied to cars. Brent Staples tells how this catastrophe was covered up and only recently brought to light.

18. **Scandal in the Oval Office,** Carl Sferrazza Anthony, *Washington Post National Weekly Edition,* June 15, 1998.   104

"Whitewater, Iran-Contra and Watergate are better known today," Carl Anthony writes, "but the granddaddy of them all was Teapot Dome, a political maelstrom that broke 75 years ago . . . and is still hard to top in terms of sheer outrageousness." He discusses the events leading up to the **Harding administration scandals** and their aftermath.

19. **The Abduction of Aimee,** J. Kingston Pierce, *American History,* February 2000.   108

By the mid-1920s, California evangelist **Aimee Semple McPherson** had become famous for her radio sermons and her vaudeville-style Sunday services conducted before packed crowds in her ornate Angelus Temple. On May 18, 1926, she told her mother that she was going to spend the afternoon at the beach, but she did not return. The national sensation caused by McPherson's mysterious disappearance and her return 5 weeks later provides a glimpse of society in the "Roaring Twenties."

UNIT 4

From the Great Depression to World War II

The seven selections in this unit discuss the severe economic and social trials of the Great Depression of the thirties, the slow recovery process, and the enormous impact of World War II on America's domestic and foreign social consciousness.

Overview   114

20. **'Brother, Can You Spare a Dime?'** Henry Allen, *Washington Post National Weekly Edition,* October 25, 1999.   116

"It's not like you go out on your porch and see **the Depression** standing there like King Kong," Henry Allen writes. "Most neighborhoods, things look pretty normal . . . ." But beneath the appearance of normality, many people were leading lives of desperation from which they saw no escape.

21. **A Monumental Man,** Gerald Parshall, *U.S. News & World Report,* April 28, 1997.   119

Gerald Parshall discusses **Franklin D. Roosevelt's personal characteristics:** his famous smile, his speeches, "fireside chats," and his ability to "treat kings like commoners and commoners like kings." Special attention is paid to "FDR's splendid deception"—his determination to conceal the fact that a 1921 bout with polio had left him unable to walk.

The concepts in bold italics are developed in the article. For further expansion please refer to the Topic Guide and the Index.

22. **Eleanor Roosevelt,** Doris Kearns Goodwin, *Time,* April 13, 1998. 122

"Eleanor shattered the ceremonial mold in which the **role of the First Lady** had traditionally been fashioned," writes Doris Kearns Goodwin, "and reshaped it around her own skills and commitment to social reform." Goodwin pays special attention to Eleanor's influence on her husband and to her own deep **commitment to civil rights.**

23. **The Lone Dissenting Voice,** Glen Jeansonne, *American History,* April 1999. 124

Jeannette Rankin was the first woman to be elected to the House of Representatives. Four days after she took her seat, she cast one of the few dissenting votes against America's entry into World War I. After serving only one term, she was again elected to the House in 1940. One day after the attack on Pearl Harbor, she cast the sole vote against the declaration of war against Japan. "As a woman I can't go to war," she said, "and I refuse to send anyone else."

24. **Our Greatest Land Battle,** Edward Oxford, *American History,* February 1995. 127

In the autumn of 1944, as Allied forces moved across France following the breakout from the Normandy beaches, some thought Germany would be defeated by Christmas. Secretly, however, Adolf **Hitler** was amassing powerful forces for a counterattack through the Ardennes forest. Beginning on December 16, the German army made alarming advances until it was halted at a few key areas by brave and determined men. What has become known as the **"Battle of the Bulge"** involved 600,000 American troops.

25. **"I Learn a Lot from the Veterans,"** Stephen E. Ambrose, *American Heritage,* November 1998. 136

Generals and admirals command campaigns; soldiers and sailors fight them. After publishing a book about the conduct of ordinary soldiers in World War II, distinguished historian Stephen Ambrose received many letters from ex-GIs. These letters provide direct testimony about the **experience of combat.**

26. **The Biggest Decision: Why We Had to Drop the Atomic Bomb,** Robert James Maddox, *American Heritage,* May/June 1995. 141

Some critics have argued that Japan was so close to surrender during the summer of 1945 that the **use of atomic bombs** was unnecessary to end the war. Robert Maddox shows that this criticism is mistaken. The Japanese army, which controlled the situation, was prepared to fight to the finish, and it hoped to inflict such hideous casualties on invading forces that the United States would agree to a negotiated peace.

The concepts in bold italics are developed in the article. For further expansion please refer to the Topic Guide and the Index.

UNIT 5

From the Cold War to 2000

The section's eight articles cover the post–World War II period, and address numerous issues that include the presidency, race and sports issues, the cold war, and changing lifestyles.

Overview   146

27. **1948: The Presidential Election,** Michael D. Haydock, *American History,* June 1998.   148

 Few believed **Harry S. Truman** had much of a chance to win the presidential election of 1948. With his party riven by defections from both right and left, Truman staged a vigorous campaign against the "do-nothing Congress" and against his well-financed opponent, Thomas E. Dewey. Polls nonetheless predicted a Dewey landslide. They were wrong.

28. **Baseball's *Noble* Experiment,** William Kashatus, *American History,* March/April 1997.   153

 Jackie Robinson broke the color line in ***major league baseball*** when he began playing for the Brooklyn Dodgers in 1947. This article explains the role of Dodger president Branch Rickey and the hardships that Robinson had to endure. Robinson triumphed and went on to a Hall-of-Fame career. He inspired countless young blacks, "and in the process taught many white Americans to respect others regardless of the color of their skin."

29. **The Split-Level Years, 1950–1960: Elvis, Howdy Doody Time, McDonald's and the Rumblings of Rebellion,** Henry Allen, *Washington Post National Weekly Edition,* November 8, 1999.   161

 The 1950s brought us Elvis, Howdy Doody, and McDonald's. There were also rumblings of discontent during this decade of conformity. Henry Allen guides us through the era of Marilyn Monroe, "Ozzie & Harriet," and teenage rebellion.

30. **Point of Order!** Thomas Doherty, *History Today,* August 1998.   164

 Senator Joseph R. McCarthy emerged in the early 1950s as one of the most powerful men in the country. His allegations of Communist influence in practically all aspects of American life created a climate of fear and suspicion. Thomas Doherty shows how the televised hearings on McCarthy's charges against the United States Army helped bring about the senator's demise.

31. **Martin Luther King's Half-Forgotten Dream,** Peter Ling, *History Today,* April 1998.   167

 The Reverend ***Martin Luther King Jr.*** is best remembered for his dramatic "I Have a Dream" speech, delivered from the steps of the Lincoln Memorial in 1963. Peter Ling maintains that the emphasis on King has diminished the roles of other ***civil rights activists.*** He also discusses King's concept of the "guilty bystander"—those who by inaction permit injustices to continue.

32. **The Spirit of '68,** John B. Judis, *The New Republic,* August 31, 1998.   171

 According to John Judis, "America passed irreversibly during ***the Sixties*** from a culture of toil, sacrifice, saving, and abstinence to a culture of consumption, lifestyle, and quality of life." He attributes these changes to the emergence of consumer capitalism, in response to which the counterculture as well as the religious right emerged.

The concepts in bold italics are developed in the article. For further expansion please refer to the Topic Guide and the Index.

33. Nixon's America, Michael Barone, *U.S. News & World Report,* September 20, 1999. — 178

Richard M. Nixon is best remembered for the scandals that forced him to become the first president to resign from office. Watergate, Michael Barone argues, should not blind us to his very real accomplishments. "Postwar America did not move gracefully into the quite different America we know today," he writes, "but its movement was shaped in many ways by Richard Nixon and it cannot be imagined without him."

34. Face-Off, John Lewis Gaddis, *U.S. News & World Report,* October 18, 1999. — 183

To many people, the essentially **peaceful breakup of the Soviet Union** could only have happened the way it did. Those who lived through **the cold war** could not have known the outcome, which at times seemed in doubt. John Gaddis analyzes the evolution of this global struggle, concluding that tension between East and West defined the cold war but that it left a legacy of the victory of hope over fear.

Overview — 188

35. The Near-Myth of Our Failing Schools, Peter Schrag, *The Atlantic Monthly,* October 1997. — 190

Peter Schrag rejects the notion that **American schools** are doing as badly as many people claim. He examines a number of myths, including what he regards as **misleading comparisons** with education in other countries. He calls for "a far more realistic appreciation of what we have done in our educational system in the past, what we are doing now, and what we think we want to do."

36. Divided We Sprawl, Bruce Katz and Jennifer Bradley, *The Atlantic Monthly,* December 1999. — 195

Many leading cities are rapidly losing population **to the suburbs** because of high crime rates, steep taxes, and poor schools. Bruce Katz and Jennifer Bradley argue that the old "city vs. suburb" view is outdated. They make a number of recommendations involving issues such as public transportation that would help integrate cities with their surrounding communities.

37. A Politics for Generation X, Ted Halstead, *The Atlantic Monthly,* August 1999. — 201

According to Ted Halstead, **today's young adults** may indeed be more disengaged politically than any others in American history. He claims they have less confidence in government and a weaker allegiance to country or party. They are also more materialistic. Will their political agendas become the wave of the future in this country?

Index — 209
Test Your Knowledge Form — 212
Article Rating Form — 213

UNIT 6

New Directions for American History

Three articles discuss the current state of American society and the role the United States plays throughout the world.

The concepts in bold italics are developed in the article. For further expansion please refer to the Topic Guide and the Index.

Topic Guide

This topic guide suggests how the selections and World Wide Web sites found in the next section of this book relate to topics of traditional concern to American history students and professionals. It is useful for locating interrelated articles and Web sites for reading and research. The guide is arranged alphabetically according to topic.

The relevant Web sites, which are numbered and annotated on pages 4 and 5, are easily identified by the Web icon (●) under the topic articles. By linking the articles and the Web sites by topic, this ANNUAL EDITIONS reader becomes a powerful learning and research tool.

TOPIC AREA	TREATED IN	TOPIC AREA	TREATED IN
African Americans	1. New View of Reconstruction 3. Buffalo Soldiers 13. Blacks and the Progressive Movement 17. Unearthing a Riot 28. Baseball's *Noble* Experiment 31. Martin Luther King's Half-Forgotten Dream ● 6, 9, 19, 20, 27, 30		10. Electing the President, 1896 13. Blacks and the Progressive Movement 14. Ambiguous Legacies of Women's Progressivism 15. Woodrow Wilson, Politician 18. Scandal in the Oval Office 21. Monumental Man 23. Lone Dissenting Voice 27. 1948: The Presidential Election 30. Point of Order! 33. Nixon's America ● 2, 3, 4, 5, 6, 7, 8, 10, 12, 18, 19, 20, 23, 26, 27, 28, 31
Asians	5. 'Chinese Must Go' 11. Our First Southeast Asian War ● 11, 15, 18, 27, 29, 30, 31		
Atomic Bomb	26. Biggest Decision ● 1, 3, 4, 20, 21	Harding, Warren	18. Scandal in the Oval Office ● 3, 4, 5, 6, 8
Bean, Judge Roy	8. "Hang 'em First, Try 'em Later" ● 3	Immigrants	5. 'Chinese Must Go' ● 15, 18, 27, 29, 30, 31
Birth Control	16. Margaret Sanger ● 3, 27	King, Martin L. Jr.	31. Martin Luther King's Half-Forgotten Dream ● 3, 6, 9, 27, 31
Business	6. Nickel & Dime Empire ● 2, 25, 28	Labor	4. Undermining the Molly Maguires 9. "If You Men Don't Withdraw . . ." ● 2, 3, 17, 27
Cold War	30. Point of Order! 33. Nixon's America 34. Face-Off ● 1, 3, 4, 8, 21	McCarthy, Joseph	30. Point of Order! ● 3, 4, 5, 6, 27
Culture	7. Captain Pratt's School 12. American Century, 1900–1910 13. Blacks and the Progressive Movement 14. Ambiguous Legacies of Women's Progressivism 16. Margaret Sanger 19. Abduction of Aimee 28. Baseball's *Noble* Experiment 29. Split-Level Years, 1950–1960 31. Martin Luther King's Half-Forgotten Dream 32. Spirit of '68 35. Near Myth of Our Failing Schools 36. Divided We Sprawl 37. Politics for Generation X ● 4, 6, 9, 19, 24, 27, 29, 30	McPherson, Aimee Semple	19. Abduction of Aimee ● 3, 4, 5, 6
		Native Americans	2. Road They Did Not Know 7. Captain Pratt's School ● 3, 5, 6, 7, 27, 30
		Nixon, Richard	33. Nixon's America ● 1, 3, 4, 5, 8
		Politics	10. Electing the President, 1896 13. Blacks and the Progressive Movement 14. Ambiguous Legacies of Women's Progressivism 15. Woodrow Wilson, Politician 18. Scandal in the Oval Office 21. Monumental Man 27. 1948: The Presidential Election 30. Point of Order! 33. Nixon's America 37. Politics for Generation X ● 2, 3, 4, 8, 13, 16, 20, 21, 24, 27, 28
Depression, Great	20 'Brother, Can You Spare a Dime?' ● 3, 4, 5, 6, 19		
Diplomacy	11. Our First Southeast Asian War 33. Nixon's America 34. Face-Off ● 3, 11, 22, 26, 28		
Education	35. Near Myth of Our Failing Schools ● 19, 25	Progressivism	13. Blacks and the Progressive Movement 14. Ambiguous Legacies of Women's Progressivism 15. Woodrow Wilson, Politician ● 3, 4, 5, 6
Government	1. New View of Reconstruction		

TOPIC AREA	TREATED IN	TOPIC AREA	TREATED IN
Racism	1. New View of Reconstruction 2. Road They Did Not Know 3. Buffalo Soldiers 5. 'Chinese Must Go' 7. Captain Pratt's School 13. Blacks and the Progressive Movement 17. Unearthing a Riot 28. Baseball's *Noble* Experiment 31. Martin Luther King's Half-Forgotten Dream ● *6, 9, 19, 20, 27, 30, 31*		20. 'Brother, Can You Spare a Dime?' 28. Baseball's *Noble* Experiment 29. Split-Level Years, 1950–1960 31. Martin Luther King's Half-Forgotten Dream 32. Spirit of '68 35. Near Myth of Our Failing Schools 36. Divided We Sprawl 37. Politics for Generation X ● *1, 2, 3, 4, 6, 9, 11, 13, 14, 15, 18, 19, 20, 24, 25, 27*
Rankin, Jeannette	23. Lone Dissenting Voice ● *3, 6*	**Truman, Harry S.**	27. 1948: The Presidential Election ● *3, 4, 5, 6, 8, 20*
Reconstruction	1. New View of Reconstruction ● *3, 4, 6, 9*	**Urban Problems**	36. Divided We Sprawl ● *27*
Reform	13. Blacks and the Progressive Movement 14. Ambiguous Legacies of Women's Progressivism 15. Woodrow Wilson, Politician 16. Margaret Sanger 21. Monumental Man 22. Eleanor Roosevelt 28. Baseball's *Noble* Experiment 31. Martin Luther King's Half-Forgotten Dream 32. Spirit of '68	**Western Expansion**	2. Road They Did Not Know 3. Buffalo Soldiers 8. "Hang 'em First, Try 'em Later" ● *1, 3, 4, 6, 10, 11*
		Wilson, Woodrow	15. Woodrow Wilson, Politician ● *3, 4, 5, 6, 8, 16*
		Women	14. Ambiguous Legacies of Women's Progressivism 16. Margaret Sanger 19. Abduction of Aimee 22. Eleanor Roosevelt 23. Lone Dissenting Voice ● *3, 4, 6, 27*
Robinson, Jackie	28. Baseball's *Noble* Experiment ● *27*		
Roosevelt, Eleanor	22. Eleanor Roosevelt ● *3, 4, 5, 6, 8, 27*	**Woolworth**	6. Nickel and Dime Empire ● *2, 4, 6, 17*
Roosevelt, Franklin D.	21. Monumental Man ● *3, 4, 5, 6, 8, 20*	**World War II**	24. Our Greatest Land Battle 25. "I Learn a Lot From the Veterans" 26. Biggest Decision ● *3, 4, 5, 6, 8, 20, 21, 27*
Sanger, Margaret	16. Margaret Sanger ● *3, 6*		
Society	6. Nickel & Dime Empire 12. American Century, 1900–1910 17. Unearthing a Riot		

AE: American History, Volume II

The following World Wide Web sites have been carefully researched and selected to support the articles found in this reader. If you are interested in learning more about specific topics found in this book, these Web sites are a good place to start. The sites are cross-referenced by number and appear in the topic guide on the previous two pages. Also, you can link to these Web sites through our DUSHKIN ONLINE support site at *http://www.dushkin.com/online/*.

The following sites were available at the time of publication. Visit our Web site—we update DUSHKIN ONLINE regularly to reflect any changes.

General Sources

1. American Historical Association
http://www.theaha.org
This is the logical first visitation site for someone interested in virtually any topic in American history. All affiliated societies and publications are noted, and AHA links present material related to myriad fields of history for students with different levels of education.

2. Harvard's John F. Kennedy School of Government
http://www.ksg.harvard.edu
Starting from this home page, click on a huge variety of links to information about American history, ranging from data about political parties to general debates of enduring issues.

3. History Net
http://www.thehistorynet.com/THNarchives/AmericanHistory/
Supported by the National Historical Society, this frequently updated site provides information on a wide range of topics. The articles are of excellent quality, and the site has book reviews and even special interviews.

4. Library of Congress
http://www.loc.gov
Examine this Web site to learn about the extensive resource tools, library services/resources, exhibitions, and databases available through the Library of Congress in many different subfields that are related to American history.

5. National Archives and Records Administration
http://www.nara.gov/nara/nail.html
It is possible to access over 125,000 digital images from this National Archives and Records site. A vast array of American subjects are available.

6. Smithsonian Institution
http://www.si.edu
This site provides access to the enormous resources of the Smithsonian, which holds some 140 million artifacts and specimens in its trust for "the increase and diffusion of knowledge." Here you can learn about American social, cultural, economic, and political history from a variety of viewpoints.

7. U.S. Founding Documents/Emory University
http://www.law.emory.edu/FEDERAL/
It is possible to view scanned originals of the Declaration of Independence, the Constitution, and the Bill of Rights from this site. The transcribed texts are also available, as are *The Federalist Papers*.

8. The White House
http://www.whitehouse.gov/WH/Welcome.html
Visit the home page of the White House for direct access to information about commonly requested federal services, the White House Briefing Room, and the presidents and vice presidents. The "Virtual Library" allows you to search White House documents, listen to speeches, and view photos.

Reconstruction and the Gilded Age

9. Anacostia Museum/Smithsonian Institution
http://www.si.edu/organiza/museums/anacost/
This is the home page of the Center for African American History and Culture of the Smithsonian Institution. Explore its many avenues. This is expected to become a major repository of information.

10. BoondocksNet.com
http://www.boondocksnet.com
Jim Zwick's site explores the often-forgotten Filipino revolt against U.S. acquisition of the Philippines after the Spanish-American War. Zwick also discusses anti-imperialist crusades within the United States during the Gilded Age.

The Emergence of Modern America

11. The Age of Imperialism
http://www.smplanet.com/imperialism/toc.html
During the late nineteenth and early twentieth centuries, the United States pursued an aggressive policy of expansionism, extending its political and economic influence around the globe. That pivotal era in the nation's history is the subject of this interactive site. Maps and photographs are provided.

12. Anti-Imperialism in the United States, 1898–1935
http://boondocksnet.com/ail98-35.html
Jim Zwick created this interesting site that explores American imperialism from the Spanish-American War years to 1935. It provides valuable primary resources on a variety of related topics.

13. The Era of William McKinley
http://www.cohums.ohio-state.edu/history/projects/McKinley/
Browse through this Ohio State University Department of History site for insight into the era of William McKinley, including discussion of the Spanish-American War.

14. Great Chicago Fire and the Web of Memory
http://www.chicagohs.org/fire/
This site, created by the Academic Technologies unit of Northwestern University and the Chicago Historical Society, is interesting and well constructed. Besides discussing the Great Chicago Fire at length, the materials provide insight into the era in which the event took place.

From Progressivism to the 1920s

15. International Channel
http://www.i-channel.com/features/
Immigrants helped to create modern America. Visit this interesting site to experience "the memories, sounds, even tastes of Ellis Island. Hear immigrants describe in their own words their experiences upon entering the gateway to America."

16. World War I—Trenches on the Web
http://www.worldwar1.com
Mike Lawrence's interesting site supplies extensive resources about the Great War and is the appropriate place to begin exploration of this topic as regards the American experience in World War I. There are "virtual tours" on certain topics, such as "Life on the Homefront."

17. World Wide Web Virtual Library
http://www.iisg.nl/~w3vl/
This site focuses on labor and business history. As an index site, this is a good place to start exploring these two vast topics.

From the Great Depression to World War II

18. Japanese American Internment
http://www.geocities.com/Athens/8420/main.html
Created by C. John Yu, this site, which focuses on the Japanese American internment during World War II, is especially useful for links to other related sites.

19. Works Progress Administration/Folklore Project
http://lcweb2.loc.gov/ammem/wpaintro/wpalife.html
Open this home page of the Folklore Project of the Works Progress Administration (WPA) Federal Writers' Project to gain access to thousands of documents on the life histories of ordinary Americans from all walks of life during the Great Depression.

20. World War II WWW Sites
http://www.lib.muohio.edu/inet/subj/history/wwii/general.html
Visit this site as a starting point to find research links for World War II, including topics specific to the United States' participation and the impact on the country.

From the Cold War to 2000

21. Coldwar0
http://ac.acusd.edu/history/20th/coldwar0.html
This site presents U.S. government policies during the cold war, listed year by year from 1945 through 1991. It is extensive, with Web links to many other sites.

22. The Federal Web Locator
http://www.infoctr.edu/fwl
Use this handy site as a launching pad for the Web sites of federal U.S. agencies, departments, and organizations. It is well organized and easy to use for informational and research purposes.

23. Federalism: Relationship between Local and National Governments
http://www.infidels.org/~nap/index.federalism.html
Federalism versus states' rights has always been a spirited topic of debate in American government. Visit this site for links to many articles and reports on the subject.

24. The Gallup Organization
http://www.gallup.com
Open this Gallup Organization home page to access an extensive archive of public opinion poll results and special reports on a huge variety of topics related to American society, politics, and government.

25. STAT-USA
http://www.stat-usa.gov/stat-usa.html
This essential site, a service of the Department of Commerce, contains daily economic news, frequently requested statistical releases, information on export and international trade, domestic economic news, and statistical series and databases.

26. U.S. Department of State
http://www.state.gov
View this site for an understanding into the workings of what has become a major U.S. executive-branch department. Links explain what exactly the department does, what services it provides, what it says about U.S. interests around the world, and much more.

New Directions for American History

27. American Studies Web
http://www.georgetown.edu/crossroads/asw/
This eclectic site provides links to a wealth of Internet resources for research in American studies, from agriculture and rural development, to history and government, to race and ethnicity.

28. National Center for Policy Analysis
http://www.public-policy.org/~ncpa/pd/pdindex.html
Through this site, you can click onto links to read discussions of an array of topics that are of major interest in the study of American history, from regulatory policy and privatization to economy and income.

29. The National Network for Immigrant and Refugee Rights (NNIRR)
http://www.nnirr.org
The NNIRR serves as a forum to share information and analysis, to educate communities and the general public, and to develop and coordinate plans of action on important immigrant and refugee issues. Visit this site and its many links to explore these issues.

30. STANDARDS: An International Journal of Multicultural Studies
http://www.colorado.edu/journals/standards
This fascinating site provides access to the *Standards* archives and a seemingly infinite number of links to topics of interest in the study of cultural pluralism.

31. Supreme Court/Legal Information Institute
http://supct.law.cornell.edu/supct/index.html
Open this site for current and historical information about the Supreme Court. The archive contains many opinions issued since May 1990 as well as a collection of nearly 600 of the most historic decisions of the Court.

We highly recommend that you review our Web site for expanded information and our other product lines. We are continually updating and adding links to our Web site in order to offer you the most usable and useful information that will support and expand the value of your Annual Editions. You can reach us at:
http://www.dushkin.com/annualeditions/.

Unit 1

Unit Selections

1. **The New View of Reconstruction,** Eric Foner
2. **A Road They Did Not Know,** Larry McMurtry
3. **Buffalo Soldiers,** T. J. Stiles
4. **Undermining the Molly Maguires,** Joseph H. Bloom
5. **'The Chinese Must Go,'** Bernard A. Weisberger
6. **The Nickel & Dime Empire,** Joseph Gustaitis

Key Points to Consider

❖ Radical Reconstruction was an attempt to ensure full citizenship to freedpeople in a society that for centuries had embraced slavery. In view of such fierce resistance by white Southerners, could this attempt have succeeded? How?

❖ How do those who want to exclude members of another race from society justify their position? Discuss the similarities between the anti-Chinese sentiment of the late nineteenth century and present-day opposition to immigration from Asia and South America.

❖ Early labor conditions were extremely difficult. Were there any other alternatives available to the Pennsylvania miners who suffered from deplorable working conditions? Explain.

 **Links**   www.dushkin.com/online/

9. **Anacostia Museum/Smithsonian Institution**
   http://www.si.edu/organiza/museums/anacost/
10. **BoondocksNet.com**
    http://www.boondocksnet.com

These sites are annotated on pages 4 and 5.

Reconstruction and the Gilded Age

The South lay prostrate after the Civil War. Its economy had been shattered, its government had ceased to exist, and many areas had suffered great physical devastation. Recovery would have been difficult under any circumstances, but the problems were compounded by the fact that many of those who had composed the South's labor force were unavailable to work the farms and plantations as they had done under the old system. The Civil War had destroyed the institution of slavery but left the political, social, and economic status of freed people undefined. Northern "Radical" Republicans wished to use the power of the federal government to ensure that former slaves enjoyed full civil and legal rights. These Republicans had their way, after a grueling struggle with the moderate President Andrew Johnson, and the South was divided into five military districts. White Southerners used every means possible to keep blacks "in their place," including terrorist organizations such as the Ku Klux Klan. Eric Foner's article, "The New View of Reconstruction," shows how Radical Reconstruction failed to achieve its goals in the short run but provided what he calls an "enduring vision."

Next, best-selling author Larry McMurtry explains the dilemma that the Sioux Indians faced when, following the discovery of gold in the Black Hills of South Dakota, the government prepared to take back lands previously granted to them. "A Road They Did Not Know" is about the decisions the Sioux made, even in the face of overwhelming odds.

A number of blacks, some of them freedmen, joined the army. "Buffalo Soldiers," which is what the Indians called these men, tells of those who served in the West. They helped spearhead Western expansion and served in combat in far greater proportion than their numbers warranted. Author T. J. Stiles describes how these soldiers persevered in spite of having to make do with poor equipment, bad food, and the prejudice they faced wherever they were stationed.

Mine workers in Pennsylvania led hard and dangerous lives. They worked long, back-breaking hours under constant threat of cave-ins and flooding. Their wages were kept as low as possible, often making it difficult even to subsist. Some miners, hoping to improve their miserable conditions, joined secret organizations that became known as "Molly Maguires." Mine operators tried to destroy these groups, as the essay "Undermining the Molly Maguires" shows, by any means possible. In 1876, a number of men accused of being Mollys were brought to trial. Twenty were found guilty of murder, 10 of whom were hanged.

Racial prejudice has always been with us. It was particularly virulent on the west coast with regard to Asians during the latter part of the nineteenth century. The article " 'The Chinese Must Go' " describes how the Chinese population of San Francisco became the target of mob violence in 1877. Anti-Chinese sentiment continued to grow and in 1882 resulted in a ban on all Chinese immigration for 10 years.

During the years following the Civil War new types of enterprise were developed to take advantage of the population movement from farms to towns and cities. In "The Nickel & Dime Empire," Joseph Gustaitis tells how F. W. Woolworth made available to customers a bewildering variety of inexpensive goods in his 5 and 10 cent stores. The idea caught on, and his chain of stores spread from coast to coast. The demise of the Woolworth empire marked the end of an era.

The New View of Reconstruction

Whatever you were taught or thought you knew about the post–Civil War era is probably wrong in the light of recent study

Eric Foner

Eric Foner is Professor of History at Columbia University and author of Nothing but Freedom: Emancipation and Its Legacy.

In the past twenty years, no period of American history has been the subject of a more thoroughgoing reevaluation than Reconstruction—the violent, dramatic, and still controversial era following the Civil War. Race relations, politics, social life, and economic change during Reconstruction have all been reinterpreted in the light of changed attitudes toward the place of blacks within American society. If historians have not yet forged a fully satisfying portrait of Reconstruction as a whole, the traditional interpretation that dominated historical writing for much of this century has irrevocably been laid to rest.

Anyone who attended high school before 1960 learned that Reconstruction was a era of unrelieved sordidness in American political and social life. The martyred Lincoln, according to this view, had planned a quick and painless readmission of the Southern states as equal members of the national family. President Andrew Johnson, his successor, attempted to carry out Lincoln's policies but was foiled by the Radical Republicans (also known as Vindictives or Jacobins). Motivated by an irrational hatred of Rebels or by ties with Northern capitalists out to plunder the South, the Radicals swept aside Johnson's lenient program and fastened black supremacy upon the defeated Confederacy. An orgy of corruption followed, presided over by unscrupulous carpetbaggers (Northerners who ventured south to reap the spoils of office), traitorous scalawags (Southern whites who cooperated with the new governments for personal gain), and the ignorant and childlike freedmen, who were incapable of properly exercising the political power that had been thrust upon them. After much needless suffering, the white community of the South banded together to overthrow these "black" governments and restore home rule (their euphemism for white supremacy). All told, Reconstruction was just about the darkest page in the American saga.

Originating in anti-Reconstruction propaganda of Southern Democrats during the 1870s, this traditional interpretation achieved scholarly legitimacy around the turn of the century through the work of William Dunning and his students at Columbia University. It reached the larger public through films like *Birth of a Nation* and *Gone With the Wind* and that best-selling work of myth-making masquerading as history, *The Tragic Era* by Claude G. Bowers. In language as exaggerated as it was colorful, Bowers told how Andrew Johnson "fought the bravest battle for constitutional liberty and for the preservation of our institutions ever waged by an Executive" but was overwhelmed by the "poisonous propaganda" of the Radicals. Southern whites, as a result, "literally were put to the torture" by "emissaries of hate" who manipulated the "simple-minded" freedmen, inflaming the negroes' "egotism" and even inspiring "iustful assaults" by blacks upon white womanhood.

In a discipline that sometimes seems to pride itself on the rapid rise and fall of historical interpretations, this traditional portrait of Reconstruction enjoyed remarkable staying power. The long reign of the old interpretation is not difficult to explain. It presented a set of easily identifiable heroes and villains. It enjoyed the imprimatur of the nation's leading scholars. And it accorded with the political and social realities of the first half of this century. This image of Reconstruction helped freeze the mind of the white South in unalterable opposition to any movement for breaching the ascendancy of the Democratic party, eliminating segregation, or readmitting disfranchised blacks to the vote.

Nevertheless, the demise of the traditional interpretation was inevitable, for it ignored the testimony of the central participant in the drama of Reconstruction—the black freedman. Furthermore, it was grounded in the conviction that blacks were unfit to share in political power. As Dunning's Columbia colleague John W. Burgess put it, "A black skin means membership in a race of men which has never of itself succeeded in subjecting passion to reason, has never, therefore, created any civilization of any kind." Once objective scholarship and modern experience rendered that assumption untenable, the entire edifice was bound to fall.

The work of "revising" the history of Reconstruction began with the writings of a handful of survivors of the era, such as John R. Lynch, who had served as a black congressman from Mississippi after the Civil War. In the 1930s white scholars like Francis Simkins and Robert Woody carried the task forward. Then, in 1935, the black historian and activist W. E. B. Du Bois produced *Black Reconstruction in America,* a monumental revaluation that closed with an irrefutable indictment of a historical profession that had sacrificed scholarly objectivity on the altar of racial bias. "One fact and one alone," he wrote, "explains the attitude of most recent writers toward Reconstruction; they cannot conceive of Negroes as men." Du Bois's work, however, was ignored by most historians.

It was not until the 1960s that the full force of the revisionist wave broke over the field. Then, in rapid succession, virtually every assumption of the traditional viewpoint was systematically dismantled. A drastically different portrait emerged to take its place. President Lincoln did not have a coherent "plan" for Reconstruction, but at the time of his assassination he had been cautiously contemplating black suffrage. Andrew Johnson was a stubborn, racist politician who lacked the ability to compromise. By isolating himself from the broad currents of public opinion that had nourished Lincoln's career, Johnson created an impasse with Congress that Lincoln would certainly have avoided, thus throwing away his political power and destroying his own plans for reconstructing the South.

The Radicals in Congress were acquitted of both vindictive motives and the charge of serving as the stalking-horses of Northern capitalism. They emerged instead as idealists in the best nineteenth-century reform tradition. Radical leaders like Charles Sumner and Thaddeus Stevens had worked for the rights of blacks long before any conceivable political advantage flowed from such a commitment. Stevens refused to sign the Pennsylvania Constitution of 1838 because it disfranchised the state's black citizens; Sumner led a fight in the 1850s to integrate Boston's public schools. Their Reconstruction policies were based on principle, not petty political advantage, for the central issue dividing Johnson and these Radical Republicans was the civil rights of freedmen. Studies of congressional policy-making, such as Eric L. McKitrick's *Andrew Johnson and Reconstruction,* also revealed that Reconstruction legislation, ranging from the Civil Rights Act of 1866 to the Fourteenth and Fifteenth Amendments, enjoyed broad support from moderate and conservative Republicans. It was not simply the work of a narrow radical faction.

Even more startling was the revised portrait of Reconstruction in the South itself. Imbued with the spirit of the civil rights movement and rejecting entirely the racial assumptions that had underpinned the traditional interpretation, these historians evaluated Reconstruction from the black point of view. Works like Joel Williamson's *After Slavery* portrayed the period as a time of extraordinary political, social, and economic progress for blacks. The establishment of public school systems, the granting of equal citizenship to blacks, the effort to restore the devastated Southern economy, the attempt to construct an interracial political democracy from the ashes of slavery, all these were commendable achievements, not the elements of Bowers's "tragic era."

> *Black initiative established as many schools as did Northern religious societies and the Freedmen's Bureau. The right to vote was not simply thrust upon them by meddling outsiders, since blacks began agitating for the suffrage as soon as they were freed.*

> *Until recently, Thaddeus Stevens had been viewed as motivated by irrational hatred of the Rebels (left). Now he has emerged as an idealist in the best reform tradition.*

NEW YORK PUBLIC LIBRARY, PRINT ROOM

LIBRARY OF CONGRESS

1 ❖ RECONSTRUCTION AND THE GILDED AGE

EDWARD S. ELLIS. *The History of Our Country.* VOL. 5, 1900

Reconstruction governments were portrayed as disastrous failures because elected blacks were ignorant or corrupt. In fact, postwar corruption cannot be blamed on former slaves.

SCHOMBERG CENTER, NEW YORK PUBLIC LIBRARY

Unlike earlier writers, the revisionists stressed the active role of the freedmen in shaping Reconstruction. Black initiative established as many schools as did Northern religious societies and the Freedmen's Bureau. The right to vote was not simply thrust upon them by meddling outsiders, since blacks began agitating for the suffrage as soon as they were freed. In 1865 black conventions throughout the South issued eloquent, though unheeded, appeals for equal civil and political rights.

With the advent of Radical Reconstruction in 1867, the freedmen did enjoy a real measure of political power. But black supremacy never existed. In most states blacks held only a small fraction of political offices, and even in South Carolina, where they comprised a majority of the state legislature's lower house, effective power remained in white hands. As for corruption, moral standards in both government and private enterprise were at low ebb throughout the nation in the postwar years—the era of Boss Tweed, the Credit Mobilier scandal, and the Whiskey Ring. Southern corruption could hardly be blamed on former slaves.

Other actors in the Reconstruction drama also came in for reevaluation. Most carpetbaggers were former Union soldiers seeking economic opportunity in the postwar South, not unscrupulous adventurers. Their motives, a typically American amalgam of humanitarianism and the pursuit of profit, were no more insidious than those of Western pioneers. Scalawags, previously seen as traitors to the white race, now emerged as "Old Line" Whig Unionists who had opposed secession in the first place or as poor whites who had long resented planters' domination of Southern life and who saw in Reconstruction a chance to recast Southern society along more democratic lines. Strongholds of Southern white Republicanism like east Tennessee and western North Carolina had been the scene of resistance to Confederate rule throughout the civil War; now,

---

Under slavery most blacks had lived in nuclear family units, although they faced the constant threat of separation from loved ones by sale. Reconstruction provided the opportunity for blacks to solidify their preexisting family ties.

---

as one scalawag newspaper put it, the choice was "between salvation at the hand of the Negro or destruction at the hand of the rebels."

At the same time, the Ku Klux Klan and kindred groups, whose campaign of violence against black and white Republicans had been minimized or excused in older writings, were portrayed as they really were. Earlier scholars had conveyed the impression that the Klan intimidated blacks mainly by dressing as ghosts and playing on the freedmen's superstitions. In fact, black fears were all too real: the Klan was a terrorist organization that beat and killed its political opponents to deprive blacks of their newly won rights. The complicity of the Democratic party and the silence of prominent whites in the face of such outrages stood as an indictment of the moral code the South had inherited from the days of slavery.

By the end of the 1960s, then, the old interpretation had been completely reversed. Southern freedmen were the heroes, the "Redeemers" who overthrew Reconstruction were the villains, and if the era was "tragic," it was because change did not go far enough. Reconstruction had been a time of real progress and its failure a lost opportunity for the South and the nation. But the legacy of Reconstruction—the Fourteenth and Fifteenth Amendments—endured to inspire future efforts for civil rights. As Kenneth Stampp wrote in *The Era of Reconstruction,* a superb summary of revisionist findings published in 1965, "if it was worth four years of civil war to save the Union, it was worth a few years of radical reconstruction to give the American Negro the ultimate promise of equal civil and political rights."

As Stampp's statement suggests, the reevaluation of the first Reconstruction was inspired in large measure by the impact of the second—the modern civil rights movement. And with the waning of that movement in recent years, writing on Reconstruction has undergone still another transformation. Instead of seeing the Civil War and its aftermath as a second American Revolution (as Charles Beard had), a regression into barbarism (as Bowers argued), or a golden opportunity squandered (as the revisionists saw it), recent writers argue that Radical Reconstruction was not really very radical. Since land was not distributed to the former slaves, the remained economically dependent upon their former owners. The planter class survived both the war and Reconstruction with its property (apart from slaves) and prestige more or less intact.

Not only changing times but also the changing concerns of historians have contributed to this latest reassessment of Reconstruction. The hallmark of the pst decade's historical writing has been an emphasis upon "social history"—the evocation of the past lives of ordinary Americans—and the downplaying of strictly political events. When applied to Reconstruction, this concern with the "social" suggested that black suffrage and officeholding, once seen as the most radical departures of the Reconstruction era, were relatively insignificant.

Recent historians have focused their investigations not upon the politics of Reconstruction but upon the social and economic aspects of the transition from slavery to freedom. Herbert Gutman's influential study of the black family during and after slavery found little change in family structure or relations between men and women resulting from emancipation. Under slavery most blacks had lived in nuclear family units, although they faced the constant threat of separation from loved ones by sale. Reconstruction provided the opportunity for blacks to solidify their preexisting family ties. Conflicts over whether black women should work in the cotton fields (planters said yes, many black families said no) and over white attempts to "apprentice" black children revealed that the autonomy of family life was a major preoccupation of the freedmen. Indeed, whether manifested in their withdrawal from churches controlled by whites, in the blossoming of black fraternal, benevolent, and self-improvement organizations, or in the demise of the slave quarters and their replacement by small tenant farms occupied by individual families, the quest for independence from white authority and control over their own day-to-day lives shaped the black response to emancipation.

In the post–Civil War South the surest guarantee of economic autonomy, blacks believed, was land. To the freedmen the justice of a claim to land based on their years of unrequited labor appeared self-evident. As an Alabama black convention put it, "The property which they [the planters] hold was nearly all earned by the sweat of *our* brows." As Leon Litwack showed in *Been in the Storm So Long*, a Pultizer Prize–winning account of the black response to emancipation, many freedmen in 1865 and 1866 refused to sign labor contracts, expecting the federal government to give them land. In some localities, as one Alabama overseer reported, they "set up claims to the plantation and all on it."

The Civil War raised the decisive questions of American's national existence: the relations between local and national authority, the definition of citizenship, the balance between force and consent in generating obedience to authority.

In the end, of course, the vast majority of Southern blacks remained propertyless and poor. But exactly why the South, and especially its black population, suffered from dire poverty and economic retardation in the decades following the Civil War is a matter of much dispute. In *One Kind of Freedom* economists Roger Ransom and Richard Sutch indicted country merchants for monopolizing credit and charging usurious interest rates, forcing black tenants into debt and locking the South into a dependence on cotton production that impoverished the entire region. But Jonathan Wiener, in his study of postwar Alabama, argued that planters used their political power to compel blacks to remain on the plantations. Planters succeeded in stabilizing the plantation system, but only by blocking the growth of alternative enterprises, like factories, that might draw off black laborers, thus locking the region into a pattern of economic backwardness.

If the trust of recent writing has emphasized the social and economic aspects of Reconstruction, politics has not been entirely neglected. But political studies have also reflected the postrevisionist mood summarized by C. Vann Woodward when he observed "how essentially nonrevolutionary and conservative Reconstruction really was." Recent writers, unlike their revisionist predecessors, have found little to praise in federal policy toward the emancipated blacks.

A new sensitivity to the strength of prejudice and laissez-faire ideas in the nineteenth-century North has led many historians to doubt whether the Republican party ever made a genuine commitment to racial justice in the South. The granting of black suffrage was an alternative to a long-term federal responsibility for protecting the rights of the former slaves. Once enfranchised, blacks could be left to fend for themselves. With the exception of a few Radicals like Thaddeus Stevens, nearly all Northern policy-makers and educators are criticized today for assuming that, so long as the unfettered operations of the marketplace afforded blacks the opportunity to advance through diligent labor, federal efforts to assist them in acquiring land were unnecessary.

Probably the most innovative recent writing on Reconstruction politics has centered on a broad reassessment of black Republicanism, largely undertaken by a new generation of black historians. Scholars like Thomas Holt and

1 ❖ RECONSTRUCTION AND THE GILDED AGE

COURTESY OF THE ATLANTA *Constitution*

Some scholars exalted the motives of the Ku Klux Klan (left). Actually, its members were part of a terrorist organization that beat and killed its political opponents to deprive blacks of their rights.

RUTHERFORD B. HAYES LIBRARY, FREMONT, OHIO

Nell Painter insist that Reconstruction was not simply a matter of black and white. Conflicts within the black community, no less than divisions among whites, shaped Reconstruction politics. Where revisionist scholars, both black and white, had celebrated the accomplishments of black political leaders, Holt, Painter, and others charge that they failed to address the economic plight of the black masses. Painter criticized "representative colored men," as national black leaders were called, for failing to provide ordinary freedmen with effective political leadership. Holt found that black officeholders in South Carolina most emerged from the old free mulatto class of Charleston, which shared many assumptions with prominent whites. "Basically bourgeois in their origins and orientation," he wrote, they "failed to act in the interest of black peasants."

In emphasizing the persistence from slavery of divisions between free blacks and slaves, these writers reflect the increasing concern with continuity and conservatism in Reconstruction. Their work reflects a startling extension of revisionist premises. If, as has been argued for the past twenty years, blacks were active agents rather than mere victims of manipulation, then they could not be absolved of blame for the ultimate failure of Reconstruction.

Despite the excellence of recent writings and the continual expansion of our knowledge of the period, historians of Reconstruction today face a unique dilemma. An old interpretation has been overthrown, but a coherent new synthesis has yet to take its place. The revisionists of the 1960s effectively established a series of negative points: the Reconstruction governments were not as bad as had been portrayed, black supremacy was a myth, the Radicals were not cynical manipulators of the freedmen. Yet no convincing overall portrait of the quality of political and social life emerged from their writings. More recent historians have rightly pointed to elements of continuity that spanned the nineteenth-century Southern experience, especially the survival, in modified form, of the plantation system. Nevertheless, by denying the real changes that did occur, they have failed to provide a convincing portrait of an era characterized above all by drama, turmoil, and social change.

Building upon the findings of the past twenty years of scholarship, a new portrait of Reconstruction ought to begin by viewing it not as a specific time period, bounded by the years 1865 and 1877, but as an episode in a prolonged historical process—American society's adjustment to the consequences of the Civil War and emancipation. The Civil War, of course, raised the decisive questions of America's national existence: the relations between local and national authority, the definition of citizenship, the balance between force and consent in generating obedience to authority. The war and Reconstruction, as Allan Nevins observed over fifty years ago, marked the "emergence of modern America." This was the era of the completion of the national railroad network, the creation of the modern steel industry, the conquest of the West and final subduing of the Indians, and the expansion of the mining frontier. Lincoln's America—the world of the small farm and artisan shop—gave way to a rapidly industrializing economy. The issues that galvanized postwar Northern politics—from the question of the greenback currency to the mode of paying holders of the national debt—arose from the economic changes unleased by the Civil War.

Above all, the war irrevocably abolished slavery. Since 1619, when "twenty negars" disembarked from a Dutch ship in Virginia, racial injustice had haunted American life, mocking its professed ideals even as tobacco and cotton, the products of slave labor, helped finance the nation's economic development. Now the implications of the black presence could no longer be ignored. The Civil War resolved the problem of slavery but, as the Philadelphia diarist Sydney George Fisher observed in June 1865, it opened an even more intractable problem: "What shall we do with the Negro?" Indeed, he went on, this was a problem "*incapable* of any solution that will satisfy both North and South."

1. New View of Reconstruction

As Fisher realized, the focal point of Reconstruction was the social revolution known as emancipation. Plantation slavery was simultaneously a system of labor, a form of racial domination, and the foundation upon which arose a distinctive ruling class within the South. Its demise threw open the most fundamental questions of economy, society, and politics. A new system of labor, social, racial, and political relations had to be created to replace slavery.

The United States was not the only nation to experience emancipation in the nineteenth century. Neither plantation slavery nor abolition were unique to the United States. But Reconstruction was. In a comparative perspective Radical Reconstruction stands as a remarkable experiment, the only effort of a society experiencing abolition to bring the former slaves within the umbrella of equal citizenship. Because the Radicals did not achieve everything they wanted, historians have lately tended to play down the stunning departure represented by black suffrage and officeholding. Former slaves, most fewer than two years removed from bondage, debated the fundamental questions of the polity: what is a republican form of government? Should the state provide equal education for all? How could political equality be reconciled with a society in which property was so unequally distributed? There was something inspiring in the way such men met the challenge of Reconstruction. "I knew nothing more than to obey my master," James K. Greene, an Alabama black politician later recalled. "But the tocsin of freedom sounded and knocked at the door and we walked out like free men and we met the exigencies as they grew up, and shouldered the responsibilities."

You never saw a people more excited on the subject of politics than are the negroes of the south," one planter observed in 1867. And there were more than a few Southern whites as well who in these years shook off the prejudices of the past to embrace the revision of a new South dedicated to the principles of equal citizenship and social justice. One ordinary South Carolinian expressed the new sense of possibility in 1868 to the Republican governor of the state: "I am sorry that I cannot write an elegant stiled letter to your excellency. But I rejoice to think that God almighty has given to the poor of S.C. a Gov. to hear to feel to protect the humble poor without distinction to race or color. . . . I am a native borned S.C. a poor man never owned a Negro in my life nor my father before me. . . . Remember the true and loyal are the poor of the whites and blacks, outside of these you can find none loyal."

Few modern scholars believe the Reconstruction governments established in the South in 1867 and 1868 fulfilled the aspirations of their humble constituents. While their achievements in such realms as education, civil rights, and the economic rebuilding of the South are now widely appreciated, historians today believe they failed to affect either the economic plight of the emancipated slave or the ongoing transformation of independent white farmers into cotton tenants. Yet their opponents did perceive the Reconstruction governments in precisely this way—as representatives of a revolution that had put the bottom rail, both racial and economic, on top. This perception helps explain the ferocity of the attacks leveled against them and the pervasiveness of violence in the post-emancipation South.

The spectacle of black men voting and holding office was anathema to large numbers of Southern whites. Even more disturbing, at least in the view of those who still controlled the plantation regions of the South, was the emergence of local officials, black and white, who sympathized with the plight of the black laborer. Alabama's vagrancy law was a "dead letter" in 1870, "because those who are charged with its enforcement are indebted to the vagrant vote for their offices and emoluments." Political debates over the level and incidence of taxation, the control of crops, and the resolution of contract disputes revealed that a primary issue of Reconstruction was the role of government in a plantation society. During presidential Reconstruction, and after "Redemption," with planters and their allies in control of politics, the law emerged as a means of stabilizing and promoting the plantation system. If Radical Reconstruction failed to redistribute the land of the South, the ouster of the planter class from control of politics as least ensured that the sanctions of the criminal law would not be employed to discipline the black labor force.

An understanding of this fundamental conflict over the relation between government and society helps explain the pervasive complaints concerning corruption and "extravagance" during Radical Reconstruction. Corruption there was aplenty; tax rates did rise sharply. More significant than the rate of taxation, however, was the change in its incidence. For the first time, planters and white farmers had to pay a significant portion of their income to the government, while propertyless blacks often escaped scot-free. Several states, moreover, enacted heavy taxes on uncultivated land to discourage land speculation and force land onto the market, benefiting, it was hoped, the freedmen.

In the end neither the abolition of slavery nor Reconstruction succeeded in resolving the debate over the meaning of freedom in American life.

As time passed, complaints about the "extravagance" and corruption of Southern governments found a sympathetic audience among influential Northerners. The Democratic charge that universal suffrage in the South was responsible for high taxes and governmental extravagance coincided with a rising conviction among the urban middle classes of the North that city government had to be taken out o the hands of the immigrant poor and returned to the "best men"—the educated, professional, financially independent citizens unable to exert much political influence at a time of mass parties and machine politics. Increasingly the "respectable" middle classes began to retreat from the very notion of universal suffrage. The poor were not longer perceived as honest producers, the backbone of the social order; now they became the "dangerous classes," the "mob." As the historian Francis Parkman put it, too much power rested with "masses of imported ignorance and hereditary ineptitude." To Parkman the Irish of the Northern cities and the blacks of the South were equally incapable of utilizing the ballot: "Witness the municipal corruptions of New York, and the monstrosities of negro rule in South Carolina." Such attitudes helped to justify Northern inaction as, one by one, the Reconstruction regimes of the South were overthrown by political violence.

In the end, then, neither the abolition of slavery nor Reconstruction succeeded in resolving the debate over the meaning of freedom in American life. Twenty years before the American Civil War, writing about the prospect of abolition in France's colonies, Alexis de Tocqueville had written, "If the Negroes have the right to become free, the [planters] have the incontestable right not to be ruined by the Negroes' freedom." And in the United States, as in nearly every plantation society that experienced the end of slavery, a rigid social and political dichotomy between former master and former slave, an ideology of racism, and a dependent labor force with limited economic opportunities all survived abolition. Unless one means by freedom the simple fact of not being a slave, emancipation thrust blacks into a kind of no-man's land, a partial freedom that made a mockery of the American ideal of equal citizenship.

Yet by the same token the ultimate outcome underscores the uniqueness of Reconstruction itself. Alone among the societies that abolished slavery in the nineteenth century, the United States, for a moment, offered the freedmen a measure of political control over their own destinies. However brief its sway, Reconstruction allowed scope for a remarkable political and social mobilization of the black community. It opened doors of opportunity that could never be completely closed. Reconstruction transformed the lives of Southern blacks in ways unmeasurable by statistics and unreachable by law. It raised their expectations and aspirations, redefined their status in relation to the larger society, and allowed space for the creation of institutions that enabled them to survive the repression that followed. And it established constitutional principles of civil and political equality that, while flagrantly violated after Redemption, planted the seeds of future struggle.

Certainly, it terms of the sense of possibility with which it opened, Reconstruction failed. But as Du Bois observed, it was a "splendid failure." For its animating vision—a society in which social advancement would be open to all on the basis of individual merit, not inherited caste distinctions—is as old as America itself and remains relevant to a nation still grappling with the unresolved legacy of emancipation.

A Road They Did Not Know

*Our greatest Western novelist deciphers
Crazy Horse, Custer, and the hard year of the Little Bighorn*

By Larry McMurtry

BY THE SUMMER OF 1875 A CRISIS OVER the Black Hills of South Dakota could no longer be postponed. Lt. Col. George Armstrong Custer had made a grand announcement that there was gold in the hills, and it caught the nation's attention. After that miners could not be held back. The government was obviously going to find a way to take back the Black Hills, but just as obviously, it was not going to be able to do so without difficulty and without criticism. The whites in the peace party were vocal; they and others of various parties thought the government ought to at least try to honor its agreements, particularly those made as solemnly and as publicly as the one from 1868 giving the Sioux the Black Hills and other lands. So there ensued a period of wiggling and squirming, on the part of the government and the part of the Sioux, many of whom had become agency Indians by this time. The free life of the hunting Sioux was still just possible, but only in certain areas: the Powder River, parts of Montana, and present-day South Dakota west of the Missouri River, where the buffalo still existed in some numbers.

By this time most of the major indian leaders had made a realistic assessment of the situation and drawn the obvious conclusion, which was that their old way of life was rapidly coming to an end. One way or another they were going to have to walk the white man's road—or else fight until they were all killed. The greatest Sioux warriors, Crazy Horse and Sitting Bull, were among the most determined of the hostiles; two others, Red Cloud and Spotted Tail, rivals at this point, both had settled constituencies. They were administrators essentially, struggling to get more food and better goods out of their respective agents. As more and more Indians came in and enrollment lists swelled, this became a full-time job, and a vexing and frustrating one at that.

> **Most of the major Indian leaders had already drawn the obvious conclusion that their old way of life was rapidly coming to an end.**

There were of course many Indians who tried to walk a middle road, unwilling to give up the old ways completely but recognizing that the presence of whites in what had once been their country was now a fact of life. Young Man Afraid of His Horses, son of the revered Old Man Afraid of His Horses, was one of the middle-of-the-roaders.

The whites at first tried pomp and circumstance, bringing the usual suspects yet again to Washington, hoping to tempt them—Red Cloud, Spotted Tail, anyone—to sell the Black Hills. They would have liked to have had Sitting Bull and Crazy Horse at this grand parley, or even a moderate, such as Young Man Afraid of His Horses, but none of these men or any of the principal hostiles wanted anything to do with this mini-summit. Red Cloud and Spotted Tail had no authority to sell the Black Hills, or to do anything about them at all, a fact the white authorities should have realized by this time. There were still thousands of Sioux on the northern plains who had not given their consent to anything. The mini-summit fizzled.

Many Indians by this time had taken to wintering in the agencies and then drifting off again once the weather improved. Thousands came in, but when spring came, many of them went out again.

Crazy Horse, who was about thirty-five years old, enjoyed in 1875–76 what was to be his last more or less unharassed winter as a free Indian. How well or how clearly he realized that his time was ending, we don't know. Perhaps he still thought that if the people fought fiercely and didn't relent, they could beat back the whites, not all the way to the Platte perhaps, but at least out of the Powder River country. We don't really know what he was thinking and should be cautious about making him more geopolitically attuned than he may have been. At this juncture nobody had really agreed to anything, but as the spring of 1876 approached, the Army directed a number of its major players toward the northern plains. To the south, on the plains of Texas, the so-called Red River War was over. The holdouts among the Comanches and the Kiowas had been defeated and their horse herd destroyed. Ranald S. Mackenzie and Nelson A. Miles both distinguished themselves in the Red River War and were soon sent north to help subdue the Cheyennes and the northern Sioux. Gen. George Crook was already in the field, and Col. John Gibbon, Gen. Alfred Terry, and, of course, George Armstrong Custer were soon on their way.

BY MARCH OF 1876 A GREAT MANY INdians were moving north, toward Sitting Bull and the Hunkpapa band of Sioux, ready for a big hunt and possibly for a big fight with the whites, if the whites insisted on it, as in fact they did. The Little Bighorn in eastern Montana was the place chosen for this great gathering of native peoples, which swelled with more and more Indians as warmer weather came.

General Crook—also known as Three Stars, or the Grey Fox—struck first. He located what the scout Frank Grouard assured him was Crazy Horse's village, made a dawn attack, captured the village, destroyed the ample provender it contained (some of which his own hungry men could happily have eaten), but killed few Indians. Where Crazy Horse actually was at this time is a matter much debated, but the camp Crook destroyed seems not to have been his. For Crook the encounter was more vexation than triumph. The Sioux regrouped that night and got back most of their horses, and the fight drove these peace-seeking Indians back north toward Sitting Bull. Crook continued to suppose that he had destroyed Crazy Horse's village; no doubt some of the Indian's friends were there, but the man himself was elsewhere.

A vast amount had been written about the great gathering of Indians who assembled in Montana in the early summer of 1876. It was to be the last mighty grouping of native peoples on the Great Plains of America, For the older people it evoked memories of earlier summer gatherings—reunions of a sort—such as had once been held at Bear Butte, near

Perhaps Crazy Horse thought that if the people fought fiercely, they could beat back the whites, at least out of the Powder River country.

Crazy Horse's birthplace. Many of these Indians probably knew that what was occurring was in the nature of a last fling; there might be no opportunity for such a grand occasion again. Most of the Indians who gathered knew that the soldiers were coming, but they didn't care; their numbers were so great that they considered themselves invincible. Many Indians, from many tribes, remembered it as a last great meeting and mingling, a last good time. Historically, from this point on, there is a swelling body of reminiscence about the events of the spring and summer of 1876. Indeed, from the time the armies went into the field in 1876 to the end of the conflict, there is a voluminous memoir literature to be sifted through—most of it military memoirs written by whites. Much of this found its way into the small-town newspapers that by then dotted the plains. These memoirs are still emerging. In 1996 four letters written by the wife of a captain who was at Fort Robinson when Crazy Horse was killed were discovered and published. The woman's name was Angie Johnson. It had taken more than a century for this literature to trickle out of the attics and scrapbooks of America, and it is still trickling. Of course it didn't take that long for the stately memoirs of Generals Sheridan and Sherman and Miles and the rest to be published.

Though the bulk of this memoir literature is by white soldiers, quite a few of the Sioux and the Cheyennes who fought at the Little Bighorn managed to get themselves interviewed here and there. It is part of the wonder of the book *Son of the Morning Star* that Evan S. Connell has patiently located many of these obscurely published reminiscences from both sides of the fight and placed them in his narrative in such a way as to create a kind of mosaic of firsthand comment. These memoirs don't answer all the questions, or even very many of them, but it is still nice to know what the participants *thought* happened, even if what we're left with is a kind of mesquite thicket of opinion, dense with guessing, theory, and speculation. Any great military conflict—Waterloo, Gettysburg, et cetera—leaves behind a similar confusion, a museum of memories but an extremely untidy one. Did the general say that or do this? Was Chief Gall behind Custer or in front of him or nowhere near him? The mind that is troubled by unanswered and possibly unanswerable questions should perhaps avoid military history entirely. Battles are messy things. Military historians often have to resort to such statements as "it would at this juncture probably be safe to assume...." Stephen E. Ambrose is precisely right (and uncommonly frank) when he says plainly that much of the fun of studying the Battle of the Little Bighorn is the free rein it offers to the imagination. Once pointed toward this battle, the historical imagination tends to bolt; certainly the field of battle that the Indians called the Greasy Grass has caused many imaginations to bolt.

WHAT WE KNOW FOR SURE IS THAT when June rolled around in 1876, there were a great many Indians, of several tribes, camped in southern Montana, with a fair number of soldiers moving west and north to fight them. Early June of that year may have been a last moment of confidence for the Plains Indians: They were many, they had meat, and they were in *their* place. Let the soldiers come.

This buildup of confidence was capped by what was probably the best-reported dream vision in Native American history—namely, Sitting Bull's vision of soldiers falling upside down into camp. This important vision did not come to the great Hunkpapa spontaneously; instead it was elaborately prepared for. Sitting Bull allowed a friend to cut one hundred small pieces of flesh from his arms, after which he danced, staring at the sun until he fainted. When

2. Road They Did Not Know

he came out of his swoon, he heard a voice and had a vision of soldiers as numerous as grasshoppers falling upside down into camp. There were some who were skeptical of Sitting Bull—he could be a difficult sort—but this vision, coming as it did at the end of a great Sun Dance, convinced most of his people that if the soldiers did come, they would fall. (It is worth mentioning that Sitting Bull had mixed luck with visions. Not long before his death a meadowlark, speaking in Sioux, told him that his own people would kill him—which is what occurred.)

Shortly after this great vision of soldiers falling had been reported and considered, some Cheyenne scouts arrived with the news that General Crook was coming from the south with a lot of soldiers and a considerable body of Crow and Shoshone scouts. This was a sign that Sitting Bull had not danced in vain, although Crook never got very close to the great encampment, because Crazy Horse, Sitting Bull, and a large force immediately went south to challenge him on the Rosebud Creek, where the first of the two famous battles fought that summer was joined.

When the Indians attacked, Crook's thousand-man force was very strung out, with soldiers on both sides of the river, in terrain that was broken and difficult. Crow scouts were the first to spot the great party from the north; by common agreement the Crows and Shoshones fought their hearts out that day, probably saving Crook from the embarrassment of an absolute rout. But Crazy Horse, Black Twin, Bad Heart Bull, and many others were just as determined. Once or twice Crook almost succeeded in forming an effective battle line, but Crazy Horse and the others kept dashing right into it, fragmenting Crook's force and preventing a serious counterattack. There was much close-quarter, hand-to-hand fighting. In a rare anticipation of women in combat, a Cheyenne woman rushed in at some point and saved her brother, who was surrounded. (The Cheyennes afterward referred to the Battle of the Rosebud as the Battle Where the Girl Saved Her Brother.) Crook struggled all day, trying to mount a strong offensive, but the attackers were

The Indians' last moment of confidence was capped by Sitting Bull's famous dream vision of soldiers falling upside down into camp.

so persistent that they thwarted him. Finally the day waned, and shadows began to fall across the Rosebud. The Indians, having enjoyed a glorious day of battle, went home. They had turned Three Stars back, allowing him nowhere near the great gathering on the Little Bighorn.

BECAUSE THE INDIANS LEFT THE field when the day was over, Crook claimed a victory, but nobody believed him, including, probably, himself. The Battle of the Rosebud was one of his most frustrating memories. It was indeed a remarkable battle between forces almost equally matched; in some ways it was more interesting than the fight at the Little Bighorn eight days later. Neither side could mount a fully decisive offensive, and both sides suffered unusually high casualties but kept fighting. The whites had no choice, of course; their adversaries in this case fought with extreme determination. The body count for the two sides varies with the commentator. Among historians who have written about the battle, George Hyde puts Crook's loss as high as fifty-seven men, a number that presumably includes many Crows and Shoshones who fell that day. Stephen Ambrose says it was twenty-eight men; Stanley Vestal says it was ten; and Robert Utley and Evan Connell claim it was nine. The attacking Sioux and Cheyennes may themselves have lost more than thirty men, an enormous casualty rate for a native force. Accustomed as we are to the wholesale slaughter of the two world wars, or even of the Civil War, it is hard to keep in mind that when Indian fought Indian, a death count of more than three or four was unusual.

At the end of the day, General Crook at last accepted the advice his scouts had offered him earlier, which was that there were too many Indians up ahead for him to fight.

Had the full extent of Crook's difficulties on the Rosebud been known to the forces moving west into Montana, the sensible officers—that is, Gibbon and Terry—would have then proceeded with extreme caution, but it is unlikely that any trouble of Crook's would have slowed Custer one whit. Even if he had known that the Indians had sent Crook packing, it is hard to imagine that he would have proceeded differently. He had plenty of explicit—and, at the last, desperate—warnings from his own scouts, but he brushed these aside as he hurried the 7th Cavalry on to its doom. He plainly did not want to give his pessimistic scouts the time of day. He refused the offer of extra troops and also refused a Gatling gun, for fear that it might slow him down and allow the Indians to get away. It was only in the last minutes of his life that Custer finally realized that the Indians were fighting, not running. Custer was convinced that he could whip whatever body of Indians he could persuade to face him. He meant to win, he meant to win alone, and be meant to win rapidly, before any other officers arrived to dilute his glory.

Custer, that erratic egotist, has been studied more than enough; he has even been the subject of one of the best books written about the West, Evan Connell's *Son of the Morning Star*. Historians have speculated endlessly about why he did what he did at the Little Bighorn on the twenty-fifth of June, 1876; and yet what he did was perfectly in keeping with his nature. He did what he had always done: push ahead, disregard orders, start a fight, win it unassisted if possible, then start another fight. He had seldom done otherwise, and there was no reason at all to expect him to do otherwise in Montana that summer.

It may be true, as several writers have suggested, that he was covertly running for President that summer. The Democratic National Convention was just convening; a flashy victory and a timely telegram might have put him in contention for the nomination. Maybe, as Connell suggests, he thought he could mop up on the Sioux, race down to the Yellowstone River, hop on the steamer *Far*

West, and make it to the big opening of the Philadelphia Centennial Exposition on July 4. So he marched his men most of the night and flung them into battle when—as a number of Indians noted—they were so tired their legs shook as they dismounted. As usual, he did only minimal reconnaissance, and convinced himself on no evidence whatever that the Indians must be running away from him, not toward him. The highly experienced scouts who were with him—the half-breed Mitch Bouyer and the Ankara Bloody Knife and the Crow Half Yellow Face—all told Custer that they would die if they descended into the valley where the Indians were. None of them, in all their many years on the plains, had ever seen anything to match this great encampment. All the scouts knew that the valley ahead was for them the valley of death. Half Yellow Face, poetically, told Custer that they would all go home that day by a road they did not know. The fatalism of these scouts is a story in itself. Bouyer, who knew exactly what was coming, sent the young scout Curly away but then himself rode on with Custer, to his death.

WHATEVER THEY SAID, WHAT WISdom they offered, Custer ignored. It may be that he *was* running for President, but it is hard to believe that he would have done anything differently even if it had been an off year politically. Maj. Marcus Reno and Capt. Frederick Benteen, whom he had forced to split off, both testified much later that they didn't believe Custer had any plan when he pressed his attack. He was—and long had been—the most aggressive general in the American army. It didn't matter to him how many Indians there were. When he saw an enemy, he attacked, and would likely have done so even if he had had no political prospects.

In the week between the fight on the Rosebud and the one at the Little Bighorn, Crazy Horse went back to the big party. The great General Crook had been whipped; the Indians felt invincible again. Everyone knew that more soldiers were coming, but no one was particularly concerned. These soldiers could be whipped in turn.

Some commentators have suggested that a sense of doom and foreboding hung over the northern plains during this fatal week; Indian and soldier alike were said to feel it. Something dark and terrible was about to happen—and yet it was high summer in one of the most beautiful places in Montana, the one time when that vast plain is usually free of rain clouds or snow clouds. But this summer, Death was coming to a feast, and many felt his approach. On the morning of the battle, when most of the Sioux and Cheyennes were happily and securely going about their domestic business, never supposing that any soldiers would be foolish enough to attack them, Crazy Horse, it is said, marked a bloody band in red pigment on both of his horse's hips and drew an arrow and a bloody scalp on both sides of his horse's neck. Oglala scouts had been keeping watch on Custer, following his movements closely. Crazy Horse either knew or sensed that the fatal day had come.

THE BATTLE OF THE LITTLE BIGHORN, June 25 and 26, 1876, is one of the most famous battles in world history. I doubt that any other American battle—not the Alamo, not Gettysburg—has spawned a more extensive or more diverse literature. There are books, journals, newsletters, one or another of which has by now printed every scrap of reminiscence that has been dredged up. Historians, both professional and amateur, have poured forth voluminous speculations, wondering what would have happened if somebody—usually the unfortunate Major Reno—had done something differently, or if Custer hadn't foolishly split his command, or if and if and if. Though the battle took place more than 120 years ago, debate has not much slackened. In fact the sudden rise in Native American studies has resulted in increased reprinting of Indian as opposed to white reminiscences; now the Sioux and the Cheyennes are pressing the debate.

A number of white historians have argued that one or another Indian leader made the decisive moves that doomed Custer and the 7th; for these historians the battle was decided by strategy and generalship, not numbers. Both Stephen Ambrose and Mari Sandoz have written many pages about the brilliance of Crazy Horse in flanking Custer and seizing the high ground—today called Custer Hill—thus ending Custer's last hope of establishing a defensive position that might have held until reinforcements arrived. Others argue for their favorite chief, whether Gall, Two Moon, or another. Evan Connell, in his lengthy account of the battle, scarcely mentions Crazy Horse's part in it. All these arguments, of course, depend on Indian memory, plus study of the battleground itself. To me they seem to be permanently ambiguous, potent rather than conclusive. It is indeed an area of study where historians can give free rein to their imaginations; what Stephen Ambrose doesn't mention is that the Sioux and the Cheyennes, in remembering this battle, might be giving their imaginations a little running room as well. A world in which all whites are poets and all Indians sober reporters is not the world as most of us know it.

Custer was certainly very foolish, a glory hound who ignored orders and charged, all but blindly, into an overwhelming situation.

We are likely never to know for sure who killed Custer. He had his famous hair short for this campaign; had it still been long, many Indians might have recognized him. It is as well to keep in mind that as many as two thousand horses may have been in motion during this battle; between the dust they raised and the gun smoke, the scene would have become phantasmagorical; it would have been difficult for anyone to see well, or far. It is thus little wonder that no one recognized Custer. At some sharp moment Custer must have realized that his reasoning had been flawed. The Indians he had assumed were running away were actually coming to kill him, and there were a lot of them. Whether he much regretted his error is doubtful. Fighting was what Custer did, battle thrilled him, and now he was right in the dead thick of the biggest Indian fight of all. He may have enjoyed himself right up to the moment he fell.

For his men, of course, it was a different story. They had been marching since the middle of the night; a lot of them were so tired they could barely lift their guns. For them it was dust, weariness, terror, and death.

No one knows for certain how many Indians fought in this battle, but two thousand is a fair estimate, give or take a few hundred. Besides their overpowering numbers they were also highly psyched by the great Sun Dance and their recent victory over Crook. When Major Reno and his men appeared at the south end of the great four-mile village, the Indians were primed. Reno might have charged them and produced, at least, disarray, but he didn't; the Indians soon chased him back across the Little Bighorn and up a bluff, where he survived, just barely. A lucky shot hit Bloody Knife, the Arikara scout, square in the head; Major Reno, standing near, was splattered with his brain matter. Some think this gory accident undid Major Reno, but we will never know the state of his undoneness, if any. Gall, the Hunkpapa warrior, who, by common agreement, was a major factor in this battle, soon had fifteen hundred warriors mounted and ready to fight. If Reno *had* charged the south end of the village, he might have been massacred as thoroughly as Custer.

Exactly when Crazy Horse entered the battle is a matter of debate. Some say he rode out and skirmished a little with Reno's men; others believe he was still in his lodge when Reno arrived and that he was interested only in the larger fight with Custer. Most students of the battle think that when it dawned on Custer that he was in a fight for survival, not glory, he turned north, toward the high ground, hoping to establish a defensive redoubt on the hill, or rise, that is now named for him. But Crazy Horse, perhaps at the head of as many as a thousand warriors himself, flanked him and seized that high ground, sealing Custer's doom while, incidentally, making an excellent movie role for Errol Flynn and a number of other leading men.

What did the victors feel? The tribes may have recognized that they were likely never to be so unified again, and they were not.

So Crazy Horse may have done, but it was Gall and *his* thousand or so warriors who turned back Reno and then harried Custer so hard that the 7th Cavalry—the soldiers who fell into camp, as in Sitting Bull's vision—could never really establish *any* position. If Crazy Horse did flank Custer, it was of course good quarter-backing, but it hardly seems possible now to insist that any one move was decisive. Gall and his men might have finished Custer without much help from anyone; Gall had lost two of his wives and three of his children early in the battle and was fighting out his anger and his grief.

FROM THIS DISTANCE OF YEARS THE historians can argue until their teeth rot that one man or another was decisive in this battle, but all these arguments are unprovable now. What's certain is that George Armstrong Custer was very foolish, a glory hound who ignored orders, skipped or disregarded his reconnaissance, and charged, all but blindly, into a situation in which, whatever the quality of Indian generalship, he was quickly overwhelmed by numbers.

What I think of when I walk that battleground is dust. Once or twice in my life I rode out with as many as thirty cowboys; I remember the dust that small, unhurried group made. The dust of two thousand milling, charging horses would have been something else altogether; the battleground would soon have been a hell of dust, smoke, shooting, hacking; once the two groups of fighting men closed with each other, visibility could not have been good. Custer received a wound in the breast and one in the temple, either of which would have been fatal. His corpse was neither scalped nor mutilated. Bad Soup, a Hunkpapa, is said to have pointed out Custer's corpse to White Bull. "There he lies," he said. "He thought he was going to be the greatest man in the world. But there he is."

Most of the poetic remarks that come to us from this battle are the work of writers who interviewed Indians, or those who knew Indians, who thought they remembered Bad Soup saying something, or Half Yellow Face making (probably in sign) the remark about the road we do not know, or Bloody Knife staring long at the sun that morning, knowing that he would not be alive to see it go down behind the hills that evening. All we can conclude now is that Bloody Knife and Bad Soup and Half Yellow Face were right, even if they didn't say the words that have been attributed to them.

Hundreds of commentators, from survivors who fought in the battle to historians who would not be born until long years after the dust had settled in the valley of the Little Bighorn, have developed opinions about scores of issues that remain, in the end, completely opaque. Possibly Crazy Horse fought as brilliantly as some think—we will never really know—but he and Sitting Bull and Two Moon survived the battle and Custer didn't. General Grant, no sentimentalist, put the blame for the defeat squarely on Custer, and said so bluntly. The Indians made no serious attempt to root out and destroy Reno, though they could have. Victory over Long Hair was enough; Custer's famous 1868 dawn attack on the Cheyenne chief Black Kettle was well avenged.

The next day, to Major Reno's vast relief, the great gathering broke up, the Indians melting away into the sheltering vastness of the plains.

What did the Sioux and Cheyenne leaders think at this point? What did they feel? Several commentators have suggested that once the jubilation of victory subsided, a mood of foreboding returned. Perhaps the tribes recognized that they were likely never to be so unified again, and they were not. Perhaps the leaders knew that they were likely never to have such a one-sided military victory again either—a victory that was thrown them because of the vainglory of one white officer.

Or perhaps they didn't think in these terms at all—not yet. With the great rally over, the great battle won, they broke up and got on with their hunting. Perhaps a few did reckon that something was over now, but it is doubtful that many experienced the sense of climax and decline as poetically as Old Lodge Skins in Thomas Berger's novel *Little Big Man:* "Yes, my son," he says, "it is finished now, because what more can you do to an enemy than beat him? Were we fighting red men against red men—the way we used to, because that is a man's profession, and besides it is enjoyable—it would now be the turn of the other side to whip us. We would fight as hard as ever and perhaps win again, but they would definitely start with an advantage, because that is the *right* way. There is no permanent winning or losing when things move, as they should, in a circle. . . .

"But white men, who live in straight lines and squares, do not believe as I do. With them it is everything or nothing: Washita or Greasy Grass. . . . Winning is all they care about, and if they can do that by scratching a pen across a paper or saying something into the wind, they are much happier. . . ."

Old Lodge Skins was right about the Army's wanting to win. Crook's defeat at the Rosebud had embarrassed the Army, and the debacle at the Little Bighorn shamed it. The nation, of course, was outraged. By August of 1876 Crook and Terry were lumbering around with a reassuring force of some four thousand soldiers. Naturally they found few Indians. Crazy Horse was somewhere near Bear Butte, harrying the miners in the Black Hills pretty much as the mood struck him. There was a minor engagement or two, of little note. The Indians were not suicidal; they left the massive force alone. Crook and Terry were such respecters now that they were bogged down by their own might.

I N THE FALL OF THAT YEAR, THE whites, having failed to buy the Black Hills, simply took them, with a travesty of a treaty council at which the Indians lost not only the Black Hills but the Powder River, the Yellowstone, the Bighorns. By the end of what was in some ways a year of glory, 1876, Crazy Horse had to face the fact that his people had come to a desperate pass. It was a terrible winter, with subzero temperatures day after day. The Indians were ragged and hungry; the soldiers who opposed them were warmly clothed and well equipped. The victories of the previous summer were, to the Sioux and the Cheyennes, now just memories. They had little ammunition and were hard pressed to find game enough to feed themselves.

During this hard period, with the soldiers just waiting for spring to begin another series of attacks, Sitting Bull decided to take himself and his people to Canada. Crazy Horse perhaps considered this option and then rejected it because in Canada the weather was even colder, or maybe he just didn't want to leave home. But in early May of 1877, he had eleven hundred people with him, and more than two thousand horses, when he came into Red Cloud's agency at Fort Robinson in northwestern Nebraska. Probably neither the generals nor Crazy Horse himself ever quite believed that a true surrender had taken place, but this august event, the surrender of "Chief" Crazy Horse, was reported in *The New York Times* on May 8, 1877.

Larry McMurtry is the author of twenty-one novels, including Lonesome Dove *and* The Last Picture Show. *This article is excerpted from his new biography,* Crazy Horse, *published by Viking Penguin.*

Buffalo Soldiers

For decades, African-American regulars were the most effective troops on the western frontier

By T. J. Stiles

ON SEPTEMBER 24, 1868, MAJ. George A. Forsyth must have wondered if he would live to see the next morning. He lay stretched out beside the rotting carcass of his dead horse, in the willow brush and tall grass that covered a small island in the dry bed of the Arikaree River, on the vast plains of eastern Colorado Territory. All around him lay dead and wounded men—his men. And beyond the empty riverbanks, just out of rifle shot, circled the 700 Cheyenne and Oglala warriors who had kept the major's detachment trapped on this island since the 17th.

Full-scale war with the tribes of the Great Plains had just erupted; Forsyth had taken his 50 handpicked scouts out of Fort Hays in Kansas on a march to find the enemy. But the Native Americans had found Forsyth first.

On the 17th, the Cheyenne war chief the soldiers called Roman Nose had led hundreds of fighters on a dawn charge against Forsyth's camp. Their storm of bullets and arrows laid waste to his horse herd and left many of his men dead or wounded. The major himself collapsed as a slug tore into each leg and another creased his scalp. By the 24th, repeated charges and stealthy sniping had turned half his scouts into casualties; a horrific stench now rose from the dead men and animals. The survivors, who at first had used their fallen mounts as protection, now resorted to eating the horses' decaying flesh.

The beleaguered scouts saw their foes had drawn off. Then they saw why: cavalrymen... black cavalrymen.

Unknown to Forsyth, a company of cavalry was searching for him. Two of his scouts had slipped through the besieging Indians and made their way to Fort Wallace in Kansas, where they had alerted Capt. Louis H. Carpenter, an old Civil War comrade of the major's.

The next day, the beleaguered scouts on that malodorous little island noticed that the Indians had drawn off. Then they saw why: in the distance they discovered movement, which gradually took the form of mounted men... cavalrymen... black cavalrymen. They were Captain Carpenter's troopers, pounding across the dry grass. This unit went by the name of Company H, 10th Cavalry—but Forsyth's men may indeed have known them by the name that the African-American troops earned from their Indian foes: they were the buffalo soldiers.

Forsyth's fight entered Western legend as the Battle of Beecher's Island, but few remember that he was rescued so dramatically by black troops. Despite a recent wave of interest in the professional African-American soldiers of the 19th century, many writers have treated them as a footnote to the history of the frontier. In fact, black regulars took center stage in the Army's great Western drama, shouldering combat responsibilities far out of proportion to their numbers (which averaged 10 percent of the military's total strength). Over the course of three decades on the frontier, the buffalo soldiers emerged as the most professional experienced and effective troops in the service.

When Carpenter led his company into Forsyth's grim camp, only three years had passed since the end of the Civil War. Some 180,000 African-Americans had carried arms for the Union, filling out regiments, divisions, even an entire corps (the 25th, part of which occupied Richmond in the war's closing days). These were all-volunteer units, however, established for the duration of the war. Not one company in the standing Regular Army was open to African-American recruits. But on July 28, 1866, Congress provided for four Regular Army infantry regiments (the 38th, 39th, 40th and 41st) and two of cavalry (the 9th and 10th), to be composed exclusively of black enlisted men. The Army would *have* to accept African-Americans.

Almost immediately, the new black regulars found themselves in combat on the frontier. Lt. Col. George Armstrong

Illustration by Arthur Shilstone

Custer's wife, Elizabeth, described an incident in June 1867 (based on an account in one of her husband's letters), when 300 Cheyennes swept down on Fort Wallace, where Custer was in command. A squad of black infantrymen from the 38th had arrived to pick up supplies, when the white garrison spilled out to form a firing line.

Suddenly, a wagon pulled by four mules tore out to the line of battle, Elizabeth wrote. "It was filled with Negroes, standing up, all firing in the direction of the Indians. The driver lashed the mules with his blacksnake, and roared at them as they ran. When the skirmish line was reached, the colored men leaped out and began firing again. No one had ordered them to leave their picket-station, but they were determined that no soldiering should be carried on in which their valor was not proved."

Despite the brave showing, the 38th Infantry was not to last. On March 3, 1869, a new law ordained a general reduction in the Army: the 38th and 41st regiments were consolidated into the new 24th Infantry, and the 39th and 40th merged to create the 25th Infantry. Oc-

> *For hours they fought, pumping bullets out of the carbines so fast the barrels grew blisteringly hot.*

casionally, companies from the 24th and 25th infantries served with their mounted counterparts, sometimes engaging in heavy combat. The lion's share of adventure fell to the special corps of black Seminole scouts—Indians of largely African descent (SMITHSONIAN, August 1991)—who served with the 24th Infantry under Lt. John Bullis. On the whole, however, the African-American infantry regiments missed out on much of the glory won by the black cavalry.

Throughout the frontier era, black soldiers endured nearly unbearable conditions. Indeed, they complained of receiving the worst of everything, including surplus equipment and cast-off horses; many white officers openly be-

moaned their assignments and some abused their troops. Maybe worst of all was local prejudice—and the Army did little if anything to help. In Texas, for example, when a sheriff killed a black Medal of Honor recipient, shooting him in the back, nothing was done. A Nebraskan who killed three black soldiers, including another Medal of Honor winner, also went unpunished. And it was nearly impossible for African-American soldiers to get commissions. One man from the 9th Cavalry said of the regiments at Fort Robinson, late in the century, "not a single colored soldier has been promoted from the ranks to the grade of an officer... the army is decidedly against it."

The demands of frontier warfare, however, led to wide dispersion of most regiments, which placed tremendous importance on the leadership qualities of noncommissioned officers. That was certainly true of the 9th Cavalry, scattered across the rough Texas landscape in tiny, undermanned posts. Yet the 9th's sergeants and corporals were precisely the men whom the Army thought most unsuited to soldiering and command: in

3. Buffalo Soldiers

Corporal Greaves arced his empty weapon in the air, slamming it into the body of the warrior.

Illustration by Arthur Shilstone

the early years they were mostly former slaves, drawn primarily from the plantation country of Louisiana and Mississippi. Often illiterate in the beginning, these officers—and their troopers—displayed a voracious appetite for education, and they ultimately set the standard for professionalism. Desertion rates for many regiments surpassed 25 percent a year; not so among the buffalo soldiers. As the service newspaper reported, "The Ninth Cavalry astonished the Army by reporting not a single desertion for twelve months."

Before 1867 came to a close, the 9th Cavalry's raw recruits won the respect of every armed opponent anywhere close to Texas. Christmas day found Capt. William Frohock and Company K on a patrol at the Pecos River, 75 miles east of Fort Stockton. The troopers settled for the night in empty Fort Lancaster, a long-abandoned post. Three men, privates Anderson Trimble, Edward Bowers and William Sharpe, stood guard over the horse herd as the troops stretched out to sleep.

The next day, Trimble, Bowers and Sharpe found themselves surrounded by armed men on horseback. They were lassoed and dragged to their deaths behind their assailants' horses. Meanwhile, the strangers turned to the company holed up in Fort Lancaster.

Captain Frohock had trouble making out just who was firing on his detachment (the attackers were most likely Lipans, Kickapoos and Mexican outlaws). In the flurry of shouting men, ricocheting bullets, swirling dust and pounding hooves, he estimated that at least 900 opponents encircled his men. If his guess was correct, it meant that Company K—fewer than 70 troopers—faced more men than served in the entire 9th Cavalry.

The inexperienced buffalo soldiers threw down a curtain of fire from their seven-shot Spencer carbines. For hours they fought, pumping bullets out of their carbines so fast the barrels grew blisteringly hot. Finally the enemy drew off, carrying away 20 dead and scores of wounded. The buffalo soldiers had triumphed; never again would the Lipans and Kickapoos dare to attack them so directly.

For eight years, the 9th Cavalry fought numerous pitched battles against Lipans, Kickapoos, Kiowas, Comanches—and the people destined to be their most determined foes, the Apaches. Then in late 1875, Col. Edward Hatch took the regiment into the Apache homeland, the New Mexico Territory. There he assumed the role of department commander, and his men devoted themselves to battling various Apache war parties that frequently struck out on raids off the reservations.

These warriors had long since mastered mountain guerrilla warfare. Unlike the Sioux, Cheyennes, Kiowas or Comanches, who fought primarily to keep ranchers and hunters off their homelands, the Apaches had lived for centuries among Hispanic settlements, alternately raiding and trading with neighboring villages. They knew how to lay expert ambushes in the steep cliffs lining the valleys of the Southwest, how to throw off pursuers by leaving behind elaborate dummy camps, how to camouflage cuts in telegraph lines by splicing them with leather thongs.

The 9th was in the field constantly. Pvt. Henry Bush remembered being "continuously on scouting service which subjected us to great exposure, such as sleeping in rains and snows in the mountains unprotected from the elements, sometimes no sleep for two days, sometimes subsisting on the most meager diet, sometimes marches of ninety miles . . . in a hot scorching sun." And when they did make contact, the fighting was ferocious.

In January 1877, Capt. Charles D. Beyer learned that a party of Apaches had broken out of the San Carlos reservation in Arizona and had crossed into New Mexico. He issued orders to Lt. Henry Wright to mount six troopers and three Navajo scouts and find their trail. On a cold, clear, winter day, the detachment of buffalo soldiers clambered up through the rocky Florida Mountains, riding right up to the edge of a camp of more than 40 Apaches.

The troops immediately saw how precarious their situation was: ten men, deep in the mountains and far from help, surrounded by nearly five times their number. Even worse, they no longer carried the rapid-firing Spencer carbines, which carried seven rounds in a tubular

1 ❖ RECONSTRUCTION AND THE GILDED AGE

> *"When they recognized us as troops, they came out of their houses waving their towels and handkerchiefs for joy."*

magazine; they now used single-shot Springfields, while many Apaches wielded new multi-shot Winchesters.

Lieutenant Wright decided to brazen it out. He trotted his horse straight into the heart of the camp, followed by his tiny squad, and shouted for the Apache chiefs to meet him in council. The troopers slid off their saddles as Wright spoke to the Indians through a Navajo scout. He and his men, he said, would be happy to accept their surrender. The chiefs apparently did not laugh; as the negotiations continued, the soldiers noticed that the women and children were silently slipping away while the warriors encircled the detachment.

Suddenly Wright shouted for his men to break through the ring. At the first step forward, the Apaches shouldered their rifles. In an instant, 26-year-old Cpl. Clinton Greaves swiveled his carbine toward the closest warrior and squeezed off its single round. Leaping toward the line of warriors, he seized the barrel of his weapon and arced its wooden shoulder stock through the air, slamming it into the body of one of his foes.

As this powerful trooper—"a big fine looking soldier," another trooper recalled—swung left and right, the rest of the detachment fired and reloaded madly. Lieutenant Wright shot down a nearby Apache; privates Dick Mackadoo and Richard Epps shot three more warriors as lead snapped through the air in every direction. The troopers frantically mounted and galloped through the opening Corporal Greaves had created. After a few seconds more of intense fighting, the Apaches themselves scattered to the mountain peaks for cover, intending to challenge the soldiers from afar. The troopers not only managed to get away unscathed, but left with 11 Apache horses.

Illustration by Arthur Shilstone

Wright and his men earned nearly legendary status within the regiment for their brave stand in the Florida Mountains. But the highest recognition of all went to Corporal Greaves: on June 26, 1879, he became the second trooper in the 9th Cavalry to earn the Medal of Honor.

Soon the regiment came to grips with the leader who would prove to be its deadliest enemy of all: Victorio, chief of the Warm Springs band of Apaches. Tension had been building as the Bureau of Indian Affairs tried to shift his people to the San Carlos reservation in Arizona. After two escapes from San Carlos, Victorio and his band were permitted to remain at a reservation in their native New Mexico. Just when a measure of peace seemed to be in hand, lawmen arrived to arrest the chief for murder. In August 1879, he fled the reservation with 60 followers, soon to multiply to more than 300. The Victorio War had begun.

The men of the 9th Cavalry quickly learned how Victorio had won his reputation as a great war chief. He selected as one of his first targets the horse herd of Company E; on September 4, the Indians killed five troopers, wounded three more and rode off with 46 animals. Shortly afterward, Victorio unleashed a well-planned ambush in the canyon of the Los Animas River, leaving as many as eight buffalo soldiers dead or wounded.

After these setbacks, Col. Hatch assigned Maj. Albert B. Morrow to lead the pursuit. Morrow's hard-riding troopers repeatedly made contact with Victorio's forces, engaging in bitter but indecisive fighting. The skillful Apache would slip away over the border into Mexico, where the 9th Cavalry's scouts could not follow.

On May 13, 1880, Sgt. George Jordan of Company K learned precisely where the Apaches were. This native of Tennessee had just made camp with 25 men at a stage station, having spent a long day escorting a train of supply wagons. As the detachment prepared for a well-earned night of rest, a courier rode in with a desperate message: Victorio was headed for the settlement of Fort Tularosa.

The sergeant called his men together. "They all said they would go on as far as they could," Jordan reported. At 8 o'clock in the evening, they began a hard march for the endangered village. At about 6 the next morning, the tired troopers rode into the silent town, its women and children peering out apprehensively through shuttered windows. "When they recognized us as troops," he recalled, "they came out of their houses waving towels and handkerchiefs for joy."

Sergeant Jordan boasted more than ten years of experience in the 9th Cavalry; he knew what it meant to command a detachment, and he knew how to fight the Apaches. After a brief rest, he set his men to work building a stockade. By the end of the afternoon, they were done; the men had not slept for at least 24 hours, but they could now lead the residents inside a hastily built fort.

As the sun dipped down to the west, Sergeant Jordan stood outside the stockade talking to a civilian when a shot cracked the quiet evening. Instantly dozens of bullets spattered the ground as Jordan and his companion sprinted for the fort. Soon scores of Apache warriors charged across the dry desert floor. "[They] tried time and time again to enter our works," Jordan reported, "but we repulsed them each time, and when they finally saw that we were masters of the situation they turned their attention to the stock and tried to run it off." Head-on attacks against an entrenched foe were not the Apache way; Victorio soon pulled away. "The whole action was short but exciting while it lasted, and after it was all over the townspeople congratulated us for having repulsed a band of more than 100." Congress congratulated Jordan with the Medal of Honor.

Nine days later, a unit of Indian scouts severely shot up Victorio's camp, sending the chief flying into Mexico with Morrow's command snapping at his heels. The move set the stage for the final, decisive phase of the campaign—and shifted the burden to the rest of the buffalo soldiers: the men of the 10th Cavalry, led by Col. Benjamin Grierson, and those of the 24th and 25th infantries.

Grierson believed Victorio would reenter the United States in western Texas; to stop him, he decided to cast a net to ensnare the chief no matter which direction he turned. The key was water: only a handful of springs dotted the dry mountains southeast of El Paso. By guarding the most important water holes, and by posting a network of scouts along the Rio Grande, he could block any attempt to penetrate West Texas.

The night of July 29 found Grierson at Tenaja de los Palmos, a strategic water hole between Fort Quitman (to the west on the Rio Grande) and Eagle Springs (15 miles to the east). He had with him a half-dozen buffalo soldiers, one white officer and his 20-year-old son, Robert. Earlier that day, Grierson and his men had been met by three African-American troopers bearing a critical dispatch from the Rio Grande: the Apaches had been seen crossing the river into Texas.

It was no ordinary buffalo soldier who led the couriers; it was Lt. Henry O. Flipper, the first black graduate of West Point and an officer of the 10th Cavalry. "I rode 98 miles in 22 hours mostly at night, through a country the Indians were expected to traverse," he wrote. "I had no bad effects from the hard ride till I reached [Grierson's] tent. When I attempted to dismount, I found I was stiff and sore and fell from my horse to the ground. . . ."

After resting, Flipper left with orders that all available troops should make haste for Grierson's position. Meanwhile the colonel and his men spent the night throwing up two stone breastworks atop the rocky ridge overlooking the water hole. Despite the desperate odds, Grierson had decided to make a stand. If he could deny Victorio access to the water in that canyon, he was certain that the Apaches would have to turn back to Mexico. The next morning, at about 4 o'clock, Lt. Leighton Finley rode in with reinforcements: a mere ten cavalrymen.

Young Robert Grierson would later scrawl in his journal a vivid account of the events that followed. Sometime after 8, as the little party finished breakfast, the scouts south of camp sent up the cry "Here come the Indians!" Then he saw them: dozens of long-haired warriors, rifles held at the ready as they nudged their horses through the canyon southeast of their position on the ridge.

As a dense cluster of Apaches rode slowly across the rough trail, the Indians heard the sound of galloping horses. Down Finley's buffalo soldiers came, snapping off shots as they thundered into the valley. "Several Indians hid in a hollow till Lt. F. passed, & then fired on his party," Robert wrote. "He had them on both sides of him & poured it into them thick & vice versa. The rifles sounded splendidly and you could hear the balls singing. Just as Lt. Finley was about to dislodge the Indians from behind a ledge, Capt. Viele's and Lt. Colladay's companies came & in the smoke and dust took F. for Indians and fired on him."

Capt. Charles Viele, Lieutenant Flipper and the troopers of Company C had just arrived from Fort Quitman. Now they fired on Finley by mistake; fortunately, both Viele and Finley pulled their men back to Grierson's breastworks. "All got back about the same time," wrote Robert, except one black trooper whose horse had been shot; after him galloped the resurgent warriors, convinced now that the battle had turned in their favor. "He got along as best he could—the Indians were nearly on him—he turned & fired his revolver & this checked them some."

Grierson ordered his men to fire. "We then let fly from our fortifications at the Indians about 300 yards off & golly!! You ought to've seen 'em turn tail & strike for the hills." In four hours of desperate fighting, the Apaches lost seven men; the 10th Cavalry, one trooper. The battle left Victorio short on food and water, and saddled with dead and wounded; he had no choice but to retreat to Mexico.

In early August, he returned and slipped past Grierson's men on his way to another strategic water hole, Rattlesnake Springs. Determined to get there first, Grierson and his men covered 65 miles in 21 hours. The buffalo soldiers outpaced their fast-moving Indian foes as Grierson led them on a parallel path, keeping to the far side of a mountain range to mask their presence from the enemy.

The 10th Cavalry won the race, arriving in the early hours of August 6. "We got there and at once took position for a fight," Flipper recalled. Grierson laid out an elaborate ambush, sending Captain Viele with companies C and G to occupy the walls of the valley above the springs. "No lights or fires were allowed and we had to eat cold suppers without coffee," Flipper continued. "If [the Apaches] once got in as far as the spring, we would have them surrounded and every vantage point occupied."

At 2 in the afternoon, the long, ragged band of Apaches rode into sight, ambling slowly through the bunchgrass and rocks and cactus on their tired horses. The Indians in the lead sensed that something was wrong and stopped their advance. When Viele saw them grow cautious, he gave orders to commence firing. The first of eight volleys of rifle fire erupted from the valley walls; Victorio's men scrambled for cover.

The master of the ambush had been ambushed himself—but the trap had been sprung too soon, and the long-range fire did little damage to the Indians. The Apaches, however, were desperate for water. Victorio rallied his men for an attack. Warriors on horseback surged across the valley floor, screaming their defiance and loosing shots at the dug-in buffalo soldiers. Just as the Apaches neared the springs, Capt. Louis H. Carpenter and Lt. Thaddeus Winfield Jones led companies H and B on a charge from one flank, crashing into the Apaches with carbines blazing. Victorio's men withdrew once again.

Over the next two hours, the firing died away to silence; Grierson knew better than to stage a pointless assault on Apaches holed up in the rocks. Then, as so often happened in battle, the unexpected occurred. At 4 o'clock a line of wagons rounded a mountain eight miles southeast of the water hole. A party of warriors emerged from the rocks and scampered onto their ponies, undoubtedly relieved to find an easy target beyond the reach of Grierson's men (and probably hoping to get some water as well).

Suddenly the Apaches pulled up short—for out of the wagons poured the buffalo soldiers of the 24th Infantry, the escort for this supply train for the 10th Cavalry. These foot soldiers unleashed a devastating fire across the valley floor. The Indians turned and fled; and within a few days they fell back to Mexico.

On October 14, 1880, Mexican troops trapped Victorio's badly reduced forces, killing the great chief in the final assault. But the victory had already been won. The Victorio War was perhaps the most difficult campaign ever waged against the Apaches. It was also one of the few Apache wars fought largely by regular troops, not Apache scouts enlisted by the Army—and those troops were largely buffalo soldiers. They outmarched, out-fought and out-generaled a foe often considered to be the hardest marching, hardest fighting, most skillful enemy in frontier history.

Over the remaining years of the frontier era, the buffalo soldiers stayed at the center of events. The 10th Cavalry, for example, played a significant role in the last major act of Indian warfare in the Southwest: the Geronimo Campaign of 1885–86. The 9th Cavalry and the 25th Infantry also joined operations against the Sioux in 1890–91.

Lieutenant Flipper, however, endured a sad sequel to the Victorio War. As the only African-American line officer in the 10th, he remained the object of special hatred by many of his fellow officers. As quartermaster at Fort Davis, Texas, in July 1881 he discovered commissary money was missing from his trunk. On December 8, 1881, a court-martial found Flipper innocent of embezzling the funds—but guilty of "conduct unbecoming an officer. (Historians believe the court-martial occurred as a result of Flipper's friendship, albeit platonic, with a white woman.) Expelled from the military, he worked as a civil engineer, and as a translator, but he failed in his unceasing efforts to clear his name. Finally, on December 13, 1976, after long campaigning by Flipper's descendants and defenders, the Army's board of corrections exonerated him, issuing an honorable discharge 36 years after his death.

As the buffalo soldiers watched the promising age of Reconstruction—the nation's first civil rights era—come crashing down into the rubble of segregation, they saw themselves as the last bastion of public service for African-Americans. "They are possessed of the notion," wrote one chaplain, "that the colored people of the whole country are more or less affected by their conduct in the Army."

In the Spanish-American War and in the Philippine insurrections, these regiments added pages to their thick record of accomplishments. Ironically, these units were largely kept out of combat in the two world wars, although African-American volunteers and draftees fought courageously in France, Italy and Germany. Yet even those who saw combat suffered severe prejudice; only a handful received awards for valor. On January 13, 1997, President Bill Clinton took a small step to rectify this injustice by awarding the Medal of Honor to seven African-Americans who had served in World War II.

In recent years, interest in the buffalo soldiers has flourished. They have been commemorated with a postage stamp, historical-reenactment groups and a 1997 cable television movie. Much of the new recognition stems from the efforts of one black officer who strongly identifies with his 19th-century predecessors. In 1982 he arrived at Fort Leavenworth, Kansas (birthplace of the 10th Cavalry), and was dismayed to find not one memorial to the buffalo soldiers' "incredible contribution to the American West." That officer was Colin Powell. In 1992, he returned to Fort Leavenworth—this time as chairman of the Joint Chiefs of Staff—to dedicate a monument by sculptor Eddie Dixon. It was a fitting tribute from a military that hesitated to accept African-Americans, learned to depend on them, and finally—under the leadership of a modern black soldier—has come to honor their memory.

T. J. Stiles, who has written several books on American history, is working on a biography of Jesse James, to be published by Alfred A. Knopf. Arthur Shilstone has illustrated numerous SMITHSONIAN *stories.*

Undermining the Molly Maguires

A series of violent crimes was plaguing Pennsylvania's coal country. Mine owners placed the blame on a secret society of Irishmen—and took steps to wipe it out.

by Joseph H. Bloom

ON October 27, 1873, a slightly built, bespectacled, and unshaven man calling himself James McKenna alighted from a train at the station in Port Clinton, a small community on the southern border of Pennsylvania's Schuylkill County. It was a coal-mining country, a rough part of the world suffering from the effects of what one newspaper had called a "reign of terror" orchestrated by a shadowy organization dubbed the Molly Maguires. Since 1862 the Mollies had been blamed for numerous murders, beatings, knifings, armed robberies, and incidents of arson.

The exploits of the Molly Maguires had been detailed in many colorful newspaper articles throughout the country, but that hadn't discouraged McKenna. In fact, he arrived in Schuylkill County determined to join the secret society. He wasn't sure how, but he was confident that his naturally friendly demeanor and quick wit would help him make the proper contacts.

BOTH: HISTORICAL SOCIETY OF SCHUYLKILL COUNTY

This man, going by the name James McKenna, arrived in eastern Pennsylvania's coal country during a time of labor unrest.

His Irish background would help too. The Mollies were all Irish Catholics, drawn mainly from the desperately poor men who worked in the coal mines of eastern Pennsylvania. Theirs was a hard life of cave-ins, explosions, flooded mines, and long hours of backbreaking labor in the darkness, all for wages that were barely sufficient to support a family. The mine workers even had to buy their own work tools and dynamite at the company store for elevated prices. The terrible conditions led many of the miners to join the Workingmen's Benevolent Association, a trade union that fought for better conditions in the mines. The mine owners, however, were equally determined to smash the union. The resulting conflict between workers and owners sparked the creation of the Molly Maguires, who vowed to fight the exploitation of the workers by predominantly Protestant mine owners and supervisors.

It was in this tense atmosphere that James McKenna found himself when he stepped off the train. At first he wan-

Individuals sometimes received "coffin notices," supposedly from the Mollies.

1 ❖ RECONSTRUCTION AND THE GILDED AGE

BOTH: HISTORICAL SOCIETY OF SCHUYLKILL COUNTY
Jack Kehoe, dubbed "The King of the Molly Maguires" by prosecuting attorneys, was a leader of the Irish community in Girardville.

James "Powder Keg" Kerrigan's testimony during the trials helped convict some of the accused Mollies.

Scholarly writer Francis P. Dewees summed up the era of the Molly Maguires as "a reign of blood... they held communities terror bound, and wantonly defied the law, destroyed property and sported human life."

dered through the region's small towns, seeking out Irishmen who might have Molly Maguire connections, but he couldn't get more than a passing word from anybody. After reaching Pottsville in December 1873, he began to frequent the Sheridan House, a popular saloon run by a loquacious Irishman named "Big Pat" Dormer. McKenna soon became a popular character around the bar, entertaining customers by spinning tall tales and dancing Irish jigs. In conversation, McKenna let it be known that he was wanted for murder and counterfeiting in Buffalo, New York. He proved himself to be handy with his fists and soon gained a reputation among the rougher elements who drank at Dormer's bar. His standing was secured after the Coal & Iron Police, a private constabulary raised by the mine owners and railroad operators to help protect their interests, arrested McKenna at the bar, interrogated him, and roughed him up.

Dormer himself was impressed with McKenna, and in February 1874 took him to the neighboring town of Shenandoah to meet fellow saloonkeeper Muff Lawler. With Lawler's backing, McKenna got work at the Indian Ridge Shaft and later at the West Shenandoah Colliery. Lawler also took McKenna to see—or more accurately to be seen by—John "Jack" Kehoe. Jack Kehoe ran the Hibernian House saloon in Girardville, an important Molly headquarters, and was a kingpin in the organization. Without McKenna knowing how, Kehoe secretly signaled his approval of the newcomer, and McKenna soon received an invitation to a secret meeting of the Ancient Order of the Hibernians.

The A.O.H. was a nationwide fraternal organization whose membership was limited to those of Irish-Catholic descent. In the coal region, however, the A.O.H. served as the cover organization for the Molly Maguires. Although not all members of the local A.O.H. lodges were Mollies, all of the Molly Maguires eventually tried and convicted of crimes were members of the A.O.H.

At an A.O.H. meeting on April 14, 1874, as McKenna later related, he was "ordered to go to my knees, and take my hat off, and there was a document read to me by the Division Master, Mr. Lawler... the substance of which that I obey my superiors in everything connected with the organization, in things lawful and not otherwise. It also contained a clause that I should keep everything secret pertaining to this organization. I then kissed the Test, the same as I would a Bible in a Court of Justice." When he rose, McKenna was a confirmed member of the Molly Maguires.

MCKENNA ROSE HIGH in the organization over the next two years, in large measure because he could read and write, accomplishments not shared by many of the brethren. He became secretary and later bodymaster (president) of the Shenandoah lodge and a trusted advisor in many matters. On one occasion, when members of the Shenandoah lodge planned to strike a blow against the mine owners by dynamiting the Ringtown bridge, a railway bridge used by coal trains, McKenna warned them that the authorities kept a close watch on the structure. Fearing arrest, the men abandoned the plan.

Several highly publicized murders took place during McKenna's stay in the coal region, including that of Benjamin Yost, a police officer who had crossed the Mollies by arresting and beating member Thomas Duffy. In the early morning hours of July 14, 1875, three men waited in a cemetery near the end of Yost's beat in Tamaqua. As the police officer climbed a ladder to extinguish a street lamp, Hugh McGehan and James

4. Undermining the Molly Maguires

HISTORICAL SOCIETY OF SCHUYLKILL COUNTY

James Roarity was implicated in the death of police officer Benjamin Yost. According to informer James Kerrigan, Roarity arranged for Hugh McGehan and James Boyle to commit the murder. Roarity was found guilty and was hanged in Pottsville on June 21, 1877, for his part in the police officer's murder.

Boyle stepped forward and shot him. Yost fell mortally wounded while his attackers, along with their guide, James "Powder Keg" Kerrigan, made their escape.

The organization sometimes asked members from one lodge to carry out violent assignments in another lodge's jurisdiction, the advantage being that Mollies from outside the area would not be recognized. The plot to kill Yost was allegedly hatched in the Tamaqua tavern run by James Carroll and carried out by McGehan and Boyle of Summit Hill. After the Yost killing, two Mollies from the Laffee district, Michael J. Doyle and Edward Kelly, were commissioned to gun down Welsh mine superintendent John P. Jones of Tamaqua. The Mollies had accused the superintendent of blacklisting miners who had taken part in a strike. On September 3 Jones was shot in the back as he walked along the pipeline that led to the Lehigh and Wilkes-Barre Coal Company mine in Lansford, Carbon County.

In a similar fashion, Thomas Sanger, foreman of Heaton's Colliery in Raven Run near Girardville, and miner William Uren had been gunned down two days earlier as they walked along an empty street to work. Sanger died because of an alleged workplace grievance, while Uren, who boarded with the Sanger family, was slain to eliminate him as a witness.

The violence, however, was not all one-sided. The most noteworthy case of the tables being turned took place in Wiggans Patch, near Mahanoy City. Early in the morning of December 10, 1875, a group of armed and masked men burst into the home of the three men believed to be involved in the deaths of Sanger and Uren. The vigilantes killed suspected murderer Charles O'Donnell and also the pregnant wife of Charles McAllister. (McAllister was wounded but survived.) Moreover, in the frenzy and confusion, one of the attackers pistol-whipped McAllister's mother-in-law. The true identity of the Wiggans Patch attackers was never established, but rumors blamed the attack on a group of irate valley residents trained by Captain Robert Linden of the Coal & Iron Police.

The Wiggans Patch incident came as a shock to the Molly Maguires. How had the attackers known that McAllister and O'Donnell had been involved in the Sanger and Uren killings? The organization was further shaken by a series of recent arrests, indicating that there was an informer within the Molly Maguires. On February 23, Shenandoah bodymaster Frank McAndrew warned McKenna that Jack Kehoe was laying bets that he, McKenna, was the spy among them. Instead of fleeing for his life, however, McKenna confronted Kehoe at his bar in Girardville and demanded that he call a conclave of the organization's leaders so that McKenna could defend himself. Kehoe agreed to the meeting but secretly assigned men to murder McKenna instead. Two weeks later, James McKenna disappeared from the region.

THE FIRST OF THE MOLLY MACQUIRE trials was held in Mauch Chunk (renamed Jim Thorpe in 1954) in January 1876 and in Pottsville in May, after the Coal & Iron Police had rounded up dozens of men on charges ranging from beatings to murder. During the Pottsville trial of James Carroll, Thomas Duffy, James Roarity, Hugh McGehan, and James Boyle for the murder of Benjamin Yost, the prosecution announced a surprise witness. On May 6, 1876, an impeccably dressed, clean-shaven man strode into the courthouse, took the stand, and testified. "My name is James McParlan," he said. "I came into Schuylkill County in October 1873 under the name of James McKenna. I am a detective. I belong to the National Detective Agency commonly known as Pinkerton's Detective Force. I was sent here by Major Allan Pinkerton of Chicago, the chief. I came to discover as to who were connected with an organization known as the Molly Maguires."

Before a stunned courtroom, McParlan recounted how Yost's murder was planned in Carroll's bar. He testified that some time after the murder Hugh McGehan showed him the pistol he had used to kill the police officer. When defense lawyers accused the detective of being an *agent provocateur* who participated willingly in Molly outrages, McParlan responded that he was often unable to forewarn intended victims in time and was forced to appear to participate in the Mollies' plans in order to protect not just his undercover mission but very probably his life.

McParlan had been hired through the efforts of the sworn enemy of the Molly Maguires, Franklin Benjamin Gowen, president of the Philadelphia & Reading Railroad. Gowen's company held a monopoly on rail transport in and out of the southern anthracite region. Determined to forestall the rise of a strong union movement and break the Mollies, Gowen turned to Allan Pinkerton, the head of America's most famous private detective agency.

Born in Scotland, Pinkerton had come to the United States and eventually settled in Chicago, where he founded the Pinkerton National Detective Agency in 1850. While working for the Illinois Central Railroad, Pinkerton met the line's vice president, George B. McClellan, who later employed him to handle intelligence for the Army of the Potomac during the Civil War. As General McClellan's intelligence chief in the Peninsula Campaign, Pinkerton substantially overstated the enemy's numbers, reinforcing the general's belief that he faced overwhelming odds. McClellan

1 ❖ RECONSTRUCTION AND THE GILDED AGE

WITH PERMISSION-PINKERTON, INC. LIBRARY OF CONGRESS

Above: Alan Pinkerton, head of the detective agency that bore his name, was hired by mine owners to help break up the Molly Maguires. Right: Franklin B. Gowen, president of the Philadelphia & Reading Railroad, conducted some prosecutions himself.

eventually lost his command, so Pinkerton returned to detective work and opened agency branches in Philadelphia and New York. He concentrated on railroad robberies and security but also became involved in helping industrialists fight labor disputes.

Gowen and Pinkerton decided that the best way to bring the Mollies to heel was to plant a trusted Pinkerton detective within the organization. Pinkerton reasoned that the man for the job would have to be an "Irishman and a Catholic, as only this class of person can find admission to the Mollie Maguires. My detective should become, to all intents and purposes, one of the order, and continue so while he remains in the case before us." Pinkerton decided that 29-year-old James McParlan was the best man for the assignment.

Pennsylvania Governor Milton J. Shapp said, "We can be proud of the men known as the Molly Maguires, because they defiantly faced allegations which attempted to make trade unionism a criminal conspiracy."

Born in Ulster's County Armagh in 1844, McParlan came to the United States in 1867. He made his way to Chicago, where he filled a number of billets, ranging from entertainer in a German beer garden to "preventive policeman" with a small Chicago detective agency. He joined the Pinkerton National Detective Agency in 1871 and once went undercover to expose pilferers on the streetcars of Chicago.

What the Irish detective lacked in experience he made up for in other ways. McParlan possessed an outgoing personality, with a good sense of humor and a knack for quickly ingratiating himself to those he met. He was an excellent boxer and an even more effective rough-and-tumble fighter, a nimble dancer of Irish jigs, a sweet-voiced tenor, a ladies' man of considerable sophistication, and a man who could drink unbelievably large quantities of whisky and retain his fac-

4. Undermining the Molly Maguires

How Did They Get That Name?

Theories abound about the origin of the Molly Maguires' name, but all refer it back to Ireland. They include stories of peasants who banded together to avenge Molly Maguire, an old woman who had been evicted from her house; a tavern owner of that name who allowed a secret society to meet on her premises; and a fierce, pistol-packing woman who led her male followers on raids through the countryside. Most likely, the name came from groups of Irishmen who called themselves the Molly Maguires, and who engaged in violence against the agents of their English landlords during the eighteenth and nineteenth centuries. These men dressed in women's clothes and blackened their faces, not only as a disguise but to indicate their dedication to a mythical Molly Maguire who symbolized their struggle against injustice.

There is no evidence to suggest that the men who acted against the Pennsylvania mine owners named themselves after the Irish Molly Maguires. In 1857 Benjamin Bannan, editor of the Schuylkill County *Miners' Journal*, brought the name to the attention of the American public when he used it as a term for all the aspects of the Irish character that he found unsavory. He kept the name alive for several years in newspaper articles with headings such as "A Molly on the Rampage" and "Molly Beating." Franklin B. Gowen perpetuated the name during legislative hearings for rate raises for his railroad in 1871. He suggested to the committee that the area was under attack by a group of men he referred to as the Molly Maguires.

---

ulties. McParlan put these "talents" to good use during his undercover work, although the full story of McParlan's more than two years in the coal region will probably never be known. The detective, who died in 1919, never set down a full account of his adventures. Historians consider Pinkerton's own version, *The Mollie Maguires and the Detectives*, to be semi-fictional.

The only person in the coal region who knew McParlan's true identity was Captain Linden of the Coal & Iron Police. Linden was also employed by Pinkerton, and his arrests and interrogations of McParlan were orchestrated opportunities to exchange information. Whenever possible, McParlan used Linden to pass word of upcoming outrages and to warn victims. At other times, such as in the case of the Ringtown bridge episode, he sought to scuttle or at least delay plans. McParlan reported on numerous Molly crimes by train mail sent to the head of the Pinkerton office in Philadelphia. His cover was nearly blown when a letter from the Philadelphia office arrived at the Pottsville post office addressed to James McParlan instead of James McKenna.

The strain of undercover work took a toll of McParlan's health. He suffered from several bouts of illness but steadfastly continued his work until he learned of the Wiggans Patch incident. The detective became so incensed that he tendered his resignation in a letter to Benjamin Franklin of the Pinkerton office in Philadelphia, saying he was not "going to be accessory to the murder of women and children." Franklin immediately wrote a letter to Pinkerton: "This morning I received a report from 'Mac' of which I sent you a copy, and in which he seems to be very much surprised at the shooting of these men; and he offers his resignation. I telegraphed 'Mac' to come here from Pottsville as I am anxious to satisfy him that we had nothing to do with what has taken place in regard to these men. Of course, I do not want 'Mac' to resign." In the end, McParlan decided to see the assignment through.

Once the arrests began, McParlan faced his final crisis. When he made his bold demand for a meeting of the organization's leaders, ostensibly to defend himself against charges of being an informer, he was actually planning a mass roundup of the Molly bosses. Unaware that Kehoe never planned to hold the meeting, McParlan notified Captain Linden by slipping an invitation to him along with those mailed to Molly leaders. When he learned that Kehoe planned to have him killed, McParlan left the region on March 7, 1876, on an early morning train bound for Philadelphia.

IN THE YEARS SINCE the accused Mollies went on trial, opinion about the organization has been divided. At the conclusion of the court proceedings, scholarly writer Francis P. Dewees summed up the era of the Molly Maguires as "a reign of blood.... [T]hey held communities terror bound, and wantonly defied the law, destroyed property and sported human life." Other writers have characterized the Mollies as more sinned against than sinning, the victims of mine owners bent on destroying the nascent labor movement. The trials were held at a time of strong anti-Irish prejudice and were often preceded by prejudicial newspaper ac-

WITH PERMISSION-PINKERTON, INC.

The Pinkerton agency produced this list of Molly Maguire fugitives in 1879. Of the men on the list, only Thomas Hurley was ever apprehended. He admitted to a murder in Shenandoah, Pennsylvania, and committed suicide in a Colorado jail in 1886.

1 ❖ RECONSTRUCTION AND THE GILDED AGE

Frustration on both sides led to violence through intimidation, beatings, industrial sabotage, and military intervention, but the founding of the United Mine Workers of America changed the lives of the miners.

counts. Labor leaders, the clergy, and hierarchy of the Catholic church, afraid of being linked with the Molly Maguires, were quick to condemn them as well. The juries in many of the trials were composed largely of German immigrants, some of whom readily confessed that their limited knowledge of English made it difficult for them to follow the proceedings. Not a single Irish American was empaneled on any of the juries. Sympathetic judges allowed Gowen, who conducted several of the prosecutions himself, to rant on endlessly about the Molly Maguires, often painting an even more sinister picture than the facts supported. As Carbon County Judge John P. Lavelle noted in his 1994 book, *The Hard Coal Docket*, "[A]ny objective study of the... entire record of these cases must conclude that they [the Molly Maguires]... did not have fair and impartial juries. They were, therefore, denied one of the fundamental rights that William Penn guaranteed to all of Pennsylvania's citizens."

All told, 20 men were found guilty of murder and were sentenced to death. Ten of them were hanged—four at Mauch Chunk and six at Pottsville—on June 21, 1877, a date remembered as "Black Thursday." Some Molly Maguire members were probably innocent of the crimes for which they were accused. One of the more questionable convictions was that of Alexander Campbell, who was charged with masterminding the slayings of mine superintendent Morgan Powell in 1871 and John P. Jones in 1875. A prominent tavern owner and A.O.H. lodge treasurer, Campbell was never proven to be connected with the actual perpetration of any Molly Maguire crimes, but the testimony of "Powder Keg" Kerrigan, who turned state's evidence and escaped punishment, sent Campbell to the gallows.

Jack Kehoe was hanged in 1878 for the 1862 murder of mine foreman Frank

HISTORICAL SOCIETY OF SCHUYLKILL COUNTY

A photograph of Pottsville in the 1800s shows the Schuylkill County jail on the left and the courthouse—scene of some Molly Maguire trials—on the right. The jail is still operating, but the courthouse was replaced in 1889.

W. Langdon. A century later Pennsylvania Governor Milton J. Shapp granted Kehoe a posthumous pardon, prompted by the efforts of some of Kehoe's relatives and several members of the Pennsylvania Labor History Society. The governor wrote, "...[I]t is impossible for us to imagine the plight of the 19th Century miners in Pennsylvania's anthracite region," and that it was John Kehoe's popularity among the miners that led Gowen "to fear, despise and ultimately destroy [him]." Shapp continued, "We can be proud of the men known as the Molly Maguires, because they defiantly faced allegations which attempted to make trade unionism a criminal conspiracy."

The Molly Maguire hangings ended the first wave of violence in the Pennsylvania coal regions. Labor relations throughout the United States remained turbulent, however, and the battle between mine owners and mine workers continued. Frustration on both sides led to violence through intimidation, beatings, industrial sabotage, and military intervention, but the founding of the United Mine Workers of America in 1890 ultimately changed the lives of the miners. The union advocated an eight-hour workday and opposed the compulsory buying of goods in company stores, employment for children under 14, and the use of hired gunmen to enforce company rules. Even with these regulations, coal mining remained a difficult and dangerous way to make a living, but no longer one that would have to rely on the Molly Maguires and their brand of justice.

Joseph Bloom is a full-time freelance medical writer currently living in western North Carolina.

'The Chinese Must Go'

By Bernard A. Weisberger

One splendid morning during a recent West Coast vacation, I was turning the pages of a San Francisco newspaper over my coffee when I came upon a headline that clouded my cheerful mood: GERMAN POLL FINDS SENTIMENT AGAINST FOREIGNERS RUNS DEEP. According to the story below it, one-quarter of a group of Germans polled in a survey agreed entirely or partly with the slogan "Germany for the Germans," which right-wing extremists had been chanting during several weeks of rampages against foreign refugees. Included in the atrocities were the rock-throwing attacks on refugee shelters and the torching of foreigners' homes. "Shades of the 1930s," I thought with the automatic shudder that any possible neo-Nazi activity sends through me—in Germany or anywhere else.

Then I thought a bit longer. Something tickled my memory, and it flashed a new message: "Shades of the 1870s too. And not in Europe but in San Francisco, California!" I remembered that San Francisco had been seized, in 1877, by a violent spasm of antiforeign, specifically anti-Chinese, feeling that broke into murderous riots against innocents of the "wrong" ancestry. The fever started among working-class whites, but before it ran its full course, it infected the governments of both California and the United States, with long-lasting results.

Please understand that I have no intention of drawing farfetched comparisons, or of calling Americans of the 1870s neo-Nazis—quite the contrary. Nor do I aim to exonerate the 1990s neo-Nazis by trite reminders that they are not the first, last, or only haters to sully history's pages with brutality. Still, one of the best things about *good* history is its power to reduce national arrogance and to promote reflection and caution. So this story needs telling.

Xenophobia wasn't new in the United States a century and a quarter ago. A strong nativist movement before the Civil War had been responsible for discrimination and occasional violence against foreign-born Catholics. In the 1850s the Protestant crusade went political in the shape of the American (or "Know-Nothing") party and scored some short-term gains. But California's nativism in 1877 was especially sharp after four years of a bitter depression that had begun in 1873. (Economic pain will do that every time; the 1992 wave of German antiforeignism is strongest in formerly Communist East Germany, where unemployment is high and living standards low.)

America in 1877 was hurting all over, but as is often the case, the situation was special in California, particularly in San Francisco. It was less than thirty years since the gold rush had filled the city with brazen fortune seekers. The giddiness of their expectations was now offset by brutal reality, and most of them were facing the fact that they would spend their lives in a post-boom economy. Gold and silver production was down, and unemployment now hovered around 20 percent. Where land had been plentiful, the best acreage was being concentrated into great estates.

Where San Francisco grocers had made fortunes selling infrequent ships loads of coveted goods, they now faced tough competition in a national market created by the newly completed transcontinental railroad line. And that same railroad, once hailed as the salvation of California, had become a monster monopoly that was charged with gouging the state's shippers and buying exemption from the law by bribing and lobbying.

The Big Four who built and owned the Southern Pacific Railroad—Mark Hopkins, Charles Crocker, Collis P. Huntington, and Leland Stanford—typified the widening social chasm. Basically storekeepers who had struck it rich by their timely investment in the rails, they and other new millionaires built, on San Francisco's Nob Hill, gingerbread mansions tended by liveried servants. Thus the social cast of San Francisco included a restless down-at-the-heels population, a class of power-flaunting neo-aristocrats, a supervillain in the shape of a railroad monopoly—and, finally, a set of scapegoats in the Chinese.

There were between twelve thousand and twenty-two thousand of them in the city, all recent immigrants and visibly, achingly different in their Manchu pigtails and their "bizarre" customs. They had been run out of the mining camps by discriminatory state laws and vigilante violence and settled in the cities to cook and wash for the Anglo-Saxons. Then the Big Four had discovered that they made wonderful railroad-construction workers—patient, diligent, and, above all, vulnerable and therefore cheap. Crocker imported thousands of them. So did other employers through wholesale contracts with Chinese labor agents. The Chinese composed perhaps only 15 percent of the San Francisco labor force, but they were blamed and hated by apparently every unemployed or underemployed white San Franciscan.

On July 23, 1877, the trigger on violence was pulled by news from the East. Between July 14 and 26 striking rail workers had clashed with militia in Pittsburgh, Baltimore, Chicago, and Martinsburg, West Virginia. At least seventy people had been murdered in the tumult. A meeting in support of the strikers was called in an empty downtown sandlot in San Francisco by sympathizers associated with the ten-year-old Marxist International Association of Workingmen. The crowd shouted its approval of anticapitalist resolutions. Then, inevitably, someone cried, "On to Chinatown," and the mob boiled out to look for victims. Twenty laundries were burned that night. On the next, there was an attack on a woolen mill employing many Chinese workers. At that the city fathers, alarmed about threats to property, formed a Committee of Safety and called out the militia. On the third night the rioters attacked the docks of the Pacific Steamship Company and set fire to a lumberyard. Police charged their ranks; four rioters were killed and fourteen wounded. That was the end of the collective violence.

But not of the anti-Chinese revolt. Two months later the crowd found a leader in a thirty-year-old Irish-born small businessman named Denis Kearney. Self-made and self-educated, Kearney was the guiding spirit in creating a new organization, the Workingmen's Party of California (WPC). Night after night he held forth to sandlot crowds in speeches full of political brimstone, like his pronouncement that "the dignity of labor must be sustained, even if we have to kill every wretch that opposes it." He frightened the city fathers enough to have him arrested in November, but since his threats were always vaguely conditional rather than immediate, he was acquitted. Actually, he mainly urged his audiences to vote for delegates to a forthcoming state constitutional convention that he hoped would empower "the people" by tightly regulating corporations and their lobbyists and subsidies. But his most powerful attention-getter was a demand for an end to the immigration and hiring of Chinese. "We intend to try and vote the Chinamen out, to frighten him out, and if this won't do, to kill him out.... The heathen slaves must leave this coast." He boiled it down to a sledgehammer four-word cry: "The Chinese must go!"

Kearney touched on worker anxieties with his hints of a scheme by the rich to bring feudalism to the United States through the replacement of American workingmen with "coolies" who would neither expect nor receive a living wage or democratic rights.

He enjoyed fleeting political success. The Workingmen's Party of California won many local and state offices in 1878 and named fifty-two delegates to the convention, which did include some of their proposals in the new Constitution of 1879. But the anti-business strictures were gradually eviscerated by the courts and by lack of implementation, and the WPC faded away, though Kearney himself lived on until 1907. Kearney's legislative influence was brief, but the evil that he did to the Chinese lived after him.

That was because "The Chinese must go" had more than local impact. It struck powerful echoes in a time of social Darwinist racism. The Chinese were almost universally disdained by the "advanced" Americans. The newspaper baron James Gordon Bennett discouraged their immigration with the comment that only "on the Caucasian element can we hope to build up such an empire as the world has never seen." Other opinion makers, lumping all classes and conditions of Chinese together, labeled them "ignorant of civilized life" or "listless, stagnant [and] unprogressive." In the popular image they were criminals, gamblers, prostitutes, and opium smokers. In Far Western towns Chinese storekeepers were often beaten and robbed by drunken miners and cowboys, or at a minimum tormented by teen-age hoodlums. And in 1885 twenty-eight Chinese were massacred in Rock Springs, Wyoming.

Therefore, legal exclusion was easily enacted. California in 1880 virtually shut the door on the importation and use of Chinese labor. The Congress of the United States followed suit with the Exclusion Act of 1882, barring all Chinese immigration for ten years. Renewed and renewed, the exclusion policy remained in force until World War II, when it began to be modified gradually until it was finally dropped, after eighty-six years, in a 1968 overhaul of immigration legislation.

It would be possible and pleasant to conclude this column on an upbeat note. Anti-Asian prejudice in the United States is only a glimmer of its former self, and the Chinese are even considered a "model minority," held up for others' emulation. That is certainly a credit to American pluralism. But the virus of xenophobia is never really extinguished in any multiethnic body politic. It merely becomes temporarily inactive. And as for racism—enough said. Human beings have an inextinguishable capacity to be cruel to one another, particularly in groups. It takes constant self-reminders of how bad things can get to keep alive the energy to make them better.

The Nickel & Dime Empire

When F. W. Woolworth opened his first five-and-ten in 1879, he never dreamed that his business would become a monument of American marketing.

By Joseph Gustaitis

July 1997 was a melancholy month for admirers of a vanishing American way of life—the era of family values, corner grocery stores, day baseball, unlocked front doors, and twice-a-day mail delivery.

On July 3 the nation's newspapers reported the death of film star Jimmy Stewart, and obituaries paid tribute to his folksiness and the way he captured the core of American individualism—characteristics people like to associate with a time that was less frantic, more diffident, and more concerned with the folks next door than the celebrities on television.

Two weeks later an equally woeful event transpired. The Woolworth Corporation announced that it was closing its 400 remaining five-and-ten-cent stores. Once again, the media cranked up the nostalgia machine as reporters fanned out across the country to assess this latest left hook to the national psyche. "It's the passing of an era," a real estate executive in San Francisco said. "They've been on Main Street forever," echoed one shopper in Denver, "I'm sure we're going to feel this loss." New York's *Daily News* pretty much summed it up with the words, "We aren't just losing stores. We're losing pieces of Americana."

Like many retail empires, this one started small. Frank Winfield Woolworth was born in Rodman, New York, just south of Watertown, on April 13, 1852. He grew up on a 108-acre farm near Great Bend that his father managed, but young Frank couldn't wait to escape the agrarian life and its relentless labor. He later recalled that his parents "worked hard to make ends meet. My father would think nothing of getting up at four in the morning and work till eight at night in the summertime at hard manual labor. Everything that came into farm labor I had experience in, and my mother would break me into housework, too. I got both ends of the stick."

For a lad with no financial advantages and a modest education, the position of store clerk sounded like a ticket to emancipation, so the 20-year-old presented himself eagerly to William Harvey Moore, part owner of the dry goods firm of Augsbury & Moore—later to become Moore & Smith—in the heart of Watertown. Moore took him on for a six-month trial.

F. W. Woolworth started at the bottom, cleaning cuspidors, delivering packages, and washing windows. He received no salary at all for the first three months, after which he earned $3.50 a week. Although he was a rather ineffective sales clerk, Woolworth showed a talent for window dressing, which then became a part of his job. He also made himself useful in the stock room and soon was considered a valued employee, earning the respectable weekly salary of $10.00. That enabled him to propose to Jennie Creighton, a 23-year-old seamstress from Canada. The couple was married on June 11, 1876.

Around 1878, when Moore & Smith found itself groaning under the burden of surplus inventory, a traveling salesman told the store's management of an interesting experiment conducted by a shop in Michigan. The proprietors had set up a display, affixed a sign to it reading, "Any Article on This Counter, 5¢," and sold the goods at a dizzy pace. The idea seemed to be worth a try and Moore told Woolworth to erect a similar counter and tack up a similar sign. Sure enough, as Frank later recalled, "Like magic, the goods on the 5¢ counter faded away and money flowed into the cash drawer."

1 ❖ RECONSTRUCTION AND THE GILDED AGE

Woolworth's store in Lancaster, Pennsylvania, was the first of his many stores that were filled with a mass of five-and-ten-cent goods.

For Woolworth, it was as if he had seen his future. The young man was convinced that an entire store dedicated to selling items for a nickel could be a success. Frank's employers were willing to back their ambitious employee, lending him $315.41 so that he could purchase the notions needed to stock his proposed emporium.

Woolworth chose Utica, New York, as the site of his enterprise. He distributed handbills and opened the doors of his store on February 22, 1879. Frank's first customer was a woman who wanted to buy one of his advertised 5-cent fire shovels. Many years later, Woolworth reminisced, "She was my first customer and had I dreamed of the things that were destined to happen to me in subsequent years, I most certainly would have taken her name and kept that first money. As it is, I don't even know who she was."

The "Great 5¢ Store" was a success at first, and Woolworth paid off his loan, but then business began to decline. Still, he remained confident; the problem, he concluded, was his location on a poorly traveled side street. When a friend gave him a glowing account of business in Lancaster, Pennsylvania, the young entrepreneur wasted no time in relocating south. He unveiled a much grander outlet in Lancaster on June 21, 1879. This store had a corner location, three show windows, seven clerks, and a rent bill of $30 a month.

Woolworth's new store was a hit from the start, and soon the merchandise was moving so swiftly that he was faced with supply problems. Lacking the purchasing power to buy five-cent items in bulk, he added a new tier of higher-priced merchandise, making his 5¢ store into a five-and-ten.

Woolworth also opened stores in the Pennsylvania cities of York and Harrisburg, but these outlets flamed brightly and then burned out. In November 1880, however, Woolworth scored with a store in Scranton. "By the end of 1880," Woolworth later recalled, "I was so rich that I decided to take the first vacation I had ever enjoyed. I was worth $2,000, which looked bigger to me than $20,000,000 would now. In fact, I felt quite as rich then as I do now because I had the consciousness and the satisfaction of having made a success in business." Woolworth's holiday was not especially ambitious. The once impecunious youth succumbed to the temptation to show off, and he took his wife, all decked out in a new dress and a feather-trimmed hat, back to Watertown, where old acquaintances admired the local man who had done so well.

F. W. Woolworth, of course, was just beginning. But as he looked to the future he vowed that he would never go into debt again. It was a vow he never broke. Instead of borrowing, Woolworth sought entrepreneurs who would put up the cash to become partners in new stores. His first collaborators were his younger brother Charles Sumner, his cousin Seymour Horace Knox, and his former employer, W. H. Moore. Another businessman, Fred Kirby, also became a partner.

From then on, the Woolworth phenomenon grew. In addition to a lengthening list of Pennsylvania stores, he had locations in Trenton, New Jersey, and Elmira, New York, by late 1886. Even the emporium of Moore & Smith transformed itself into a five-and-ten in 1885.

In order to move into the big time, however, Woolworth had to conquer the citadel of commerce, New York City. And so, in 1886 he and his family moved to a new home in Brooklyn, and F. W. opened an office on Chambers Street in Manhattan. Two years later he moved to the Stewart Building at 280 Broadway, where he remained until he opened his own building 25 years later. By this time Woolworth no longer needed partners and so became the sole owner of all new Woolworth stores. His four associates opened up retail chains of their own, but all remained on friendly terms.

In 1890, Woolworth decided to go to Europe after a business associate told him about inexpensive merchandise there. In Germany he found dolls reasonably priced but was appalled that women and children toiled cruelly making them "while the men drink beer." In one town he found a good source of glass marbles and Christmas tree ornaments. He passed through Vienna and Bohemia, inspecting the vases and glassware, then he journeyed to the Leipzig Fair and to Berlin before spending a week in Paris. Shortly after Woolworth's return to the United States, customers began finding imported goods on his store shelves. By 1907, Woolworth was annually importing more than $2 million worth of European merchandise.

Soon after his homecoming, Woolworth sent the following message to his managers: "I have been looking over a census of the United States and I am convinced that there are one hundred cities and towns where we can locate five-and-ten-cent stores and we can sell a million dollars' worth of goods a year!"

It has often been remarked that when bad times assail a nation's economy some businesses—like shoe repair, used cars, and relocation services—flourish. When the Panic of 1893, the worst depression the nation had experienced up to that time, struck the United States, F. W. Woolworth easily rode out the storm. True to his vow he incurred no debts, and when wholesale prices dropped he was able to snap up merchandise cheaper than ever. Besides, his low prices seemed even more of a bargain to hard-pressed consumers.

Between 1895 and 1897, Woolworth opened major emporia in Washington, D.C., Brooklyn, Philadelphia, and Boston. Then, on the last day of October 1896, he unveiled his grandest achievement—a store in Manhattan itself. The outlet, at 17th Street and 6th Avenue, was such a hit that four years later he opened an even larger store on 14th Street. This "world's largest five-and-ten" boasted a pipe organ and 12,000 square feet of space; it sold everything from candy and jewelry to toys, perfume, hardware, knitted goods, stationery frames, and novels.

In 1901 the Woolworth family moved into a 30-room mansion on 5th Avenue and 80th Street in Manhattan—the so-called "Millionaire's Row"—which he had built to impress members of New York Society, who to this point had ignored the man they considered nothing more than an upstart tradesman. Later, when his three daughters, Helena, Edna, and Jessie, were wed, F. W. purchased lots further down East 80th Street and built houses for all of them.

Life was good for the retail magnate. On May 25, 1907, his company conducted a census of the 170 stores it had in 23 states and the District of Columbia and found that 1,137,449 customers entered the establishments on that day—82 percent of whom made purchases. Two years later, Woolworth expanded overseas to Britain, where his outlets were called "Three-and-Sixpence" stores.

That same year the Woolworth store in Philadelphia opened a small food counter, and three years later, customers were welcomed at the first of the true Woolworth lunch counters at the 14th Street store in Manhattan. It began a tradition of grilled cheese sandwiches, malted milk, the 60¢ turkey dinner, hot dogs on a rotating cooker, cream pie, and coffee that became as much a part of Woolworth's stores as the merchandise.

With companies such as J. G. McCrory and S. S. Kresge offering competition, Woolworth merged his chain in 1912 with five others—four owned by his former partners, plus a chain west of the Rocky Mountains owned by Earle Perry Charlton—and created an empire, the F. W. Woolworth Company with 596 stores and annual sales of more than $50 million.

On his trips to Europe, Woolworth did more than ferret out merchandise. He enjoyed attending the opera, and he gamely tried to master both the French and German languages. Architecture also enthralled him. He found the Gothic Revival Houses of Parliament in London very impressive, and

1 ❖ RECONSTRUCTION AND THE GILDED AGE

The Woolworth Building still ranks as one of the world's most distinguished structures.

when he began planning a new building for his headquarters he selected the same style.

The architect Woolworth chose to design the building was Cass Gilbert, who had already made a name for himself with his brilliant designs for the Minnesota State Capitol and the New York Customs House. When Gilbert asked his employer how tall the new building should be, Woolworth told him, "750 feet." "Am I limited to that?" the architect queried. "That's the minimum," Woolworth answered.

Woolworth's new building on Broadway at Park Place in Manhattan was completed in 1913. It topped out at 792 feet, the tallest building in the world, until the 1,046-foot-high Chrysler Building was completed in 1930. Although the Woolworth Building had only 60 stories, each floor averaged more than 13 feet in height. The lowest ceiling was 11 feet, and some were as high as 20 feet. With its soaring lines, sumptuous mosaic lobby and flamboyant Gothic spire, the Woolworth Building was, and still is, a landmark in New York City

True to his promise never to borrow money, Woolworth carried no mortgage on his tower, paying for it in cash—$13.5 million. Yet, for all the building's grandeur, there's one indication that Woolworth didn't see himself as an Ozymandian figure. In one of the upper corners of the lobby there is a gargoyle of F. W. himself, clutching the nickels and dimes that built his kingdom.

World War I put a dent in Woolworth's European supply chain, but by then the company was too big to let even a war put a stop to it. In 1916 alone, 115 stores opened their doors, and sales were solid even in war-torn Britain. At the same time, sadness began to shadow the empire. The spring of 1915 brought the deaths of Carson Peck, Woolworth's general manager for 25 years, and Woolworth's cousin Seymour Knox.

The retail magnate's own health was declining, as was his wife's mental capacities (her symptoms bore the signs of Alzheimer's disease). In 1916, Woolworth's first employer and friend of many years, W. H. Moore, died of a stroke. Two years later Woolworth's second daughter Edna (Hutton) died at age 35. The coroner's verdict was mastoiditis, which "had caused contraction of the tongue muscles and consequent suffocation." Others were suspicious that her death could have been suicide by poisoning.

Moore had had the majority of his teeth removed shortly before he died. Woolworth thought the action had contributed to his friend's death, so he vowed to refuse dental care for his own teeth, which were in poor condition. He began to have increasing problems with them and could eat only soft foods, his favorite being overripe bananas. Despite warnings from his physicians that septic poisoning would set in, Woolworth would not visit a dentist. On April 4, 1919, Woolworth began to run a high fever. Doctors diagnosed his condition as gallstones and uremic and septic poisoning, and he died on April 8, just five days short of his 67th birthday.

Woolworth had built a personal fortune estimated at $65 million, which he left to his wife. She was by that time totally incompetent and, without knowing it, had become one of the richest people in America. When Jennie died five years later, the estate went in equal parts to their surviving daughters, Helena and Jessie, and to Barbara Hutton, the only child of Woolworth's deceased daughter, Edna.

The Woolworth Empire, however, had many years to live. By its 50th anniversary in 1929, the company had 2,247 stores in the United States, Canada, Cuba, England, and Germany. The directors had managed for a remarkably long time to hold the maximum price of merchandise to a dime, but by the early 1930s, although the term "five-and-ten" was still used, it was an anachronism, as many items were going for 20¢ and more.

After World War II, the great migration to the suburbs began, eventually gutting American downtown areas as buyers shifted to the malls. The situation deteriorated rapidly for the company and its 1953 earnings hit a five-year low of $29.8 million. A series of presidents addressed some of the problems, but the company was still not growing at the rate of its competitors. By 1996, Woolworth stores were selling items that a customer could find elsewhere, and usually at a lower price. The newer chains, such as Wal-Mart and Target, were offering a wider range of merchandise at a bigger discount, while franchise specialty stores and a host of supersized drugstores were providing a greater variety of the same type of merchandise.

To make matters worse, the Woolworth stores themselves had deteriorated, offering poor service, uninspiring displays, unappealing merchandise, and a general air of shabbiness. Customers got the feeling that the company had lost interest. One analyst put it this way: "F. W. Woolworth and the entire variety-store concept became defunct 20 years ago and began to decline 35 years ago. It was a company that had completely lost its reason for being. It died many years ago, but it just wasn't buried."

Yet Woolworth Corporation survives as the owner of several profitable divisions—Foot Locker and Kinney Shoes among them. And it may get stronger now that it has shed its biggest liability. It could be taken as a lamentable sign of the unsentimental, bottom-line view of the modern economy, but after the Woolworth Corporation announced the closings of its five-and-tens, company stock went up ten percent.

New York writer Joseph Gustaitis is a frequent contributor to American History *magazine.*

Unit 2

Unit Selections

7. **Captain Pratt's School,** Mary Kay Morel
8. **"Hang 'em First, Try 'em Later,"** Bruce Watson
9. **"If You Men Don't Withdraw, We Will Mow Every One of You Down,"** William C. Kashatus
10. **Electing the President, 1896,** Edward Ranson
11. **Our First Southeast Asian War,** David R. Kohler and James W. Wensyel
12. **The American Century, 1900–1910: How It Felt When Everything Seemed Possible,** Henry Allen

Key Points to Consider

❖ Discuss the assumptions that underlay the approach of Captain Pratt's school. Have we learned any lessons from that experiment? Are there "superior" and "inferior" cultures? Defend your answer.

❖ Analyze labor-management strife as described in the article on the Homestead massacre. What options did workers have to try to better wages and working conditions?

❖ What were the outstanding issues of the presidential election of 1896? Why did the Democrat-Populist, William Jennings Bryan, fail to appeal to urban workers?

❖ Discuss the consequences of the Spanish-American War on world power alignments. Did the Philippine insurrection offer any lessons we might have learned for the war in Vietnam?

 **Links**   www.dushkin.com/online/

11. **The Age of Imperialism**
    http://www.smplanet.com/imperialism/toc.html
12. **Anti-Imperialism in the United States, 1898–1935**
    http://www.boondocks.com/ai/9835.html
13. **The Era of William McKinley**
    http://www.cohums.ohio-state.edu/history/projects/McKinley/
14. **Great Chicago Fire and the Web of Memory**
    http://www.chicagohs.org/fire/

These sites are annotated on pages 4 and 5.

The Emergence of Modern America

The United States underwent significant changes during the decades following the Civil War. Although many people continued to live on isolated farms or in small towns, others flocked to cities as did immigrants from abroad. Similarly, although small- and medium-sized businesses continued to exist, corporations on a scale previously unheard of came to dominate the marketplace. The gross national product increased dramatically, but the gap between rich and poor steadily widened. Corporate leaders, on the one hand, amassed unprecedented fortunes on which they paid no income taxes. Urban working families, on the other, often lived in unhealthy squalor even though all their members, including young children, worked in some shop or factory. Depressions, one beginning in 1873 and another in 1893, threw more people out of work than ever before. Farmers had to sell what they produced in markets that fluctuated widely. They also had to contend with the monopolistic practices of railroads, which charged "all the traffic would bear" for shipping and storing farm products. Minority groups, such as Indians and blacks, continued to suffer socially and economically through good times as well as bad.

The unit begins with the article "Captain Pratt's School" in which an account of a well-meaning attempt to bring Indian children into the mainstream is provided. The school's philosophy was based on the assumption that Indian cultures were inferior to the "American way." In order to escape poverty and deprivation, therefore, Indian children must be made to cast off the customs and dress of their ancestors and become more like whites. Mostly, the result was to produce young people who were caught between both cultures but who belonged to neither one.

Although the days of the "Wild West" were numbered, there still were regions in which the law was administered in haphazard fashion. Bruce Watson, in "Hang 'em First, Try 'em Later," describes how Judge Roy Bean meted out "justice" as he saw fit from 1882 to 1902 in Langtry, Texas. Bean became a mythic figure around whom all sorts of legends have been spun. In this essay, Watson tries to separate the known facts from the fictions.

There was a great deal of violence between labor and management during the 1880s and 1890s. Labor was treated pretty much like any raw material used in industry; the idea was to purchase it as cheaply as possible regardless of the human consequences. Workers often regarded going on strike as the only means to redress their grievances. Some companies used the Pinkerton National Detective Agency to break these strikes. "If You Men Don't Withdraw, We Will Mow Every One of You Down" discusses events leading up to the "massacre" in Homestead, Pennsylvania, in 1892.

Farm organizations grew in response to the many grievances harbored by those who tilled the land. Some created cooperatives to get higher prices for the goods they produced and lower prices for the supplies they purchased. When it appeared that neither the Republican nor Democratic Party was responsive to the needs of farmers, they moved to form the People's Party, known as the Populists. The Populists favored more government intervention against the corporations they dealt with and looked to the government to provide, among other things, cheaper credit for farmers. The Populists formed a third party in 1892, but the combination of an uninspiring presidential candidate, lack of funds, and the taint of "radicalism" prevented them from doing very well.

The onset of a major depression in 1893 resulted in large scale unemployment, violent labor disputes, and an unprecedented number of farm foreclosures. Populist strength grew in rural areas, but the doubt that they could win a national election even under these conditions caused them to endorse the Democratic candidate, William Jennings Bryan, in 1896. Bryan attached himself to the cause of "free silver," which farmers thought would result in higher prices for agricultural products. The article "Electing the President, 1896" discusses that campaign and concludes that Bryan lost because he championed an older, rural America against those who represented a modernizing, industrial nation. The return of prosperity and the outbreak of the Spanish-American War ended the Populist crusade.

American foreign policy became more assertive during the 1880s and 1890s. Various theories were put forward to justify American expansion into the Pacific: The need for Asian markets, the acquisition of coaling stations for merchant and naval vessels, and taking up the "white man's burden" were among them. The Spanish-American War provided an opportunity to put these ideas in practice. Although events in Cuba provided the immediate cause of the war, by its end the United States had acquired the Philippines and other Pacific islands. Although it lasted only a few months and casualties were relatively low, what a contemporary referred to as a "splendid little war" actually had very significant consequences.

Rebels in the Philippine Islands had been fighting for liberation from Spanish rule for years. They had reason to believe that if they collaborated with the United States in its war against the Spanish they would receive independence. When it became clear that this was not to be, Filipino rebels, led by Emilio Aguinald, launched a guerrilla war against the United States that lasted until 1902. Casualties on both sides during this conflict far exceeded those of the Spanish-American War. "Our First Southeast Asian War" describes this bloody endeavor and draws parallels with the more recent Vietnam War.

The essay "The American Century, 1990–1910: How it Felt When Everything Seemed Possible" provides an impressionistic account of life in the United States during the years 1900–1910. Relative prosperity had returned after the onset of the Spanish-American War in 1898 and a new optimism prevailed in many quarters. It was during these years that Progressivism, to be discussed in the next unit, began to develop. Many people believed that although there were a great many wrongs in the society, they could be corrected through reform.

Captain Pratt's School

BY MARY KAY MOREL *Between 1879 and 1918, the Carlisle Indian Industrial School in Pennsylvania, brainchild of Captain Richard Henry Pratt, educated young Native Americans for life in the white man's world.*

FOR THE LAKOTA BOY, it seemed the perfect kind of day. The cool autumn air made playtime pleasant and hardly hinted at the winter snows that would soon blanket the ground on South Dakota's Rosebud Reservation. But the fun near his father's store was interrupted for Ota Kte, or "Plenty Kill," and his friends when they noticed people gathered in front of the nearby agency buildings. Stopping long enough to peek through the window, Plenty Kill had no idea that the white visitors inside would change his life forever.

One of the men he observed—Richard Henry Pratt—was a career military officer, who was about to embark on a new endeavor. He had come to the Rosebud Reservation that September day in 1879 with a 63-year-old school teacher named Sarah Mather, who had recently taught Indian prisoners at Fort Marion in St. Augustine, Florida. The pair were in search of recruits, Native-American children to attend Pratt's recently founded boarding school in the distant state of Pennsylvania. Removed from the influence of their own people, the children attending what would become known as the Carlisle Indian Industrial School would be given a "white" education that would prepare them, Pratt believed, to make their way in the white man's world.

Seeing the boys at the window, Pratt proffered sticks of candy to win them over. Afraid at first, they were eventually coaxed inside, where they met Pratt's party, which included two Santee Sioux boys who had been educated in the white man's ways. Although unswayed by the chance to become like these young men, Plenty Kill, after obtaining his father's permission, decided to attend Pratt's school, and within a few days, found himself heading east with Pratt and Miss Mather.

In 1928, writing as Luther Standing Bear, the name he was given at Carlisle, Plenty Kill recalled with both pride and poignancy his reason for going to the new boarding school. He chose to attend Carlisle, he explained in his memoirs, in order to prove to his father that he was brave. By 1879, few opportunities ex-

isted for young Sioux males to demonstrate their courage, the most prized of all character traits among their people. To the youth, going east and facing the unknown white man's world was a way to show his bravery.

What made Richard Henry Pratt think that he knew what was best for Plenty Kill and other American Indians? And how did this career military man grow into a crusader and lobbyist for a cause where even missionaries were often reluctant to tread? Pratt was born on December 6, 1840, in Rushford, New York, in a part of the country where the forests had already been cleared and the Indians pushed west. When he was six, his family also headed west, moving to the banks of the Wabash River in Indiana. But family life was disrupted for the Pratts when Richard's father, lured by the promise of gold, headed alone for California, where he was robbed and murdered. In 1853, Richard, the oldest of three sons, left school to help support the household.

At the age of twenty young Pratt, by then a tinsmith, got his first taste of military life during the Civil War, when he joined the Union Army. After the war, Pratt, who had spent four years fighting, found it hard to readjust to peacetime quiet. So, on March 7, 1867, he rejoined the U.S. Army, becoming a second lieutenant in the 10th United States Cavalry, an all-black unit commanded by white officers.

In addition to rubbing elbows with black soldiers, Pratt soon found himself in charge of Caddo and Washita Indian scouts at Fort Arbuckle in the Indian Territory (Oklahoma). It was during this period that Pratt, who showed an unusual aptitude for working with both black troops and Indians, began scrutinizing the problems of the indigenous people in the West. He concluded that what Native Americans needed were ways to become acclimated to the white man's way of doing things. Since the Indians were capable people, he reasoned, education would solve the problem of how they could best fit into the Anglo world.

Pratt's vision was hardly unique, and his ideas were shaped as much by the times as by his experiences. Many Americans believed that "reforming" Indians meant eradicating their centuries-old traditions. Dress an Indian in white man's clothes, cut his hair, show him the white man's technological achievements and creature comforts, the theory went, and he would want to embrace the white man's world.

Although this theory was shared by many, differences of opinion existed

7. Captain Pratt's School

Captain Richard Henry Pratt's philosophy of "total immersion" made a change in his Indian students' physical appearance as necessary as their classroom studies. Soon after their arrival at the school, the children received uniform suits or dresses and had their traditional long hair cut short. These 11 Chiricahua Apaches (left), who reached Pratt's Carlisle, Pennsylvania, school in November 1883, were photographed again four months after their arrival, having been transformed by Pratt and his staff (below).

CUMBERLAND COUNTY HISTORICAL SOCIETY

CUMBERLAND COUNTY HISTORICAL SOCIETY

2 ❖ THE EMERGENCE OF MODERN AMERICA

CUMBERLAND COUNTY HISTORICAL SOCIETY

NATIONAL PARK SERVICE

Despite his beliefs, Pratt did not shirk the day-to-day military duties of chasing down renegades and returning them to the reservations. During his seven years in the Indian Territory at Camp Supply and Forts Sill and Arbuckle, from 1867 to '74, Pratt and his "Buffalo Soldiers"* spent much of their time pursuing Kiowa, Comanche, Cheyenne, and other tribes who were determined to maintain their traditional way of life.

Privately Pratt blamed corruption within the Indian Bureau for many of the problems with the tribes. He could see for himself that even the notoriously bad army rations were vastly superior in quality and quantity to the supplies and food doled out to the reservation Indians by the U.S. government. It hardly sur-

Pratt (left, top), who eventually retired as a brigadier general, got his first experience working with Indians while serving with the U.S. Army in the Southwest. In 1875, he was assigned the task of holding a group of troublesome Indian leaders (left, bottom), including Chief Lone Wolf of the Kiowas.

prised him that men would be tempted to slip away for the hunt, especially in the late 1860s, when game was still plentiful

By 1874, white hunters had severely depleted the game herds, forcing the last of the freewheeling Indians to settle down to reservation life or face starvation. With such changed circumstances, Pratt found his opportunity to attempt to remake the Native peoples. In the spring of 1875, he was put in charge of 72 of the most recalcitrant members of the Arapaho, Cheyenne, Kiowa, and Comanche nations, a group that included some of those tribes' most important leaders. Chained to wagons, the men were hauled away to Fort Leavenworth, Kansas, from where they were transported to imprisonment in St. Augustine's Fort Marion.** Situated near the ocean, the dank and musty fortification offered its new inhabitants an environment very

about how best to implement it. During his administration, President Ulysses S. Grant confidently claimed that recruiting Quakers to act as Indian agents on reservations would solve all problems. "If you make Quakers out of Indians," he naively told a gathering of the pacifist sect, "it will take the fight out of them."

Pratt belonged to a school of thought that disapproved of the reservation system that President Grant had blessed. He believed that isolating the Indian would cause him to hold onto old traditions, alienate him from white society, and cripple his chances of competing in the white man's world.

---
*The 9th and 10th U.S. Cavalry, segregated units composed of black troops, were dubbed "Buffalo Soldiers" by the Cheyennes, who admired their fighting ability.
**Renamed Fort Marion after the United States took control of Florida, the fortification was originally Spain's Castillo de San Marcos.

7. Captain Pratt's School

different from the arid plains that they had once roamed.

Afflicted by Florida's climate, the Indians grew sullen and demoralized. To counteract the effects of their new surroundings, Pratt first set the men to work building a barracks above the old Spanish dungeons in which they had been assigned to sleep each night. During the hottest months of the summer, Pratt moved the prisoners out of the building and allowed them to camp on a nearby island, giving them some relief from the oppressive heat and humidity. On June 11, 1875, he wrote to the adjutant general of the Army asking permission to have the prisoners' wives and families join them in the East. Although the military approved the idea, the Indian Bureau denied his request.

Generally sympathetic to the plight of his charges, Pratt wrote to the War Department that "the duty of the Government to these Indians seems to me to be the teaching of them something that will be permanently useful to them." Thus, Pratt encouraged the prisoners, who had asked to be permitted to work, in all kinds of enterprises, from polishing sea beans and drawing pictures to sell to those who came to tour the prison and teaching archery to townspeople and tourists, to performing such jobs as fishing and bread baking.

Determined that visitors to the prison not view the Native Americans as freaks, Pratt insisted that they cut their hair and dress in cast-off army uniforms. When white soldiers guarding the Indians drank and fell asleep while on duty, Pratt dismissed them. Then, to show his faith in the prisoners, he allowed them to guard themselves. They did not let him down.

To put into practice his theory about educating the Indians, Pratt brought Miss Mather, a schoolteacher in St. Augustine, to the prison. Soon, the likes of Kiowa chiefs White Horse and Lone Wolf were sitting in classrooms, learning their ABCs from Miss Mather and Pratt's wife, Anna. And on Sundays, Pratt's prisoners attended church services and learned to pray to the white man's God.

By 1878, Pratt's success at Fort Marion brought freedom to the Indians being held there and recognition for himself. When some of these Indians requested to be allowed to remain in the East, Pratt attempted to find places for them in schools where they could learn to be farmers, agriculture being the only way that the government would allow Indians to earn a living. Finally he persuaded Samuel Chapman Armstrong, who had commanded black troops during the Civil War and now ran an agricultural school for blacks in Virginia, to admit 17 of the former Indian prisoners into his Hampton Institute.

Pratt's concept of solving the so-called "Indian problem" through education was beginning to catch on. The 17 Indians whom Pratt had brought to the Hampton Institute did so well that he was asked by the War Department to head west to the Dakotas to recruit fifty additional students for the school.

Pratt reveled in his new vocation, but had come to see blacks and Indians as having different needs, and he espoused a philosophy different from that of Armstrong, who believed that blacks' requirements could only be met in a segregated atmosphere. To prove his theories, Pratt longed for an Indian school of his own.

Although still on the Army's roster, Pratt had ceased to be a military man and had become a crusader who spent his time at the capitol in Washington,

CUMBERLAND COUNTY HISTORICAL SOCIETY

Pratt was assisted in his recruitment for the school by Sarah Mather, who had taught the Indian prisoners in Florida and went on to teach the children at Carlisle.

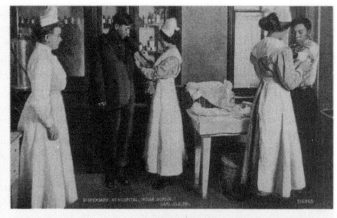

ALL: CUMBERLAND COUNTY HISTORICAL SOCIETY

As the three postcards included here demonstrate, Pratt was always eager to show the world what his school was accomplishing. Pictured above (clockwise from top, left) are postcards featuring the exterior of the former cavalry barracks that housed the school, the hospital dispensary, and the library, as well as a photograph of one of the many shop classes that taught trades to male students.

D.C., elbowing his way through the halls of Congress and lobbying for his cause. Pratt's absence from the frontier did not go unnoticed by his critics, who charged him with shirking his duties in the West. These same critics believed that educating the Indian was the business of the Indian Bureau, not a job for the Army to tackle.

But Pratt was a man with a mission, who was not about to be stopped by naysayers. He found a soul mate in President Rutherford B. Hayes's secretary of the interior, Carl Schurz. Pratt convinced the German-born Schurz of the validity of his views by asking him if he would have risen to the rank of general during the Civil War as he had, or be serving in the president's cabinet, if he had "been reservated in any of the solid German communities we have permitted to grow up in some sections of America."

In the spring of 1879, the two men concocted a scheme to create Pratt's dream school at a shabby unused cavalry barracks in Carlisle, Pennsylvania. Then, after persuading the Army to allow his use of the barracks complex, Pratt set out to find Indian recruits. He had wanted to return to the Southwest tribes familiar to him, but Schurz sent Pratt north to the Pine Ridge and Rosebud reservations of the discontented Sioux, who were selected, Pratt explained, "on the principle of taking the most pains with those who give the most trouble." And, the "children [of the Sioux chiefs] would serve as hostages for the good behavior of their people."

Pratt had no previous experience with the Lakota. Word was sent in advance to Cicero Newell, the Indian agent at Rosebud, to have 36 male and female students ready to be turned over to the determined Pratt. When he and Miss Mather reached Rosebud on the spring wagon, however, they found opposition to their mission, led by Spotted Tail of the Brulé Sioux. The concerned father and Indian leader told them that "white people are all thieves and liars, and we refuse to send our children because we do not want them to learn such things."

Pratt rose to the occasion, first praising Spotted Tail and then reminding him that he had been cheated by whites because he could not read, write, or understand their language. Eventually Pratt eloquently persuaded Spotted Tail to send his sons to the school. Plenty Kill may have volunteered to go to Carlisle as an act of bravery, but many other less-willing Sioux young people went because their parents were convinced to surrender them for the good of Pratt's cause.*

To these Sioux parents, east was the sacred direction toward which they turned their tipis, the place where the sun rose. East was not a specific destination, and the state of Pennsylvania was as inconceivable to them as the Arctic Circle. Thus, the moment of parting

---

*Recruitment for the Carlisle school was also carried on by former prisoners from St. Augustine's Fort Marion, who returned to their tribes in the Southwest to enlist students. And Alfred J. Standing, a Quaker and friend of Pratt's who became the assistant superintendent at the school, signed up youngsters from among the Pawnee.

7. Captain Pratt's School

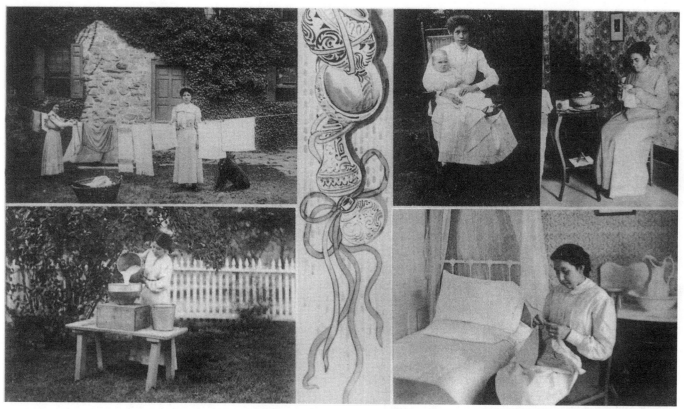

Another postcard published by the Carlisle Indian School called attention to the "outing" program that saw students spend time working in homes and businesses or on farms (above). In order to practice the domestic arts learned in the school, girls worked in homes doing laundry, caring for children, knitting and sewing, and helping with such chores as separating cream from milk. Students who belonged to the school's marching band had the opportunity to travel to fairs and parades, such as the one held in Philadelphia in 1887 to commemorate the centennial of the U.S. Constitution (below).

CUMBERLAND COUNTY HISTORICAL SOCIETY

was an anxious and fearful one for those whose children were being wrenched from the family nest. Most had no idea whether they would ever see their offspring again. And, in fact, some would not.

As for the young people themselves, it was a bewildering experience. Many Carlisle recruits were teenagers who had lived their entire lives in tipis. They had never slept on a bed, nor eaten at a table. Some had probably never set foot in any building other than a trading post. Born in precarious times for their people, their few contacts with whites had been unpleasant.

The trip to Carlisle by steamboat and then by rail turned into a fearful adventure. Most frightening were the throngs of whites who showed up at all the railroad stations to see the children of the feared Red Cloud and Spotted Tail, whom they heard would be passing through. The youngsters were baffled by these people who threw money to them, shouted in words that they did not understand, laughed at them, or made loud war whoops. Missing their families and wondering if they would ever go home again, the boys sang their death songs at night, and the girls wept loudly

Finally on October 6, 1879, Captain Pratt and 84 students reached Carlisle, only to find that the necessary provisions had not been sent by the Indian Bureau. There was no food, no clothing, and no desks or books for the school's first scholars. Weeks after the children's

CUMBERLAND COUNTY HISTORICAL SOCIETY

2 ❖ THE EMERGENCE OF MODERN AMERICA

A Modern Approach

For countless generations before the arrival of the white man in the New World, Native Americans educated their children in the life ways and traditions of their people through word of mouth. That began to change in the sixteenth century, when European explorers and settlers attempted to "civilize and Christianize" the Indians they encountered here. By the mid-1800s in the United States, the prevailing belief was in the systematized, forced education of native peoples in the white man's ways. "They should be educated, not as Indians, but as Americans," Indian Affairs Commissioner Thomas Morgan explained in 1889. It was necessary to "kill the Indian"—figuratively, if not in fact—by weaning him away from his former beliefs and lifestyle, the theory went, in order to save the individual and help him find his place in American society.

During the twentieth century, attitudes gradually changed. A 1976 report from the National Advisory Council on Indian Education, recognizing the educational uniqueness of Native Americans, advocated a method of teaching that "revives an appreciation for Indian heritage and generates a positive self-image...." One product of this more enlightened attitude is the Institute of American Indian Arts (IAIA) in Santa Fe, New Mexico, which acknowledges that the arts provide a link for Native Americans to the traditions of their ancestors, and fosters that idea through instruction that encourages the preservation of American and Alaskan Native art forms and cultural life.

Established in 1962 by the Bureau of Indian Affairs as an arts education facility for high school and college students, the IAIA became a two-year higher education institution in 1971. Since 1988, it has operated as a fully-accredited, federally-chartered cultural arts college that is governed by a 19-member Board of Trustees, a majority of whom must be Native Americans.

More than three thousand men and women from across the country and from nearly all of the 547 federally-recognized tribes have passed through the IAIA's doors since its inception. And during that time, the school has acquired a well-deserved reputation for developing Native-American talent. Many of the best known, contemporary Indian artists have attended or taught at the school, including 1969 graduate Dan Namingha (Hopi-Tewa), a leading painter and sculptor and a 1994 winner of the Harvard Foundation Award.

The passing of the Indian Education Act of 1972, which acknowledged the special needs of Indian students, served as a catalyst for colleges such as the IAIA, which encourage students to identify with their own heritage and thus ensure its survival. The IAIA Museum, founded with the school, houses the world's largest collection of contemporary Native-American artworks along with textiles, photographs, and a documentary record of the school's history.

arrival, a church organ was delivered; hardly a necessity, it was one of the first requested items to trickle in.

Without supplies, the youngsters spent their first days at play often hungry, due to the scanty provisions available. At night, they lay on hard, wood floors, homesick for the softness of a buffalo robe. Eventually each child made a mattress to sleep on by stuffing a bag with straw from a haystack on the grounds. When more food began to appear on the dining-room tables, a mad rush ensued among students at meal time, as they fought for the plates with the most meat.

While adapting to their new surroundings, the children also underwent a physical transformation that was part of Pratt's philosophy of "total immersion," or civilizing the Indians by altering their physical appearance as well as their thinking. Their long hair, an important cultural symbol, was cut short. Itchy woolen uniforms replaced their own clothes, which were taken out and burned. Before-and-after photographs, which recorded the startling changes in appearance, were taken and sent by Pratt to his superiors in Washington, D.C.

The children's native tongues became forbidden languages, and they were called by new Anglo names that had no meaning for them. At home, the culture of their Indian camps had been driven by tradition, not oriented by time; children ate when they were hungry, slept when they were tired. Now meals, bedtime, life itself, all ran on a strict schedule. And the white man's diet of starchy foods, so foreign to their bodies, along with exposure to new diseases, wreaked havoc with the health of the students. Some of the children did not survive. White Thunder, a Sioux chief, did not even learn of his son Wica-karpa's death until he stopped at the school for a visit while on his way to Washington, in 1880.*

During his visit to Carlisle that same year, Spotted Tail openly criticized Pratt's dream school; then, when Pratt refused to allow Spotted Tail's son-in-law to remain there as an interpreter, he gathered up his children and took them home. In 1881, when word reached the school that Spotted Tail had been killed, the children assumed that whites had been involved and feared that war had again come to their people. Some of the older boys told the younger children that they were in danger at the school. Having gone east to prove his bravery Luther Standing Bear (Plenty Kill) remembered that this "suited me, as I was willing to die right there, just as I had promised when leaving home." Soon, however, the children learned that Spotted Tail had died at the hands of an Indian named Crow Dog and that war was not imminent.

In addition to learning to read and write and deal with numbers, the male students received instruction in trades such as blacksmithing, wagon building, harness making, and other industrial trades. Their wares were shipped back to the reservation for use by their people. Girls spent their time learning domestic arts, Anglo style.

Every summer, Indian students participated in what were called "outings." While living with white families, they would work in homes or businesses, or on farms. Girls baked pies and sewed for their hosts, and boys helped with haying and other farm chores. Luther Standing Bear's outing was more urbane; in 1882, he was, as one of the "best boys" in the school, selected to work at Wanamaker's department store in Philadelphia.

---

*In 1880, the Hayes administration brought 31 Sioux chiefs and their principal men to Washington for a conference. Those with relatives in Carlisle stopped there for a visit.

7. Captain Pratt's School

It was Pratt's hope that Carlisle would inspire more schools of its kind. Although some 24 others did spring up, not all educators agreed with Pratt's concept of a military-style boarding school. Those who ran reservation day schools, convinced that Indian children would learn more readily in their own environment and adapt better to the new ways over a period of time, fought Pratt vehemently The children at the school run by the famous Indian educator and missionary Alfred Riggs on the Santee Sioux reservation in northern Nebraska received instruction in their native tongue; English was taught as a second language.

Despite his controversial views, Pratt's school became famous, largely thanks to his propensity for keeping it in the public eye. Sports played a large part in promoting the Carlisle institution, whose teams enjoyed great success against such universities as Harvard, Yale, and Cornell [see "Triumph and Tragedy," page 34, *American History,* June 1997].* In the field of music, the Carlisle marching band, which consisted of more than three hundred boys and girls, participated in a variety of events, including the October 1892 parades in New York City and Chicago commemorating the quadricentennial of Columbus's voyages of discovery to the New World.

Despite the high-profile image of his school, Pratt remained critical of the administrative policies of the Bureau of Indian Affairs. In May 1904, Pratt declared in a speech at a Baptist ministers' conference that "Nothing better could happen to the Indians than the complete destruction of the [Indian] Bureau." Shortly after the speech, the Army relieved Pratt of his duties at Carlisle.

During his 24 years at the school, Pratt had seen 4,903 Native-American students from 77 different tribes pass through its doors. The Carlisle Indian School continued on for another 14 years without Pratt at the helm, closing in 1918,

---

*Although teams from Carlisle played against universities, the Indian School was not on an academic par with those institutions. Students at Carlisle could not progress beyond the high school level.

a victim, in large measure, of a governmental overhaul of Indian schools.

In retirement, Richard Henry Pratt dictated his memoirs to his daughter and continued to speak out on the subject of Indian education. He retired as a brigadier general, but to the Indian students who remembered him from their days in Carlisle, he was always Captain Pratt. He passed away in a San Francisco army hospital on April 23, 1924, and was buried in Arlington National Cemetery, where a monument at his gravesite reads, "Erected in Loving Memory by His Students and Other Indians."

Did this tireless crusader succeed in making life better for the American Indian? No one can deny that Pratt fought long and hard to eliminate corruption in the Bureau of Indian Affairs and to more quickly blend the nation's indigenous people into white society

Although he sincerely believed that he was doing what was best for the Indian, Pratt never really understood the people that he was so determined to help. Unlike Alfred Riggs, Pratt never lived among the Indians on their own terms and had no interest in their customs, language, or culture.

Luther Standing Bear returned home in 1882. Once back on the reservation, he took a wife, ran his father's dry-goods store, and taught school. Later, he hired on with William "Buffalo Bill" Cody's Wild West show, and eventually ended up in Hollywood as one of the first Native Americans to make a career in talking pictures. Like Pratt, Standing Bear wrote his memoirs, as well as several other books that he hoped would raise awareness of his people's plight.

Many other Carlisle students were not as lucky as Standing Bear. They had been taught to fend for themselves in the white man's world, but when they returned to their reservations, they discovered that their new-found skills did them little good there. Moreover, their education had made them strangers to the old ways.

In March 1891, a Lakota named Plenty Horses stood trial for the murder of Lieutenant Edward W. Casey at Pine Ridge. The killing had taken place two

CUMBERLAND COUNTY HISTORICAL SOCIETY

Luther Standing Bear (above) was among the first group of students to enter the Carlisle Indian School. Originally named Ota Kte (Plenty Kill), he decided to attend the school in order to prove his bravery. Supported by his father who believed in the need to learn the white man's ways, he adapted to life at the school better than many of his fellow students.

months earlier when the Lakota people frantically tried to Ghost Dance their way to better times. At his hearing in Deadwood, South Dakota, Plenty Horses told the court: "I am Indian. Five years I attended Carlisle and was educated in the ways of the white man. I was lonely. I shot the lieutenant so I might make a place for myself among my people. Now I am one of them. I shall be hung and the Indian will bury me as a warrior. They will be proud of me. I am satisfied."

Instead of hanging, however, Plenty Horses went free when the judge ruled that he had killed while a state of war existed. Thus, Plenty Horses suffered the pain of having to live a life straddled between two cultures.

The Carlisle Indian School taught students many things. But in the end, the school's founder, his crusading staff, and their supporters had themselves failed to learn one of the most fundamental lessons—that it takes more than a hair cut and a few years of classroom instruction to eradicate a person's cultural heritage. It was a lesson that the Indian students knew all too well.

Mary Kay Morel is a freelance writer from Colorado Springs, Colorado.

Article 8

"Hang 'em first, try 'em later"

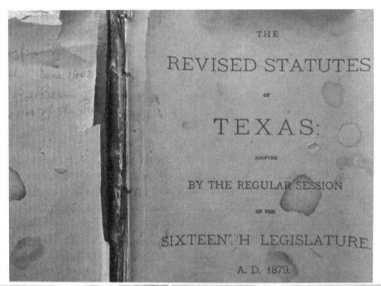

"The only law west of the Pecos," Judge Bean appears in a formal portrait and on his horse Bayo in front of a rebuilt version of the Jersey Lilly, which served as saloon, pool hall and courthouse. At top right is the only law book Bean ever consulted.

From *Smithsonian*, June 1998, pp. 96-107. © 1998 by Bruce Watson. Reprinted by permission.

8. "Hang 'em First, Try 'em Later"

By gobs! There was nothing judicious about Judge Roy Bean

By Bruce Watson

BEHIND THE BAR OF A RICKETY wooden saloon in a lonesome corner of the Old West stood a grizzled bear of a barkeep. His crooked neck was hidden by a beard. His soiled bandanna reeked of bourbon and sweat. No stranger to these parts would have suspected him a judge, but without warning he shouted, "Order, by Gobs! Order in this court!" Lumbering across the saloon, he took off his apron and donned a dirty alpaca coat. He seated himself behind the bar and drew his pistol. "Hear ye! Hear ye!" he proclaimed, banging the gun like a gavel. "This honorable court is now in session, and if any galoot wants a snort before we start, let him step up to the bar and name his pizen."

Judge Roy Bean never attended law school, but he knew how to hold court. His saloon, scorched by the West Texas sun, served some of the finest hooch in the territory. It also had two poker tables, a beer-keg table holding the judge's only law book, and a porch hard by the Rio Grande. In this venue, the judge set many legal precedents. Take the case in which a corpse found near the Pecos River was brought back to Judge Bean's saloon. The dead man's pocket held $40 and a pistol. "I hereby fine this corpse $40 for carrying a concealed weapon," the judge declared, pocketing the money. At least, some say he did. Then there was the highfalutin lawyer who demanded Bean issue a writ of habeas corpus. The judge threatened to hang him for using foul language in his courtroom. According to legend. And some folks still talk about the San Antonio slicker who tried to appeal a fine. The judge listened carefully, then set his six-shooter on the bar. 'There is no appeal from this court," he said. "And that's my rulin'." Appeal denied. So the story goes.

Many Wild West legends have been tamed by truth. Billy the Kid (SMITHSONIAN, February 1991) didn't kill 21 men—4 is more like it. Butch Cassidy and the Sundance Kid looked very little like Paul Newman and Robert Redford. But nearly a century after his death, Judge Roy Bean remains a blur of fiction and fact. Did he really sentence dozens to the gallows, saying "Hang 'em first, try 'em later"? Did he name his town and saloon after his true-love, a British actress he'd never met? Did he keep a pet bear in his courtroom? Rendering a verdict on most Bean legends, the jury remains, well . . . hung. Yet this much is certain: in a brutal landscape where the only other law was nature's own, Judge Roy Bean was, as he claimed to be, the "Law West of the Pecos."

In 1882, when the Galveston, Harrisburg and San Antonio Railroad reached Pecos County, it faced one mean stretch of Texas turf. To link San Antonio with El Paso, railroad crews had to cross 530 miles of sagebrush, leading, one wag said, "from no place through nothing to nowhere." The high, hilly desert was a cactus garden infested with bobcats, rattlers and scorpions, locally called vinegaroons. Summer temperatures topped 100 in the shade, if you could find any shade. Water was as scarce as a smiling face. Yet by the spring of that year, 3,000 men were cutting the railroad's course along the Rio Grande. Serving them whiskey from a tent was a leathery saloon keeper named Roy Bean.

Bean had taken the scenic route to West Texas. Almost nothing is known about his childhood, not even his birth date sometime in the 1830s. But at about 15, he left his hardscrabble Kentucky home to follow two older brothers westward toward adventure. For the next 30 years, he studied pre-law, Old West-style. With brother Sam, he joined a

TODD WILLIAMS AND MARK MATSON

Judge Bean's bar still looks much as it did when he used to shortchange customers and brag about his "acquaintance with Miss Langtry."

TODD WILLIAMS AND MARK MATSON

Today a refurbished Jersey Lilly draws 80,000 visitors a year from around the world, wherever the American West is romanticized.

He soon built a small saloon and hung a tattered picture of Miss Lillie behind the bar.

Vast stretches of range and sky separated the Pecos from Beanville. Bean, his beard now salted in gray, had crossed the barren country in a wagon loaded with whiskey barrels and tent canvas. At the edge of a railroad camp called Vinegaroon, he pitched his tent and began selling liquor to thirsty railroad workers. Business was good, but risky. "There is the worst lot of roughs, gamblers, robbers and pickpockets collected here I ever saw," a Texas Ranger lamented. An old Texas saying proclaimed "West of the Pecos there is no law; West of El Paso there is no God." In Vinegaroon, rangers could round up the usual suspects, but the nearest courtroom was a week's ride away. Some sort of law was needed, and—with three months of formal education to his credit—Roy Bean seemed to be the man. As his own best saloon customer, he was often drunk and disorderly. But Bean could talk circles around anyone who crossed him. And while a reasonable man wouldn't dare lay down the law to a bunch of railroad rowdies, Roy Bean was crazy enough to try it. "The camp is as quiet as can be," he'd say. "There hasn't been a man killed for four hours." When he came to the Pecos, he just wanted to be a saloon keeper. But on August 2, 1882, Pecos County Commissioners "ordered that Roy Bean be and is hereby appointed the Justice of the Peace for Precinct No. 6, Pecos County, Texas."

Bean packed up and moved north to a small settlement on a bluff above the Rio Grande. When he arrived, the town was a tent city, a ragtag cluster of dance halls and drinking establishments surrounded by sagebrush and solitude. Langtry was its name, in honor of a railroad boss who had run the Southern Pacific's tracks through it. But by coin-

wagon train into New Mexico, then crossed the Rio Grande and set up a trading post in Chihuahua, Mexico. Los Frijoles, as the locals called the Beans, did business for a few months before going their separate ways at the Mexican border. That was after Roy had got into a bit of a dustup when an hombre died from one of his bullets. So he rode on alone across the Southwest and, in 1849, dropped in on brother Joshua, who would soon become the first mayor of a little pueblo called San Diego. There he began romancing his own image. He strutted the streets in a sombrero and embroidered pants, with two guns in his belt and a bowie knife in one boot. The darling of local senoritas, he developed a reputation for bragging, dueling, and gambling on cockfights. To tame his wild brother, Mayor Josh Bean made Roy a lieutenant in the state militia and bartender of the Headquarters, the mayor's own saloon. The taming worked for a while, but in 1852, Roy wounded a man in a duel. Arrested, he broke out of jail. A few months later, Josh was killed by his rival in a romantic triangle, and Roy rambled back to New Mexico where Sam Bean had become a sheriff

Roy quietly tended bar in Sam's saloon for several years. When the Civil War broke out, he began running the Union blockade, bringing goods by wagon from the Mexican border into Texas. After the war, and pushing 40, he married a Mexican teenager and settled in San Antonio. Throughout the 1870s while various parts of Texas exploded in range wars, Bean was a dishonest working man supporting five children. He peddled firewood (cut without permission on another man's land) and sold milk (watered down). Once when a customer found a minnow in his milk, Roy responded, "By Cobs, that's what I get for waterin' them cows down at the river." His notorious business schemes earned his San Antonio neighborhood the nickname "Beanville." But when his marriage began to fail, Roy resurrected his romance with the untamed West.

In the summer of 1882, the San Antonio *Express* published a brief notice from Eagle's Nest Springs, in Pecos County:

> I would announce to my friends and the public in general, that I have opened another saloon at the above place, where can be found the best of wines, liquors and cigars. . . . Visitors will always find a quiet, orderly place, where they can get a good drink. The water is good and the scenery grand. Will be pleased to see any of my friends at all times.—Roy Bean.

8. "Hang 'em First, Try 'em Later"

There stood a woman, regal, Titian-haired and as beautiful as her picture on the wall of the saloon.

cidence, the name also belonged to a beautiful British actress Bean had read about in the newspaper. Captivated by Lillie Langtry, Bean began claiming he named the town for her. Like many of his boasts—that he had fought in the Mexican War, that he was related to Daniel Boone—this one was pure Texas bull. But he soon built a small saloon and hung a tattered picture of Miss Lillie behind the bar. She was known and billed as the "Jersey Lily," so he named his saloon after her-with an extra *l*, thanks to an orthographically challenged sign painter. Above the door, he posted signs proclaiming "ICE COLD BEER" and "LAW WEST OF THE PECOS." From the capacious barroom, which doubled as his home, Bean began dispensing liquor and the law.

His lone law book was *The Revised Statutes of Texas, 1879.* "They send me a new book every year or so," he said, "but I use it to light fires with." He had two pistols, a muzzle-loading rifle and colossal nerve. He quickly became his own court jester, astounding criminals with his demeanor and decisions. "It is the judgment of this court that you are hereby tried and convicted of illegally and unlawfully committing certain grave offenses against the peace and dignity of the State of Texas, particularly in my bailiwick," a typical Bean ruling went. "I fine you two dollars; then get the hell out of here and never show yourself in this court again. That's my rulin'." If his justice was arbitrary, it was consistently arbitrary. Though he could swear in English or Spanish, Bean rarely tolerated cursing in his courtroom. Those using invective harsher than his "By Gobs!" were sometimes fined, often the exact amount Roy owed them in change at his bar. He roamed the Pecos region carrying blank warrants that he served at the slightest offense. Once he boarded the train to ride up line and fine two men for fighting: "You know," he told the conductor, "this court of mine has to be self-sustaining."

Unfettered by legalities, Roy Bean's justice was governed by greed, prejudice and a dash of common sense. If a marriage "didn't take," then Bean granted a divorce. Once, after divorcing two couples, he married each man to the other man's ex-wife, collecting two dollars for each divorce and five for each marriage. One day a railroad bridge in the Pecos River Canyon collapsed, and ten workers fell 300 feet to the canyon floor. The judge, who earned five dollars for each coroner's inquest, soon rode up on a mule. Three of the victims were still alive, but Bean pronounced all ten deceased, picking up an extra 15 dollars in the process. Of the injured he said, "Them three fellers is bound to die."

Despite such capers, Bean, once duly appointed, was duly elected in 1884. He was often reelected, so that between 1882 and 1902, most of the time Bean's peculiar rulings were the law. Given the circumstances, his law wasn't all that peculiar. Those quick to judge him should visit Langtry, where the Jersey Lilly still stands. From the saloon's

TODD WILLIAMS AND MARK MATSON
With only 20 residents left in town, Langtry's Sample Cafe has fallen on hard times.

steps, one can see a dozen dusty buildings. Beyond these lie nothing but barren land and cactus baking in the sun. The nearest jail is 50 miles away in Del Rio, and the nearest mercy meted out by nature is well beyond the horizon.

In legend, Judge Roy Bean is a merciless arbiter, but folks in Langtry like to tell a different story. Rancher Jack Skiles grew up in the town, whose population has petered out from 300 in Bean's heyday to about 20 nowadays. In 1963, Skiles began interviewing old-timers who remembered Bean from their childhoods. By 1968 he had become the first director of the Judge Roy Bean Visitor Center. 'The term I always heard Langtry people use for Roy Bean was 'that old reprobate,'" Skiles told me over lunch in his house on a bluff above the Rio Grande. "Now, 'reprobate' is not the kind of word Langtry people used a lot." Thumbing through a dictionary, he read: "'*Reprobate*—depraved, corrupt, a scoundrel or mischievous rogue.' Well, I guess that's a pretty good word for old Roy."

But when compared with his contemporaries, "that old reprobate" was a solon of the Southwest. In most one-horse towns, justice was a one-man job. Familiarity with the law was optional. The phrase "sober as a judge" contains a wealth of irony since many Western judges were drunk as skunks, even in court. To enforce their authority, they used canes, fists, sometimes pistols. In the mining town of Sonora, California, justice Richard Barry once fined and jailed a lawyer for merely suggesting that the court had no authority. "I told him that I didn't care a damn for his book law, that I was the law myself," the honorable Barry said. The decision was a warning to "unrooly" persons not to contradict. And although Bean is often called "the hangin' judge," the West's hangingest judge was Isaac Parker of Fort Smith, Arkansas. Parker sentenced 172 men to hang and strung up 88 of them. Measured against these "suspended" sentences, Roy Bean's rule was evenhanded, even wise.

Bean prevailed because he was the right man in the right place. "That man did a world of good," said an El Paso judge who had known Bean. "The rough

2 ❖ THE EMERGENCE OF MODERN AMERICA

TODD WILLIAMS AND MARK MATSON
At the edge of nowhere and nothing, Bob Fitzsimmons fought Peter Maher for the world title.

community where he had settled would have tolerated no enforcement of the law as it was printed on the statute books. But they tolerated Bean, because he was both law and equity, right and justice." Geography was also on Bean's side. In more populous parts of Texas, violent factions waged war over sheep and cattle, but there wasn't much to fight over in Bean's territory. Except for the occasional murder, his cases consisted of misdemeanors, counts of drunkenness and the crimes of small-time con men like himself. Bean spent most of his days sitting on the porch of his saloon, with rifle handy. In his spare time, he served customers. His favorites were railroad passengers, desperate for something to drink while their train took on water. Bean served them quickly, then lingered giving them change. And lingered. When the train's warning whistle blew, customers swore and demanded their money. The judge hereby fined them the exact amount and sent them cursing back to their coach.

Bean regularly boasted of his "acquaintance with Miss Langtry." Someday, he said, he hoped she would come to Langtry and sing. In 1896, after his first saloon burned, Bean rebuilt the Jersey Lilly and then put up a home for himself across the street. Miss Lillie would someday perform there, of course, so Bean called his home the Opera House. His dreams of Lillie were not as wild as they seemed. Langtry, whose beauty partly inspired Oscar Wilde to write *Lady Windermere's Fan,* sometimes toured Western theaters. In 1888 she performed in San Antonio. When Bean learned of the upcoming show, he dressed up, took the train to the big city and bought a front-row seat. He had hoped to meet her backstage but at the last minute was struck by a rare fit of shyness. He never met Miss Lillie, but back home he celebrated his sighting for a week. He continued to yearn and often wrote her. Once she wrote back and even offered to give her eponymous town an ornamental drinking fountain. Bean replied that the fountain wouldn't be necessary because "if there's anything these hombres of Langtry don't drink, it's water." Yet Bean cherished two fancy pistols some say Miss Lillie sent him, and her picture was a fixture in the Jersey Lilly. Someday . . .

There were plenty of Judge Roy Bean stories in the Texas newspapers. But you can't believe everything you read in the papers. Did the judge once flag down millionaire Jay Gould's train, then sip champagne with the railroad tycoon in the Jersey Lilly? Unlikely. And what about Bean's bear, Bruno? Once, a story goes, a woman's little dog strayed too close to Bruno. The frantic woman begged the judge to free her precious pet from the bear's clutches. "Well, lady," Bean said, "if you buy your dog 50 cents' worth of meat at my market, I'll feed it to the bear and he'll forget about the pup." Photographs of Bruno exist, yet few old-timers would swear to this story under oath.

Of all the legends, none is more outrageous than Bean's ruling on the murder of a Chinese man. When it came to race, Bean's law was far from color-blind. He loved the free-spending Irish who frequented his bar, but had less regard for the more thrifty Chinese. When an Irishman killed a Chinese worker, friends of the accused said they'd tear down the Jersey Lilly if Bean found him guilty. The tale of what happened goes something like this. Searching for another legal precedent, Bean rapped his pistol. "Hear ye! Hear ye!" The court was in session. He then browsed through his law book, turning page after page. "Gentlemen," he said at length. "I find the law very explicit on murdering your fellow man, but there's nothing here about killing a Chinaman. Case dismissed." Unfortunately, this one is probably true.

Many of Bean's rulings were amusing, but there's nothing funny about getting away with murder. Or getting your son off for murder. Sam Bean was the youngest and wildest of Roy's five children. One day in the saloon, a certain Mr. George Upshaw made fun of Sam's fine Mexican blanket. The two men argued, and Upshaw slapped Sam in the face, drawing blood. Roy said simply, "Shoot him, Sam—shoot him." Obeying his father, Sam blew the man away. For the next year, Roy corralled witnesses and promised favors. In a Del Rio courtroom in 1899, Sam Bean was acquitted. The verdict, a Langtry old-timer remembered, cost Roy "many a bottle of beer" and nearly all the money he'd managed to save.

Bean kept no record of his cases. "I have got the cleanest docket in the state of Texas," he gloated; "not a scratch of a pen on it." But as his legend grew, he enjoyed bullying the tourists who came to see him at the Jersey Lilly. Nearly every Bean story has the smoky scent of a tale told round a campfire. Yet in

An unfortunate star at Judge Bean's bar was a black bear named Bruno, one of whose charms was that he could drink beer after pulling the cork with his teeth.

his book *Judge Roy Bean Country,* Jack Skiles refutes the most fanciful claims against the judge. Bean threatened to hang hundreds. One or two were even taken to the gallows, then allowed to escape. But rumors to the contrary, says Skiles, "there's no evidence to suggest that Judge Roy Bean ever hung anybody." And by the way, he adds. This tough man? This hangin' judge? His first name wasn't Roy, but Phantly. Phantly Roy Bean. That's Skiles' rulin', based on Kentucky census records.

Judge Roy Bean stories are like a plant that grows in the Pecos region. Along the Rio Grande, the resurrection plant lies withering on dry rocks. But put it in water, and within a day, it stands tall again. Bean legends, refuted by historians, are watered by our need to believe in Western myth. About 80,000 visitors come to Langtry each year. Tour buses arrive laden with sightseers from Germany, Japan, Slovenia and anywhere else the American West is romanticized. Tourists' most common question is, "Where's your hangin' tree?" Tour guides jokingly point to the remnants of a mesquite tree in the center of town. Its skinny limbs couldn't support a rope swing, let alone a noose, but it makes a good story. "Everyone waits to know how many people he killed, how many he hung," says Sarah Rangel, a Texas state travel counselor based in Langtry. "Some are real disappointed to hear that he didn't hang anyone."

Yet one Bean story, documented and photographed, is as colorful as legend. By the 1890s, as reformers fought to civilize the West, prizefighting had been made illegal in most Western states. Fans were eager for a fight, however, and promoters were eager to dodge the law. A Dallas man, having booked two boxers for a world heavyweight title bout, needed a venue. The fight was first scheduled to take place in Arkansas, but state authorities blocked it. It was to be held in Juarez, but the Mexican governor said he wouldn't allow it. New Mexico was considered as a likely site until Congress intervened, outlawing boxing in all federal territories. By February 1896, fighters, sportswriters and hundreds of fans were hanging around El Paso waiting to hold the fight *somewhere*. Twenty-six Texas Rangers were on hand to make sure it wouldn't happen in Texas. But then a telegram arrived inviting the entourage down to a tiny town on the Southern Pacific line.

8. "Hang 'em First, Try 'em Later"

Boxers, fans and rangers boarded the train. When it stopped in Langtry, it was met by the "Law West of the Pecos."

On the afternoon of February 22, the Jersey Lilly was packed. Following rounds of drinks for all, Bean led the crowd down the bluff to the *vega*, the river's bottomland beneath towering cliffs. There local laborers had put up a small jerry-built bridge. While Texas Rangers watched helplessly from atop the cliff, the fighters and about 200 fans crossed the bridge and made their way to a sandbar near the Mexican shore of the Rio Grande. In a makeshift ring on the edge of nowhere and nothing, Bob Fitzsimmons fought Peter Maher for the world title. Fitzsimmons made quick work of it, decking Maher with a vicious right after only 95 seconds. Then the crowd followed Bean up the bluff to the Jersey Lilly for more drinks. That night, the entourage returned to El Paso, where sportswriters sent the story around the country. Soon the name of Judge Roy Bean was known far beyond Texas.

By the dawn of the new century, Roy Bean was a tired man. A life of raw adventure had made him older than his years. Yet his legend was being born. In the traditional "Ballad of Judge Roy Bean," the judge smiles "his six-gun smile," and shouts, "By Gobs, gents, . . . that's my rulin'!" In newspapers and dime novels, the myth grew and grew. Bean's saga soon became a part of Texas folklore. In 1936, the Texas centennial fairgrounds featured replicas of Bean's saloon and office. Then in 1940, the judge went to Hollywood.

In *The Westerner,* Walter Brennan played Bean opposite Gary Cooper. Salty, constantly hitting the bottle, Brennan's Bean fights *against* justice, siding with cattlemen in a range war. Cooper, a lone, lean drifter, urges the judge to "be a real judge for all the people!" But Bean burns out home steaders and hangs anyone who crosses him. When he goes to see Miss Lillie in nearby Fort Davis, "Coop" guns him down. He dies backstage at Miss Lillie's feet. Brennan won an Oscar for the role, and the myth was set in stone. Always concerned about the shifting sands of the law, we use Judge Roy Bean to recall a time when justice was firm, if not always fair. In 1956, gravel-voiced Edgar Buchanan played Bean in a weekly TV series. Later the myth became farce in the 1972 shoot-em-up *The Life and Times of Judge Roy Bean*. As the judge, Paul Newman is nearly hanged when he first visits Langtry. He shoots everyone in the saloon and appoints himself judge. Newman's Bean hangs 'em all before dying in a hail of gunfire, shouting "For Texas, and Miss Lillie!"

Roy Bean was not killed in a blaze of bullets. Contrary to the Larry McMurtry novel and movie *Streets of Laredo*, he was not gunned down by a Mexican outlaw on the steps of the Jersey Lilly. In March 1903, Bean went on a drinking binge in Del Rio. The next afternoon, friends found him wandering helplessly around his saloon courtroom. A doctor was sent for, but it was too late. His Honor died peacefully in bed the following morning. Not much of an ending to a legend, except....

Ten months after Bean passed on to his reward, the Southern Pacific stopped at Langtry. A small ensemble of well-dressed visitors stepped from a luxurious coach. At the center of attention stood a woman, regal, Titian-haired and as beautiful as her picture on the wall of the local saloon. On her way from New Orleans to San Francisco, Lillie Langtry had decided to take the judge up on his invitation. The whole town came out to greet Judge Roy Bean's "someday" sweetheart. Miss Lillie shook hands with grizzled ranchers and greeted women and children dressed in their finest. She set foot in the saloon whose sign still bore her nickname and perhaps even saw her faded picture on its wall. Folks told her stories: how Roy Bean had fined a corpse, freed a murderer, and lined his pockets by short-changing train passengers. The town's new justice of the peace presented the actress with Bean's pistol and his bear, who quickly fled into the desert. Those gathered gave her some resurrection plants, which she later revived with water. "It was a short visit," Langtry recalled in her autobiography, "but an unforgettable one."

Bruce Watson is a frequent contributor to the magazine. He has lately written articles on Jack London and Ferraris.

"If you men don't withdraw, we will mow every one of you down."

When the Carnegie Steel Company hired the Pinkerton National Detective Agency to end a labor dispute at one of its mills, it set the stage for a bloody encounter between the forces of labor and management.

by William C. Kashatus

The Pinkertons, 300 of them, came on July 6, 1892. Early that morning a lookout posted along the Monongahela River had spotted the two barges coming from Pittsburgh toward the shabby industrial town of Homestead. The Pinkerton National Detective Agency was notorious for breaking strikes, and the men on the barges were coming to reclaim the Carnegie Steel Company mill in Homestead from disgruntled workers who had seized it. As the barges advanced up the polluted river, some 10,000 people—steelworkers and their wives and children—stood ready to defend their position.

The barges attempted to land around 4:00 A.M., but Hugh O'Donnell, a spokesman for the steelworkers, stopped them at the river's edge. O'Donnell insisted that under no circumstances could the Pinkertons come ashore to take possession of the works. He shouted an impassioned plea to the men in the barges: "I beg of you to leave here at once. I don't know who you are nor from whence you came, but I do know that you have no business here, and if you remain there will be more bloodshed."

On one of the boats Captain Frederick Heinde stepped forward and identified himself and his men as agents of the Pinkerton agency. "We don't wish to shed blood, but we are determined to go up there and shall do so," Heinde said. "If you men don't withdraw, we will mow every one of you down and enter in spite of you." Several agents lowered a gangplank and Heinde ordered his men forward.

No one could say who fired first, but suddenly shots rang out, wounding Heinde and William Foy, a union leader on the landing. The crowd on shore smashed through a makeshift fence at the river's edge and began throwing rocks at the despised Pinkertons. Then both sides opened a murderous barrage.

THE END OF THE nineteenth century was a time of increasing labor unrest in the United States. Rapid technological advancement and the unchecked pursuit of profits by wealthy industrialists like Andrew Carnegie (see "Man of Steel") increased the tensions between workers and management. At the 90-acre Homestead steel mill—originally built in 1881 by a syndicate of Pittsburgh manufacturers who sold it to Carnegie two years later—conditions created a natural climate for the union movement. While the town's steel-making industry provided employment for 3,800 workers who resided there, the work was dangerous and miserable. Men worked 12-hour shifts for meager pay while facing the possibility of death from a variety of sources: white-hot ingots, fast-moving overhead cranes, and exploding furnaces.

In 1892, the country's most powerful union was the Amalgamated Association of Iron and Steel Workers (AAISW). Organized in Pittsburgh on August 4, 1876, the AAISW committed itself to improving the job security and social conditions of its members and had

THE EMERGENCE OF MODERN AMERICA

Steel magnate Andrew Carnegie.

gained major strongholds in the iron mills of western Pennsylvania and Ohio. In 1887 the AAISW had aligned with the new American Federation of Labor, and during the next five years, AAISW membership exploded to 20,975 as it became one of the Federation's largest unions and helped shape and direct national labor policy.

The AAISW did suffer from internal tensions among its various craft unions, but Homestead, in particular, seemed to enjoy harmonious relations within the work force as well as between labor and management. The skilled workers—predominantly English, German, Irish, Scottish, and Welsh—who belonged to the AAISW had achieved a significant measure of solidarity with their non-union brethren, mostly unskilled Hungarians and Slavs, who held the worst jobs in the mill. Whenever possible, the union and the work force cooperated with

Union leader Hugh O'Donnell.

management, mainly due to the seemingly receptive nature of mill owner Andrew Carnegie, who believed that trade unions were "beneficial, both to labor and capital." Insisting that he would rather negotiate with his workers than hire strikebreakers, Carnegie swore by "an unwritten law—'Thou shalt not take thy neighbor's job.'" In 1889 Carnegie agreed to recognize the AAISW at Homestead, yet by 1892 he had come to believe that the union had acquired excessive power and he began planning to destroy it even as he portrayed himself as a friend of the working man.

During the ensuing conflict, Carnegie would remove himself from the fray. His chief instrument for breaking the union would be his chairman and plant manager, Henry Clay Frick. Like Carnegie, Frick had risen from humble origins. As a youth, he worked on his father's Pennsylvania farm and, later, his grandfather's distillery. In 1871, Frick invested in bituminous coal and in the beehive ovens used to convert coal into coke for iron production. Not only did the 21-year-old budding entrepreneur possess the business acumen to succeed, but he also had the confidence and iron-fisted will to squelch any labor movement that got in his way. Within a year, Frick's company controlled 100 ovens; by the end of the decade he was a millionaire. When he joined his business with Carnegie's in the 1880s, Frick's financial fortunes grew even more dramatically. Despite a sometimes combative relationship, Carnegie trusted Frick and made him chairman of Carnegie Bros. & Company. In 1892, Frick took over as manager of all plants within the Carnegie empire and amalgamated the mining, milling, and transportation operations.

In January 1892, superintendent of the Homestead mill John Potter initiated negotiations with the AAISW to change the wage structure. Wages were fixed to the price of steel, rising or falling as the price did, with an agreed-on minimum price fixed at $25 a ton. Carnegie's company wanted to lower the minimum to $22 per ton. Frick defended the decrease by insisting that the company had "spent large sums of money on new machinery" which, in turn, enabled the work-

men to increase both the "daily output" of steel and the "amount of their own earnings." AAISW rejected the lower price and negotiations deadlocked.

That spring, Carnegie and his wife departed for Britain, where they remained for the rest of the year. With tension rising between management and labor, Carnegie chose to protect his public image as a beneficent capitalist, and he left Frick—who had severely criticized Carnegie's decision to recognize the AAISW back in 1889—to enforce his anti-union policy. Carnegie told Frick that he "approved of anything you do, not stopping short of a contest with labor." By July the Carnegies were on their way to Rannoch Lodge, a rented retreat in a remote section of the Scottish Highlands.

Men worked 12-hour shifts for meager pay while facing the possibility of death from a variety of sources.

Before he left the United States, however, Carnegie sent Frick a notice that he wanted posted at the Homestead works. It announced that due to the planned amalgamation of other Carnegie steel mills to form the Carnegie Steel Company, Homestead would have to become non-union just as the other mills were. Frick quietly filed the notice away. Although the plant manager agreed with Carnegie's position, he favored more devious tactics. His idea was to offer such severe terms to the AAISW that the union would not accept them, thus placing the onus for non-agreement on labor and not on management.

On May 29 Frick issued an ultimatum to the AAISW: accept the company's new wage structure by June 24 or force a lockout. Soon after, he lined the plant's periphery with a three-mile-long, 11-foot-high fence made of two-inch thick wooden planks and topped by barbed wire, leaving it open only on the riverside. Frick's workers erected searchlights on 12-foot towers and bored holes in the fence every few yards so sharpshooters could thwart any attack by strikers. Now, in the event of a strike, boatloads of strikebreakers could safely reach company property. The infuriated steelworkers saw the fence as a declaration of war and renamed the mill "Fort Frick."

Determined to force a showdown, Frick wrote to the Pinkerton National Detective Agency on June 2, requesting a force of 300 guards to "deal with the trouble we anticipate" when the company "reopens non-union on July 6th." It proved to be the decisive step in the conflict. The Pinkerton agents were widely regarded as the enemy of workers across the nation, and their mere presence seemed to provide the catalyst for labor violence. The agency's suppression of the Molly Maguires, a secret organization of Irish-American coal miners who challenged mine owners in eastern Pennsylvania in the 1870s, was especially well known (See "Undermining the Molly Maguires," August 1999). The Pinkertons were also instrumental in combating strikes at the McCormick Reaper Works in Chicago, the iron molders lockout in Troy, New York, and the Burlington Railroad strike during the 1880s. Their involvement at Homestead would only reinforce the agency's reputation.

On June 19, more than 3,000 delegates to the AAISW annual convention in Pittsburgh assembled in the Homestead opera house to hear John McLuckie, the town's burgess (mayor), address the impending crisis. The epitome of labor republicanism, McLuckie fancied himself a "citizen-reformer." Though he had little more than a grade-school education and worked as a semi-skilled hand in the local steel mills, the 40-year-old burgess had distinguished himself in the union's earlier fights against the forces that sought "to deprive the working men of their rights under the constitution of this government." A legion of admirers within the AAISW knew McLuckie as "Honest John," and the union appointed him to its advisory committee to negotiate a new contract with Carnegie Steel. Doubting that Carnegie had the stomach to spill blood for the sake of profits, McLuckie urged the steelworkers to take a hard line.

While Honest John rallied the rank-and-file, several hundred unskilled workers formed their own amalgamated lodge and voted unanimously to follow the AAISW lead in case of a strike.

Negotiations ended in failure on June 23, when Frick refused to accept the AAISW offer of a sliding-scale minimum of $24 per ton instead of the $22 the company wanted. Six days later, Frick ordered the closing of the mill's open-hearth and armor-plate departments, locking out 800 men; on June 30, other department closings locked out 300 more workers. At a 10:00 A.M. mass meeting in Homestead on June 30, steelworkers and union members agreed not to accept Frick's offer. A union delegation met men who had been working at the time of the meeting and asked them not to return to work the following day. "What if we don't want to come out?" cried one worker. "Come out anyway, or if you don't you'll have to be a rapid runner," shouted another. On July 1 the remaining 2,700 steelworkers refused to report to work, and the strike was on.

The AAISW responded quickly. In early July its members seized the Homestead mill but did not interfere with the few watchmen and government steel inspectors left on the premises. The union-appointed advisory committee was determined to preserve order and protect the life and property of the town's residents. Its members visited liquor saloons and warned proprietors against drunkenness and disorderly gatherings on their premises, advised McLuckie that he could ask the committee for assistance in preserving the peace, and sealed off the town to prevent any strikebreakers from resuming operations. The union stationed patrols at the entrances to the town and on the river and posted pickets around the works. When Allegheny County Sheriff William H. McCleary and his 11 deputies tried to take possession of the mill on behalf of the company, members of the rank-and-file escorted them out of town. The advisory committee now controlled Homestead.

McLuckie understood that the union had no legal right to invade Carnegie's property or to interfere with his effort to hire strikebreakers, but he insisted that it had no choice in the matter. "We

Henry Clay Frick enforced Carnegie's policies.

do not propose that Andrew Carnegie's representatives shall bulldoze us," he said. "We have our homes in this town, we have our churches here, our societies and our cemeteries. We are bound to Homestead by all the ties that men hold dearest and most sacred." Then, late in the evening of July 5, the Pinkertons made their way up the river from Pittsburgh.

FOUR HOURS AFTER the initial confrontation at Homestead on July 6, the Pinkertons, armed with rifles and revolvers, made a second attempt to come ashore, only to meet another volley of fire. Sporadic shooting continued throughout the day. "It was a place of torment," recalled one Pinkerton guard.

Homestead's burgess John McLuckie miscalculated management's resolve.

"Men were lying around wounded and bleeding and piteously begging for someone to help them. The booming of cannon, the bursting of dynamite bombs, the burning of oil on the river, and the yells and shouts on the shore made our position appalling. It is a wonder we did not commit suicide." The shooting finally ceased in the late afternoon when the Pinkertons surrendered. The *Pittsburgh Post* reported that as the agents marched up the river embankment, "No mercy was shown them.... The men were knocked on the head and struck in the face, begging for the mercy which they received not." When the conflict finally ended, six steelworkers and two Pinkertons lay dead and dozens were injured.

The Pinkertons may have surrendered, but the shoot-out proved to be a strategic blunder for the strikers. It only served to strengthen Frick's resolve to destroy the union. Publicly, he made every effort to make the AAISW members appear as if they were the offenders. "The question at issue is a very grave one," he told the *Pittsburgh Commercial Gazette*. "It is whether the Carnegie Company or the Amalgamated Association shall have absolute control of our plant and business at Homestead. We have decided to operate the plant ourselves." Frick insisted that he had done everything in his power to avert the calamity, and he placed the blame for it squarely on the strikers' shoulders. "Not a man known to raise a rifle or a revolver in the bloody fight, or openly asserting his affiliation with any union will ever be employed in the Carnegie Works again," he said emphatically.

Four days later, at Frick's insistence, Pennsylvania Governor Robert E. Pattison called out the entire state militia of 8,615 National Guardsmen to occupy Homestead. The strikers welcomed the news, anticipating a quick resolution of differences with the company now that the state was involved. At a rally, McLuckie announced that "any man who insults the militia shall be taken to the river and ducked," and the crowd greeted his words with cheers. To their great dismay, the men soon discovered that the militia intended to enforce the company's position and protect the strikebreakers who were hired to resume production at the mill. When Major General George R. Snowden, commander of the Pennsylvania National Guard, arrived on July 13, he brusquely dismissed the citizens' delegation that had come to greet his troops and ordered

> *On May 29 Frick issued an ultimatum to the AAISW: accept the company's terms by June 24 or force a lockout.*

COURTESY OF RIVERS OF STEEL

After Frick ordered the construction of a three-mile long fence topped with barbed wire around the Homestead plant, steelworkers angrily dubbed the place "Fort Frick." The Homestead works general office building, pictured here, was among the buildings behind the barricade. Frick, who liked all his operations in good order, hired a man to whitewash the fence.

9. "If You Men Don't Withdraw, We Will Mow Every One of You Down"

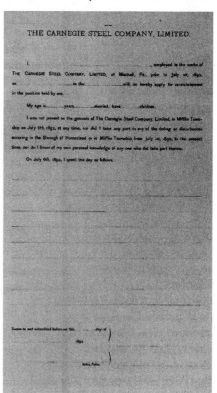

Above: Members of the Pennsylvania state militia drilled on the outskirts of the town during their occupation of Homestead. Pennsylvania governor Robert E. Pattison called out the troops to prevent further violence and to secure the property for its owners. Right: Before workers could return to their jobs after the strike, management made them sign a legal document affirming that they had not taken "part in any rioting or disturbances." Workers also had to state where they were and what they were doing on July 6, 1892.

them to "go home and behave yourselves." McLuckie appealed to the governor in Harrisburg, but to no avail. In September, McLuckie, O'Donnell, and 13 others were arrested for the murders of the Pinkerton agents. Although the men were acquitted, McLuckie felt powerless in the eyes of the local people, his strategic plan a failure, and he resigned as burgess in November and left town.

ON JULY 23, 25-YEAR-OLD Alexander Berman burst into Frick's office in downtown Pittsburgh, stabbed him three times in the back and both legs, and shot him in the ear and neck. Berkman, a Russian-born anarchist who wanted to champion the cause of a worker's revolution, had no connection to the strike. Frick survived the attack, however, and even remained at his desk to complete his day's work after his wounds had been treated. He was just as unyielding in his defense of company profit as he was in his opposition to unionism. "I do not think I shall die," he said, "but whether I do or not, the company will pursue the same policy and it will win."

Ultimately, Frick emerged the victor. Not only did he fully recover from the

THE MAN OF STEEL

Andrew Carnegie's life story was the classic "rags-to-riches" dream. The son of a poor weaver in Dunfermline, Scotland, Andrew immigrated with his family to the United States in 1848. There the 12-year-old found a job as a bobbin boy in a Pittsburgh textile mill, earning $1.20 for a 60-hour workweek. He still managed to find time to take a night course in double-entry bookkeeping. A year later, Carnegie became a Western Union messenger boy and learned how to operate the telegraph. As he handled messages for every major business in Pittsburgh, the youngster quickly gained an insider's view of their operations.

Carnegie's big break came in 1852 when Thomas Scott, superintendent of Pennsylvania Railroad's western division, hired him as his secretary and personal telegrapher. The ambitious young Scotsman soon mastered the complex details of the era's most innovative industry, and when Scott became vice president of the Pennsylvania Railroad in 1859, Carnegie succeeded him as head of the line's western division. Not only did he more than double the railroad's mileage by running trains around the clock, Carnegie also slashed commuter fares to keep ridership at capacity and developed other innovative cost-cutting techniques. Professional success guaranteed his personal financial success. By 1868, Carnegie earned more than $56,000 a year on investments alone. In the early 1870s, he decided to enhance his fortune by building his own steel mill, a logical choice considering that railroads were the nation's largest purchaser of steel.

Widely known for his salesmanship, Carnegie cultivated the personal friendship of railroad executives, securing their steel orders for rails, bridges, and other related structures. In 1891, he acquired a substantial interest in the vast western Pennsylvania coal and coke holdings of Henry Clay Frick. This gave the Scotsman guaranteed supplies of coke, which, together with iron and limestone, is a major ingredient of steel.

By the 1890s, Carnegie had become the nation's foremost steel magnate, owning three large mills in western Pennsylvania at Homestead, Braddock, and Dusquesne. He mechanized each one, using the latest technology to fabricate the steel beams, sheets, and plates used by urban America to build the metal skeletons of the Gilded Age. In 1901 he sold the Carnegie Company to U.S. Steel for $480 million, retired, and concentrated on his philanthropic work.

> *When the conflict ended, six steelworkers and two Pinkertons lay dead and dozens were injured.*

assassination attempt, but he also triumphed over the union. On November 20, the workers declared the strike over and returned to the mill without a contract. The combined authority of the state and the steel industry had forced the AAISW to capitulate. It was a severe blow to unions throughout the United States.

Carnegie's concern for his public image was so great that he refused to accept any responsibility for his role in instigating the bloody strike, emphasizing instead the "reward the comes from the feeling that you and your employees are friends." Still, he was excoriated in the press and shunned as the "arch-sneak of his age" by both liberals and conservatives alike. He tried to distance himself from the criticism by continuing to plow his money into trusts, university endowments, and public libraries.

Years later Carnegie was still seeking absolution from John McLuckie, saying he "would rather risk McLuckie's verdict as a passport to Paradise than all the theological dogmas invented by man." Blacklisted from employment in the steel industry and ignored by the rank-and-file, the former burgess wound up in Mexico, looking for mining work. When Carnegie learned of McLuckie's whereabouts he dispatched an associate to offer him money. The steel magnate would have to look elsewhere for his passport to Paradise, however. McLuckie turned down the offer.

William C. Kashatus is a professional historian who works at the Chester County Historical Society, West Chester, Pennsylvania.

For more about labor and management struggles, read "Undermining the Molly Maguires," by Joseph H. Bloom. You can find it starting February 28 on the World Wide Web at TheHistoryNet, http://www.thehistorynet.com.

Electing The President, 1896

Edward Ranson *on the White House race that split and defined a fin-de-siècle US.*

On the eve of the American presidential and congressional elections in November 1896 the mood of the country was tense. In some quarters, especially in the ranks of nervous bankers, financiers, businessmen and property owners it approached hysteria. Both major parties warned of the dire consequences of a victory for the other side, of the cataclysmic economic results that would follow, of the resultant sectional hostility and of class conflict. Politicians, editors and clergymen all used military metaphors in their appeals to the electorate. Although feelings ran high and voting was heavy (nearly 14 million ballots were cast—a figure that would not be exceeded until 1908), polling day, November 3rd, passed without serious incident.

William McKinley, the Republican candidate, achieved a clear victory, though not a landslide, receiving 7,102,246 votes (51 per cent) to the 6,492,559 (46 per cent) cast for William Jennings Bryan, the Democratic standard-bearer, minor candidates sharing the remaining 3 per cent. Although McKinley carried only twenty-three states to Bryan's twenty-two he won in the electoral college 271–176 because his appeal was greatest in the most populous areas of the country; the demographic and economic trends of the 1890s were in the Republicans' favour. Urban and industrial America, the backbone of McKinley's support, was growing, and Bryan failed to attract the working classes in these areas. On the other hand, rural and agrarian America, the natural constituency of Bryan and the Democrats, was losing its economic and political influence.

True, presidential elections between the end of the American Civil War in 1865 and 1896 had often stimulated high levels of voter interest and participation and provoked intense partisan passions. Bitter recollections of the Civil War and Reconstruction on both sides, and the rough political equilibrium which existed at the national level between the Democrats and the Republicans, ensured that political managers would stoop to any expedient to win over particular groups in the electorate or to carry key states. As Republican Senator Ingalls of Kansas wrote in 1890, 'The Decalogue and the Golden Rule have no place in a political campaign. The object is success.'

Yet for most of this period, party and presidential politics were not concerned with philosophies, programmes or policies, but focused rather upon personalities and patronage. Party loyalty was fierce, political apostasy despised, and breakaway movements and third parties rarely exercised more than temporary influence. Success could rest on wafer

On the stump: (far left) the charismatic orator and Democratic candidate for the Presidency, William Jennings Bryan, on the campaign trail leaving Galion, Ohio, by train with his wife and supporters.

thin margins in pivotal states like Indiana, Illinois or New York, and candidates were chosen, in part at least, because of their local associations and their perceived ability to win in these vital areas. Hence it came to be said that while some men were born great, and some had greatness thrust upon them, others came from Ohio.

The political battles of the late nineteenth century were fought against a background of social, economic and cultural change. The population grew from 39.8 million in 1870 to 75.9 million in 1900, an increase of 25 per cent in each decade. At the same time the nation experienced rapid urbanisation and industrialisation. The costs of these changes included heightened urban-rural tensions, growing hostility between capital and labour, increasing poverty and rising resentment against social inequalities. Although the Republican Party usually supported a high protective tariff, as a means of aiding American industry and securing full employment, while the Democrats favoured a tariff for revenue purposes only as a way of helping American farmers, politicians of the 1870s and 1880s, imbued with *laissez-faire* ideas, generally chose to ignore domestic social and economic problems.

By the 1890s social, economic and political discord had created a climate close to national crisis. Men of power and property even pondered the likelihood of revolution. It was in such an atmosphere that the presidential campaign of 1896 was conducted, a campaign that for the first time in decades saw serious debate on economic and social issues which deeply divided America along unfamiliar socio-economic fissures, rather than according to traditional party lines.

The Democrats, led by Grover Cleveland, had won control of Congress and the White House in 1892, and the prospects seemed set for Cleveland to redeem his campaign promise to reduce the tariff. Within weeks of his taking office in March 1893, however, economic confidence evaporated, stock prices fell, production slowed and unemployment rose alarmingly to 2,500,000 by January 1894. By that time 642 banks had closed, and by mid-1894 156 railroads with 30,000 miles of track were in the hands of receivers. Agricultural prices dropped precipitously, tens of thousands of farmers faced bankruptcy and foreclosure of their mortgages, and agrarian distress was widespread.

Republican contender (and victor in the 1896 White House race) William McKinley pictured here with his wife; a stiff pose that reflected his rather 'stuffed shirt' persona.

The nation blamed the Democratic Party in general, and the Cleveland administration in particular, for their tribulations, with public soup kitchens being christened 'Cleveland Cafés.' The political prospects of the Democrats depended on how the administration responded to this crisis, but, in fact, both the economic and political situations quickly went from bad to worse. In the face of Republican opposition, and Democratic defections by those who believed the circumstances had changed or had special interests to protect, Cleveland was unable to persuade Congress to agree [on] a significantly lower tariff. The resultant act of August 1894 was referred to by the President as falling 'far short of the consummation for which we have long labored', and as the result of 'party perfidy and party dishonor'. The new tariff became law without his signature, an action which amounted to a public acknowledgement of the deep rifts apparent in Democratic ranks.

Other problems also had to be faced in 1893–94. Several 'armies' of unemployed men marched on Washington, including the group led by 'General' Jacob S. Coxey, an Ohio businessman, who sympathised with the victims of the depression. The march, which began on March 25th, 1894, never exceeded a few hundred men, but attracted considerable publicity. Although the episode ended in farce on May 1st, when Coxey and other leaders were arrested for trespassing on the grass outside the Capitol Building, it was a graphic illustration of the plight and desperation of many.

Labour-capital relations were also at a low ebb, sometimes approaching a state of industrial warfare. The best known confrontations of the period included the Homestead strike of 1892, which took place before the panic and Depression of 1893 began. The refusal of the management at the Homestead, Pennsylvania, iron and steel works to negotiate conditions or to grant full union recognition led to a strike in July 1892. Violence flared with a pitched battle between the strikers and Pinkerton agents, but the end result was a victory for the management which left bad feelings on both sides.

10. Electing the President, 1896

Hard times served only to intensify labour problems as shown by the Pullman strike of 1894. George M. Pullman, head of the Pullman Palace Car Company which built and operated railroad diner, parlor and sleeping cars, saw himself as a philanthropist, but his employees resented high rents and service charges for company housing and the stifling paternalism. Despite the Depression Pullman maintained profits and dividends, but he repeatedly cut wages and his workers turned to the new American Railway Union headed by Eugene V. Debs. When his workers went on strike in May 1894, Pullman assumed an intransigent position, and the dispute escalated into a national railroad strike.

The workers were eventually defeated when the conservative Railroad Brotherhoods and the American Federation of Labor declined to help, when the General Managers Association co-ordinated the activities of the railroads and when the Federal Government, on the excuse that the mails were being interfered with, employed court injunctions and deployed troops. Just as the battle over the tariff had opened up divisions in the Democratic Party so too did the administration's actions during the Pullman strike. Conservatives supported the President, while radicals sympathised with the strikers.

The Depression, the tariff fiasco, Coxey's army, the Pullman strike, all undermined the unity of the Democrats and their chances in the 1894 mid-term elections. To compound their troubles the Democrats also divided bitterly over whether to repeal the 1890 Sherman Silver Purchase Act. Under its provisions the Secretary of the Treasury was required to purchase 4.5 million ounces of silver every month—the estimated American production—and to issue in payment treasury notes of full legal-tender value redeemable in gold or silver at the discretion of the government. The act also proclaimed it to be 'the established policy of the United States to maintain the two metals on a parity with each other upon the present legal ratio or such ratio as may be provided by law'.

To understand the importance of the money question during this period one must remember that gold had become a symbol of conservative eastern and northern financial and business corporations. These institutions were perceived to be ruthlessly exploiting western and southern debtors, mainly farmers, who favoured inflationist policies, including the monetarisation of silver, as a means of raising prices, restoring prosperity and escape from their burdens of debts. While the debate was sometimes conducted with the intellectual dexterity and complexity of a medieval theological dispute, there was often a tendency on both sides to simplify the arguments, to take extreme positions, and to appeal to emotions and morality as much as to economic theory.

In the straightened financial circumstances of 1893 the obligations to purchase large quantities of silver and to redeem treasury notes were considered by the administration to be too onerous, and Cleveland called for the repeal of the Silver Purchase Act. The ensuing debate in Congress divided both parties on sectional lines, with members from the north and east favouring repeal and those from the south and west making impassioned appeals to retain the legislation. Young William Jennings Bryan, a Democratic representative from Nebraska, made a brilliant three-hour speech that presaged the 1896 campaign, claiming the debate was between over-privileged corporate interests and the frequently ignored down-trodden masses. The repeal of the Act in October 1893 was achieved by a ruthless use of patronage, but it led to a further serious breach in the ranks of the Democrats.

The Republicans skillfully placed the blame for the Depression, unemployment and the farmers' woes on the shoulders of the Democrats, but they said nothing as severe as the Democrats were saying about each other. Republican representative Thomas Reed predicted, 'The Democratic mortality will be so great next fall that their dead will be buried in trenches and marked "Unknown",' and events bore him out. The great Democratic majorities of 1892 were overturned and one Democrat, Champ Clark of Missouri, referred to 1894 as the greatest 'slaughter of the innocents' since the days of Herod.

Rising partisan, sectional and class antagonisms were soon exacerbated by three ultra-conservative Supreme Court decisions in 1895. In January the Court held in the E. C. Knight case that the American Sugar Refining Company, which processed 94 percent of the nation's sugar, had not violated the Sherman Anti-trust Act. In May, in Pollock v. Farmers' Loan and Trust Company, the Court outlawed the income tax provisions of the 1894 Tariff Act, provisions that men of poverty had seen as a dangerous assault on wealth. The same month the Court upheld the use of an injunction issued in 1894 against Eugene V. Debs during the Pullman strike.

By 1895 the money question, and the belief in the merits of deliberately inflating the currency, so-called 'free silver', had become the dominant political and economic issue. President Cleveland, whose belief in conservative fiscal policies and 'sound' money was unshakeable, tried in vain to prevent the spread of the silver infection through his party. His efforts only intensified the strong, indeed bitter, feelings against him, without preventing the silverites gaining additional converts in both country and party.

The growth of pro-silver sentiment among the Democrats posed a dilemma for the Populist or People's Party which had supported free silver since 1892. Their candidate for President in 1892, General James B. Weaver of Iowa, had polled over one million votes and won 22 electoral votes, a good result for a third party. The Populist problem was whether to continue to fight for a broad spectrum of political and economic reforms or to concentrate on silver. They had also to decide whether to co-operate with their political rivals, the Democrats, or to remain independent.

Even the Republicans were not immune from the growing silver sentiment. Republicans from the western farming states had at least to express sympathy with free silver ideas in order to win re-election. For Senator Henry Moore Teller of Colorado, a silver mining state, free silver was not just a tactical necessity, but a matter of conscience, and he threatened to leave the Republican Party in 1896. However, the disaffection in Republican ranks was limited, and in any case they hoped to fight the election on the issue of the protective tariff which had added electoral attractions in a depression.

Democratic disarray foretold Republican success in 1896, and there was no shortage of aspirants for the Grand Old Party's nomination. The anticipated prominence of the tariff issue gave the advantage to fifty-three year-old William McKinley from the key state of Ohio. 'Major' McKinley had a respectable Civil War record, and had served in Congress between 1877–91 followed by two successive terms as Governor of Ohio. He was best-known as an expert on the tariff, was sometimes called the High Priest of Protection—the 1890 Tariff Act carried his name. In the 1894 elections, though not a candidate himself, he was much in demand as a speaker and he enhanced his personal reputation by making 371 appearances in sixteen states, including twenty-three speeches in a single day.

The genial McKinley was a moderate in politics, had led a blameless personal life, and inspired trust and loyalty. Even those who disagreed with him found it difficult to dislike him. McKinley also had the advantage of a talented political manager and personal friend in the energetic Cleveland industrialist, Marcus Monzo Hanna. By the time the Republican national convention opened in St Louis in June 1896 Hanna had corralled enough delegates virtually to ensure McKinley's nomination.

The Republican platform damned the Democrats and all their works, blaming them for the Depression and all its consequences. The Republicans declared 'unreservedly for sound money', but devoted their greatest attention to the tariff issue. Unable to support the platform Senator Teller and twenty-one other delegates walked out to cries of 'Go to Chicago', where the Democrats were due to meet. Thereafter McKinley was easily nominated on the first ballot.

Whereas the silver rebellion in the Republican ranks was minor, the advocates of free silver in the Democratic Party experienced sweeping successes in 1895 and 1896, winning control over one state delegation to Chicago after another. When the Democratic national convention opened on July 8th it was soon clear that silver men were in the saddle and they wrote into the platform the statement: 'We demand the free and unlimited coinage of both silver and gold at the present legal ratio of 16 to 1'. The platform also preferred a lowering of the tariff, but not 'until the money question is settled.'

While the silver forces had indeed captured the Democratic Party, repudiated President Cleveland and written the platform, no outstanding spokesman and potential presidential nominee had emerged. To some extent this was deliberate as silver supporters believed the cause was greater than the ambitions of any individual. Leading possibilities included former congressman Richard Parks 'Silver Dick' Bland of Missouri who had a long and distinguished history of supporting free silver. 'Bland's major political liabilities were the facts that he came from a relatively unimportant state and was *persona non grata* with the Populists whose support was necessary for any silver Democrat to avoid splitting the anti-gold vote. Former governor Horace Boies of Iowa was another hopeful, and there was even a suggestion that Senator Teller, the silver Republican, might be selected to unite the silver vote.

One of the myths of the 1896 campaign is that William Jennings Bryan, the eventual Democratic nominee, was virtually unknown before the Chicago convention. Bryan, who was born in Illinois in 1860, had moved to Lincoln, Nebraska, in 1887 and made a name for himself as a politician, a supporter of free silver and a noted public speaker. Known as 'the boy orator from the Platte', or as 'the silver tongued orator', he had served four years in Congress, but failed to get elected to the Senate in 1894. Only thirty-six in 1896 Bryan was a man with a deep religious commitment, impeccable moral standards, a social conscience and a magnetic personality. He inspired supporters with his sincerity and could captivate audiences with his wonderful voice and dramatic abilities. Bryan's weaknesses were his inexperience and his tendency to suggest simple answers to complicated problems. He conducted a skillful campaign for two years before the Chicago convention to advance the cause of free silver and to win personal recognition within the ranks of the silverites.

At Chicago good fortune and deft manipulation gave Bryan the opportunity to speak last in the debate on the party platform. He delivered a carefully rehearsed address that came to be known as 'The Cross of Gold speech', but made it appear to be spontaneous. He began by telling his listeners that he came to speak to them in defence of a cause as holy as that of liberty, namely the cause of humanity. He reviewed the history of the struggle over money, paraded the arguments in favour of free silver, then reached a thrilling climax with the words:

> ... Having behind us the producing masses of this nation and the world, supported by the commercial interests, the laboring interests, and the toilers everywhere, we will answer their demand for a gold standard by saying to them: You shall not press down upon the brow of labor this crown of thorns, you shall not crucify mankind upon a cross of gold.

Bryan was nominated the next day with Arthur Sewall of Maine as his running mate. Subsequently the silver Republicans and the small National Silver Party endorsed these selections.

The Populist Party problems now came to a head. Should they accept Bryan and Sewall and the Chicago platform, and effectively fuse with the Democrats, thus sacrificing their independence and broad programme of reforms? If they stubbornly maintained their independence they would probably suffer major desertions to the stronger Democrats and bear the responsibility of handing the election to McKinley and the Republicans. With much heart-searching and many cries of betrayal the Populists, in a turbulent convention, solved their dilemma by adopting their own platform while nominating Bryan, but rejecting Sewall in favour of their own candidate for Vice-President, Tom Watson of Georgia. Thus Bryan actually had the nomination of four political groups, while McKinley was the standard bearer only for the Republican. The gold Democrats, who did not walk out at Chicago, could not bring themselves to vote for either of the major candidates and later made the gesture of selecting Senator John M. Palmer of Illinois for President and former Confederate General Simon Bolivar Buckner of Kentucky for Vice-President.

The two major candidates conducted quite different campaigns. The Democrats had a cause and a leader, but they lacked organisation, money and press support—in the past these had been supplied by the conservatives in the party who now stood aside. Bryan compensated in part by undertaking strenuous speaking tours. He travelled 18,000 miles in twenty-seven states making hundreds of appearances, often before very large crowds, including twenty-seven speeches on the final day. For Bryan silver became the symbol of the aspirations of the exploited masses, but his speeches were stronger on rhetoric than in dealing with economic realities; the beneficial effects of free silver were taken as articles of faith.

Bryan's effort was heroic, especially as he was often left to arrange details of his tours that should have been handled by others. Yet, despite the Democrats' promises of social and economic reform, Bryan converted few eastern working men to his cause. His platform rhetoric appealed to southern and western farmers.

Meanwhile McKinley, billed as the advance agent of prosperity, conducted a front porch campaign. He knew he could not compete with Bryan as an orator, and moreover, believed that to tour the country in pursuit of the presidency demeaned the office. Instead hundreds of delegations of faithful Republicans made a pilgrimage to McKinley's home in Canton, Ohio. Perhaps 750,000 people came to listen to his well-rehearsed responses to their prearranged addresses and questions. Thus it was said that while Bryan went to the people, the people came to McKinley.

The Republicans enjoyed many advantages thanks to Mark Hanna who ran the election campaign as Chairman of the National Republican Committee. He created the finest political organisation yet seen, with headquarters in New York and Chicago, and raised a campaign chest of between $3\frac{1}{2}$ and 4 million dollars via contributions from businesses with an interest in a Republican victory. The electorate was educated as to the advantages of the gold standard and to the threat of free silver through millions of pamphlets published in several languages relating to the currency and tariff issues. Appeals were often aimed at particular economic, ethnic or special interests groups, even to cyclists! Newspapers and magazines were supplied with articles, posters, cartoons and campaign badges. Hundreds of speakers were employed and the party strategists even appropriated the national flag as a partisan symbol. It was also to their advantage that the Republican message—that a high tariff protected American living standards against cheap foreign competition and that free silver would unsettle business conditions—was far easier to understand than the Democratic theories which sometimes approached the metaphysical. As Hanna said of Bryan 'He's talking silver all the time, and that's where we've got him.' Republicans portrayed Bryan as a wild-eyed radical, even a revolutionary and as a dangerous free trader.

Businessmen indoctrinated their employees with placards in the work place, pamphlets and lunchtime speeches. Printed slips in pay packets warned that the election of Bryan and the adoption of radical financial policies might mean job losses and a fall in the purchasing power of wages. Some business contracts were signed with let-out clauses in case of a Democratic victory, insurance companies put pressure on their policy holders, and mortgage companies threatened to curtail credit, though it is difficult to know how effective this was. Some clergymen, both Protestant and Catholic, broke with the practice of political neutrality by endorsing McKinley, as they saw Bryan as a dangerous socialist, and because they objected to his use of phrases like 'crown of thorns' and 'cross of gold' as blasphemous.

Unable to find a chink in McKinley's political or personal armour the Democrats concentrated much of their fire upon Hanna, an acknowledgement of his importance in the campaign and the later source of the popular, though erroneous, belief that he possessed a dominating influence over McKinley.

The election had its lighter side, of course. The Democrats sang to the tune 'Marching Through Georgia':

> Sound the good old bugle with a bi-metallic ring,
> Silver free from sea to sea with lusty voice-sing,
> Our banner with its silver stars to waiting breezes fling,
> While we go marching to victory.

Republicans replied to the tune 'Battle Cry of Freedom' with:

> We will welcome to our numbers all honest men and true,
> Shouting sound money and protection,
> And the rich and poor shall share in the wages when they're due,
> Shouting sound money and protection.
> Protection forever, hurrah! boys, hurrah!
> Down with 'free silver,' and stop Bryan's 'jaw,'
> Then we'll rally 'round McKinley, we'll rally once again,
> Shouting sound money and protection.

The 1896 election allowed the demands for reform to be channelled via the established political processes rather than be disputed on the streets. Both the Republican and Democratic parties were affected by the campaign as they had to face up to new policies, new methods and a changing electorate. The presentation of candidates and issues, the refinement of campaign techniques, the use of slogans and images were all advanced at this time.

In reality both sides were offering the electorate panaceas, the Democrats free silver and the Republicans protection. The Democrats lost because of inferior organisation, pitifully inadequate funds, and because their remedy for the nation's ills was both too radical and untried compared to the Republican programme. Not that the election was a simple fight between the two major parties. The presence of the Populists helped to bring the silver question into the limelight, though Bryan found their endorsement a mixed blessing. Both the Populists and the Democrats concentrated in 1896 on the currency issue at the expense of the rest of their programme and there is some truth, at least, in the comment of the noted reformer Henry Demarest Lloyd that free silver 'was the cowbird of the Reform movement', which 'waited until the nest had been built by the sacrifices and labour of others, and then laid its egg in it, pushing out the others which lie smashed on the ground'.

While the Democrats did eventually win the White House in 1912, the Populists would never recover from their defeat in 1896. Yet many of the reforms they advocated in the 1890s, like the direct election of United States senators, a federal income tax, and stricter regulation of banks and corporations, measures considered dangerous innovations at the time, were actually achieved in the early twentieth century during the calmer Progressive Era.

Bryan fought a courageous campaign in 1896, which he referred to as 'The First Battle', intending to continue the fight. Indeed, 1900 was a rematch between McKinley and Bryan, but by then prosperity had returned and the emergence of imperialism as an issue after the 1898 Spanish-American War made free silver redundant. Bryan and the Democrats, the intellectual heirs of Thomas Jefferson and his belief in the virtues of rural life and the vices of urban living, were unable to adapt to the fact that political power had shifted to the burgeoning industrial towns. Whether he realised it or not Bryan was the champion of old America in a vain struggle against an emerging twentieth-century new America.

FOR FURTHER READING:

William M. Bryan, *The First Battle, A Story of the Campaign of 1896* (Chicago, 1896); Robert F. Durden, *The Climax of Populism: The Election of 1896* (University of Kentucky Press, 1965); Paul W. Glad, *McKinley, Bryan and the People* (Philadelphia, Lippincott, 1964); Stanley L. Jones, *The Presidential Election of 1896* (University of Wisconsin Press, 1964); Lewis L. Gould, *The Presidency of William McKinley* (University of Kansas Press, 1980); H. Wayne Morgan, *From Hayes to McKinley, National Party Politics, 1877–1896* (Syracuse University Press, 1969); Arthur M. Schlesinger, Jr., (ed), *History of American Presidential Elections 1789–1968, Vol II* (Chelsea, New York, 1971).

Edward Ranson is Lecturer in American History at the University of Aberdeen and author of British Defence Policy and Appeasement Between the Wars 1919–1939 *(The Historical Association, 1993)*

BATTLES WON AND LOST

Our First Southeast Asian War

America's turn-of-the-century military campaign against Philippine insurgents consumed three years, involved 126,000 troops, and cost 4,000 lives. The lessons we learned could have been used in Vietnam sixty years later.

David R. Kohler and James W. Wensyel

David R. Kohler, Commander, U.S. Navy, is a Naval Special Warfare officer who has served multiple tours in UDT (underwater demolition) and SEAL (sea, air, land) teams. He has a master's degree in national security affairs from the Naval Postgraduate School in Monterey, California.

James W. Wensyel, a retired Army officer, is the author of three published books and numerous articles. His article on the crash of the dirigible Shenandoah *appeared in the February 1989 issue of* American History Illustrated. *He resides with his wife Jean in Newville, Pennsylvania.*

Guerrilla warfare... jungle terrain... search and destroy missions... benevolent pacification... strategic hamlets... terrorism... ambushes... free-fire zones... booby traps... waning support from civilians at home. These words call forth from the national consciousness uncomfortable images of a war Americans fought and died in not long ago in Southeast Asia. But while the phrases may first bring to mind America's painful experience in Vietnam during the 1960s and '70s, they also aptly describe a much earlier conflict—the Philippine Insurrection—that foreshadowed this and other insurgent wars in Asia.

The Philippine-American War of 1898–1902 is one of our nation's most obscure and least-understood campaigns. Sometimes called the "Bolo War" because of the Filipino insurgents' lethally effective use of razor-sharp bolo knives or machetes against the American expeditionary force occupying the islands, it is often viewed as a mere appendage of the one-hundred-day Spanish-American War. But suppressing the guerrilla warfare waged by Philippine nationalists seeking self-rule proved far more difficult, protracted, and costly for American forces than the conventional war with Spain that had preceded it.

America's campaign to smash the Philippine Insurrection was, ironically, a direct consequence of U.S. efforts to secure independence for other *insurrectos* halfway around the world in Cuba. On May 1, 1898, less than a week after Congress declared war against Spain, a naval squadron commanded by Commodore George Dewey steamed into Manila Bay to engage the Spanish warships defending that nation's Pacific possession. In a brief action Dewey achieved a stunning victory, sinking all of the enemy vessels with no significant American losses. Destroying the Spanish fleet, however, did not ensure U.S. possession of the Philippines. An estimated 15,000 Spanish soldiers still occupied Manila and the surrounding region. Those forces would have to be rooted out by infantry.

President William McKinley had already ordered a Philippine Expeditionary Force of volunteer and regular army infantry, artillery and cavalry units (nearly seven thousand men), under the command of Major General Wesley Merritt, to "reduce Spanish power in that quarter [Philippine Islands] and give order and security to the islands while in the possession of the United States."

Sent to the Philippines in the summer of 1898, this limited force was committed without fully considering the operation's potential length and cost. American military and government leaders also failed to anticipate the consequences of ignoring the Filipino rebels who, under Generalissimo Don Emilio Aguinaldo y Famy, had been waging a war for independence against Spain for the past two years. And when American insensitivity toward Aguinaldo eventually led to open warfare with the rebels, the American leaders grossly underestimated the determination of the seemingly ill-trained and poorly armed insurgents. They additionally failed to perceive the difficulties involved in conducting military operations in a tropical environment and among a hostile native population, and they did not recognize the burden of fighting at the end of a seven-thousand-mile-long logistics trail.

Asian engagements, the Americans learned for the first time, are costly. The enterprise, so modestly begun, eventually saw more than 126,000 American officers and men deployed to the Philippines. Four times as many soldiers served in this undeclared war in the Pacific as had been sent to the Caribbean during the Spanish-American War. During the three-year conflict, American troops and Filipino insurgents fought in more than 2,800 engagements. American casualties ultimately totaled 4,234 killed and 2,818 wounded, and the insurgents lost about 16,000 men. The civilian population suffered even more; as many as 200,000 Filipinos died from famine, pestilence, or the unfortunate happenstance of being too close to the fighting. The Philippine war cost the United States $600 million before the insurgents were subdued.

The costly experience offered valuable and timeless lessons about guerrilla warfare in Asia; unfortunately, those lessons had to be relearned sixty years later in another war that, despite the modern technology involved, bore surprising parallels to America's first Southeast Asian campaign.

ORIGINS

America's war with Spain, formally declared by the United States on April 25, 1898, had been several years in the making. During that time the American "yellow press," led by Joseph Pulitzer's *New York World* and William Randolph Hearst's *New York Journal,* trumpeted reports of heroic Cuban *insurrectos* revolting against their cruel Spanish rulers. Journalists vividly described harsh measures taken by Spanish officials to quell the Cuban revolution. The sensational accounts, often exaggerated, reminded Americans of their own uphill fight for independence and nourished the feeling that America was destined to intervene so that the Cuban people might also taste freedom.

Furthermore, expansionists suggested that the revolt against a European power, taking place less than one hundred miles from American shores, offered a splendid opportunity to turn the Caribbean into an American sea. Businessmen pointed out that $50 million in American capital was invested in the Cuban sugar and mining industries. Revolutions resulting in burned cane fields jeopardized that investment. As 1898 opened, American relations with Spain quickly declined.

In January 1898 the U.S. battleship *Maine* was sent to Cuba, ostensibly on a courtesy visit. On February 15 the warship was destroyed by a mysterious explosion while at anchor in Havana harbor, killing 262 of her 350-man crew. The navy's formal inquiry, completed on March 28, suggested that the explosion was due to an external force—a mine.

On March 29, the Spanish government received an ultimatum from Washington, D.C.: Spain's army in Cuba was to lay down its arms while the United States negotiated between the rebels and the Spaniards. The Spanish forces were

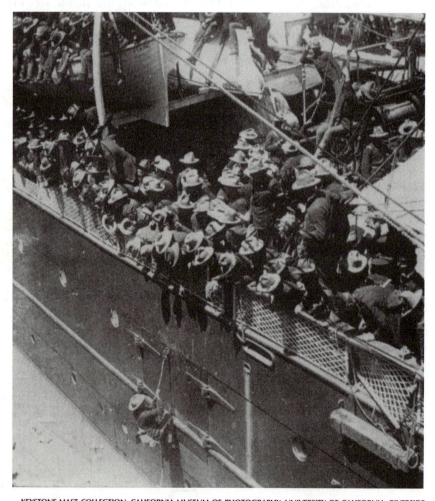

KEYSTONE-MAST COLLECTION. CALIFORNIA MUSEUM OF PHOTOGRAPHY, UNIVERSITY OF CALIFORNIA, RIVERSIDE

Manila-bound soldiers on a troopship pulling away from a San Francisco pier watch as the last man climbs aboard (right). At the height of the Spanish-American War, President William McKinley sent a seven-thousand-man expeditionary force to occupy the Philippines; during the next three years nearly twenty times that number of Americans would become involved in operations against Filipino insurgents.

11. Our First Southeast Asian War

also told to abolish all *reconcentrado* camps (tightly controlled areas, similar to the strategic hamlets later tried in Vietnam, where peasants were regrouped to deny food and intelligence to insurgents and to promote tighter security). Spain initially rejected the humiliation of surrendering its arms in the field but they capitulated on all points. The Americans were not satisfied.

On April 11, declaring that Spanish responses were inadequate, President McKinley told a joint session of Congress that "I have exhausted every effort to relieve the intolerable condition at our doors. I now ask the Congress to empower the president to take measures to secure a full and final termination of hostilities in Cuba, to secure . . . the establishment of a stable government, and to use the military and naval forces of the United States . . . for these purposes . . ."

Congress adopted the proposed resolution on April 19. Learning this, Spain declared war on the 24th. The following day, the United States responded with its own declaration of war.

The bulk of the American navy quickly gathered on the Atlantic coast. McKinley called for 125,000 volunteers to bolster the less than eighty-thousand-man regular army. His call was quickly oversubscribed; volunteers fought to be the first to land on Cuba's beaches.

The first major battle of the war, however, was fought not in Cuba but seven thousand miles to the west—in Manila Bay. Dewey's victory over Spanish Admiral Patricio Montojo y Pasarón (a rather hollow victory as Montojo's fleet consisted of seven unarmored ships, three of which had wooden hulls and one that had to be towed to the battle area) was wildly acclaimed in America.

American leaders, believing that the Philippines would now fall into America's grasp like a ripe plum, had to decide what to do with their prize. They could not return the islands to Spain, nor could they allow them to pass to France or Germany, America's commercial rivals in the Orient. The American press rejected the idea of a British protectorate. And, after four hundred years of despotic Spanish rule in which Filipinos had little or no chance to practice self-government, native leaders seemed unlikely candidates for managing their own affairs. McKinley faced a grand opportunity for imperialistic expansion that could not be ignored.

The debate sharply divided his cabinet—and the country. American public opinion over acquisition of the Philippines divided into two basic factions: imperialists versus anti-imperialists.

The imperialists, mostly Republicans, included such figures as Theodore Roosevelt (then assistant secretary of the navy), Henry Cabot Lodge (Massachusetts senator), and Albert Beveridge (Indiana senator). These individuals were, for the most part, disciples of Alfred Thayer Mahan, a naval strategist who touted theories of national power and prestige through sea power and acquisition of overseas colonies for trade purposes and naval coaling stations.

The anti-imperalists, staunchly against American annexation of the Philippines, were mainly Democrats. Such men as former presidents Grover Cleveland and Rutherford B. Hayes, steel magnate Andrew Carnegie, William Jennings Bryan, union leader Samuel Gompers, and Mark Twain warned that by taking the Philippines the United States would march the road to ruin earlier traveled by the Roman Empire. Furthermore, they argued, America would be denying Filipinos the right of self-determination guaranteed by our own Constitution. The more practical-minded also pointed out that imperialistic policy would require maintaining an expensive army and navy there.

Racism, though demonstrated in different ways, pervaded the arguments of both sides. Imperialists spoke of the "white man's burden" and moral responsibility to "uplift the child races everywhere" and to provide "orderly development for the unfortunate and less able races." They spoke of America's "civilizing mission" of pacifying Filipinos by "benevolent assimilation" and saw the opening of the overseas frontier much as their forefathers had viewed the western frontier. The "subjugation of the Injun" (wherever he might be found) was a concept grasped by American youth—the war's most enthusiastic supporters (in contrast to young America's opposition to the war in Vietnam many years later).

The anti-imperialists extolled the sacredness of independence and self-determination for the Filipinos. Racism, however, also crept into their argument, for they believed that "protection against race mingling" was a historic American policy that would be reversed by imperialism. To them, annexation of the Philippines would admit "alien, inferior, and mongrel races to our nationality."

As the debate raged, Dewey continued to hold Manila Bay, and the Philippines seemed to await America's pleasure. President McKinley would ultimately cast the deciding vote in determining America's role in that country. McKinley, a genial, rather laid-back, former congressman from Ohio and one-time major in the Union army, remains a rather ambiguous figure during this period. In his Inaugural Address he had affirmed that "We want no wars of conquest; we must avoid the temptation of territorial aggression." Thereafter, however, he made few comments on pacifism, and, fourteen weeks after becoming president, signed the bill annexing Hawaii.

Speaking of Cuba in December 1897, McKinley said, "I speak not of forcible annexation, for that cannot be thought of. That, by our code of morality, would be criminal aggression." Nevertheless, he constantly pressured Madrid to end Spanish rule in Cuba, leading four months later to America's war with Spain.

McKinley described experiencing extreme turmoil, soul-searching, and prayer over the Philippine annexation issue until, he declared, one night in a dream the Lord revealed to him that "there was nothing left for us to do but to take them all [the Philippine Islands] and to educate the Filipinos, and uplift, and civilize, and Christianize them." He apparently didn't realize that the Philippines had been staunchly Roman Catholic for more than 350 years under Spanish colonialism. Nor could he anticipate the difficulties that, having cast

THE EMERGENCE OF MODERN AMERICA

its fortune with the expansionists, America would now face in the Philippines.

PROSECUTING THE WAR

Meanwhile, in the Philippine Islands, Major General Wesley Merritt's Philippine Expeditionary Force went about its job. In late June, General Thomas Anderson led an advance party ashore at Cavite. He then established Camp Merritt, visited General Aguinaldo's rebel forces entrenched around Manila, and made plans for seizing that city once Merritt arrived with the main body of armed forces.

Anderson quickly learned that military operations in the Philippines could be difficult. His soldiers, hastily assembled and dispatched with limited prior training, were poorly disciplined and inadequately equipped. Many still wore woolen uniforms despite the tropical climate. A staff officer described the army's baptism at Manila: "... the heat was oppressive and the rain kept falling. At times the trenches were filled with two feet of water, and soon the men's shoes were ruined. Their heavy khaki uniforms were a nuisance; they perspired constantly, the loss of body salts inducing chronic fatigue. Prickly heat broke out, inflamed by scratching and rubbing. Within a week the first cases of dysentery, malaria, cholera, and dengue fever showed up at sick call."

During his first meeting with Dewey, Anderson remarked that some American leaders were considering annexation of the Philippines. "If the United States intends to hold the Philippine Islands," Dewey responded, "it will make things awkward, because just a week ago Aguinaldo proclaimed the independence of the Philippine Islands from Spain and seems intent on establishing his own government."

A Filipino independence movement led by Aguinaldo had been active in the islands since 1896 and, within weeks of Dewey's victory, Aguinaldo's revolutionaries controlled most of the archipelago.

Aguinaldo, twenty-nine years old in 1898, had taken over his father's position as mayor of his hometown of Kawit before becoming a revolutionary. In a minor skirmish with Spanish soldiers, he had rallied the Filipinos to victory. Thereafter, his popularity grew as did his ragtag but determined army. Aguinaldo was slight of build, shy, and soft-spoken, but a strict disciplinarian.

As his rebel force besieged Manila, Aguinaldo declared a formal government for the Philippines with himself as president and generalissimo. He proclaimed his "nation's" independence and called for Filipinos to rally to his army and to the Americans, declaring that "the Americans ... extend their protecting mantle to our beloved country. When you see the American flag flying, assemble in numbers: they are our redeemers!" But his enthusiasm for the United States later waned.

Sytmied by the Filipinos' use of guerrilla warfare, the Americans were forced to change their strategy.

Merritt put off Aguinaldo's increasingly strident demands that America recognize his government and guarantee the Filipinos' independence. Aguinaldo perceived the American general's attitude as condescending and demeaning.

On August 13, Merritt's forces occupied Manila almost without firing a shot; in a face-saving maneuver the Spanish defenders had agreed to surrender to the Americans to avoid being captured—and perhaps massacred—by the Filipino insurgents. Merritt's troops physically blocked Aguinaldo's rebels, who had spent weeks in the trenches around the city, from participating in the assault. The Filipino general and his followers felt betrayed at being denied a share in the victory.

Further disenchanted, Aguinaldo would later find his revolutionary government unrepresented at the Paris peace talks determining his country's fate. He would learn that Spain had ceded the Philippines to the United States for $20 million.

Officers at Merritt's headquarters had little faith in the Filipinos' ability to govern themselves. "Should our power ... be withdrawn," an early report declared, "the Philippines would speedily lapse into anarchy, which would excuse ... the intervention of other powers and the division of the islands among them."

Meanwhile, friction between American soldiers and the Filipinos increased. Much of the Americans' conduct betrayed their racial bias. Soldiers referred to the natives as "niggers" and "gugus," epithets whose meanings were clear to the Filipinos. In retaliation, the island inhabitants refused to give way on sidewalks and muscled American officers into the streets. Men of the expeditionary force in turn escalated tensions by stopping Filipinos at gunpoint, searching them without cause, "confiscating" shopkeepers' goods, and beating those who resisted.

On the night of February 4, 1899, the simmering pot finally boiled over. Private William "Willie" Walter Grayson and several other soldiers of Company D, 1st Nebraska Volunteer Infantry, apprehended a group of armed insurgents within their regimental picket line. Shots were exchanged, and three Filipino *insurrectos* fell dead. Heavy firing erupted between the two camps.

In the bloody battle that followed, the Filipinos suffered tremendous casualties (an estimated two thousand to five thousand dead, contrasted with fifty-nine Americans killed) and were forced to withdraw. The Philippine Insurrection had begun.

GUERRILLA WARFARE

The Americans, hampered by a shortage of troops and the oncoming rainy season, could initially do little more than extend their defensive perimeter beyond Manila and establish a toehold on several islands to the south. By the end of March, however, American forces seized Malolos, the seat of Aguinaldo's revolutionary government. But Aguinaldo escaped, simply melting into the jungle. In the fall, using conventional methods

11. Our First Southeast Asian War

of warfare, the Americans first struck south, then north of Manila across the central Luzon plain. After hard marching and tough fighting, the expeditionary force occupied northern Luzon, dispersed the rebel army, and barely missed capturing Aguinaldo.

Believing that occupying the remainder of the Philippines would be easy, the Americans wrongly concluded that the war was virtually ended. But when the troops attempted to control the territory they had seized, they found that the Filipino revolutionaries were not defeated but had merely changed strategies. Abandoning western-style conventional warfare, Aguinaldo had decided to adopt guerrilla tactics.

Aguinaldo moved to a secret mountain headquarters at Palanan in northern Luzon, ordering his troops to disperse and avoid pitched battles in favor of hit-and-run operations by small bands. Ambushing parties of Americans and applying terror to coerce support from other Filipinos, the insurrectionists now blended into the countryside, where they enjoyed superior intelligence information, ample supplies, and tight security. The guerrillas moved freely between the scattered American units, cutting telegraph lines, attacking supply trains, and assaulting straggling infantrymen. When the Americans pursued their tormentors, they fell into well-planned ambushes. The insurgents' barbarity and ruthlessness during these attacks were notorious.

The guerrilla tactics helped to offset the inequities that existed between the two armies. The American troops were far better armed, for example, carrying .45-caliber Springfield single-shot rifles, Mausers, and then-modern .30-caliber repeating Krag-Jorgensen rifles. They also had field artillery and machine guns. The revolutionaries, on the other hand, were limited to a miscellaneous assortment of handguns, a few Mauser repeating rifles taken from the Spanish, and antique muzzle-loaders. The sharp-edged bolo knife was the revolutionary's primary weapon, and he used it well. Probably more American soldiers were hacked to death by bolos than were killed by Mauser bullets.

KEYSTONE-MAST COLLECTION, CALIFORNIA MUSEUM OF PHOTOGRAPHY, UNIVERSITY OF CALIFORNIA, RIVERSIDE

U.S. troops found the tropical climate and Southeast Asian terrain almost as deadly as combat. Thousands of soldiers were incapacitated by dysentery, malaria, and other tropical maladies. The first troopse sent to the archipelago wore unsuitable woolen uniforms; these men, photographed in 1900, had at least been issued ponchos for use during the rainy season.

As would later be the case in Vietnam, the guerrillas had some clear advantages. They knew the terrain, were inured to the climate, and could generally count on a friendly population. As in Vietnam, villages controlled by the insurgents provided havens from which the guerrillas could attack, then fade back into hiding.

Americans soon began to feel that they were under siege in a land of enemies, and their fears were heightened because they never could be sure who among the population was hostile. A seemingly friendly peasant might actually be a murderer. Lieutenant Colonel J. T. Wickham, commanding the 26th Infantry Regiment, recorded that "a large flag of truce enticed officers into ambushes... Privates Dugan, Hayes, and Tracy were murdered by town authorities... Private Nolan [was] tied up by ladies while in a stupor; the insurgents cut his throat... The body of Corporal Doneley was dug up, burned, and mutilated... Private O'Hearn, captured by apparently friendly people, was tied to a tree, burned over a slow fire, and slashed up... Lieutenant Max Wagner was assassinated by insurgents disguised in American uniforms."

As in later guerrilla movements, such terrorism became a standard tactic for the insurgents. Both Filipinos and Americans were their victims. In preying on their countrymen, the guerrillas had a dual purpose: to discourage any Filipinos disposed to cooperate with the

Americans, and to demonstrate to people in a particular region that they ruled that area and could destroy inhabitants and villages not supporting the revolution. The most favored terroristic weapon was assassination of local leaders, who were usually executed in a manner (such as beheading or burying alive) calculated to horrify everyone.

By the spring of 1900 the war was going badly for the Americans. Their task forces, sent out to search and destroy, found little and destroyed less.

The monsoon rains, jungle terrain, hostile native population, and a determined guerrilla force made the American soldiers' marches long and miserable. One described a five-week-long infantry operation: "... our troops had been on half rations for two weeks. Wallowing through hipdeep muck, lugging a ten-pound rifle and a belt... with 200 rounds of ammunition, drenched to the skin and with their feet becoming heavier with mud at every step, the infantry became discouraged. Some men simply cried, others slipped down in the mud and refused to rise. Threats and appeals by the officers were of no avail. Only a promise of food in the next town and the threat that if they remained behind they would be butchered by marauding bands of insurgents forced some to their feet to struggle on."

News reports of the army's difficulties began to erode the American public's support for the war. "To chase barefooted insurgents with water buffalo carts as a wagon train may be simply ridiculous," charged one correspondent, "but to load volunteers down with 200 rounds of ammunition and one day's rations, and to put on their heads felt hats used by no other army in the tropics.... to trot these same soldiers in the boiling sun over a country without roads, is positively criminal.... There are over five thousand men in the general hospital."

Another reported that the American outlook "is blacker now than it has been since the beginning of the war... the whole population... sympathizes with the insurgents. The insurgents came to Pasig [a local area whose government cooperated with the Americans] and their first act was to hang the 'Presidente' for treason in surrendering to Americans. 'Presidentes' do not surrender to us anymore."

NEW STRATEGIES

Early in the war U.S. military commanders had realized that, unlike the American Indians who had been herded onto reservations, eight million Filipinos (many of them hostile) would have to be governed in place. The Americans chose to emphasize pacification through good works rather than by harsh measures, hoping to convince Filipinos that the American colonial government had a sincere interest in their welfare and could be trusted.

As the army expanded its control across the islands, it reorganized local municipal governments and trained Filipinos to take over civil functions in the democratic political structure the Americans planned to establish. American soldiers performed police duties, distributed food, established and taught at schools, and built roads and telegraph lines.

As the war progressed, however, the U.S. commanders saw that the terrorism practiced by Aguinaldo's guerrillas was far more effective in controlling the populace than was their own benevolent approach. Although the Americans did not abandon pacification through good works, it was thereafter subordinated to the "civilize 'em with a Krag" (Krag Jorgensen rifle) philosophy. From December 1900 onward, captured revolutionaries faced deportation, imprisonment, or execution.

The American army also changed its combat strategy to counter that of its enemy. As in the insurgents' army, the new tactics emphasized mobility and surprise. Breaking into small units—the battalion became the largest maneuver force—the Americans gradually spread over the islands until each of the larger towns was occupied by one or two rifle companies. From these bases American troops began platoon- and company-size operations to pressure local guerrilla bands.

Because of the difficult terrain, limited visibility, and requirement for mobility, artillery now saw limited use except as a defensive weapon. The infantry became the main offensive arm, with mounted riflemen used to pursue the fleeing enemy. Cavalry patrols were so valued for their mobility that American military leaders hired trusted Filipinos as mounted scouts and cavalrymen.

The Americans made other efforts to "Filipizize" the war—letting Asians fight Asians. (A similar tactic had been used in the American Indian campaigns twenty years before; it would resurface in Vietnam sixty years later as "Vietnamization.") In the Philippines the Americans recruited five thousand Macabebes, mercenaries from the central Luzon province of Pampanga, to form the American officered Philippine Scouts. The Macabebes had for centuries fought in native battalions under the Spanish flag—even against their own countrymen when the revolution began in 1896.

Just as a later generation of American soldiers would react to the guerrilla war in Vietnam, American soldiers in the Philippines responded to insurgent terrorism in kind, matching cruelty with cruelty. Such actions vented their frustration at being unable to find and destroy the enemy. An increasing number of Americans viewed all Filipinos as enemies.

"We make everyone get into his house by 7 P.M. and we only tell a man once," Corporal Sam Gillis of the 1st California Volunteer Regiment wrote to his family. "If he refuses, we shoot him. We killed over 300 natives the first night.... If they fire a shot from a house, we burn the house and every house near it."

Another infantryman frankly admitted that "with an enemy like this to fight, it is not surprising that the boys should soon adopt 'no quarter' as a motto and fill the blacks full of lead before finding out whether they are friends or enemies."

That attitude should not have been too surprising. The army's campaigns against the Plains Indians were reference points for the generation of Americans that took the Philippines. Many of

11. Our First Southeast Asian War

the senior officers and noncommissioned officers—often veterans of the Indian wars—considered Filipinos to be "as full of treachery as our Arizona Apache." "The country won't be pacified," one soldier told a reporter, "until the niggers are killed off like the Indians." A popular soldiers' refrain, sung to the tune of "Tramp, tramp, tramp, the boys are marching," began, "Damn, damn, damn the Filipinos," and again spoke of "civilizing 'em with a Krag."

Reprisals against civilians by Americans as well as insurgents became common. General Lloyd Wheaton, leading a U.S. offensive southeast of Manila, found his men impaled on the bamboo prongs of booby traps and with throats slit while they slept. After two of his companies were ambushed, Wheaton ordered that every town and village within twelve miles be burned.

The Americans developed their own terrorist methods, many of which would be used in later Southeast Asian wars. One was torturing suspected guerrillas or insurgent sympathizers to force them to reveal locations of other guerrillas and their supplies. An often-utilized form of persuasion was the "water cure," placing a bamboo reed in the victim's mouth and pouring water (some used salt water or dirty water) down his throat, thus painfully distending the victim's stomach. The subject, allowed to void this, would, under threat of repetition, usually talk freely. Another method of torture, the "rope cure," consisted of wrapping a rope around the victim's neck and torso until it formed a sort of girdle. A stick (or Krag rifle), placed between the ropes and twisted, then effectively created a combination of smothering and garroting.

The anti-imperialist press reported such American brutality in lurid detail. As a result, a number of officers and soldiers were court-martialed for torturing and other cruelties. Their punishments, however, seemed remarkably lenient. Of ten officers tried for "looting, torture, and murder," three were acquitted; of the seven convicted, five were reprimanded, one was reprimanded and fined $300, and one lost thirty-five places in the army's seniority list and forfeited half his pay for nine months.

Officers and soldiers, fighting a cruel, determined, and dangerous enemy, could not understand public condemnation of the brutality they felt was necessary to win. They had not experienced such criticism during the Indian wars, where total extermination of the enemy was condoned by the press and the American public, and they failed to grasp the difference now. Press reports, loss of public support, and the soldiers' feeling of betrayal—features of an insurgent war—would resurface decades later during the Vietnam conflict.

SUCCESS

Although U.S. military leaders were frustrated by the guerrillas' determination on one hand and by eroding American support for the war on the other, most believed that the insurgents could be subdued. Especially optimistic was General Arthur MacArthur, who in 1900 assumed command of the seventy thousand American troops in the Philippines. MacArthur adopted a strategy like that successfully used by General Zachary Taylor in the Second Seminole War in 1835; he believed that success depended upon the Americans' ability to isolate the guerrillas from their support in the villages. Thus were born "strategic hamlets," "free-fire zones," and "search and destroy" missions, concepts the American army would revive decades later in Vietnam.

MacArthur strengthened the more than five hundred small strong points held by Americans throughout the Philippine Islands. Each post was garrisoned by at least one company of American infantrymen. The natives around each base were driven from their homes, which were then destroyed. Soldiers herded the displaced natives into *reconcentrado* camps, where they could be "protected" by the nearby garrisons. Crops, food stores, and houses outside the camps were destroyed to deny them to the guerrillas. Surrounding each camp was a "dead line," within which anyone appearing would be shot on sight.

Operating from these small garrisons, the Americans pressured the guerrillas, allowing them no rest. Kept off balance, short of supplies, and constantly pursued by the American army, the Filipino guerrillas, suffering from sickness, hunger, and dwindling popular support, began to lose their will to fight. Many insurgent leaders surrendered, signaling that the tide at last had turned in the Americans' favor

In March 1901, a group of Macabebe Scouts, commanded by American Colonel Frederick "Fighting Fred" Funston, captured Aguinaldo. Aguinaldo's subsequent proclamation that he would fight no more, and his pledge of loyalty to the United States, sped the collapse of the insurrection.

As in the past, and as would happen again during the Vietnam conflict of the l960s and '70s, American optimism was premature. Although a civilian commission headed by William H. Taft took control of the colonial government from the American army in July 1901, the army faced more bitter fighting in its "pacification" of the islands.

As the war sputtered, the insurgents' massacre of fifty-nine American soldiers at Balangiga on the island of Samar caused Brigadier General Jacob W. "Hell-Roaring Jake" Smith, veteran of the Wounded Knee massacre of the Sioux in 1890, to order his officers to turn Samar into a "howling wilderness." His orders to a battalion of three hundred Marines headed for Samar were precise: "I want no prisoners. I wish you to kill and burn, the more you kill and burn the better it will please me. I want all persons killed who are capable of bearing arms against the United States." Fortunately, the Marines did not take Smith's orders literally and, later, Smith would be court-martialed.

On July 4, 1902, the Philippine Insurrection officially ended. Although it took the American army another eleven years to crush the fierce Moros of the southern Philippines, the civil government's security force (the Philippine Constabulary), aided by the army's Philippine Scouts, maintained a fitful peace throughout the islands. The army's campaign to secure the Philippines as an American colony had succeeded.

American commanders would have experienced vastly greater difficulties

2 ❖ THE EMERGENCE OF MODERN AMERICA

except for two distinct advantages: 1) the enemy had to operate in a restricted area, in isolated islands, and was prevented by the U.S. Navy from importing weapons and other needed supplies; and 2) though the insurgents attempted to enlist help from Japan, no outside power intervened. These conditions would not prevail in some subsequent guerrilla conflicts in Asia.

In addition to the many tactical lessons the army learned from fighting a guerrilla war in a tropical climate, other problems experienced during this campaign validated the need for several military reforms that were subsequently carried out, including improved logistics, tropical medicine, and communications.

The combination of harsh and unrelenting military force against the guerrillas, complemented by the exercise of fair and equitable civil government and civic action toward those who cooperated, proved to be the Americans' most effective tactic for dealing with the insurgency. This probably was the most significant lesson to be learned from the Philippine Insurrection.

LESSONS FOR THE FUTURE

Vietnam veterans reading this account might nod in recollection of a personal, perhaps painful experience from their own war.

Many similarities exist between America's three-year struggle with the Filipino *insurrectos* and the decade-long campaign against the Communists in Vietnam. Both wars, modestly begun, went far beyond what anyone had foreseen in time, money, equipment, manpower, casualties, and suffering.

Both wars featured small-unit infantry actions. Young infantrymen, if they had any initial enthusiasm, usually lost it once they saw the war's true nature; they nevertheless learned to endure their allotted time while adopting personal self-survival measures as months "in-country" lengthened and casualty lists grew.

Both wars were harsh, brutal, cruel. Both had their Samar Islands and their My Lais. Human nature being what it is, both conflicts also included acts of great heroism, kindness, compassion, and self-sacrifice.

Both wars saw an increasingly disenchanted American public withdrawing its support (and even disavowing its servicemen) as the campaigns dragged on, casualties mounted, and news accounts vividly described the horror of the battlefields.

Some useful lessons might be gleaned from a comparison of the two conflicts. Human nature really does not change—war will bring out the best and the worst in the tired, wet, hungry, and fearful men who are doing the fighting. Guerrilla campaigns—particularly where local military and civic reforms cannot be effected to separate the guerrilla from his base of popular support—will be long and difficult, and will demand tremendous commitments in resources and national will. Finally, before America commits its armed forces to similar ventures in the future, it would do well to recall the lessons learned from previous campaigns. For, as the Spanish-born American educator, poet, and philosopher George Santayana reminded us, those who do not learn from the past are doomed to repeat it.

Recommended additional reading: Benevolent Assimilation: The American Conquest of the Philippines, 1899–1902 by *Stuart C. Miller (Yale University Press, 1982)*; In Our Image: America's Empire in the Philippines by *Stanley Karnow (Random House, 1989)*; Little Brown Brother *by Leon Wolff (Doubleday and Co., Inc., 1961)*; Muddy Glory *by Russell Roth (Christopher Publishing house, 1981); and* Soldiers in the Sun *by William T. Sexton (Books for Libraries Press, 1971)*.

The American Century

1900–1910: How it felt when everything seemed possible

By Henry Allen
Washington Post Staff Writer

You'd ask your mother, "What was it like in the olden days?"

Answer: stricter, poorer, more polite.

No: You wanted to know what it felt like to be alive then. How could she explain... the dusty heat of old television sets, the smell of Vitalis on men's hair ... women in gloves that felt sexy touching your skin, the warmth... men who whistled (with trills) and wore hats tipped to one side and got killed in wars ... the champagne disenchantment of the tuxedo '20s, husbands who lost Depression jobs and hid in their houses for shame, the October-morning energy of the postwar '40s, the barefoot LSD weddings when the universe seems a conspiracy in everyone's favor...

Charles Baudelaire, a hip 19th-century French poet, said that each age has "a deportment, a glance, a smile of its own."

In his high school yearbook, your father seems older at 18 than you did at 35. His age had a deportment of its own. So does yours.

Ages don't match decades, of course. Maybe the '60s ran from 1965 to 1975, but never mind. Some ages coincided with decades—the Roaring '20s, the Depression '30s. Some didn't. Either way, decades are handy pigeonholes for lives and times.

No one denies the importance of history—newsreel dive bombers, Olympic medals, dates and facts. Yes, the Titanic sank and Martin Luther King Jr. changed America.

But what did it feel like to be alive back then when everything or nothing seemed possible? When you lay awake listening to train whistles that weren't so much noise as a heightening of your bedroom silence? When you smelled wood smoke walking home in the early dark?

What it felt like... Back in the first decade of the 20th century, the Oughts, the Good Years, the Age of Confidence. People fought over solutions, not problems: the gold standard vs. free silver, the flying machine—tool or toy? And Teddy Roosevelt busted the trusts, started digging the Panama Canal and sent the Great White Fleet around the world.

In the century's first decade, America's destiny was shaped by, clockwise, a newfangled contraption called the automobile, the telephone, and the immigrants who passed through Ellis Island.

What it felt like just to walk down the street on a morning in early spring?—the smell of dank, dark wool and the ragged sparking of streetcar wires, men with derbies and level stares, women holding skirts above the muck and manure, immigrants audacious with ambition, the dead sweet smell of coal smoke, and soot on the last yellow, melting snow . . .

Back when health, wealth and happiness seemed not just possible but inevitable and there were Gibson girls with their confident, lifted hair and their hands in fur muffs . . . photographs of families lined up from tallest to shortest, like organ pipes . . . the whistle of stiff bristle brushes on porch floors . . . wiseacres saying "Make like a hoop and roll out of here" . . . grimy children crippled in textile mills . . .

John D. Rockefeller said, "God gave me my money." Things were dark and deliberate. Fathers knew best.

You want to know what if felt like to have the nervous system of a striker wrecking two trains near Wilkes-Barre, Pa., or a baseball player sleeping in barns and living on bread and beefsteak, or a schoolteacher thinking about the science of Marie Curie and the bared legs of Isadora Duncan, and then going home to hand her sealed pay envelope to Father.

In 1900, there were 75 million people in the 45 states and by 1910 a million immigrants a year, and who knows what it felt like for each one of them?

Davy Jones, outfielder for the Chicago Cubs, in "The Glory of Their Times":

"Back at the turn of the century, you know, we didn't have the mass communication and mass transportation that exist nowadays. We didn't have as much schooling, either. As a result, people were more unique then, more unusual, more different from each other. Now people are all more or less alike, company men, security minded, conformity—that kind of stuff. In everything, not just baseball."

YOU ALREADY KNOW TEDDY Roosevelt shot bears and the Wright brothers flew an airplane on that cold beach in 1903. You've seen the crowd photographs. Everything seemed to happen in crowds: the masses huddled in slum flats, the sea-bathing ladies in bloomers, boys in knickers playing marbles. Things flashed around in newsreels: horses, smiles, top hats, parasols and dimity dresses.

Sen. Albert Beveridge of Indiana announced: "God has marked the American people as his chosen nation to finally lead in the regeneration of the world. This is the divine mission of. . . ."

Henry James said: "The will to grow was everywhere written large, and to grow at no matter what or whose expense." The expense of the working man? The immigrant? The farmer? Anarchists and atheists? The conquered Filipino?

But what it felt like is lost and gone forever, O my darling Clementine.

No telling what it was like for W. K. Vanderbilt—the dining room of his Newport "cottage" had bronze furniture and Algerian marble walls—or for farmers driven off the land by railroads, or for parents with children dying of diphtheria, whooping cough, typhoid and malaria. Or terrified families dressing up for the minister's visit. Or blacks: W. E. B. Du Bois, who went to Harvard and then studied racial theory in Germany, said American blacks had "two-ness—an American, a Negro, two souls, two thoughts, two unreconciled strivings."

But you have ideas. You have an idea of ashmen and icemen. The circus with miraculous foreigners in tights. Croquet. Resort hotels that burned down. So many blind people, harelips, clubfeet, hunchbacks, Chestnut trees, Hydrangeas.

Vaudeville comics: "I sent my wife to the Thousand Islands for a vacation: a week on each island." Dogs: Loyal Newfoundlands and smart pugs are good with children.

On Sunday afternoons, Aunt Lil sings "'Tis the Last Rose of Summer." You cringe when the high note nears. Your mother mouths at you: "Don't." With the gramophone you can listen to Caruso singing "Vesti la giubba." He always makes the high note.

Machines will solve all our problems.

The New York Times: "We step upon the threshold of 1900 . . . facing a still brighter dawn of civilization."

The Cheyenne Sun-Leader: "Never has a year been ushered in with more promise."

Your father shaves with King Gillette's new safety razor. It's not as manly as the straight razor, somehow. But that Gillette! What a man! He says he's going to take the electricity from Niagara Falls and build a city for 60 million people! And he's not the only one—he's racing against Albert Love with his "Model City" and Love Canal.

Drain the swamps! Clear the forests! The city skyline gets higher every day, and the wind tears the smoke and steam out of stacks, banners of progress, electric Camelot.

But how it felt . . . You have an idea of dark houses with fringed couches and tables of golden oak.

A MOTHER WEEPS IN HER BEDroom for no reason she can tell. The doctor calls it neurasthenia. She feels asphyxiated, as if the whole world smelled like a clothes closet. She drinks another tablespoon of Lydia Pinkham's Vegetable Tonic, 18 percent alcohol.

Sitting by a kitchen window, a daughter wonders what real love will be like and studies the Sears, Roebuck catalogue ad for "La Dores Bust Food—for developing the bust and making it firm and round." There is linoleum on the floor. They can make anything now in factories. She watches the streetcar turn the corner with a waltzy pivot that isn't quite graceful in the way that the metronome on the parlor organ isn't quite rhythm.

Aunt Lil says no machine will ever create beauty, though some European artists think art must be like machines in the future . . . anarchists, probably, or socialists. And what about the Pianola playing those beautiful rolls of sad Chopin! He lived with George Sand, a woman. Unmarried. Why not?

In his bedroom, a son lifts dumbbells and wonders if he is magnetic, masterful and fascinating. Perhaps if he learned to play Ping-Pong. Or smoked cigarettes. Or bought penny stocks . . . oil wells in Mexico . . . that turned him into the youngest millionaire in the history of Wall Street and when he ran into old classmates they'd say, "If only we'd known then..."

Outside, an Italian family walks past with eyes you can't see into, the women shrouded in black, the men carrying knives, or so the son has heard. In the spring, they ask to pick your dandelions. To make wine? Some people don't like Italians. They lynched 11 of them one day in New Orleans. But who was it who invented the radio? Marconi! Put that in your pipe and smoke it.

Off in the city, a father thinks about the lady "typewriters" clacking away outside his office in their shirtwaists with big shoulders that make their hands look small. He wears a high, stiff collar that makes his chin look bigger. Chins show character. He wishes his son cared more about character and less about what young people call "personality." Personality didn't decide to dig the Panama Canal. It's one of those words that Walt Whitman slung around.

Wanting to have fame instead of a good reputation. Dancing the bunny hug. A fellow named Simon Nelson Patten saying that it is better to consume than produce. Everything new and scientific. Magazines telling you the best ways to comb your hair and cook your dinner—Edward Bok and his Ladies' Home Journal calling for an end to corsetry. And "The Call of the Wild" with Jack London telling you to live outdoors and be free of the same civilization that publishes his books.

Things feel a little unreal. Distant corporations can your food, light your house, ready-make your clothes without even measuring you, and give you music with machines when you used to make it yourself. McCall's, McClure's, all these magazines tell you how to beat rugs, cure female troubles and raise your children.

When Father was a boy, people knew these things. They didn't need some dude in a city to tell them. Though we've still got some grit. After the San Francisco earthquake America turned down foreign offers of help and said we'd handle it ourselves, by God.

Father locks his desk. He wouldn't want anybody to open it and find Boccaccio's "Decameron," which may be a classic in Europe but it's smut here in these United States.

On his way to the saloon, he dodges the clatter of a wagonload of shingles. He thinks of the fellow in the paper saying soon the streets would be clean, silent and uncrowded thanks to the automobile. It takes less space than the horse and wagon, and is quiet with no iron-rimmed wheels or hooves on cobblestones with the sharp, dark crack that feels like it'll make your ears ring. But with less than 150 miles of paved roads in 1900, how soon could it happen?

PROGRESS. DESTINY. BUT WILL there be the men to make it happen? A doctor has written, "Is it not shameful to think of a big, well-built man, brought up on the farm... spending his days... whispering into a Dictaphone?" On the other hand, a commentator named John Bates Clark says: "A certain manly quality in our people gives assurance that we have the personal material out of which a millennium will grow."

Bill the bartender emerges from the tangy haze of cigar smoke, pickle brine and beer-damp sawdust. He says to Father: "Here's one you can tell the wife. It seems Paddy tells Mike that Mrs. O'Hara has died. 'Has she now, Paddy? And what did she die of?' 'Why, she died of a Tuesday.'"

"That's a corker," Father says, while he tries to figure it out. Ah: the way the Irish say "of" a Tuesday not "on" a Tuesday. "A corker indeed, Bill."

We leave our family now, with mother feeling better and going down the cellar stairs to fetch an apronful of potatoes sprouting the occasional white tendril in a bin that smells mildewy and dusty at the same time. And apples for apple brown betty. She sets the salt cod to soak.

The daughter decides on molded ice cream for her birthday party, angels for the girls and George Washingtons for the boys. Though it's spring now and the milk tastes of onion sprouts the cows have been eating. Will the ice cream smell of onions, too? Well, as long as Aunt Lil doesn't sing....

IS THIS FAMILY WHAT FAMILIES where like back then? Is so, they were a lot like families now. Maybe people don't change that much. Though smells change, and some day this son and daughter will remember this house by the smell of hominy, pipe smoke, ill-fitted plumbing, rice pudding, cloves, radiator air, fried doughnuts, and the way you could follow summer into fall by the pies: strawberry, raspberry, blue- and blackberry, apple, grape, pumpkin, yam. ... Then it's winter with canned peas, bread and the root vegetables in cellar bins—turnips, onions....

Outside, in the twilight chill, wood smoke makes your nostrils flare. The sky over the city horizon twitches with glare from smelters. Down at the station, there's ice on the tracks. A locomotive, steam punching at the air, gets a little start and then the wheels lose purchase and they spin puffpuffpuff... puff, to silence, and it starts again.

Unit 3

Unit Selections

13. **Blacks and the Progressive Movement: Emergence of a New Synthesis,** Jimmie Franklin
14. **The Ambiguous Legacies of Women's Progressivism,** Robyn Muncy
15. **Woodrow Wilson, Politician,** Robert Dallek
16. **Margaret Sanger,** Gloria Steinem
17. **Unearthing a Riot,** Brent Staples
18. **Scandal in the Oval Office,** Carl Sferrazza Anthony
19. **The Abduction of Aimee,** J. Kingston Pierce

Key Points to Consider

❖ The Populist reform movement developed in response to economic hardship, made worse by the onset of depression. How do you account for the rise of progressivism in times of relative prosperity? Discuss the legislation passed during Woodrow Wilson's presidency. Did it succeed in achieving its goals? Why or why not?

❖ Why was Margaret Sanger's campaign to disseminate information about birth control so controversial? Which groups opposed her and why?

❖ Discuss Warren Harding's presidency with regard to the wrongdoing that went on during his tenure. No one has accused him of being directly involved, but what share of blame does he deserve for what went on under his nose?

❖ It is easy to scoff at Aimee Semple McPherson as a consumate showperson who was of little substance. But what does her popularity tell us about the society of the time? Why do you suppose people were attracted to her rather than to the traditional churches all about them?

 **Links**   www.dushkin.com/online/

15. **International Channel**
    http://www.i-channel.com/features/
16. **World War I—Trenches on the Web**
    http://www.worldwar1.com
17. **World Wide Web Virtual Library**
    http://www.iisg.nl/~w3vl/

These sites are annotated on pages 4 and 5.

From Progressivism to the 1920s

Reform movements in the United States have most often developed in the face of economic dislocation. The Populist crusade in the 1890s and the New Deal in the 1930s are typical. Progressivism was an exception. It developed during a period of relative prosperity. Yet more and more people became dissatisfied with existing conditions. A group that became known as the "muckrakers" published books and articles that exposed the seamier side of American life. Some concentrated on corruption and mismanagement at all levels of government. Others focused on the shady business practices of corporations and on the inordinate influence that they wielded in politics. Still others described the terrible conditions people on the bottom of the economic ladder had to endure in sweatshops and factories and in the slums that they inhabited. The popularity of muckraking in newspapers, journals, and books showed that many segments of the public were receptive to such exposures.

The Progressive movement generally was led by white, educated, middle or upper-middle class men and women. They were not radicals, though their opponents often called them that, and they had no wish to destroy the capitalist system. Instead they wanted to reform it to eliminate corruption, to make it function more efficiently, and to provide what we would call a "safety net" for the less fortunate. The reforms they proposed were modest ones such as replacing political appointees with trained experts, having senators elected directly by the people, and conducting referenda on important issues. The movement arose on local levels, then percolated upward to state governments, then into the national arena.

As president, Teddy Roosevelt had responded to Progressive sentiment through actions such as his "trust busting." He did not seek a third term in 1908, and anointed William Howard Taft as the Republican candidate for the presidency. Taft won the election but managed to alienate both progressives and conservatives during his tenure of office. By 1912 progressivism was so strong that the Democratic Party nominated Woodrow Wilson, who had compiled an impressive record as a reform governor in the state of New Jersey. Roosevelt, now counting himself a full-blown Progressive, bolted the Republican Party when Taft won renomination and formed the Progressive or "Bull Moose" Party. Roosevelt was still popular, but he managed only to split Republican support with the result that Woodrow Wilson won the election with just 42 percent of the popular vote.

Those Progressives who held or competed for political offices were almost exclusively white males. Women had not yet been granted the right to vote, let alone to be elected to positions in government, and the prevailing racism ensured that blacks would be excluded from the power structure. ("Jim Crow" laws in the South had virtually pushed blacks out of the political arena altogether.) Yet members of both groups were attracted to progressivism. "Blacks and the Progressive Movement: Emergence of a New Synthesis" shows that they, like their white counterparts, "wanted to achieve a greater sense of community and order, the preservation of moral values, and the perfection of social institutions." Female Progressives shared these goals as well. In "The Ambiguous Legacies of Women's Progressivism," Robyn Muncy points out that, contrary to what one might think, the movement did not always serve to liberate women.

"Woodrow Wilson, Politician" is aptly named, for Wilson is too often remembered only for his foreign policies—his leadership during World War I, and his failure to bring the United States into the League of Nations. Author Robert Dallek evaluates the domestic policies of Wilson's presidency and concludes that his achievements should be ranked favorably along with those of Franklin D. Roosevelt and Lyndon B. Johnson.

Margaret Sanger's mother simply wore out after 18 pregnancies and 11 live births. Margaret, while working as a practical nurse and midwife, saw many other women whose health suffered from frequent, unintended, and unwanted pregnancies. She defied existing morality by preaching in favor of, and providing instructions for, birth control. To avoid prosecution for violating postal obscenity laws, she fled to Europe for a year. Later, when the case was dismissed, she continued her crusade for sex education and family planning. Gloria Steinem's article, "Margaret Sanger," highlights the career of this important forerunner of modern feminism.

Racism has been a constant factor in American life, although it was more virulent in some regions than in others. In "Unearthing a Riot," author Brent Staples reveals the facts of a bloody race riot that took place in Tulsa, Oklahoma, in 1921. Hundreds of black people were shot, burned alive, or dragged to death behind automobiles. Staples not only describes what happened but how this catastrophe was covered up for decades before being brought to light.

America's entry into World War I or "The Great War," as people at the time called it, to a great degree stifled the progressive impulse. After numerous crusades against inequities at home and the consequences of waging war abroad, the American people yearned to return to what Republican presidential candidate Warren G. Harding referred to as "normalcy." Harding was elected in a landslide. Following a recession brought about by postwar reconversion, prosperity returned again although it was not equally shared by all. The genial Harding presided over this economic boom and was an extremely popular president at the time of his death in 1923. There was a darker side to his presidency, however, the details of which began to emerge after his passing. The report "Scandal in the Oval Office" relates the skullduggery that went on behind the scenes.

"The Roaring Twenties" produced a number of colorful figures who attained wide popularity. Babe Ruth, for instance, achieved a level of renown previously unknown in the sports world. "The Sultan of Swat," as he was sometimes called, was looked upon as a lovable clown who, when he was not knocking baseballs out of parks, spent his time eating innumerable hot dogs or visiting sick children in hospitals. Actually, Ruth was a hard-drinking womanizer, with a wide mean streak. In the field of religion there were a number of popular evangelists such as Aimee Semple McPherson, who had attained a loyal following through her radio sermons and vaudville-style Sunday services. Like Ruth, however, McPherson was not quite the person she appeared to be in public. J. Kingston Pierce, in "The Abduction of Aimee," analyzes the rise and fall of this woman and tells us something about the society in which she lived.

Blacks and the Progressive Movement: Emergence of a New Synthesis

Jimmie Franklin

In his magisterial work, *Origins of the New South, 1877–1913*, historian C. Vann Woodward wrote that, in the South, Progressive-era reforms generally benefitted white men. He also implied that in the North, the era did not usher in sweeping changes for African Americans. Restrictive social customs dictated a secondary place for them in society. For nearly two decades after Woodward's study, scholars repeated the author's conclusion on the failure of progressivism to attack fundamental problems in the black community (1).

Historians of progressivism fixed their attention essentially upon a middle-class urban movement that, at best, made blacks only marginal participants in the struggle for social change. In 1968, August Meier wrote in his *Negro Thought in America, 1880–1915,* that "Negroes were practically omitted from the Progressive Era's program of reform." In a perceptive work a few years later, John Temple Kirby pointed scholarship in a slightly different direction when he suggested that *"in a way"* black people did not profit from the many changes that took place during the period. Kirby's qualification did not go unnoticed by some scholars, especially those interested in women's history and in looking at history from "the bottom up" (2).

Woodward and other historians who directed their attention toward blacks and the progressive movement gave paramount emphasis to political matters and race relations. It is hard to overlook the declining citizenship status of the race during the latter part of the nineteenth century. Indeed the infamous 1896 *Plessy* Supreme Court decision gave legal sanction to segregation; lynching also continued at an ugly pace; and both national and regional leadership seemed willing to adopt the "scientific" view of race that relegated blacks to an inferior status on the scale of humanity. Ironic as it may now seem, political "purification" in the progressive South came to mean the elimination of blacks from the electoral process, for total abrogation of the fifteenth amendment (3).

Even some northern reformers who aggressively addressed social issues in their region only reluctantly tackled problems related to the African-American community. The noted journalist Ray Stannard Baker, for example, who wrote the classic *Following the Color Line,* acquainted Americans with some of the pressing matters of the black community, but ultimately concluded that only time would remedy the problems of race in America. The distancing of Baker and other progressives from racial issues shaped the conclusions of Woodward and other scholars about blacks and progressivism (4).

In the 1970s historians began to recognize that black Americans themselves had engaged in a variety of reform endeavors that often had little if anything to do with racial protest or political progressivism, although those issues may have inadvertently overlapped. When John Temple Kirby qualified his assessment of progressivism with the phrase "in a way," he was aware of black reform efforts that, more frequently than not, paraded under the heading of self-reliance. These efforts were infused with notions of social justice and the principles of Social Christianity (or Social Gospel) that characterized many of the programs of white progressives (5).

Many reasons prompted scholars to refocus their attention or to change their emphasis in assessing progressivism and matters of race. Social and intellectual currents that followed in the wake of *Brown v. Board of Education*; the availability of new historical sources; greater concentration on class, race, and gender issues; and the broader participation of blacks and women in the historical profession all had significant impact upon writers. When scholars now speak of progressivism, they not only allude to the ideal of black self-reliance, but suggest a concern that transcends individual striving for profit and self-growth, or the acquisition of power or influence for personal gain. In its broad sense, they view progressivism as the effective use of collective organization, energy, and resources directed toward a community's growth, advancement, or uplift.

Much like white reformers, black progressives wanted to achieve a greater sense of community and order, the preservation of moral values, and the perfection of social institutions. John Dittmer undoubtedly had this in mind when he wrote in *Black Georgia in the Progressive Era, 1900–1920,* that white supremacy did not destroy a reform spirit within the black community, and that African Americans created and strengthened institutions behind the veil of segregation (6).

Black reformers came principally from a middle-class background, but constructing an accurate profile of a "typical" black progressive is as difficult as trying to define a white one. "Conservatives" such as Booker T. Washington and "radicals" such as W. E. B. DuBois both fit the characterization of "progressive" if one moves away from narrow political and ideological considerations. If Washington, for example, shied away from the protest-oriented Niagara Movement and the National Association for the Advancement of Colored People, which represented the spirit of progressivism, his emphasis on farmers' institutes to improve black rural life and his abiding concern for black health care reflected a progressive disposition toward human and social problems (7).

THE BLACK CHURCH

The leadership of the black church, the most powerful social institution within the African-American community, took on greater life and activity during this era. The prevailing view of the black church as theologically orthodox obscured some of the changes that took place during this period. It helped to shape, and was shaped by, contemporary currents of Social Christianity that characterized the Progressive Era. In reality, the black church, even many rural southern ones, had demonstrated a broader social consciousness before the turn of the twentieth century than some historians realize. The crucial point, however, is that during the Progressive Era an increasing number of churches accepted the tenets of the Social Gospel and extended their mission beyond the walls of their sanctuaries, into the streets of the city and into the countryside (8).

Among the black clergy, Reverdy Ransom stood out as the most celebrated clergy member of the Progressive Era. A powerful preacher and social activist, Ransom studied at Wilberforce, Ohio, where he came under the influence of teachers who saw the church as an instrument for altering American society and the black community. For them the church had to remain the social center of black life, a means of social control, and, potentially, a medium for black enfranchisement and political participation. Ransom's professors taught that service to others was a Christian obligation, and they stressed that salvation rested upon social responsibility and good works. Ransom learned to exalt systematic inquiry, research, institutional organization, and the role of government in the resolution of societal problems. If one could craft a stereotype, Ransom was a classic Social Gospel progressive of the age (9).

Ransom rose to become a bishop in the African Methodist Episcopal (AME) Church in the 1920s, but his most enduring work took place during the first two decades of the twentieth century. As a minister in Cleveland, he created programs for the development of young children, established a men's club in his church to carry out community activities, and appointed a Board of Deaconesses, to the chagrin of more conservative males. A literary society sponsored debates and lectures on local and national issues. When the minister moved to Bethel Church in Chicago, he joined forces with black and white reformers including activist Ida Wells-Barnett who had gone to Chicago from Memphis, the noted lawyer Clarence Darrow, and Jane Addams of Hull House. Ransom's church started an industrial school for children, a kindergarten, and programs to provide for the needs of people who lived in the church's district. Wells-Barnett recalled that Ransom had an abiding concern for the sick, the poor, and the needy (10).

Ransom transferred the tenets of the Social Gospel into his best remembered endeavor: the Institutional Church and Social Settlement (ICSS). His belief in the need for this kind of social service, writes Ralph Luker, sprang from an experience in Pennsylvania where he walked among the poor in alleys and climbed dark stairways of unhealthy tenements. Ransom believed that the black church needed to provide more than worship service and spiritual food for black migrants who had already begun to move into the city. Thus, he founded ICSS more than a decade before the formation of the National Urban League.

Although technically under the auspices of the AME Church, Ransom's creation had a mission broader than the parent organization. He presided over a structure that offered a variety of activities, including an employment bureau, print shop, kindergarten and nursery, and an athletic gymnasium that held 1,200 people. Ransom's ICSS not only served the needs of Chicago's poor, but helped pave the way for the establishment of institutional churches and settlements in other localities. Through his leadership, Ransom advanced Social Gospel activity within the black community by mentoring persons such as R. R Wright, who became a bishop in the AME Church, and George Haynes, a sociologist who was a founder of the National Urban League in 1911 (11).

THE ROLE OF WOMEN REFORMERS

When scholars look closely for the bedrock of progressivism in the black community, they must turn their attention to African-American women. While some of them—Ida Wells-Barnett, Mary Church Terrell, Mary Waring, and Lugenia Burns Hope—are well known to scholars because of their protest activity or their national club work, some lesser known reformers in small communities are just beginning to emerge with recent scholarship in women's history. The work of historians such as Cynthia Neverdon-Morton and Elizabeth Hayes Turner have enabled us to recenceptualize the role of women, especially in southern life. Whether in churches, clubs, or neighborhood unions, women provided vital energy, leadership, and knowledge that fueled reform during the Progressive Age. Examples abound, but the work of black women as agents for change is especially evident in their push for support of common schools in the South during the Progressive Era (12).

Scholars of southern history have written much about the positive impact of northern philanthropy upon black education. Funds from foundations certainly played an important role in improving and sustaining learning in the South, where most blacks lived during the Progressive Era. Unfortunately, support from the major philanthropic organizations—the Rockefeller Foundation, the General Education Board, the Jeanes Fund, and the Rosenwald Foundation—often enabled white southerners to escape responsibility for adequate funding of black schools. As Louis Harlan and Henry Bullock have shown, a wide gulf existed between black and white education during the Progressive Era. Scholars, however, often overlook the enormous contribution blacks themselves made to sustaining the life of the public school and the progressive philosophy that African Americans brought to those efforts (13).

Mollie Parker Franklin. (Courtesy of John Hope Franklin.)

James Anderson has written the most perceptive study of the black community's commitment to educational reform in the American South. Black women joined black men in carrying out various fund-raising campaigns to secure community schools across the region. In examining the activities of the Rosenwald Fund—one of the most active foundations that supported the building of black schools during the period—Anderson documents the remarkable efforts of poor southern blacks to raise money to finance buildings for their children. The Rosenwald agent for the state of Alabama related a meaningful story of an Autauga county, Alabama community where poor black tenant farmers struggled to eke out a precarious existence from the soil, where money was at a real "premium." On a hot summer day, the community gathered for a rally to collect funds to pay its share of a new Rosenwald school. Agent M. H. Griffin recalled that an elderly black woman had written him to say that "I have only one copper cent, and it goes for the children of Autaugaville." Apocryphal or not, the story symbolizes the black community's concern with education and the belief in the kind of social change it could bring. Some black men mortgaged their farms and their lands to build schools, while determined black mothers sponsored fish fries, raffles, musical programs, and other activities to raise money for education (14).

If women demonstrated a profound interest in public schools as a means of positively affecting the life chances of their children, they also initiated or sponsored a plethora of other activities. Their energy and commitment defined the very notion of agency, the instrument through which change arose. In city after city, they pressed for playgrounds, recreational centers, hospitals, better sanitation and housing, more youth facilities, and nurseries. From Boston to Tuskegee, writes Anne Firor Scott, black women tackled community problems and created institutions to solve or ameliorate them. Middle-class black women characteristically worked through the club movement, the church, or auxiliaries to men's groups such as the Prince Hall Masons. In Tulsa, Oklahoma for example, Mollie Parker Franklin, mother of the distinguished historian John Hope Franklin, started a nursery with the help of other club women; and in Atlanta Lugenia Burns Hope found support for her Neighborhood Union from women associated with the club movement and universities in the city. In Cleveland, Jane Hunter did not depend on government or men's groups in establishing her home for unwed mothers (15).

CONCLUSION

During the later part of the nineteenth century and the first decades of the twentieth, organized black men and women not only tackled Jim Crow in a variety of direct and covert ways, but also worked to improve social conditions and institutions in their communities. Much like other progressives, they sought a better life free of debilitating ills and political proscriptions. They bequeathed to the country a legacy of self-help that remains with us as America still desperately struggles for a solution to its most difficult social problem.

Shortly after the beginning of the Progressive Era, W. E. B. DuBois, black scholar and reformer, wrote that the great problem of the twentieth century was that of race. We face the new century encumbered with the same burden. In the years ahead, perhaps a new progressivism, fueled by a more dynamic democratic ethos of both blacks and whites, will help achieve meaningful reforms that will exalt the possibilities of the human spirit and enable the United States to rise above cultural provincialism, racial bigotry, and the narrowness of gender discrimination.

ENDNOTES

1. C. Vann Woodward, "Progressivism—For Whites Only," in *Origins of the New South, 1877–1913* (Baton Rouge: Louisiana State University Press, 1951), 369–95. My essay tilts slightly toward a consideration of the American South, where the overwhelming majority of blacks lived during the Progressive Era.
2. August Meier, *Negro Thought in America, 1880–1915: Racial Ideologies in the Age of Booker T. Washington* (Ann Arbor: University of Michigan Press, 1966), 165; and Jack Temple Kirby, *Darkness at the Dawning: Race and Reform in the Progressive South* (Philadelphia: Lippincott, 1972), 155.
3. Dewey W. Grantham, *Southern Progressivism: The Reconciliation of Progress and Tradition* (Knoxville: University of Tennessee Press, 1983), xvii, 112–20; and William A. Link, *The Paradox of Southern Progressivism, 1880–1930* (Chapel Hill: University of North Carolina Press, 1992), 63–70.
4. Ray Stannard Baker, *Following the Color Line: American Negro Citizenship in the Progressive Era* (1908; Reprint, New York: Harper and Row, 1964).
5. Kirby, *Darkness at the Dawning*, 155; and for the many-sided issue of social justice in the South, see Grantham, *Southern Progressivism*, especially 230–45.
6. John Dittmer, *Black Georgia in the Progressive Era, 1900–1920* (Urbana: University of Illinois Press, 1977), 50.
7. The best biography of Booker T. Washington during the Progressive Era is Louis R. Harlan, *Booker T. Washington: The Wizard of Tuskegee, 1901–1915* (New York: Oxford University Press, 1983); and of W. E. B. DuBois, David Levering Lewis, *W. E. B. Du Bois: Biography of a Race* (New York: H. Holt, 1993), 218–24, especially the section on DuBois's Atlanta University studies, which he hoped would help pave the way for social change.
8. A vast historiography now exists on the black church. An informed work that best traces the activity of the church from the Progressive Era to the early 1930s is Benjamin B. Mays and Joseph W. Nicholson, *The Negro's Church* (New York: Institute of Social and Religious Research, 1933). Many black churches across the country did not keep adequate records of their many activities, and it is possible that Mays and Nicholson underestimated the extent to which African-American religious institutions became involved in community programs. An insightful commentary on women, one particular black religious denomination, and Progressive-era reform is Evelyn Brooks Higginbotham, Righteous *Discontent: The Women's Movement in the Black Baptist Church, 1880–1920* (Cambridge: Harvard University Press, 1993), 171–79.
9. The most useful full-length study of Ransom is Calvin S. Morris, *Reverdy C. Ransom: Black Advocate of the Social Gospel* (Lanham, MD: University Press of America, 1990).
10. Ibid., 105–06; and Randall K. Burkett and Richard Newman, *Black Apostles: Afro-American Clergy Confront the Twentieth Century* (Boston: G. K. Hall, 1978), 196.
11. Ralph E. Luker, *The Social Gospel in Black and White: American Racial Reform, 1885–1912* (Chapel Hill: University of North Carolina Press, 1991), 173–76; and Peter J. Paris, *The Social Teaching of the Black Churches* (Philadelphia: Fortress, 1985), 95–98.
12. The best general work of its kind on black women in the region is Cynthia Neverdon-Morton, *Afro-American Women of the South and the Advancement of the Race, 1895–1925* (Knoxville: University of Tennessee, 1989). A superb and provocative state study that discusses black women in some detail is Elizabeth Hayes Turner, *Women, Culture, and Community: Religion and Reform in Galveston, 1880–1920* (New York: Oxford University Press, 1997), 228–60.
13. On the condition of black public schools generally during this period, see Henry Bullock, *A History of Negro Education in the South from 1619 to the Present* (Cambridge: Harvard University Press, 1967). See also, Louis Harlan, *Separate and Unequal: Public School Campaigns and Racism in the Southern Seaboard States, 1901–1915* (New York: Atheneum, 1969); and Grantham, *Southern Progressivism*, 240–47.
14. James Anderson, *The Education of Blacks in the South, 1860–1935* (Chapel Hill: University of North Carolina Press, 1988), 159, 161.
15. The black women's club movement is traced in Lindsay Davis, *Lifting as They Climb: The National Association of Colored Women* (Washington, DC: National Association of Colored Women, 1933). See also, Anne Firor Scott, *Natural Allies: Women's Associations in American History* (Urbana: University of Illinois Press, 1991), 147–48; John Hope Franklin and John Whittington Franklin, eds., *My Life and An Era: The Autobiography of Buck Colbert Franklin* (Baton Rouge: Louisiana State University Press, 1997), 211–13; and Jacqueline Anne Rouse, *Lugenia Burns Hope: Black Southern Reformer* (Athens: University of Georgia Press, 1989), 57–90. For a helpful note on the role of women in creating a settlement in one southern city, and for the subsequent activity of one progressive black woman, see Elisabeth Israels Perry, "'The Very Best Influence': Josephine Holloway and Girl Scouting in Nashville's African-American Community," *Tennessee Historical Quarterly* 53 (Summer 1993): 73–85. A useful full-length study of blacks and the settlement movement that focuses heavily upon women is Elisabeth Lasch-Quinn, *Black Neighbors: Race and the Limits of Reform in the American Settlement House Movement, 1890–1945* (Chapel Hill: University of North Carolina Press, 1993).

BIBLIOGRAPHY

Baker, Ray Stannard. *Following the Color Line: American Negro Citizenship in the Progressive Era.* New York: Harper and Row, 1908.

Dittmer, John. *Black Georgia in the Progressive Era, 1900–1920.* Urbana: University of Illinois Press, 1977.

Harlan, Louis R. *Booker T. Washington: The Wizard of Tuskegee, 1901–1915.* New York: Oxford University Press, 1983.

Kirby, Jack Temple. *Darkness at the Dawning: Race and Reform in the Progressive South.* Philadelphia: Lippincott, 1972.

Lasch-Quinn, Elisabeth. *Black Neighbors: Race and the Limits of Reform in the American Settlement House Movement, 1890–1945.* Chapel Hill: University of North Carolina Press, 1993.

Lewis, David Levering. *W. E. B. Du Bois: Biography of a Race, 1868–1919.* New York: H. Holt, 1993.

Luker, Ralph E. *The Social Gospel in Black and White: American Racial Reform, 1885–1912.* Chapel Hill: University of North Carolina Press, 1991.

Morris, Calvin. *Reverdy Ransom: Black Advocate of the Social Gospel.* Lanham, MD: University Press of America, 1990.

Neverdon-Morton, Cynthia. *Afro-American Women of the South and the Advancement of the Race, 1895–1925.* Knoxville: University of Tennessee Press, 1989.

Rouse, Jacqueline Anne. *Lugenia Burns Hope: Black Southern Reformer.* Athens: University of Georgia Press, 1989.

Turner, Elizabeth Hayes. *Women, Culture, and Community: Religion and Reform in Galveston, 1880–1920.* New York: Oxford University Press, 1997.

Woodward, C. Vann. "Progressivism—For Whites Only." In *Origins of the New South, 1877–1913.* Baton Rouge: Louisiana State University Press, 1951.

Jimmie Franklin is a professor of history at Vanderbilt University and a past president of the Southern Historical Association.

The Ambiguous Legacies of Women's Progressivism

Robyn Muncy

Most undergraduates come into my classroom convinced that men have so dominated American political life that they are responsible for all the good and evil in America's public past. The history of progressive reform usually persuades them otherwise. Students discover that black and white women, by the hundreds of thousands—even millions—threw themselves into progressive reform, helping to chart the direction of public policy and American values for the century to come. When they learn this, students want to believe that such activism and power must have tended unambiguously to liberate women. My job is to explain that this is not altogether the case.

The truth is that female progressive activism left a complicated legacy to twentieth-century American women. First, women reformers generally failed to overcome (and white activists often worked to sustain) racial divisions in American life. Second, black and white female progressives changed "the place" of American women in many important senses, especially in winning admittance to the polls and the policymaking table. Third, despite carving out significant public space for women, female progressives—mostly white in this case—embedded in public policy the notion that motherhood and economic independence were incompatible. Women reformers thus empowered successive generations of women in some ways while continuing to deny them the multiplicity of roles open to men.

Most women's activism took place through the many local, regional, and national organizations that women formed around 1900. The sheer number of women participating in these associations boggles the late-twentieth-century mind and suggests an engaged, cohesive female citizenry well before the achievement of women's suffrage. For instance, two hundred local white women's clubs joined together in 1890 to form the General Federation of Women's Clubs (GFWC), which by 1920 claimed over a million members. Along with the National Mothers' Congress (NMC), formed in 1897, the GFWC became a vehicle for moderate white women's political activism. In similar fashion, one hundred middle-class black women's clubs created the National Association of Colored Women (NACW) in 1896, and by 1914 this group claimed fifty thousand members in one thousand local clubs. Jewish women organized the National Council of Jewish Women in 1893, and black Baptist women founded the Woman's Convention of the National Baptist Convention in 1900. That organization alone embraced over one million members (1).

Although gender and race segregation were the rule among civic organizations early in this century, there were exceptions. Some women participated in gender-integrated groups like the National Child Labor Committee, which targeted child labor as an urgent public problem, and some women helped to found such gender- and race-integrated groups as the National Association for the Advancement of Colored People and the National Urban League. One of the most important progressive organizations, the National Consumers League (NCL), was ostensibly a gender-integrated group, though white women dominated it throughout the period, and thousands of women—overwhelmingly white—invigorated the Progressive party of 1912 (2).

In these organizations, women pursued an agenda that set them squarely in the social justice wing of progressiv-

From *OAH Magazine of History,* Spring 1999, pp. 15-19. © 1999 by the Organization of American Historians. Reprinted by permission.

14. Ambiguous Legacies of Women's Progressivism

The mansion of the late Chicago businessman Charles Hull served as the original home of Jane Addams's famous social settlement. This photo of Hull House was taken around 1893. (Courtesy of the Jane Addams Memorial Collection, Special Collections, The University Library, The University of Illinois at Chicago, Negative 146.)

ism. They aimed to ameliorate the worst suffering caused by rapid industrialization, immigration, and urbanization without forsaking capitalism altogether. To do so, they strove to make government at all levels more responsible for the social and economic welfare of citizens, and though many hoped ultimately to improve the lives of America's entire working class or the whole community of color, most women reformers found that they were especially effective when they spoke specifically to the needs of women and children. Their agendas ran the gamut from anti-lynching campaigns to the prohibition of alcohol, from maximum hours laws to women's suffrage, from improved educational opportunities for African-American children to the abolition of prostitution. A brief article can glimpse only a tiny portion of their work.

One example, the campaign for protective labor legislation, reveals some of the complex meanings of women's progressivism. Although many working-class women believed the solution to workplace problems lay in unionization, some accepted the middle-class preference for legislation as the surest route to job-related improvements. Thus, both groups—organized, for instance, in the National Women's Trade Union League—lobbied their states for guarantees of factory safety, maximum hours laws, and less often, minimum wage provisions as well. Many states passed such laws and even hired women as factory inspectors to enforce them.

These legislative successes were threatened in 1905, when the U.S. Supreme Court handed down its famous *Lochner* decision. In it, the Court struck down a New York law that regulated the hours of bakers, an overwhelmingly male group. The Court ruled that states could interfere in the freedom of contract only if long hours constituted a clear health risk either to the workers themselves or to the general public.

Women reformers would not see their protective laws undone. Indeed, their determination to sustain protective labor legislation led to their participation in a second case, *Muller v. Oregon*. In 1903, Oregon passed a law that limited the hours of women in industrial work to ten per day. Two years later, the state prepared a case against laundry owner Curt Muller for violation of the law. Muller took the case to the U.S. Supreme Court, where he expected the reasoning in *Lochner* to strike down Oregon's law. The NCL, with the fiery Florence Kelley at its head, took up Oregon's fight, leading the charge for protective legislation for women workers.

Kelley, who had fought for and implemented a similar law in Illinois, hired Louis Brandeis to argue against Muller. Kelley's colleague, Josephine Goldmark, aided Brandeis in preparing a precedent-setting brief. Providing over one hundred pages of evidence that showed that women workers were hurt by long hours in ways that men were not, the brief argued that women workers warranted the state's interference in freedom of contract even when men did not. In 1908, the Supreme Court accepted their arguments, concluding that "woman's physical structure and the performance of maternal functions place her at a disadvantage in the struggle for subsistence" (3).

Women reformers thus won a progressive end—government intervention in the economy on behalf of workers—by perpetuating an older belief in male/female difference and moreover inscribing that difference into law. In this crusade, activist women, mostly middle-class and white, gained public power for themselves while at the same time cementing in public policy a view of working women as peculiarly vulnerable workers. This image of working women, while justifying legislation that genuinely helped many, made it impossible for women to compete effectively with men in many sectors of the labor market. This law created a complicated bequest to later generations of American women. Moreover, these maximum hours laws, antecedents of the Fair Labor Standards Act of 1938, also supported racial difference, not explicitly as in the case of gender, but implicitly, by omitting from coverage the occupations in which African-American women were heavily represented: agricultural labor and domestic service.

Another campaign rooted in a belief in the difference between women and men was the movement for mothers' pensions. Mothers' pensions were public stipends paid to mothers—usually widows—who found themselves without male support. The purpose of these payments was to allow impoverished mothers to remain at home with their children rather than having to put them in an orphanage or neglect them while working for wages. Led especially by the NMC and the GFWC, white activists lobbied their state governments for such programs and won them in virtually every state by the mid 1920s. These programs, unfortunately poorly funded and often unjustly administered, set the precedent for Aid to Dependent Children, a federal program enacted as part of the Social Security Act in 1935 during Franklin Roosevelt's New Deal (4).

African-American women reformers, seeing that social workers often reserved mothers' pensions for white women, lobbied for their extension to qualified African-American women. Simultaneously however, they promoted day care services as an alternative response to mothers' need to work for pay. These services revealed not only black women's suspicion of government programs—based in part on the disenfranchisement of African-American men and spread of Jim Crow laws in the early twentieth century—but also their greater acceptance of working mothers. Poor wages for men were so endemic to African-American communities that black reformers could not so easily envision a world in which mothers were spared paid labor, and so they were more ready than white women to create institutions that allowed women to be both good mothers and good workers (5).

In both black and white neighborhoods, day care services were often provided by other, multifaceted progressive women's institutions. Indeed, the quintessential progressive women's institutions were social settlements and neighborhood unions. Social settlements first appeared in the United States in the 1880s. They were places where middle-class women and men lived in the midst of working-class, largely immigrant neighborhoods. Their purpose was to bridge the gap between the classes. By the turn of the century, settlements existed in most sizable cities. Educated women took the lead in the establishment of settlement communities. Once acquainted with their working-class neighbors, these middle-class women created social services that they believed their neighbors needed. Much of the time, settlement residents piloted local health services, educational series, or recreational programs and then lobbied their municipal, county, or state government to provide permanent funding and oversight. In this way, settlement residents became leaders in progressive reform.

To counter the claim that suffragists deserted their families or disrespected motherhood, suffragists often took their children on parade with them, as some did in this 1912 demonstration in New York City. (Library of Congress, Division of Prints and Photographs.)

The most famous social settlement was Hull House in Chicago. Founded in 1889 by Jane Addams and Ellen Gates Starr, Hull House set the standard for the hundreds of settlements that subsequently opened in cities all over the country. Beginning with a day nursery (considered a regrettable, stop-gap measure by the white reformers) and evening classes and clubs for its immigrant neighbors, Hull House eventually housed seventy middle-class residents, a library for the neighborhood, a community theater, a gym, playground, labor museum, many classrooms and clubhouses for adults and children, and a coffee house. It offered a visiting nurse and employment counseling to the neighborhood, as well as a meeting ground for unions and political groups. It was a vital hub of neighborhood life and provided the initiative and/or support for much progressive legislation, including protective legislation for women workers and children, women's suffrage, workers' compensation programs, increased funding for public education, and the creation of the U.S. Children's Bureau.

Besides women's suffrage, the Children's Bureau may have been progressive women's most significant national achievement. The idea for a federal agency devoted to child welfare is usually credited to Lillian Wald, founder and head resident of the Henry Street Settlement in New York City. Herself a visiting nurse, Wald joined Jane Addams in creating a female reform network that stretched across the country by 1903. That year Wald first proposed that the U.S. government create a bureau to collect information and propose legislation of benefit to the country's children. In 1912, Congress finally rewarded the women's lobbying efforts by establishing the Children's Bureau in the U.S. Department of Labor.

Addams immediately argued that a woman should head the new agency and proposed in particular Julia Lathrop, a long-time resident of Hull House. To everyone's surprise, President William Howard Taft accepted the recommendation, and Lathrop became the first woman ever to head a federal agency. She quickly hired other women to staff the bureau, which became a female beachhead in the federal government for decades to come. In 1921, Lathrop and her staff drafted and won from Congress the first piece of federal social/welfare legislation: the Sheppard-Towner Maternity and Infancy Act, which sent public health nurses into nearly every corner of America to teach pregnant women how best to care for themselves and their newborns. This set another precedent for New Deal programs (6).

Although African-American women also founded social settlements, as did some interracial groups, more typical of black women's institution building was the neighborhood union. Such entities differed from social settlements mainly in that few reformers actually lived in them, reflecting in part the tendency of black women reformers to be married while their white counterparts often remained unmarried. Many of these progressive institutions called themselves missions, community centers, institutional churches, or even schools, but like settlements, they provided meeting places and services for those living nearby, and they joined the middle and working classes in local political crusades (7).

The most famous such center was the Neighborhood Union in Atlanta. Founded in 1908 by Lugenia Burns Hope, the union provided day care services, health care and health education, and playgrounds. It sponsored clubs and classes for children and adults alike, and organized lobbying campaigns to obtain greater funding for the education of African-American children, as well as improved street lights and sanitation in black neighborhoods. Members urged public relief for the unemployed. The Neighborhood Union's appeals for governmental support remind us that even though black women had less hope for a positive response from government officials than white women, they did not—even in this hour of miserable race relations—give up entirely on obtaining government resources (8).

Just as social settlements and neighborhood unions were usually race-segregated, so were organizations that fought for women's suffrage. Ratification of the Nineteenth Amendment in 1920 stood as a monumental victory for women progressives; it is one of the signal achievements of progressive reform. But even that fight to expand democracy was marked by racial division and hierarchy. Hoping to win support from white southerners, leaders in the North refused to admit black women's clubs to the National American Woman Suf-

Lugenia Burns Hope founded the Neighborhood Union in Atlanta. While white progressives in the South usually pursued policies that assured white dominance, Hope's activism reminds us that southern African Americans were also progressives. (Courtesy of the National Park Service, Mary McLeod Bethune Council House National Historic Site, Washington DC.)

frage Association, which, with two million members in 1917, was the largest suffrage organization in U.S. history. In response, black women formed their own suffrage associations—like the Equal Suffrage League founded by Ida Wells-Barnett in Chicago—or fought for enfranchisement through multi-issue groups like the NACW or the black Baptist Women's Convention (9). Complicating black women's struggle for suffrage was their simultaneous fight for the re-enfranchisement of African-American men in the South, whose right to vote was eroding in the face of brutal violence, literacy tests, and poll taxes. When the women's suffrage amendment passed, no state could deny suffrage on the basis of sex, but the same measures that disenfranchised black men in the South also prevented most black women from approaching the polls. Thus, not until the Voting Rights Act of 1965 did women's suffrage achieve a complete victory.

Black and white women were integral to progressivism. No history of progressive reform could possibly be complete without discussing the campaign for women's suffrage, the work of neighborhood unions, or the struggle for protective legislation.

These efforts by millions of American women suggest several conclusions. This history illuminates the source of sometimes contradictory views of women embedded in public policy and personal identities since the Progressive Era: while most American women received the vote by 1920, imparting a new parity with men in public life, the same period produced legislation that construed women primarily as mothers rather than as workers and as more vulnerable, weaker workers than men. This ambiguous legacy has reverberated through the twentieth century.

The history of these women reformers moreover reveals some of the ways that race has shaped women's experience and political agendas in the past, and it embodies the ways that racism has crippled democracy and betrayed democratic movements in the United States. It reminds us that the renewed political life we might create in the twenty-first century, if it is to fulfill the promise of democracy, must strive to overcome the racial hierarchy that progressives—and all of their successors—failed to defeat.

ENDNOTES

1. Karen J. Blair, *Clubwoman as Feminist. True Womanhood Redefined, 1868–1914* (New York: Holmes and Meier, 1980); Evelyn Brooks Higginbotham, *Righteous Discontent. The Women's Movement in the Black Baptist Church* (Cambridge: Harvard University Press, 1993), 8; and Stephanie Shaw, "Black Club Women and the Creation of the National Association of Colored Women," *Journal of Women's History* 3 (Fall 1991): 10–25.
2. Dorothy Salem, *To Better Our World: Black Women in Organized Reform, 1890–1920* (Brooklyn: Carlson, 1990), 45–46, 100–14, 146–96, 274; Kathryn Kish Sklar, "The Historical Foundations of Women's Power in the Creation of the American Welfare State, 1830–1930," in *Mothers of a New World: Maternalist Politics and the Origins of Welfare States*, ed. Seth Koven and Sonya Michel (New York: Routledge, 1993), 43–93; and Robyn Muncy, "'Women Demand Recognition': Women Candidates in Colorado's Election of 1912," in *We Have Come to Stay: American Women and Political Parties, 1880–1960*, ed. Melanie Gustafson, Kristie Miller, and Elisabeth Israels Perry (Albuquerque: University of New Mexico Press, 1999), 45–54.
3. Muller v. Oregon, 208 U.S. 412; Nancy Woloch, *Muller v. Oregon: A Brief History with Documents* (Boston: Bedford Books, 1996); Sybil Lipschultz, "Social Feminism and Legal Discourse," *Yale Journal of Law and Feminism* 2 (Fall 1989): 131–60; and Kathryn

Kish Sklar, "Hull House in the 1890s: A Community of Women Reformers," *Signs* 10 (Summer 1985): 658–77.

4. Molly Ladd-Taylor, *Mother-Work: Women, Child Welfare, and the State, 1890–1930* (Urbana: University of Illinois Press, 1994), 135–66; and Theda Skócpol, *Protecting Soldiers and Mothers: The Political Origins of Social Policy in the United States* (Cambridge: Belknap Press of Harvard University, 1992), 424–79.

5. Linda Gordon, "Black and White Visions of Welfare: Women's Welfare Activism: 1890–1945," *Journal of American History* 78 (September 1991): 559–90; Eileen Boris, "The Power of Motherhood: Black and White Activist Women Redefine the 'Political,'" *Yale Journal of Law and Feminism* 2 (Fall 1989): 25–49.

6. Robyn Muncy, *Creating a Female Dominion in American Reform, 1890–1935* (New York: Oxford University Press, 1991).

7. Salem, *To Better Our World;* and Elisabeth Lasch-Quinn, *Black Neighbors: Race and the Limits of Reform in the American Settlement House Movement, 1890–1945* (Chapel Hill: University of North Carolina Press, 1993).

8. Jacqueline Anne Rouse, *Lugenia Burns Hope: Black Southern Reformer* (Athens: University of Georgia Press, 1989).

9. Rosalyn Terborg-Penn, "Discrimination Against Afro-American Women in the Woman's Movement, 1830–1920," in *The Afro-American Woman: Struggles and Images,* ed. Sharon Harley and Rosalyn Terborg-Penn (Port Washington, NY: National University Publications, 1978); and Higginbotham, *Righteous Discontent,* 226.

BIBLIOGRAPHY

In addition to the works cited in the endnotes, the following sources are helpful for studying women's activism in the Progressive Era.

Boris, Eileen. *Home to Work: Motherhood and the Politics of Industrial Homework in the United States.* New York: Cambridge University Press, 1994.

Cott, Nancy F. *The Grounding of Modern Feminism.* New Haven: Yale University Press, 1987.

Crocker, Ruth Hutchinson. *Social Work and Social Order: The Settlement Movement in Two Industrial Cities, 1889-1930.* Urbana: University of Illinois, 1992.

Goodwin, Joanne L. *Gender and the Politics of Welfare Reform: Mothers' Pensions in Chicago, 1911–4929.* Chicago: University of Chicago Press, 1997.

Gordon, Linda. *Pitied But Not Entitled: Single Mothers and the History of Welfare, 1890-1935.* New York: Maxwell MacMillan International, 1994.

Hewitt, Nancy A. and Suzanne Lebsock, eds. *Visible Women: New Essays on American Activism.* Urbana: University of Illinois Press, 1993.

Knupfer, Anne Meis. *Toward a Tenderer Humanity and a Nobler Womanhood: African American Women's Clubs in Turn-of-the-Century Chicago.* New York: New York University Press, 1996.

Neverdon-Morton, Cynthia. *Afro-American Women of the South and the Advancement of the Race, 1895–1925.* Knoxville: University of Tennessee Press, 1989.

Scott, Anne Firor. *Natural Allies: Women's Associations in American History.* Urbana: University of Illinois Press, 1991.

Robyn Muncy is an associate professor of history at the University of Maryland. She is the author of Creating a Female Dominion in American Reform, 1880–1935 *(1991) and coauthor with Sonya Michel of* Engendering America: A Documentary History, 1865-The Present *(1999).*

Woodrow Wilson, Politician

The idealistic architect of a postwar world order that never came into being: such is the popular image of President Woodrow Wilson. What it omits is the savvy, sometimes ruthless politician whose achievements in the domestic sphere were equalled by only two other 20th-century presidents, Franklin Delano Roosevelt and Lyndon Baines Johnson. Robert Dallek here restores the whole man.

Robert Dallek

Robert Dallek is professor of history at the University of California, Los Angeles. He is the author of several books on political and diplomatic history, including Franklin D. Roosevelt and American Foreign Policy, 1932–1945 *(1979), which won a Bancroft Prize, and, most recently,* Lone Star Rising: Lyndon Johnson and His Times, 1908–1960 *(1991).*

Few presidents in American history elicit more mixed feelings than Woodrow Wilson. And why not? His life and career were full of contradictions that have puzzled historians for 70 years. A victim of childhood dyslexia, he became an avid reader, a skilled academic, and a popular writer and lecturer. A deeply religious man, who some described as "a Presbyterian priest" with a dour view of man's imperfectability, he devoted himself to secular designs promising the triumph of reason and harmony in domestic and world affairs. A rigid, self-exacting personality, whose uncompromising adherence to principles barred agreement on some of his most important political goals, he was a brilliant opportunist who won stunning electoral victories and led controversial laws through the New Jersey state legislature and the U.S. Congress. A southern conservative and elitist with a profound distrust of radical ideas and such populists as William Jennings Bryan, he became the Democratic Party's most effective advocate of advanced progressivism. A leading proponent of congressional influence, or what he called "Congressional Government," he ranks with Theodore Roosevelt, Franklin D. Roosevelt, Harry S. Truman, and Lyndon B. Johnson as the century's most aggressive chief executives. An avowed pacifist who declared himself "too proud to fight" and gained reelection in 1916 partly by reminding voters that he had "kept us out of war," he made military interventions in Latin America and Europe hallmarks of his two presidential terms.

There is no greater paradox in Wilson's life and career, however, than the fact that his worst failure has become the principal source of his historical reputation as a great American president. Administrative and legislative triumphs marked Wilson's service as president of Princeton, governor of New Jersey, and president of the United States. But most Americans who would concede Wilson a place in the front ranks of U.S. chief executives would be hard pressed to name many, if any, of these achievements. To them, he is best remembered as the president who preached self-determination and a new world order. (And not only to Americans: An upcoming Wilson biography by Dutch historian J. W. Schulte Nordholt is subtitled *A Life for World Peace.*) In the 1920s and '30s, when America rejected participation in the League of Nations and a political or military role in a world hellbent on another total war, Wilson's reputation reached a low point. He was a good man whom bankers and munitions makers had duped into entering World War I. He had also led America into the fighting out of the hopelessly naive belief that he could make the world safe for democracy and end all wars.

American involvement in World War II reversed Wilson's historical standing. Now feeling guilty about their isolationism and their rejection of his vision of a world at peace, Americans celebrated him as a spurned prophet whose wisdom and idealism deserved renewed acceptance in the 1940s. A new world league of self-governing nations practicing collective security for the sake of global stability and peace became the great

American hope during World War II. When the fighting's outcome proved to be the Soviet-American Cold War, Americans saw it as another setback for Wilson's grand design. Nevertheless, they did not lose faith in his ultimate wisdom, believing that democracy and the international rule of law would eventually have to replace tyranny and lawless aggression if the world were ever to achieve lasting peace.

Now, with America's triumph in the Cold War and the Soviet-American confrontation all but over, the country has renewed faith in a world order akin to what Woodrow Wilson proposed in 1918. The idea took on fresh meaning when President Bush led a coalition of U.N.-backed forces against Iraq's attack upon and absorption of Kuwait. The triumph of coalition arms seemed to vindicate Wilson's belief that collective action through a world body could reduce the likelihood and effectiveness of attacks by strong states against weaker ones and thus make international acts of aggression obsolete.

Yet present hopes for a new world order can plummet overnight—and with them Wilson's standing. If Wilson's reputation as a great president rests upon his vision of a new era in world affairs and the fulfillment of some part of that design in our lifetimes, his place in the forefront of U.S. presidents seems less than secure.

Will the ghost of Wilson be plagued forever by the vagaries of world politics? Only if we fail to give scrutiny to his full record. A careful reassessment of Wilson's political career, especially in domestic affairs, would go far to secure his place as a great American president who has much to tell us about the effective workings of democratic political systems everywhere.

For all his idealism and elitism, Wilson's greatest triumphs throughout his career rested on his brilliance as a democratic politician. He was the "great communicator" of his day—a professor who abandoned academic language and spoke in catch phrases that inspired mass support. He was also a master practitioner of the art of the possible, a leader with an impressive talent for reading the public mood and adjusting to it in order to advance his personal ambition and larger public goals. This is not to suggest that his career was an uninterpreted success. He had his share of spectacular failures. But some of these he converted into opportunities for further advance. And even his unmitigated failures had more to do with circumstances beyond his control than with flaws in his political judgment.

Wilson's early life gave little indication of a master politician in the making. Born in 1856 in Staunton, Virginia, the third of four children, he was the offspring of devout Scotch Presbyterian divines. Thomas Woodrow, his maternal grandfather, came from Scotland to the United States, where he ministered to congregations in small Ohio towns. Jesse Woodrow Wilson, Wilson's mother, was an intensely religious, austere Victorian lady with no sense of humor and a long history of psychosomatic ailments. Joseph Ruggles Wilson, Woodrow's father, was a brilliant theologian and leading light in the southern Presbyterian church, holding pulpits in Staunton, Virginia; Augusta, Georgia; Columbia, South Carolina; and Wilmington, North Carolina. Joseph Wilson enjoyed a reputation as an eloquent and powerful speaker whose "arresting rhetoric and cogent thought" made him one of the leading southern preachers and religious teachers of his time. Woodrow Wilson described his father as the "greatest teacher" he ever knew. Yet theological disputes and clashes with other strong-willed church leaders drove Joseph, who advocated various reforms, from one pulpit to another and left him with a sense of failure that clouded his life. One Wilson biographer notes that "by mid-career, Joseph Wilson was in some ways a broken man, struggling to overcome feelings of inferiority, trying to reconcile a God of love with the frustration of his ambition for success and prominence within the church." To compensate for his sense of defeat, Joseph invested his vaunting ambition in his son Woodrow, whom he hoped would become the "very great man" Joseph himself had wished to be.

Although Joseph imparted a love of literature and politics to his son, Bible readings, daily prayers, and Sunday worship services were centerpieces of Woodrow's early years. His father also taught him the transient character of human affairs and the superiority of religious to secular concerns. Joseph left little doubt in the boy's mind that he foresaw for him a career in the ministry as "one of the Church's rarest scholars . . . one of her most illustrious reformers . . . or one of her grandest orators." But Joseph's defeats in church politics in Woodrow's formative adolescent years soured father and son on Woodrow's entrance into the ministry.

Instead, Woodrow, with his father's blessing, invested his ambitions in a political career. As Richard Hofstadter wrote, "When young Tommy Wilson sat in the pew and heard his father bring the Word to the people, he was watching the model upon which his career was to be fashioned." Before college, he hung a portrait of British Prime Minister William Gladstone above his desk and declared: "That is Gladstone, the greatest statesman that ever lived. I intend to be a statesman, too." During his years as a Princeton undergraduate (1875–79), he rationalized his determination to enter politics by describing it as a divine vocation. A career as a statesman was an expression of Christian service, he believed, a use of power for the sake of principles or moral goals. Wilson saw the "key to success in politics" as "the pursuit of perfection through hard work and the fulfillment of ideals." Politics would allow him to spread spiritual enlightenment to the yearning masses.

Yet Wilson, as one of his later political associates said, was a man of high ideals and no principles, which was another way of saying that Wilson's ambition for self-serving political ends outran his commitment to any particular philosophy or set of goals. Like every great American politician since the rise of mass democracy in the 19th century, Wilson allowed the ends to justify the means. But Wilson never thought of himself as an opportunist. Rather, he considered himself a democrat responsive to the national mood and the country's most compelling needs. It is possible to scoff at Wilson's rationalization of his willingness to bend to current demands, but we do well to remember

15. Woodrow Wilson, Politician

that the country's greatest presidents have all been men of high ideals and no principles, self-serving altruists or selfish pragmatists with a talent for evoking the vision of America as the world's last best hope.

Wilson's path to high political office, like so much else in his life, ran an erratic course. Legal studies at the University of Virginia, self-instruction, and a brief law practice in Atlanta were meant to be a prelude to a political career. But being an attorney had little appeal to Wilson, and he decided to become a professor of politics instead. Consequently, in 1883, at the age of 27, he entered the Johns Hopkins University Graduate School, where he earned a Ph.D. for *Congressional Government* (1885). His book was an argument for a Congress more like the British Parliament, a deliberative body in which debate rather than contending interests shaped legislation. For 17 years, from 1885 to 1902, he taught at Bryn Mawr, Wesleyan, and Princeton, beginning at the last in 1890. By 1898 he had grown weary of what he derisively called his "talking profession," and during the next four years he shrewdly positioned himself to become the unanimous, first-ballot choice of Princeton's trustees as the university's president.

Wilson's eight years as president of Princeton (1902–1910) were a prelude to his later political triumphs and defeats. During the first three years of his Princeton term, Wilson carried off a series of dazzling reforms. Offended by the shallowness of much instruction at Princeton and animated by a desire to make it a special university like Oxford and Cambridge, where undergraduate education emphasized critical thinking rather than "the ideal of making a living," Wilson introduced a preceptorial system. It aimed at transforming Princeton "from a place where there are youngsters doing tasks to a place where there are men doing thinking, men who are conversing about the things of thought...." As a prerequisite to the preceptorial system, Wilson persuaded the faculty to reorganize the University's curriculum and its structure, creating 11 departments corresponding to subjects and requiring upperclassmen to concentrate their studies in one of them. Wilson's reforms, biographer Arthur S. Unk asserts, "mark him as an educational statesman of originality and breadth and strength." His achievement was also a demonstration of Wilson's political mastery—a case study in how to lead strong-minded, independent academics to accept a sea change in the life of a conservative university.

The fierce struggles and bitter defeats of Wilson's next five years are a measure of how difficult fundamental changes in higher education can be without the sort of astute political management Wilson initially used. Between 1906 and 1910 Wilson fought unsuccessfully to reorganize the social life of undergraduates and to determine the location and nature of a graduate college. In the first instance, Wilson tried to deemphasize the importance of campus eating clubs, which had become the focus of undergraduate life, and replace them with residential colleges, or quadrangles, where students would live under the supervision of unmarried faculty members residing in the colleges. Wilson viewed the clubs as undemocratic, anti-intellectual, and divisive, and the quadrangle plan as a sensible alternative that would advance the university's educational goals and national standing. Wilson assumed that he could put across his plan without the sort of consultation and preparation he had relied on to win approval for the preceptorial system. But his failure to consult alumni, faculty, and trustees was a major political error that led to his defeat. Likewise, he did not effectively marshal the support he needed to win backing for his graduate-school plan, and again it made his proposal vulnerable to criticism from opponents.

Physical and emotional problems caused by strokes in 1906 and 1907 may partly account for Wilson's defeats in the quadrangle and graduate-school fights. But whatever the explanation for his poor performance in these academic struggles, they were by no means without political benefit to Wilson. In fact, what seems most striking about these conflicts is the way Wilson converted them to his larger purposes of running

Reproduction from the Library of Congress

Among Wilson's progressive measures was the Underwood Tariff of 1914, the first downward revision of the tariff since the Civil War.

first for governor of New Jersey and then for president of the United States.

Colonel George Harvey, a conservative Democrat who owned a publishing empire that included the *New York World* and *Harper's Weekly,* proposed Wilson for the presidency as early as 1906. Although Wilson made appropriate disclaimers of any interest in seeking the White House, the suggestion aroused in him the longing for high political station that he had held for some 30 years. In response to Harvey's efforts, Wilson, who was already known nationally as a speaker on issues of higher education, began speaking out on economic and political questions before non-university audiences. His initial pronouncements were essentially conservative verities calculated to identify him with the anti-Bryan, anti-Populist wing of the Democratic Party. "The nomination of Mr. Wilson," one conservative editor wrote in 1906, "would be a good thing for the country as betokening a return of his party to historic party ideals and first principles, and a sobering up after the radical 'crazes.'" In 1907 Wilson prepared a "Credo" of his views, which, Arthur Unk says, could hardly have failed to please reactionaries, "for it was conservative to the core." It justified the necessity of great trusts and combinations as efficient instruments of modern business and celebrated individualism. In

1908 Wilson refused to support Bryan for president and rejected suggestions that he become his vice-presidential running mate.

During the next two years, however, Wilson shifted decidedly to the left. Mindful of the mounting progressive temper in the country—of the growing affinity of middle-class Americans for reforms that would limit the power of corporations and political machines—Wilson identified himself with what he called the "new morality," the need to eliminate fraud and corruption from, and to restore democracy and equality of opportunity to, the nation's economic and political life. His academic fights over the quadrangles and graduate school became struggles between special privilege and democracy. In a speech to Princeton's Pittsburgh alumni in the spring of 1910, Wilson attacked the nation's universities, churches, and political parties as serving the "classes" and neglecting the "masses." He declared his determination to democratize the colleges of the country and called for moral and spiritual regeneration. Incensed at his conservative Princeton opponents, who seemed the embodiment of the privileged interests, and eager to make himself a gubernatorial and then national candidate, Wilson invested idealism in the progressive crusade, leaving no doubt that he was ready to lead a movement that might redeem America.

New Jersey Democratic boss James Smith, Jr., seeing Wilson as a conservative opportunist whose rhetoric would appease progressives and whose actions would favor the corporations and the bosses, arranged Wilson's nomination for governor. Wilson seemed to play his part perfectly during the campaign, quietly accepting Smith's help even as he declared his independence from the party machine and espoused the progressive agenda—the direct primary, a corrupt-practices law, workmen's compensation, and a regulatory commission policing the railroads and public utilities. On election day Wilson swept to victory by a 50,000-vote margin, 233,933 to 184,573, and the Democrats gained control of the normally Republican Assembly. Once in the governor's chair, Wilson made clear that he would be his own man. He defeated Smith's bid for election to the U.S. Senate by the state legislature and skillfully assured the enactment of the four principal progressive measures. As he told a friend, "I kept the pressure of opinion constantly on the legislature, and the programme was carried out to its last detail. This with the senatorial business seems, in the minds of the people looking on, little less than a miracle in the light of what has been the history of reform hitherto in the State." As Wilson himself recognized, it was less a miracle than the product of constant pressure on the legislature at a time when "opinion was ripe on all these matters." Wilson's break with the machine and drive for reform reflected a genuine commitment to improving the lot of New Jersey's citizens. Most of all, they were a demonstration of how an ambitious politician in a democracy bends to the popular will for the sake of personal gain and simultaneously serves legitimate public needs.

Wilson's nomination for president by a deeply divided Democratic convention in the summer of 1912 was an extraordinary event in the history of the party and the nation. Wilson himself called it "a sort of political miracle." Although Wilson was the frontrunner in 1911 after speaking trips to every part of the nation, by May 1912 aggressive campaigns by Missouri's Champ Clark, speaker of the House of Representatives, and Alabama Representative Oscar W. Underwood made Wilson a decided underdog. When Clark won a majority of the delegates on the 10th ballot, it seemed certain that he would eventually get the two-thirds vote needed for the nomination. In every Democratic convention since 1844, a majority vote for a candidate had translated into the required two-thirds. But 1912 was different. Wilson won the nomination on the 46th ballot after his managers struck a bargain, which kept Underwood's 100-plus delegates from going to Clark. William Jennings Bryan gave Wilson essential progressive support, and the party's most powerful political bosses—the men who, in the words of one historian, had been Wilson's "bitterest antagonists and who represented the forces against which he had been struggling"—decided to back him.

Wilson's campaign for the presidency was another milestone in his evolution as a brilliant democratic politician. He entered the election without a clear-cut campaign theme. The tariff, which he initially focused on, inspired little popular response. In late August, however, after conferring with Louis D. Brandeis, Wilson found a constructive and highly popular campaign theme. Persuading Wilson that political democracy could only follow from economic democracy or diminished control by the country's giant business trusts, Brandeis sold him on the New Freedom—the idea that regulated competition would lead to the liberation of economic enterprise in the United States. This in turn would restore grassroots political power and control. Wilson accurately sensed that the country's mood was overwhelmingly favorable to progressive reform, especially the reduction of the economic power of the trusts. He also saw correctly that Theodore Roosevelt's plea for a New Nationalism—regulated monopoly and an expanded role for federal authority in the economic and social life of the nation—impressed most voters as too paternalistic and more a threat to than an expansion of freedom. As a result, Wilson won a plurality of the popular vote in the four-way contest of 1912, 42 percent to a combined 58 percent for William Howard Taft, TR, and socialist Eugene V. Debs. Wilson's victory in the electoral column was far more one-sided, 435 to 99 for TR and Taft. His victory was also a demonstration of his talents as a speaker who could satisfy the mass yearning for a new era in national affairs.

Wilson's election represented a triumph of democratic hopes. After nearly five decades of conservative rule by the country's business interests, the nation gave its backing to a reform leader promising an end to special privilege and the economic and political democratization of American life. "Nobody owns me," Wilson declared at the end of his campaign, signaling his readiness to act in behalf of the country's working and middle classes. Despite his own largely conservative background, his po-

15. Woodrow Wilson, Politician

litical agility and sensitivity to popular demands made it likely that he would not disappoint progressive goals.

His first presidential term represents one of the three notable periods of domestic reform in 20th-century America. What makes it particularly remarkable, notes historian John Milton Cooper, is that Wilson won his reforms without the national emergencies over the economy and civil rights that respectively confronted the country during the 1930s and the 1960s. Wilson, in other words, lacked "the peculiarly favorable political conditions" aiding Franklin Roosevelt and Lyndon Johnson.

Wilson's successful leadership rested on his effective management of his party and Congress. Following the advice of Texas Representative Albert S. Burleson, a superb politician who became postmaster general, Wilson filled his cabinet with "deserving" Democrats and allowed Burleson to use patronage "ruthlessly to compel adoption of administration measures." Despite Bryan's ignorance of foreign affairs, for example, his prominence persuaded Wilson to make him secretary of state. Wilson's readiness to set a bold legislative agenda found support from both a 73-member Democratic majority in the House and a decisive majority of Democratic and Republican progressives in the Senate. The 28th president quickly proved himself to be an able manipulator of Congress. Eager to create a sense of urgency about his legislative program and to establish a mood of cooperation between the two branches of government, Wilson called a special congressional session at the start of his term and then spoke to a joint meeting of both houses. Indeed, he was the first president to appear in person before Congress since John Adams. Presenting himself as a colleague rather than "a mere department of the Government hailing Congress from some isolated island of jealous power," Wilson returned repeatedly to Capitol Hill for conferences to advance his reform program.

In the 18 months between the spring of 1913 and the fall of 1914, Wilson pushed four key laws through the Congress. The Underwood Tariff of October 1914 was the first downward revision of the tariff since the Civil War; it was inspired more by a desire to reduce the cost of living for lower- and middle-class Americans than by any obligation to serve the interests of industrial giants. Wilson drove the bill through the upper house by exposing the lobbyists representing businesses that sought "to overcome the interests of the public for their private profit." Making the tariff law all the more remarkable was the inclusion of the first graduated income tax in U.S. history. Shortly thereafter, Wilson won passage of the most enduring domestic measure of his presidency, the reform of the country's banking and money system. Insisting on pubic, centralized control of banks and the money supply rather than a private, decentralized system, Wilson once again came before Congress to influence the outcome of this debate. The Federal Reserve Act of December 1913 combined elements of both plans, providing for a mix of private and public control. Although further reforms would occur later to make the Federal Reserve system a more effective instrument for dealing with national economic problems, the Wilson law of 1913 created the basic elements of the banking system that has existed for almost 80 years. During the next nine months, by keeping Congress in continuous session for an unprecedented year and a half, Wilson won passage of the Clayton Antitrust and Federal Trade Commission acts, contributing to the more effective regulation of big business and greater power for organized labor.

In November 1914, Wilson announced that his New Freedom program had been achieved and that the progressive movement was at an end. A man of fundamentally conservative impulses (which he believed reflected those of the nation at large), Wilson did not wish to overreach himself. His announcement bewildered advanced progressives, who had been unsuccessfully advocating a variety of social-justice measures Wilson considered too radical to support. Herbert Croly, the editor of the *New Republic,* charged that "any man of President Wilson's intellectual equipment who seriously asserts that the fundamental wrongs of a modern society can be easily and quickly righted as a consequence of a few laws... casts suspicion either upon his own sincerity or upon his grasp of the realities of modern social and industrial life." Similarly, Wilson's refusal to establish a National Race Commission and his active commitment to racial segregation in the federal government incensed African-American leaders who had viewed him as a likely supporter of progressive measures for blacks.

Though he did little to reverse course on helping blacks, Wilson stood ready to return to the progressive position for the sake of reelection in 1916. "I am sorry for any President of the United States who does not recognize every great movement in the Nation," Wilson declared in July 1916. "The minute he stops recognizing it, he has become a back number." The results of the congressional elections in 1914 convinced Wilson that the key to success in two years was a campaign attracting TR's Progressive backers to his standard. Consequently, in 1916, he elevated Louis D. Brandeis to the Supreme Court and signed seven additional reform bills into law. Among other things, these laws brought relief to farmers and workers and raised income and inheritance taxes on wealthy Americans. The election results in November vindicated his strategy. Wilson gained almost three million popular votes over his 1912 total and bested Charles Evans Hughes, who headed a reunited Republican party, by 23 electoral votes. On this count alone, Wilson's two consecutive victories as the head of a minority party mark him as one of the century's exceptional American politicians.

Why did Wilson's political astuteness desert him during his second term in his handling of the Versailles Treaty and the League of Nations? The answer is not naiveté about world politics, though Wilson himself believed "it would be the irony of fate if my administration had to deal chiefly with foreign affairs." In fact, the same mastery of Congress he displayed in converting so many significant reform bills into law between 1913 and 1916 was reflected in his creation of a national consensus in 1917 for American participation in the Great War.

At the start of the fighting in 1914, Wilson declared America neutral in thought and deed. And though Wilson himself had a decidedly pro-British bias, he understood that the country then was only mildly pro-Allied and wanted no part in the war. His policies initially reflected these feelings. Only as national sentiment changed in response to events in Europe and on the high seas, where German submarine violations of U.S. neutral rights drove Americans more decisively into the Allied camp, did Wilson see fit to prepare the country for and then lead it into the war. His prewar leadership became something of a model for Franklin Roosevelt in 1939–41 as he maneuvered to maintain a national majority behind his responses to World War II.

Wilson's failure in 1919–20, or, more precisely, the collapse of his political influence in dealing with the peacemaking at the end of the war, consisted of a number of things—most of them beyond his control. His Fourteen Points, his formula for making the world safe for democracy and ending all wars, was beyond the capacity of any political leader to achieve, then and now. Yet there is every reason to believe that Wilson enunciated his peace aims assuming that he would have to accept compromise agreements on many of his goals, as indeed he did in the Versailles negotiations. A number of these compromises on the Fourteen Points went beyond what he hoped to concede, but he recognized that the conclusion of the fighting had stripped him of much of his hold over America's allies and limited his capacity to bend the strong-minded French, British, and Italian leaders to his will or to influence the radical revolutionary regime in Russia. Events were moving too fast in Europe and all over the globe for him to make the world approximate the postwar peace arrangements he had enunciated in 1918.

Faced by such circumstances, Wilson accepted the proposition that a League of Nations, including the United States, would be the world's best hope for a stable peace. Wilson's prime objective after the Versailles conference was to assure American participation in the new world body. But the political cards were stacked against him. After six years of Democratic rule and a growing conviction in Republican Party circles that the Democrats would be vulnerable in 1920, Senate Republicans made approval of the Versailles Treaty and American participation in the League partisan issues which could redound to their benefit. Moreover, between 1918 and 1920, Wilson's deteriorating health, particularly a major stroke in the fall of 1919, intensified a propensity for self-righteousness and made him uncharacteristically rigid in dealing with a political issue that cried out for flexibility and accommodation. As Edwin A. Weinstein has persuasively argued in his medical and psychological biography of Wilson, "the cerebral dysfunction which resulted from Wilson's devastating strokes prevented the ratification of the Treaty. It is almost certain that had Wilson not been so afflicted, his political skills and facility with language would have bridged the gap between [opposing Senate] resolutions, much as he had reconciled opposing views of the Federal Reserve bill ... or had accepted the modifications of the Treaty suggested in February, 1919."

Wilson's political failure in 1919–20 was a striking exception in a career marked by a substantial number of political victories. His defeat and its consequences were so stunning that they have eclipsed the record of prior achievements and partly obscured Wilson's contributions to American history.

But it is not only the disaster of 1919–20 that is responsible. Mainstream academia today dismisses political history and particularly the study of powerful leaders as distinctly secondary in importance to impersonal social forces in explaining historical change. What seems lost from view nowadays is just how essential strong and skillful political leadership remains in bringing a democracy to accept major reforms. Wilson is an excellent case in point. For all the public's receptivity to progressivism in the first two decades of the century, it took a leader of exceptional political skill to bring warring reform factions together in a coalition that could enact a liberal agenda. By contrast, Wilson's physical incapacity in 1919 assured the defeat of American participation in a world league for 25 years. This is not to say that an American presence in an international body would have dramatically altered the course of world affairs after 1920, but it might have made a difference, and the collapse of Wilson's leadership was the single most important factor in keeping the United States on the sidelines.

Did social and economic and a host of other factors influence the course of U.S. history during Wilson's time? Without a doubt. But a leader of vision and varied abilities—not all of them purely admirable—was needed to seize the opportunities provided by history and make them realities. To forget the boldness of Wilson's leadership, and the importance of political leaders generally, is to embrace a narrow vision of this nation's past—and of its future.

Margaret Sanger

Her crusade to legalize birth control spurred the movement for women's liberation

By Gloria Steinem

"The movement she started will grow to be, a hundred years from now, the most influential of all time," predicted futurist and historian H. G. Wells in 1931. "When the history of our civilization is written, it will be a biological history, and Margaret Sanger will be its heroine."

Though this prophecy of nearly 70 years ago credited one woman with the power that actually came from a wide and deep movement of women, no one person deserves it more. Now that reproductive freedom is becoming accepted and conservative groups are fighting to maintain control over women's bodies as the means of reproduction, Sanger's revolution may be even more controversial than during her 50-year career of national and international battles. Her experience can teach us many lessons.

She taught us, first, to look at the world as if women mattered. Born into an Irish working-class family, Margaret witnessed her mother's slow death, worn out after 18 pregnancies and 11 live births. While working as a practical nurse and midwife in the poorest neighborhoods of New York City in the years before World War I, she saw women deprived of their health, sexuality and ability to care for children already born. Contraceptive information was so suppressed by clergy-influenced, physician-accepted laws that it was a criminal offense to send it through the mail. Yet the educated had access to such information and could use subterfuge to buy "French" products, which were really condoms and other barrier methods, and "feminine hygiene" products, which were really spermicides.

It was this injustice that inspired Sanger to defy church and state. In a series of articles called "What Every Girl Should Know," then in her own newspaper *The Woman Rebel* and finally through neighborhood clinics that dispensed woman-controlled forms of birth control (a phrase she coined), Sanger put information and power into the hands of women.

While in Europe for a year to avoid severe criminal penalties, partly due to her political radicalism, partly for violating postal obscenity laws, she learned more about contraception, the politics of sexuality and the commonality of women's experience. Her case was dismissed after her return to the States. Sanger continued to push legal and social boundaries by initiating sex counseling, founding the American Birth Control League (which became, in 1942, the Planned Parenthood Federation of America) and organizing the first international population conference. Eventually her work would extend as far as Japan and India, where organizations she helped start still flourish.

Sanger was past 80 when she saw the first marketing of a contraceptive pill, which she had helped develop. But legal change was slow. It took until 1965, a year before her death, for the Supreme Court to strike down a Connecticut law that prohibited the use of contraception, even by married couples. Extended to unmarried couples only in 1972, this constitutionally guaranteed right to pri-

BORN Sept. 14, 1879, in Corning, N.Y.
1914 Launches The Women Rebel, a feminist monthly that advocates birth control; is indicted for inciting violence and promoting obscenity
1916 Opens the U.S.'s first family-planning clinic, in Brooklyn, N.Y.; is later jailed for 30 days
1921 Founds the American Birth Control League, the presursor to the Planned Parenthood Federation
DIED Sept. 6, 1966, in Tucson, Ariz.

Facing trial in 1916 for violating obscenity laws

> *"She made people accept that women had the right to control their own destinies."*
> Grandson ALEXANDER SANGER, head of Planned Parenthood of New York City

vacy would become as important to women's equality as the vote. In 1973 the right to privacy was extended to the abortion decision of a woman and her physician, thus making abortion a safe and legal alternative—unlike the $5 illegal butcheries of Sanger's day.

One can imagine Sanger's response to the current anti-choice lobby and congressional leadership that opposes abortion, sex education in schools, and federally funded contraceptive programs that would make abortion less necessary; that supports ownership of young women's bodies through parental-consent laws; that limits poor women's choices by denying Medicaid funding; and that holds hostage the entire U.S. billion-dollar debt to the United Nations in the hope of attaching an antiabortion rider. As in her day, the question seems to be less about what gets decided than who has the power to make the decision.

One can also imagine her response to pro-life rhetoric being used to justify an average of one clinic bombing or arson per month—sometimes the same clinics Sanger helped found—and the murder of six clinic staff members, the attempted murder of 15 others, and assault and battery against 104 more. In each case, the justification is that potential fetal life is more important than a living woman's health or freedom.

What are mistakes in our era that parallel those of Sanger's? There is still an effort to distort her goal of giving women control over their bodies by attributing such quotes to Sanger as "More children from the fit, less from the unfit—that is the chief issue of birth control." Sanger didn't say those words; in fact, she condemned them as a eugenicist argument for "cradle competition." To her, poor mental development was largely the result of poverty, overpopulation and the lack of attention to children. She correctly foresaw racism as the nation's major challenge, conducted surveys that countered stereotypes regarding the black community and birth control, and established clinics in the rural South with the help of such African-American leaders as W. E. B. Du Bois and Mary McLeod Bethune.

Nonetheless, expediency caused Sanger to distance herself from her radical past; for instance, she used soft phrases such as "family planning" instead of her original, more pointed argument that the poor were being manipulated into producing an endless supply of cheap labor. She also adopted the mainstream eugenics language of the day, partly as a tactic, since many eugenicists opposed birth control on the grounds that the educated would use it more. Though her own work was directed toward voluntary birth control and public health programs, her use of eugenics language probably helped justify sterilization abuse. Her misjudgments should cause us to wonder what parallel errors we are making now and to question any tactics that fail to embody the ends we hope to achieve.

Sanger led by example. Her brave and joyous life included fulfilling work, three children, two husbands, many lovers and an international network of friends and colleagues. She was charismatic and sometimes quixotic, but she never abandoned her focus on women's freedom and its larger implications for social justice (an inspiration that continues through Ellen Chesler's excellent biography, *Woman of Valor: Margaret Sanger and the Birth Control Movement in America*). Indeed, she lived as if she and everyone else had the right to control her or his own life. By word and deed, she pioneered the most radical, humane and transforming political movement of the century.

Gloria Steinem is a co-founder of Ms. *magazine and author of* Revolution from Within

Unearthing a Riot

After nearly 80 years of trying to forget a civic tragedy that left as many as 300 residents dead, Tulsa, Okla., is now being forced to confront the city's racist past.

By Brent Staples

Tulsa grew explosively between 1910 and 1920, built by the oil families who have dominated business, politics and cultural life right up to the present. Downtown Tulsa has changed so little in the last half-century that a traveler who returned after 50 years would find it familiar. But since 1997, Tulsans who thought they knew the city well have been startled to learn of a 1921 riot in which hundreds of people were shot, burned alive or tied to cars and dragged to death. These grim facts have been churned up by the Tulsa Race Riot Commission, created by the Oklahoma Legislature two years ago to investigate the country's bloodiest civil disturbance of the century. The commission report, due on Gov. Frank Keating's desk early next year, will attempt to fix a death toll, provide an estimate of property damage and explain what caused the disturbance in the first place. But the most controversial mission is to determine whether or not the state should pay reparations either to the black district of Greenwood or to individual survivors. The issue has spawned a contentious dispute in the city as a whole—and reopened interest in the race wars that swept the country early in this century, when whites and African-Americans engaged in armed combat in the streets.

The race war in Tulsa involved thousands of whites who destroyed most of the 35 square blocks of Greenwood, including its affluent business district, known locally as the Negro Wall Street, in riots that left as many as 300 dead. But the nightmare was soon banished from newspapers, textbooks and civil conversation, so that most Tulsans born just 20 years later grew up with no idea that it had ever happened. Older Tulsans, quiet for decades, have been talking nonstop since The Tulsa World ran a series of articles on the commission earlier this year, inviting people to call the Tulsa Historical Society with their stories. Nearly 150 people have called so far. An employee at the historical society itself tells of an aging black man who shot an unarmed white man during the riot and still cries every time he passes the spot. A nurse tells of a white man who confessed on his deathbed that he had killed many blacks during the riot and buried them near the railroad tracks—and would do it again if he had to.

The commission has located more than 50 black survivors of the riot and has begun to videotape their testimony. Among the survivors who still live in Tulsa is Kinney Booker, 86, who was 8 at the time and relates on one of the videotapes how he listened from a hiding place in the attic as white men called his father "nigger" and took him away at gunpoint: He said, 'Please don't set my house on fire.' Soon as he left, they set our house on fire and we were up in the attic.... Five kids.... [We] were able to get out without injury but bullets were zinging around there.... But when we got down, the telephone poles were burned and falling and my poor sister who was two years younger than I am [said], 'Kinney, is the world on fire?' I said, 'I don't think so, but we are in deep trouble.'"

People who have called the historical society focus mainly on corpses. Corpses stacked like cordwood on street corners, photographed for keepsakes. Corpses piled in the backs of wagons, dump trucks and along railroad sidings. Corpses buried in an underground tunnel downtown, where one caller said 123 blacks had been clubbed to death. Corpses left to rot for days in a park under the blistering Oklahoma sun. Corpses dumped in the Arkansas River and allowed to float away.

Tips have led commission investigators to three sites within the city that they suspect to be mass graves containing the riot dead, though given the way the bodies seem to have been scattered, all of them will never be found.

THE MAN WHO BROUGHT THE RIOT back to life is state representative Don Ross, who has served the Greenwood district in the Legislature for 17 years and wrote the riot commission resolution that became law in 1997. Ross has lived with the riot for more than 40 years, and since he became a senior member of the Legislature, has forced Tulsa and Oklahoma to live it with him. As a young magazine editor in 1971, Ross ran an article exposing the carnage in Greenwood that has been widely credited for breaking a 50-year conspiracy of silence. As a community gadfly in the late 70's, he helped fight to preserve the few historic buildings that remained after Greenwood had been almost completely changed by middle-class flight, urban renewal and highway construction. He was elected to the Legislature in 1982 on the basis of his civil rights activism and has since made the riot a top issue—helping to secure money in 1995 for the Greenwood Cultural Center, which contains a permanent photo exhibit of the destruction, and working to get a black granite memorial to the Negro Wall Street, which was built in 1996.

Ross is a skillful legislator. He knew in the beginning that a bill requiring the state to pay reparations would be dead on arrival. Even so, the initial bill obligated the state to pay $5 million—but mainly as a tactic. When the Legislature balked, Ross, a Democrat, allowed the provision to be stripped away, but language calling for a study of the history of the riot remained. The bill passed both houses, partly because many legislators were ignorant of the riot.

The case has attracted considerable interest from legal scholars like Alfred L. Brophy, a law professor at Oklahoma City University, who read about the case in the newspapers and volunteered to serve as the commission's legal counsel. Brophy has a keen interest in civil rights issues that predate contemporary civil rights law. He compares the Greenwood case to that of the Japanese-Americans who had property confiscated and were placed in internment camps during World War II, and then waited nearly 50 years before receiving an official apology from Ronald Reagan, in 1988, along with $1.65 billion in compensation from the federal government. What links Greenwood and the Japanese-Americans, Brophy says, is the fact that the government permitted the harm that was committed in both cases.

The case that Greenwood most resembles is that of Rosewood, Fla., a black enclave in the central part of the state that was wiped out by an invading force of whites in 1923. Told that reparations were "a moral obligation," the Florida Legislature voted in 1994 to, among other things, make reparations through a college scholarship fund for Rosewood descendants. In Florida, the government admitted that it knew of the impending disaster and failed to protect the town. But in Tulsa, the city "made the riot worse," Brophy argues, by deputizing a lynch mob. In an analysis of the case, Brophy writes that the city "clothed private citizens with the authority to arrest, almost surely instructed them to kill and quite likely instructed them to burn Greenwood." Brophy thinks Tulsa would "find some money" to pay survivors if a trial appeared imminent. In November, the riot commission's reparations committee suggested a settlement of at least $33 million, including a scholarship fund for black Tulsans and additional payments of up to $150,000 each for survivors whose families lost assets in 1921.

DON ROSS, 58, SHOULD BE CONtented now that his life's work has been vindicated. But the day I visited him at his yellow ranch house in a subdivision not far from Greenwood, I realized that the word "contented" may never apply to him. Ross seems permanently enraged by the rape of what he calls "my community." The kitchen table, the breakfast counter and his office were awash in manila envelopes and file folders containing photocopies of Tulsa city records from the 20's and newspaper clippings from The Chicago Defender, The Kansas City Call, The New York Age, The Pittsburgh Courier and several other Negro-press newspapers that covered the riot's aftermath critically, while The Tulsa Tribune swallowed whole the "official story."

"See?" Ross says, pointing to the minutes of the Tulsa City Commission in 1921. "This is where the city paid off whites who lost property in the riot and disallowed claims by blacks. This is where the city promised a fund to rebuild the community, but the fund was never created and the money was never paid!" Flipping pages, he continues. "See this! The mayor and the city commission plotted in open session—open session!—to steal black land so that the 'colored section' could be pushed farther north. It's right there, in black and white." During lulls in the conversation, Ross sat silently dreaming into the middle distance. But when he spoke of the riot, he was animated and fiery.

The Greenwood business district today consists of a one-block stretch of historic structures built after the riots that were saved from the wrecking ball during urban renewal. This museum block is surrounded by expanses of empty space, the exposed foundations of long-gone houses and ghostly driveways that start at the curb and disappear into the grass.

But the Greenwood Avenue in Ross's mental landscape is a densely built street that runs for more than a mile, a street crowded with hotels, bars, jazz joints, barbershops and poolrooms, with the premier addresses occupied by doctors, dentists and lawyers. When Ross rides these streets in his red Lincoln Town Car, he sees not just empty fields, but shades of the community as it was on the eve of the riot.

Greenwood came into being out of necessity, when black people were forbidden by law to live or own businesses in the white city—and were expected to be off the white city streets by sundown. By the eve of the riot in 1921, the black city within a city included as many as 15,000 people and supported 191 businesses, including 15 doctors, 2 dentists, one chiropractor and three law offices.

With a larger black land-owning class, Oklahoma had about 45 black municipalities—more by far than any state in the union—and was known as "the promised land," a veritable capital of black economic independence. At the beginning of the Negro Wall Street, at 102 North Greenwood Avenue, was the three-story Williams Building, the first of several properties owned by John Williams and his wife, Loula, who began their enterprises with an auto-repair business, then built a movie house, the Williams Dreamland Theater, as well as other holdings. A few doors down was the soon-to-be-famous attorney B.C. Franklin, who, like many others, went by his first initials only to prevent white folks from getting overly familiar and calling him by his first name. B.C.'s 6-year-old son, John Hope Franklin, told everyone within hearing range that he planned to be the first Negro president of the United States, but grew up to become one of the most respected historians of his era. At No. 112 lived Emma and O.W. Gurley, rich developers who built much of the black district and estimated their holdings at more than $1 million in 1921. At No. 126 stood The Tulsa Star, whose owner and publisher, A.J. Smitherman, campaigned vigorously against lynching while the white-owned Tulsa Tribune tacitly endorsed it.

Down at No. 301 stood the 65-room Stradford Hotel, the jewel of Greenwood Avenue, built by J.B. Stradford, who had come to the area in 1899 with degrees from both Oberlin and Indiana Law School. Farther along, in a less prestigious block at No. 503, were the offices of A.C. Jackson, who was described by the Mayo brothers, the founders of the Mayo Clinic, as "the most able Negro surgeon in America."

White Tulsans especially hated Stradford and Smitherman. Stradford had already sued a railroad for confining him to the Jim Crow car even though he purchased a first-class ticket. He had once beaten a white deliveryman nearly to death for a racist remark. The pistol-packing Smitherman was similarly volatile. Three years before the riot, he led an armed group of black farmers to prevent the lynching of a black prisoner in nearby Bristow. He was also brazen enough to write about them in his paper, The Star. The white hatred of these "uppity" Negroes was intensified by the city's desire for their land. Hemmed in by the river on the south and Greenwood on the north, Tulsa was burgeoning with nowhere to grow.

The tensions in Tulsa were part of a national pattern during the teens and 20's, when city after city exploded in the worst racial conflicts that the country would ever see. Fear of black independence and self-determination took a Freudian form: rape hysteria. In one town after another, racial violence was sparked by rumors that a Negro had harmed a white woman. This happened in Washington; Omaha, Neb.; Kansas City, Kan.; Knoxville, Tenn.; Longview, Tex.; and Rosewood, Fla.

RAPE HYSTERIA TOUCHED DOWN in Tulsa on the morning of Monday, May 30, at the Drexel Building on Main Street. The protagonists were a Negro shoe-shiner named Dick Rowland and a white elevator operator named Sarah Page. The Drexel Building was the only one in the vicinity that allowed Rowland and his co-workers to use its bathrooms. That morning, Rowland rode up with Page, used the bathroom and came down again as he did almost every day. When the elevator car reached the lobby, people allegedly heard Page scream and saw Rowland run from the scene. No Negro in his right mind, of course, would attack a random white woman in a public elevator, in a public building, at the height of rush hour in the busiest city in the state. Later, Rowland was acquitted when Page refused to press charges. Articles in the Negro press maintained that Rowland and Page were romantically involved.

But all that was yet to come when Rowland was arrested and taken to a jail cell atop the Tulsa County Courthouse. The Tribune had been raging for weeks against Greenwood—which it regularly called "Niggertown" and blamed for all of the city's vice and troubles. Seizing on the Rowland affair, the editors published a front-page article and an editorial that bore the headline "To Lynch Negro Tonight," essentially encouraging a lynching. (Both articles were removed from the paper's archives and presumably destroyed before The Tribune went to microfilm. The riot commission continues to search for clippings or copies.) On the evening of May 31, a white mob showed up at the courthouse in search of Rowland. As though on cue, a group of black men marched in from Greenwood to protect Rowland. The two camps exchanged words, then shots, and several men fell dead. Outgunned, the black force retreated north, across the railroad tracks into Greenwood.

Back downtown, the destruction of Greenwood was all but assured when the Tulsa police deputized perhaps hundreds from the lynch mob and, according to court records from the time, instructed them to, in effect, "go out and kill you some damn niggers."

The mob moved to the tracks that separated white Tulsa from Greenwood and began to close in on Greenwood Avenue. During the initial hours, snipers held off the white invaders from the windows overlooking the tracks. But the skirmishing continued through the night, and at dawn the snipers fell back in the face of ever-growing numbers.

Otis Clark, now 96, was eager to defend Greenwood that morning. Clark, then 18, went toward the gunfire and arrived at the Jackson Funeral Home just off Greenwood Avenue, where other blacks had gathered. White snipers had climbed into the old mill across the tracks, which offered an unobstructed view of the funeral home and its garage, where Clark says an ambulance was parked. "While [the driver] was trying to unlock the door to get the ambulance," Clark recalls, "they shot out of that mill and hit the boy on the hand while he was unlocking the door, and blood shot out his hand... and he dropped the keys and whatnot and we ran back to the back part of the funeral home by the dead folks."

Perhaps as many as 10,000 whites surged across the tracks into Greenwood. The commission has found the daughter of a waitress who recalled running into the street to sweep up a child being fired on from a passing airplane. A woman named Mary E. Jones Parrish mentions the plane strafings and the machine-gun fire in her memoir "Events of the Tulsa Disaster," published soon after the event: "There was a great shadow in the sky and, upon a second look, we discerned that this cloud was caused by fast-approaching aeroplanes.... The enemy had organized in the night and was invading our district, the same as the Germans invaded France and Belgium." Parrish watched for a long time, frozen with fear, but eventually swept up her young daughter and ran through machine-gun fire to safety. The oral tradition of Greenwood had many variations on this theme. Yet another mother is said to have strapped her baby to her back and escaped Greenwood by crawling through the storm drains.

As the morning wore on, a wall of fire worked its way across Greenwood, destroying everything in its path. The mob burst into one house after another, sometimes killing the occupants outright, often looting the house and setting it afire from within, in the manner of the pogroms that were carried out against the Jews in Eastern Europe.

Among those who survived is 83-year-old George Monroe, a black survivor located by the riot commission. Monroe was 5 at the time and at home with his mother and three siblings. "We saw coming up the walk in front of the house four men with torches in their hands," he told the riot commission. "These torches were burning. When my mother saw them coming, she says, 'You get up under the bed, get up under the bed.' ... All four of us got up under the bed. I was the last one and my sister grabbed me and pulled me under there, and while I was under the bed, one of the guys coming past the bed stepped on my finger and I was about to scream. My sister put her hand over my mouth so I couldn't be heard.... [The men] set the curtains on fire, and as a result that's how our house started to burning."

The most traumatic story comes from Elwood Lett, who died recently at the age of 82. Five white men came to his family's house but surprised them by allowing the grandfather to place his daughter and two grandchildren into a wagon so that they could leave town. "I was happy to know they didn't shoot him or kill him there at the house," Lett recalled. "He's thinking, 'They're pretty nice people by letting us get in the wagon and go on about our business.' ... We hadn't got to the town of Sperry before this white guy asked, 'Where in the hell you going?'—using the 'N' word. My grandfather said, 'We're heading out, we're going out of town.' And he said, 'Not this day you're not going out of town.' Bam! ... And he just tumbled. My mother let out a scream: 'Oh, you have killed my father, you've killed him,' and I thought he was going to do the same thing to my mother."

As the burning continued unabated, deputies who had been called to defend some of the finest houses in Greenwood—houses owned by Smitherman, A.C. Jackson and others—doused the properties with kerosene and watched them burn. By the time the Oklahoma National Guard marched into Greenwood, in the late morning of June 1, virtually all of black Tulsa had gone up in smoke and ash. About 1,200 buildings were burned or looted or both. For months afterward, black Tulsans would encounter white people on the streets wearing familiar clothing and jewelry looted from black homes.

The dead fell so thick in the streets that the National Guard was diverted from quelling the disturbance by the task of piling corpses onto wagons and trucks. The city fathers played down the horror and placed the death toll at an implausible 35. But based on new interviews and newly discovered records, the riot commission's historian, Scott Ellsworth, is convinced that as many as 300 were killed, about 90 percent of them black.

Greenwood was physically wiped out. But in the long run, the loss of leadership and spiritual vitality proved more devastating. Stradford and Smitherman were unfairly indicted for the riot and fled the city. Jackson, the surgeon, was shot while trying to surrender and bled to death. Gurley, the developer, went missing soon after the riot.

Its offices razed by fire, Franklin's law firm set up in a tent overlooking the tracks and prepared for the legal onslaught that was soon to come. The city told the outside world that it would provide a generous rebuilding fund—and actively discouraged money-raising efforts that had begun all across the country. But the city fund never materialized. In fact, the mayor and the city commission did everything they could to ensure that Greenwood was never rebuilt. The ashes were scarcely cooled before the city passed an ordinance that forbade the building of anything but "fireproof" structures—a law, expensive to comply with, that would have kept Greenwood a vacant lot had not Franklin and his colleagues defeated the ordinance in court. Black Tulsans filed a total of nearly 200 damage claims, but the insurance companies declined to pay any of them because of a riot-exclusion clause in the policies, and the city refused any claims as well.

In the years after the riot, survivors in Greenwood bragged that they had "won" the shooting war, killing more white people than the white community or The Tulsa Tribune cared to admit. But the shouts of victory faded as survivors grew older and more vulnerable. Fearful that speaking evil would summon it to life, most black Tulsans banned the riot from conversation and no longer spoke of it to young people and newcomers. As Ross put it years later, "Black folks lived with the fear that the whites who had come once might come again."

THE CONSPIRACY OF SILENCE WAS locked down tight by the time Ross was born in Greenwood in 1941. He was 15 and a sophomore at Greenwood's Booker T. Washington High School before he learned how the streets that seemed so lively and substantial to him had once been burned to the ground. The news came from a teacher, W.D. Williams, who had watched the early stages of the invasion from his family's apartment on Greenwood Avenue—and seen his family's real estate holdings reduced to ruins.

When Williams revealed this in class, Ross leapt to his feet. "I thought he was lying," Ross recalls "I challenged him almost with my finger in his face—something that got you kicked out of school in those days. I thought my community was a proud community that would never have let whites get away with burning us down." But Williams settled the matter with a collection of photographs showing scenes from the riot, including corpses with arms and legs burned away and wicker coffins stacked on the backs of trucks, being borne away to anonymous graves.

Anger at this discovery became the driving force of Ross's life. In his quest to understand and expose the riot, he dragged the city as a whole along with him. This history propelled him into journalism, where, in 1971, he joined with some friends to create a magazine in Tulsa. On the 50th anniversary of the riot, the editors of the magazine, Oklahoma Impact, were casting about for something spectacular when an article called "Profile of a Race Riot" came across his desk. A young white editor named Larry Silvey had assigned it for Tulsa, the Chamber of Commerce magazine, and was about to send it to press when officials at the chamber killed it. Silvey's bosses at the chamber argued that the article was "possibly inflammatory." But Silvey has other suspicions. "I didn't think about this back then," he said recently, "but the men who controlled the Chamber of Commerce were in their 70's in 1971. Which meant that they had been in their 20's during the riot." Given that thousands of young men in the city were in the streets at the time, Silvey said, "it is likely that these men had something to hide."

The article was written by a white amateur historian and radio host, Ed Wheeler, who had learned a great deal about Oklahoma history for his popular radio show, which dramatized historical events—including episodes based on African-American history. Black Tulsans agreed to meet him and discuss the riot—but only at night, in their churches, accompanied by their ministers.

On the white side of town, Wheeler had gotten interviews with people who had a great deal to hide. Among them were several former Ku Klux Klansmen, whom Wheeler had tracked through grandsons and great-nephews he knew from his weekend training with the Oklahoma National Guard. The K.K.K. had essentially acted as an execution squad and had crisscrossed the burning streets for the express purpose of murdering black men.

When it became known that Wheeler was moving forward with the article, he began to be harassed by telephone, both at home and at work. One afternoon in downtown Tulsa, a man in overalls tapped Wheeler on the shoulder, whispered, "You'll be sorry if you publish that story," and walked away. In the spring of 1971, his article nearly finished, Wheeler discovered a message scrawled in soap across the windshield of his blue Ford sedan: "Best Look Under Your Hood From Now On."

AFTER TULSA MAGAZINE REjected the article, wheeler took "Profile of a Race Riot" to The Tulsa World, where an editor told him that the paper would not touch the article with "an 11-foot pole." This was not surprising since the article trashed The World's sister paper, The Tribune, for the inflammatory articles that had stoked up the lynch mob in the first place. Once competitors, The World and The Tribune had since become business partners.

Shut out of white Tulsa, Wheeler's article found its way across the tracks and into Greenwood—and into the hands of Ross. The issue of his magazine, Oklahoma Impact, with "Profile of a Race Riot" on the cover, sold out in Greenwood and was largely ignored on the white side of the tracks, at least publicly.

Between the two of them, Don Ross and Ed Wheeler cracked the wall of silence and made it possible to speak openly about the riot for the first time in 50 years. But Ross and Wheeler take opposite sides of the reparations issue, chilling what was once a warm relationship. Wheeler is opposed to reparations and believes that modern-day Tulsans are not responsible for the sins of their fathers. Ross, of course, believes that reparation is the one and only issue, and will think so until the day he dies.

Brent Staples writes editorials on politics and culture for The Times and is the author of the memoir "Parallel Time: Growing Up in Black and White."

Article 18

Scandal in the Oval Office

A tale of sex, spies, snitches and suicides has an oddly familiar ring

By Carl Sferrazza Anthony
Special to The Washington Post

Fearing revelations about his illicit affair with a young campaign volunteer—which included sex in an Oval Office hideaway while under the guard of Secret Service agents—the president realized that stonewalling was ultimately futile. He stunned a private party of reporters at the National Press Club by confessing his carnal desires.

"It's a good thing I am not a woman," the president said. "I would always be pregnant. I can't say no."

In this administration, the scandals never seemed to end. There was the strange suicide of an administration official, made even more mysterious by a note that disappeared. Then came an investigation into payoffs and coverups connected to a notorious land deal. The president's friends launched smear campaigns against his perceived foes. Dossiers were compiled; private eyes and snitches deployed. Affidavits were drafted in which various women denied liaisons with the president. Jobs were arranged to keep people quiet

Through it all, a steel-willed first lady kept the press at bay and did whatever was necessary to defend her husband's reputation—even if it meant destroying evidence.

The scandals erupted at a time when technological advances in communication were feeding a nation hungry for distraction, and the economy was booming. Sex sold—and the ravenous press corps was all too happy to name names and offer seamy details. The president and his wife boosted their public image by bringing Hollywood stars to the White House; they knew the value of glamour and the power of celebrity. It also helped that he was a genial populist and inveterate shaker of hands, fond of golf and cards, a man of the people.

Ladies thought him virile and handsome; he photographed well.

For some reason, all of this seems familiar. Whatever else may be said of Warren Gamaliel Harding—whose tenure as 29th president ended with his peculiar, premature death in 1923—he was a truly modern politician. His administration, which reeked of corruption, offers a prototype for Washington scandals. Whitewater, Iran-contra and Watergate are better known today, but the granddaddy of them all was Teapot Dome, a political maelstrom that broke 75 years ago this month and is still hard to top in terms of sheer outrageousness.

Harding, a small-town Ohio newspaper publisher, was uniquely unsuited for the job of president—and he knew it. "I am not fit for this office and never should have been here," he once said. But he "looked like a president," as one major backer put it, and his wife, Florence, was instrumental in shepherding his political career. (The press considered Florence, known as the Duchess, to be the power behind the throne; one cartoon depicted the couple as "The Chief Executive and Mr. Harding.") Harding, a one-term Republican senator, won the job by promising Americans a "return to normalcy" after World War I.

Though his legacy was soiled, his domestic achievements were substantial: the 40-hour work week, improved health care for new mothers, the first balanced-budget bureau, a focus on technology. And we have to give Harding credit for establishing a venerable institution: the Washington gossip mill. Based on new documentation, here's a reprise of the Harding era.

*I love your back, I love your breasts
Darling to feel, where my face rests,
I love your skin, so soft and white,
So dear to feel and sweet to bite.
I love your poise of perfect thighs,
When they hold me in paradise....*

—A Harding poem to one of his mistresses, Carrie Phillips

No president had more "women scrapes," as his attorney general put it, than Warren G. His first affair, three years into his marriage to Florence, was with Susie Hodder—his wife's best friend from childhood—resulting in the birth of a daughter. His second affair was with Florence's closest adult friend, Carrie Fulton Phillips. It lasted 15 years.

From the *Washington Post National Weekly Edition,* June 15, 1998, pp. 6-7. © 1998 by The Washington Post Writers Group. Reprinted by permission.

18. Scandal in the Oval Office

His third enduring mistress was his Senate aide, Grace Cross.

Number four was the most infamous and the first presidential mistress to write a memoir: In the large Oval Office closet, the president had at least one tryst with Nan Britton, a campaign volunteer who had started having sex with Harding when he was 51 and she was 22. Their assignations, facilitated by Secret Service agents James Sloan and Walter Ferguson ("Harding hated to have them around, for he despised being watched," reported the chief usher), came to an abrupt stop when another agent, Harry Barker, tipped Florence off, and she ran down for a confrontation.

It was in Harding's Senate office, late one night in the winter of 1919, that Britton claimed she conceived their daughter, Elizabeth Ann. They disrobed because Harding wanted to "visualize" her while he worked there during the day. Britton worried that they lacked the "usual paraphernalia which we always took to the hotels . . . and of course, the Senate Offices do not provide preventive facilities for use in such emergencies."

He had assorted other flings, including one with Rosa Hoyle, said to have conceived his only illegitimate son, and one with Augusta Cole, whose pregnancy by Harding was terminated. He bedded a Washington Post employee known as Miss Allicott, and former chorus girls Maize Haywood and Blossom Jones—all procured by Harding's crony, Washington Post publisher and owner Ned McLean. And then there's the string of "New York women"—including one who committed suicide after Harding wouldn't marry her, and another who had a stash of incriminating love letters purchased by Harding loyalists.

The president even publicly ogled Margaret Gorman, the first Miss America, in Atlantic City, days after her crowning.

JUST WEEKS AFTER HIS INauguration in 1921, Harding approved Interior Secretary Albert Fall's request to transfer oil reserves from the Navy Department to Fall's control. Fall then secretly leased the reserve at Elks Hills, Calif., to oil man Edward Doheny and the one at Teapot Dome, Wyo., to Harry Sinclair—in exchange for a "loan" of cash and stock worth nearly $400,000, delivered in a small black satchel, and a "gift" of $100,000 from Doheny. Fall became the first Cabinet member to be thrown in prison.

Col. Charles Forbes, the first director of the U.S. Veterans Bureau, created by Harding, was particularly close to the first lady. She saw to his appointment, and entrusted him with $450 million to build hospitals and provide decent medical care for the thousands of disabled veterans of World War I, on whose behalf the Duchess was a national activist. Instead, he bilked tens of thousands out of building contractors and medical supply companies. He was eventually imprisoned—but not before Harding personally throttled him against the Red Room wall in the White House.

Although Attorney General Harry Daugherty, a Harding crony and campaign manager, eluded conviction on a variety of pardon-selling and influence-peddling charges, his Justice Department was riddled with malfeasance, kickbacks and payoffs. One of the department's central tasks was to intimidate any Harding mistress who threatened the president with blackmail.

Evalyn Walsh McLean, the Post publisher's wife, was a confidante of Mrs. Harding and an admitted intermittent morphine addict. Despite Prohibition, she also was a heavy drinker and speakeasy regular—but then, so were her husband and other ranking government officials: Albert Fall, Col. Forbes and the president's chief aide, George Christian. In the Veterans Bureau, stories eventually broke about flapper secretaries and young officers having a regular cocktail hour, with shakers and glasses at the ready, overseen by Forbes.

The president served liquor freely in the present-day Yellow Oval Room to his guests. Alice Roosevelt Longworth—a regular at poker—recalled that the first lady mixed the drinks. "No rumor could have exceeded the truth . . . trays with bottles containing every imaginable brand of whiskey stood about," she remembered. And, according to recently declassified FBI reports, Harding was drunk on whiskey during an Oval Office confrontation with railroad union leaders during their 1922 strike.

AT THE CENTER OF THE capital's most elite bootlegging service was Jess Smith—who, even though never an employee or even a volunteer at the Justice Department, used official letterhead, cars and staff, and sat in on private meetings with FBI Director Billy Burns. Smith enjoyed these perks as the bachelor companion of the attorney general. Smith also served as the first lady's favorite escort and arbiter of her jaunty '20s fashions.

Through the Justice Department, Smith had access to whiskey supplies confiscated by Prohibition agents, and some of the booze went directly to the White House, and to the McLeans, while the rest was kept for parties at the "Love Nest," the small house shared by Smith and Daugherty, complete with a pink taffeta bedroom.

Working closely with Republican National Committee Chairman Will Hays during the 1920 campaign, Florence Harding conceived of recruiting Hollywood movie stars to support her husband. Al Jolson was drafted to head the Harding-Coolidge Theatrical League, and on Aug. 24, 1920, the marriage of politics and entertainment was forged forever when Jolson brought 40 movie stars to the Harding home for a campaign rally.

The White House became a little Hollywood. On any given day, D.W. Griffith, the Gish sisters or Tom Mix might pose for newsreel cameras with the Hardings. When Hays left his job as postmaster general to become president of the Motion Picture Producers and Distributors of America, he developed a "project to link the White House with the motion picture industry" by providing a movie library. All of this was nothing short of immoral to old society. The religious press took even greater offense to Florence's ringing the stately halls with jazz for the first time. The Biblical Recorder excoriated the Hardings for "setting a bad example by joining in the modern dance with its 'jazz' music."

There was a good reason for Jess Smith having a vaguely defined association with the Justice Department. In this way, he was able to act at the implicit direction of the attorney general and FBI director and carry out a systematic intimidation of Harding mistresses who threatened to do as Carrie Phillips did and demand blackmail for their love letters. At one point, in exchange for apparently small amounts of money, affidavits disclaiming rumors of their liaisons were wrestled out of Evelyn Ruby, Augusta Cole and Cecilia Hoyle, and made their way to the first lady.

In April 1921, Ned McLean officially became an agent of the FBI, and did his utterly unethical best to destroy any anti-Harding efforts he heard about as publisher of The Post. Such responsibilities included ripping the blouse of Nan Britton to try to snatch letters she claimed to be carrying—in the privacy of his editorial office.

Even on the eve of his inauguration, Harding was providing more trouble for his troubleshooters. He had arranged a late-night rendezvous with Grace Cross, his Senate aide, in a Willard Hotel room. Some of his friends, recalled Olive Clapper, a reporter's wife, "ordered her to pack and get out of town, threatening to put the FBI on her trail if she didn't go at once. She was so frightened she left immediately."

MRS. HARDING'S DIARY, discovered last year at an Ohio barn auction, revealed her to be a true believer in crystal ball readings, the zodiac and clairvoyance. In February 1920, as a Senate wife, she had her first consultation with capital society's seer, "Madame Marcia." The psychic predicted that if Harding ran for president that year, he would be nominated—but that if he won the election, he would not live through his full term and instead die of "sudden, peculiar, violent...death by poison."

Knowing that the blackmail price of $25,000 demanded by Carrie Phillips for the love letters could never be met unless her husband became a presidential nominee, Florence pushed him through the primaries on to the nomination, ignoring the ominous prediction. During the Harding presidency, Madame Marcia was regularly fetched by the first lady's Secret Service agent, brought through the back entrance and escorted to the presidential bedroom for zodiac updates. Madame Marcia also did horoscopes for the president's public appearances; the first lady was trying to protect him from numerous assassination and bomb threats.

When Florence got early inklings of the Teapot Dome, Veterans Bureau and Justice Department scandals, she asked Marcia to do astrological charts of Cabinet members—and used the results as evidence to remove some of the crooks from the administration.

Newly discovered documents now prove that Harding was the only president successfully blackmailed by a mistress. Once he was nominated as the Republican candidate, the national GOP committee paid off Carrie Phillips's lump-sum demand of $25,000 and monthly stipend of $2,000, funneled through a secret bank account kept, apparently, under Jess Smith's name (the records were burned by Attorney General Daugherty).

Once Harding became president, Phillips returned from an all-expense-paid trip abroad and demanded that her brother and son-in-law be given federal posts. It was done. Harding even circulated the name of Phillips's husband to be ambassador to Japan—before word got out why he thought a drygoods salesman from Marion, Ohio, deserved the post and the idea was quashed.

One night, when he was a senator, Harding had such a row with aide Grace Cross that she cut his back and the police were called. Thereafter, Cross went around town talking about a "birthmark" on the president's back that she could identify—undoubtedly the wound—which became part of her arsenal in unsuccessful attempts to get blackmail money. However, former Democratic attorney general Mitchell Palmer would later use his knowledge of the Cross affair to force Harding to drop a Justice Department prosecution against him.

After a failed attempt to frame Cross with a phony affidavit claiming she was a liar and blackmailer, Smith approached Bertha Martin—a friend of Cross's—to try to get possession of the aide's love letters from Harding. Martin said she would turn on her friend on the condition that she was given the job of society editor at The Post. Smith went to McLean, who gave his nod. Martin took Cross to lunch, asked to see the letters, snatched them away and bolted out of the restaurant. She was made society editor—and still managed to stay friends with Cross, taking her on a European vacation, courtesy of the secret blackmail fund.

DURING A PARTY AT SMITH and Daugherty's "Love Nest," some New York chorus girls were brought down to entertain at a stag party. In attendance was the president. When glasses and bottles were being flung off the table so the dancing girls could perform, one Washington prostitute, identified only as a Miss Walsh, was knocked unconscious. Harding was hustled out. The woman died and was buried in a potter's field.

In recently discovered transcripts of her taped revelations, Evalyn McLean recalled that the FBI director "railroaded" the woman's brother into St. Elizabeth's mental hospital when he suggested a blackmail payment.

"The Strange Death of President Harding," written in 1930 by the notorious perjurer and former FBI agent Gaston Means, implied that Florence Harding poisoned her husband in retaliation for his adultery, but the book has long been dismissed as a fabrication. New evidence shows that while Means lied in details, he told general truths. He said that he was part of an FBI effort to seize and destroy a small, privately printed book, "The Illustrated Life of Warren Gamaliel Harding," that revealed Harding's affair with Carrie Phillips, the RNC blackmail payoff and Florence's out-of-wedlock child by a common-law first husband.

This turned out to be the only book suppressed by the government in peacetime. The entire action was illegal, and thus the boxes of books and updated manuscripts were taken not to any government property but to the McClean estate, where they were all burned. Well, not all: An original with the author's notes sits with none other than Evalyn McLean's papers at the Library of Congress.

Among Gaston Means's other sensational charges was that he spied for the first lady on Nan Britton. In fact, it was probably Grace Cross—for at least one letter sent to her from the president's office was purloined and found its way into the file on Cross in the McLeans' private papers. Post reporter Vylla Poe Wilson later admitted that both "Mrs. Harding and Mrs. McLean were very jealous women, and they hired Gaston Means to follow Harding and McLean and report on their actions." In congressional hearings on the Justice Department, it was confirmed that Agent Means not only spied on Cross but also on the president's physician, Charles Sawyer, and his mistress, the first lady's housekeeper.

CONGRESS FIRST HEARD tales of gross corruption at the Veterans Bureau in February 1923. Col. Forbes's colleague in kickbacks, Charles Cramer—the bureau's chief counsel, and the purchaser of the Hardings' Senate home—wrote out a letter to the president in his dining room, then stood before the bathroom mirror and shot himself. The letter mysteriously disappeared.

At the start of the summer, the first big Harding scandal broke with the news that Jess Smith was found in his room with his head in a trash can, and a bullet in his head. The official word went out that it was a suicide due to health and emotional problems. Bertha Martin of The Post recalled that it was "noised about" town that Smith was a known homosexual, and that he was heartbroken over Daugherty's sudden rejection of his friendship when the president learned of Smith's nefarious activities. Others, like Evalyn McLean, simply believed Daugherty, Means or Burns had Smith killed because he knew too much. As for Martin, after a second career bootlegging whiskey to embassies, she was found dressed in her fur coat, pearls and white gloves with her head on the gas range, another alleged suicide.

Beginning on June 20, 1923, the Hardings sought to escape the heat and scandal of Washington on a 15,000-mile transcontinental train trip and voyage to Alaska. The president was 57 at the time. The recently unsealed diary and notes of naval physician Joel Boone reveal Boone's grave concerns about the president's heart condition. The warnings were ignored by longtime Harding homeopath "Doc" Sawyer, who made no effort to stop Harding from speaking in the blistering heat, driving the golden spike to complete the Alaska Railroad, or doing other arduous tasks. In this Sawyer had the absolute approval of the first lady, who was now enjoying the height of her national popularity and didn't want the trip canceled. She viewed the incompetent Sawyer as her own Rasputin, who'd miraculously kept a chronic kidney ailment from killing her.

When Harding suffered a bout of food poisoning from tainted crab meat at Cordova, Alaska, Doc Sawyer ultimately weakened the president's sick heart by treating him with heavy doses of purgatives to flush out the toxins. On Aug. 2, 1923, when Boone was out of the sickroom in San Francisco's Palace Hotel, Sawyer plied one too many purgatives—in Florence's presence—and Harding died. There was a quick coverup regarding who was in the room and at precisely what time the president died. Mrs. Harding refused to permit an autopsy or a death mask, protecting her beloved Sawyer. "Now that is all over," she told Evalyn McLean after Harding's death, "I think it was all for the best"

At the McLean estate, aptly named Friendship, Evalyn permitted the widowed first lady to bring from the White House wood crates full of government documents (which may have been incriminating to Harding) and helped burn them. Even though Mrs. Harding was being spied on and her phone was tapped during the congressional investigations of the scandals, she was able to keep destroying documents within the privacy of her Willard Hotel suite.

Four months after leaving Washington, Florence died at age 64 in Marion, Ohio. She was staying in a cottage on the grounds of the Sawyer Sanitarium "for the treatment of nervous and mental diseases," amid signs that read: "Please do not stare at the Patients."

Carl Sferrazza Anthony is author of the just-published biography, "Florence Harding: The First Lady, the Jazz Age and the Death of America's Most Scandalous President" (Morrow).

The Abduction of Aimee

Evangelist Aimee Semple McPherson disappeared from a California beach in 1926, creating a national sensation. Five weeks later she reappeared, under circumstances that have never been completely explained.

by J. Kingston Pierce

WHEN AIMEE SEMPLE MCPHERson returned to Los Angeles after a three-month, work-and-play tour through Europe and the Holy Land, thousands showed up at the train station to welcome her back. The 35-year-old pastor, famous for her radio sermons and vaudeville-style Sunday services, promptly picked up where she'd left off. She worked to furnish a new Bible school and lure ever-larger crowds into her grand Angelus Temple, where she could regale them with her distinctively upbeat messages of holiness, happiness, healing, and Heaven.

Less than a month later, however, events took a dramatic turn. On the sunny afternoon of May 18, 1926,

Above, left: Aimee preached up and down the United States, reaching out to thousands with her "Foursquare Gospel." Above: In 1924 McPherson made the first broadcast over her Temple radio station. Standing behind her is Kenneth Ormiston, the radio engineer linked to her disappearance. It is the only known photograph of them together.

19. Abduction of Aimee

McPherson told her mother, Minnie Kennedy, that she and her devoted secretary, Emma Schaffer, were going to drive out to the beach at Ocean Park, just south of Santa Monica. There Aimee planned to relax and maybe pen a few new sermons. She was scheduled to be back in time to show color slides of her Holy Land excursion during that evening's service. The evangelist, however, did not return.

Schaffer reported that "Sister Aimee," as her flock called her, had gone wading into the warm Pacific surf . . . and simply vanished. The secretary's preliminary search turned up no clues regarding Sister's fate, and a subsequent sweep of the area by police and her followers found nothing. During the search a deep-sea diver died of exposure in the ocean depths, and one of Aimee's grief-stricken disciples cast herself into the sea and drowned. McPherson was an able swimmer, yet people assumed that she must have drowned too and her body been carried out to sea. "Sister is gone," her mother told the congregation that night. "We know she is with Jesus."

The press, however, thought McPherson might be keeping different company. So even as airplanes and boats sought signs of the evangelist up and down the shore, reporters plumbed juicy rumors that the prominent preacher had merely absconded for a lover's tryst with one of her former employees—a man who had been conspicuously absent from the city in recent days. They also pursued "Aimee sightings" from as far away as Canada. Psychics soon weighed in with their own suggestions about McPherson's whereabouts, and her mother fielded several ransom demands, including one threat to sell Sister Aimee into white slavery unless her kidnappers were paid a half million dollars.

"It's a shame that all these unfounded reports should gain circulation," groused Minnie Kennedy. But then she further exacerbated doubts about her daughter's demise by offering a $25,000 reward to anybody who could fetch Sister back home "unharmed." What had started out as a tragedy was turning into a mystery.

For AIMEE SEMPLE MCPHERSON, religion had always been a dominant

Sister Aimee had gone wading into the warm Pacific surf . . . and simply vanished.

part of her life. Born the daughter of James and Minnie Kennedy in Ontario, Canada, on October 9, 1890, Aimee was only six weeks old when her mother carried her to a Salvation Army event and dedicated the cooing infant to a lifetime of Christian service. Thereafter, Minnie made sure that Aimee fell asleep to hymns, rather than lullabies, and she was told Bible stories in place of traditional fairy tales.

Yet Aimee's world did not revolve solely around theological matters. Her aged father managed to share with her his love of music, horseback riding, and the abundant wonders of nature. Aimee also delighted in dancing, reading fiction, and attending the local movie theater. Yet Aimee was considered a serious child, dissatisfied with doing things halfway or having only partial answers to important questions. For example, in her mid-teens she discovered Charles Darwin's studies of natural evolution in a school geography book and grilled her parents for proof that the earth had been created in six days, rather than evolving over millions of years. Dissatisfied with their Bible-centric responses, she set off on her own determined path of research, and for a time Aimee—who'd already demonstrated elocutionary talents—was her hometown's most vocal and adamant defender of evolutionary theories.

As chagrined as Minnie must have been by this turn of events, she was more distressed to learn that her daughter had attended a local meeting of Pentecostals in 1907. Aimee went to see these "Holy Rollers" on a lark. But she was profoundly moved by the evening's speaker, a tall, blue-eyed Irishman in his mid-20s named Robert Semple. Semple exhorted his audience to experience "the baptism of the Holy Spirit" and repent of worldly pleasures: dancing, movies, music, novel reading—the very entertainments Aimee relished. For the next several days, the girl worried that she had unwittingly condemned herself to hell. She prayed desperately for redemption, until finally, as she later related, "The sky was filled with brightness, the trees, the fields, and the little snow birds flitting to and fro were praising the Lord and smiling upon me. . . . I had been redeemed!"

Minnie admonished her 17-year-old daughter to steer clear of the Pentecostals, but those words fell on deaf ears. "It is perfectly useless to argue with her," James told his wife, "for no matter what we say, she only thinks she is being persecuted and will hold to it all the more tenaciously." When, within another six months, Aimee announced that she and preacher Semple would marry and move to China as missionaries, Minnie could only acquiesce.

After raising the necessary funds, the Semples—Aimee pregnant with their first child—left for Asia in 1910. Following two months of missionary work, though, Minnie received word that her daughter was sick with malaria and dysentery in Hong Kong, and Robert Semple had died of the same illnesses. She cabled money for Aimee to come home with her newborn daughter, Roberta Star Semple, but their reunion in New York City was less than idyllic. Minnie, who had recently left her husband behind in Ontario to assist the Salvation Army in Manhattan, found her daughter fragile, despondent, and directionless. Aimee had no interest in moving back to the Kennedy's quiet Ontario farm, yet she didn't know what else to do. She tried looking for missionary work in Chicago, but little Roberta's ill health forced her to retreat to Minnie's New York apartment.

While in New York Aimee met Harold McPherson, the cashier at a Madison Square-area restaurant. In the spring of 1912, McPherson became her second husband. From the outset, theirs was a troubled partnership. The handsome, no-nonsense Harold quickly realized that his energetic new spouse was uncomfortable with the circumscribed responsibilities of a housewife and mother. Years later Aimee admitted that she married McPherson in order to give her child a home. Entrusting Roberta to her husband's care, Aimee felt free to spend more and more time doing religious work. Complaints that she was neglecting her child and husband just left her feeling guilty and depressed and prone to "tantrums." Harold resolved that if he was ever to enjoy a "normal" marriage, he must separate Aimee from her fellow Pentecostals. So he relocated his family to his hometown of Providence, Rhode Island.

Nevertheless, neither this move nor the birth of a son, Rolf, in the spring of 1913 brought Aimee peace. Her health deteriorated precipitously. She was hospitalized, and Minnie rushed to her bedside, sure that her daughter's life hung in the balance. However, as Aimee would tell her adherents in the years to come, at this low point she heard what she believed was the voice of God saying, "NOW WILL YOU GO?" She presumed that she was being given a choice: to either surrender to death or the ministry. She chose the latter. Within two weeks, Aimee "miraculously" recovered. Then one night in late June 1915, when Harold McPherson was away, she packed up her clothes and her children and left for the local train station, bound for her parents' home in Ontario ... and a 30-year preaching career that would be as controversial as it was acclaimed.

AIMEE BEGAN BY LEADING camp-style Pentecostal meetings around southern Ontario, but enthusiastic crowds soon encouraged her to extend her evangelical reach down the Atlantic seaboard, all the way to Florida. The collections from her prayer services paid for a succession of ever-larger tents (her "canvas cathedrals") to hold the poor, oppressed, and neglected folk who came to accept salvation on her upbeat terms. She also bought a 1912 Packard—dubbed her "Gospel Car"—that provided transportation and doubled as Aimee's office on wheels and a traveling billboard, plastered with Bible verses and slogans such as "JESUS IS COMING—GET READY" and "WHERE WILL YOU SPEND ETERNITY?"

"In this show-devouring city," Harper's *magazine remarked in 1927, "no entertainment compares in popularity with that of Angelus Temple."*

This itinerant and penurious existence would have been impossible for many people to take. Harold McPherson, for instance, thinking he could reconcile with his wife, made several efforts to become a fixture in Aimee's revivalist road show, but it was clearly not the life for him, and the pair wound up separating permanently in 1918.

Aimee, however, found the gypsy pace of her religious mission invigorating, and she thrived on new challenges—except when they concerned business. She had no interest in finances, was often cheated, and seemed unable to hold onto what money she did make. By the winter of 1917, Aimee was exhausted from handling both the spiritual and administrative ends of her ministry. So she did what she'd done many times before—called on her mother to help. Despite the fact that she and her daughter often butted heads, Minnie was game to follow Aimee's preaching path, even when it led clear across the country.

Hungry for a fresh start away from the East Coast evangelical circuit and figuring that the tens of thousands of Americans who were then migrating to bountiful California needed her spiritual guidance, Aimee Semple McPherson piled her family into a new Gospel Car and sped westward in the fall of 1918.

They reached Los Angeles in mid-December, "with ten dollars and a tambourine," as she'd later quip. After only a week, Aimee was drawing huge crowds to her services in rented halls and taking in collections ample enough to buy her family their first real home. But she wanted more. She wanted to raise her own house of worship. So while Minnie and the children remained in Los Angeles, Aimee set off to barnstorm the country. She preached in classic Pentecostal fashion, giving special attention to the sick, who came by the hundreds to see her, believing that her touch could cure their worst infirmities.

Minnie saved every donated dime possible, and in January 1923, mother and daughter opened (debt-free) their "glorious dream": the $1.5 million Angelus Temple in Los Angeles. Topped by a concrete dome—painted an azure blue with fleecy clouds on the inside—the circular edifice sported chandeliers, a magnificent organ, and seating for 5,300. Critics scoffed that Aimee could never fill such a hall. Yet she did, week in and week out, frequently offering more than one service a day.

Part of her success might be attributed to the explosion in local church activity set off by Los Angeles' booming population. But Sister Aimee also offered flamboyance and a joyful message. Her "Foursquare Gospel," with its message, "Jesus only Savior, Baptizer and Healer, Jesus the coming King," offered equal parts religious fundamentalism and tent revivalism. It attracted a wide cross-section of listeners, including actor Charlie Chaplin and politician William Jennings Bryan, who himself spoke twice before the congregation. Dressed in white and backed by hundreds of musicians and singers, McPherson unabashedly blended Hollywood with hallelujahs. She even had an electric theater-style marquee over the Tem-

---

"The sky was filled with brightness, the trees, the fields, and the little snow birds flitting to and fro were praising the Lord and smiling upon me. . . . I had been redeemed!"

19. Abduction of Aimee

ple's entrance, advertising her upcoming sermons.

"In this slow-devouring city," *Harper's* magazine remarked in 1927, "no entertainment compares in popularity with that of Angelus Temple." A typical tightly choreographed Sunday service included costumed musical numbers as well as elaborately staged allegorical scenes. For one such skit, Sister dressed as a policeman and rode a motorcycle onto the stage to literally arrest sin. On another occasion, she borrowed a camel from the city zoo to illustrate its inability to pass through the eye of a needle. "Many a theatrical producer would shrink from the outlay involved in staging such scenes," *Harper's* noted. "It is said that the lighting expenditure for one Sunday evening performance would make safe the streets of a dark village."

Some observers dismissed McPherson's services as "supernatural whoopee," and even *Harper's* called her sermons—delivered in a "curious nasal twang"—commonplace. Sister's local evangelical rival, the blustering and bigoted "Fighting Bob" Shuler, went further, declaring her messages and their entertaining presentation "blasphemous." Hundreds of people who were turned away from the Temple on Sundays for lack of seating, however, willingly stood outside and listened to her over loudspeakers. Starting in early 1924, thousands more from all over the West tuned in on her radio station, KFSG (Kall Foursquare Gospel), only the third broadcast station commissioned in Los Angeles. Further expanding her influence, Sister Aimee created a training institute for aspiring evangelists, erected a six-story Bible school adjacent to Angelus Temple, and set about founding branches of her Church of the Foursquare Gospel throughout Southern California.

Then Aimee Semple McPherson stepped off the beach at Ocean Park . . . and straight into the headlines.

THE FUROR OF 1926 could hardly have been greater had President Calvin Coolidge gone missing. Newspapers nationwide filled their pages with police reports and statements from Angelus Temple officials. Mother Minnie was confident that she knew her daughter had drowned, and it was about time Sister's followers accepted that, too. So on June 20, a month after the disappearance and one day after Minnie received—and promptly ignored—the latest ransom note, demanding $500,000 for Aimee's return and signed by "the Avengers," Angelus Temple hosted an elaborate, flower-filled farewell ceremony. Huge crowds attended the event, many people lining up before dawn to be there.

Still, the press continued to chase rumors, sniffing a scandal in the wind. The most fertile gossip surrounded Kenneth Ormiston, an unhappily married man in his mid-30s who had been the engineer at KFSG radio—until Minnie, wary of her daughter's attentions toward him, pressured Ormiston to resign in late 1925. Since then, there had been unsubstantiated talk that the radioman had accompanied Aimee on her Holy Land tour. More recently, Ormiston's wife had filed a missing-person report on him. The *Los Angeles Times* quickly con-

Mother Minnie was confident that she knew her daughter had drowned, and it was about time Sister's followers accepted that, too.

cluded that the engineer and the evangelist must be off together—only to have Ormiston turn up days later and deny any knowledge of Aimee's whereabouts.

Then on June 23 Minnie received a phone call from Aimee in a hospital bed in Douglas, Arizona. Accompanied by Roberta and Rolf and a deputation of reporters and district attorney office investigators, she immediately rushed down to be with her daughter.

When Minnie arrived, McPherson told her mother and a host of newspaper men and photographers that, on the day she vanished, she had been approached

Los Angeles District Attorney Asa Keyes suggested that the kidnapping might have been faked as a publicity stunt or a plot to collect on a life-insurance policy.

at the beach by a man and a woman begging her to come to their car and pray for their dying baby. When she reached the vehicle, though, Aimee was pushed inside and smothered with a cloth doused in anesthetic. Waking the next morning, she found herself in an unfamiliar bedroom, the captive of a woman and two men who called themselves "the Avengers." They told her they wanted ransom money from Minnie, and when Sister refused to help them get it, they threatened her and burned her with a lighted cigar. Later, the kidnappers moved Aimee to a shack somewhere in the northern Mexico desert. Aimee said she was never alone—until June 22, when the two men drove off and the woman tied Aimee to a cot and announced she was going into town to buy groceries. Taking advantage of the opportunity, Sister slashed her restraints on a jagged piece of metal and stumbled into the desert. She eventually reached the Mexican town of Agua Prieta, where she collapsed on the porch of a mystified resident, who took her across the border to a hospital in nearby Douglas.

The tale sounded like something out of the movie serials Aimee had enjoyed in her youth, so she shouldn't have been surprised to encounter skepticism. The local sheriff questioned why, after her supposed ordeal, Sister's clothing remained in such good repair. Ranchers, miners, and other desert hands could find no sign of the Mexican shack in which Aimee maintained she'd been held, nor of her kidnappers. Before a grand jury, impaneled to seek indictments against her abductors, Los Angeles District Attorney Asa Keyes suggested that the kidnapping might have been faked as a publicity stunt or

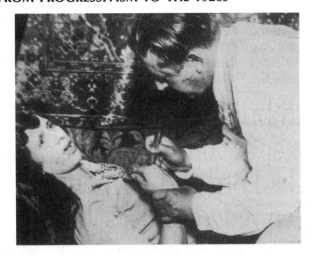
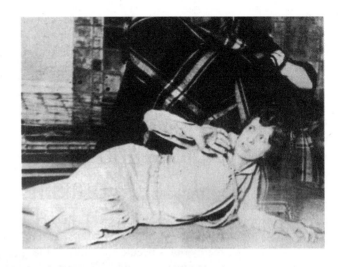
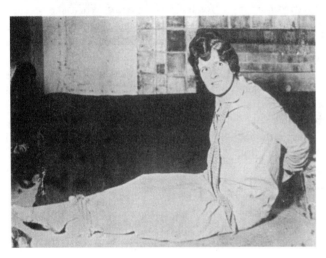

ALL: CORBIS/BETTMANN-UPI

From upper left: For the press and Temple officials, Aimee acted out her version of the kidnapping story. She claimed three people calling themselves "the Avengers" had abducted her and kept her captive in Mexico.

a plot to collect on a life-insurance policy. Yet Sister stuck to her story, asking reporters, "Why should I lie? What motive would I have?"

By late July, shortly after the grand jury disbanded—concluding that it lacked evidence enough to issue indictments—the press thought it had an answer. Witnesses had come forward to claim that during at least 10 days of her alleged imprisonment by the "Avengers," McPherson had actually been hiding out with Kenneth Ormiston in a cottage "love nest" at Carmel-by-the-Sea, a resort several hundred miles north of Los Angeles. Sister's denials only incited newspapers to hire private detectives and dig harder for proof of her perfidy. During the next few months, Americans were fed a steady stream of disclosures about disguises, grocery slips written in Aimee's hand, a trunk of her clothing found on the East Coast, and numerous other "clues" said to discredit the preacher's kidnapping account.

With this ammunition at the ready, District Attorney Keyes announced on September 16 that he was charging Aimee and her mother with corruption of public morals, obstruction of justice, and conspiracy to manufacture evidence. The two women were brought before Judge Samuel Blake on September 27, 1926. After six weeks of testimony, Judge Blake bound Aimee and her mother over for trial in Superior Court.

Newspaper and magazine readers were titillated by coverage of this sordid affair. At 35, Aimee was an appealing woman with luxuriant auburn hair and a broad smile—it was easy to imagine her enticing Ormiston or many other men to run away with her. Now, after years of mostly favorable attention, the revivalist was incensed to find herself portrayed in print and in court as a conniving seductress.

McPherson fought back from the pulpit and on the radio, contending that the district attorney—in league with the imperious Reverend Shuler—was persecuting her in order to enhance his own political profile. The curtain finally closed on this fiasco in January 1927, just before the trial was due to commence. Keyes resolved that the case against the Angelus Temple leaders was so polluted by obfuscations, contradictions, and rebuttals, that it could no longer be prosecuted "with honor or with any reasonable hope of success." He asked the court to dismiss the criminal charges against the two women and added bitterly that the judgment of McPherson's actions was now left up to "the only court of her jurisdiction—the court of public opinion."

Although many observers were disappointed at the loose ends left by this non-conclusion, Sister felt vindicated. Not only had she weathered a reputation-damaging trial, she'd come through it with the vast majority of her flock intact. She would need those followers to keep Angelus Temple running, and they would help her spread the Foursquare movement across the country and around the world.

The support of her adherents was vital, especially during a series of opéra-bouffe episodes that clouded the last two decades of McPherson's life. They included her with her daughter Roberta; Sister's 1931 marriage to actor and singer David Hutton, which ended in divorce within three years; the widowed Minnie's wedding to a charming bigamist; and imbroglios involving everything from McPherson's rumored facelift to accusations that she had been diverting Temple funds for her personal use. In the public's mind, Sister Aimee's work to feed and clothe the poor during the Great Depression and her encouragement to rural nobodies to make something of themselves in burgeoning Los Angeles tended to be overshadowed by these flaps.

Little about Aimee went unremarked by the press, and her death from an apparent accidental overdose of barbiturates on September 27, 1944, was no exception. Sensation-hungry reporters were among the crowds packing Angelus Temple and filling the surrounding streets on the day of Aimee's funeral, held October 9, on what would have been her 54th birthday. As expected, it was quite a show, with tributes and plenty of music. A motorcade of 600 cars escorted the hearse to Forest Lawn Memorial Park in Glendale, where 2,000 invited guests formed an "Avenue of Sorrow" to the tomb, one side holding American flags, the other side holding the flags of their church. The turnout would have delighted Aimee.

J. Kingston Pierce is a Seattle resident currently working on a collection of essays about that city's past. His story, "Andrew Jackson and the Tavern-Keeper's Daughter," appeared in the June 1999 issue of American History.

Unit 4

Unit Selections

20. **'Brother, Can You Spare a Dime?'** Henry Allen
21. **A Monumental Man,** Gerald Parshall
22. **Eleanor Roosevelt,** Doris Kearns Goodwin
23. **The Lone Dissenting Voice,** Glen Jeansonne
24. **Our Greatest Land Battle,** Edward Oxford
25. **"I Learn a Lot from the Veterans,"** Stephen E. Ambrose
26. **The Biggest Decision: Why We Had to Drop the Atomic Bomb,** Robert James Maddox

Key Points to Consider

❖ Based on the articles in this unit, discuss the character and personality of both Franklin and Eleanor Roosevelt.

❖ Author Stephen Ambrose provides readers with excerpts from letters that former soldiers sent him about their experiences in World War II. Do you think their attitudes about what they went through are any different from what Vietnam War veterans might have?

❖ Analyze the article on the use of atomic bombs against Japan. What alternatives did President Truman believe were available? Do you agree or disagree with his choice? Why?

 **Links**   www.dushkin.com/online/

18. **Japanese American Internment**
    http://www.geocities.com/Athens/8420/main.html
19. **Works Progress Administration/Folklore Project**
    http://lcweb2.loc.gov/ammem/wpaintro/wpalife.html
20. **World War II WWW Sites**
    http://www.lib.muohio.edu/inet/subj/history/wwii/general.html

These sites are annotated on pages 4 and 5.

From the Great Depression to World War II

Republicans liked to proclaim the prosperity of the 1920s as a "New Era." Business was booming, and more people had more surplus money to spend than ever before. When people ran out of things to buy and still had money left over they dabbled in the stock market. As stock prices rose dramatically, a kind of speculative mania developed in the latter half of the decade. In the past most people had bought stocks as investments. That is, they wanted to receive income from the dividends reliable companies would pay over the years. Speculators had no interest in the long run; they bought stocks on the assumption that they would make money when they sold on the market in a matter of months or even weeks.

By the end of the 1920s the stock market prices had soared to unprecedented heights. So long as people were confident that they would continue to rise, they did. There were a few voices warning that stocks were overpriced, but they were denounced as doomsayers. Besides, had not the highly regarded President Herbert Hoover predicted that "we are on the verge of a wave of never ending prosperity?" No one can say why this confidence began to falter when it did, but on October 24, 1929, the market crashed. "Black Thursday" set off an avalanche of selling as holders dumped their shares at whatever price they could get, thereby driving prices even lower.

President Herbert Hoover tried to restore confidence by assuring the public that what had happened was merely a glitch, a necessary readjustment of a market that had gotten out of hand. His reassurances met with increasing disbelief as time went on. Businessmen as well as stockholders were worried about the future. In order to protect themselves they laid off workers, cut back on inventory, and put off previous plans to expand or to introduce new products. But their actions, however much sense they made for an individual firm, had the collective result of making the situation worse. " 'Brother, Can You Spare a Dime?' " provides a closeup view of the pathetic lives led by those who fell prey to the widespread unemployment.

Hoover endorsed more federal programs than had any of his predecessors to combat the depression, but they failed to stop the downward slide. He became the most widely detested man in America. In the presidential election of 1932, the discredited Hoover lost by a landslide to Democratic candidate Franklin D. Roosevelt. Although Roosevelt had compiled an impressive record as governor of New York state, his greatest asset in the election was that he was not Hoover.

Roosevelt assumed the presidency without any grand design for ending the depression. Unlike Hoover, however, he was willing to act boldly and on a large scale. His "first 100 days" in office resulted in passage of an unprecedented number of measures designed to promote recovery and to restore confidence. "A Monumental Man" provides a portrait of Roosevelt as president.

Eleanor Roosevelt was America's most influential "first lady" with no close second. Her marriage to Franklin was no love story, especially when she discovered that he was involved with another woman. Their marriage continued, but Eleanor began developing her own interests quite apart from merely being Franklin's wife. When he became president, she served as both his "eyes and ears" and his conscience, particularly with regard to civil rights. They made an effective team: Franklin, the pragmatic politician not overly concerned with moral issues; Eleanor the moral uplifter "barging into cocktail hour when he wanted only to relax, cross-examining him at dinner, handing him memos to read late at night."

Roosevelt's "New Deal" mitigated the effects of the depression but did not end it. That came with the onset of war in Europe and America's preparedness program. Unlike Woodrow Wilson, Roosevelt made no effort to remain neutral when conflict engulfed Europe and Asia. He believed the United States ought to cooperate with other nations to stop aggression, but he had to contend with a Congress and public that was deeply influenced by those who thought the United States should remain aloof. After war broke out, Roosevelt took decidedly unneutral steps when he transferred 50 overage destroyers to Great Britain and later pushed through Congress a lend-lease program providing aid for those nations fighting the Axis powers. Alarmed at Japan's attempt to conquer China, Roosevelt tried to use economic pressure to get Japan to back off. His efforts only stiffened the will of Japanese hard-liners who planned and carried out the raid on Pearl Harbor on December 7, 1941. An aroused Congress almost unanimously approved the declaration of war that Roosevelt asked for. An exception was Congresswoman Jeannette Rankin. In "The Lone Dissenting Voice," Glen Jeansonne tells of this remarkable person's courage in the face of incredible pressures.

Pearl Harbor and Germany's declaration of war against the United States a few days later united Americans in their determination to win the war. For the next 6 months the Japanese ran rampant as they inflicted a string of defeats against British and American forces in the Pacific. The tide of Japanese expansion was halted during the summer of 1942 by the naval battles at the Coral Sea and at Midway.

Roosevelt and his military advisers agreed at the beginning of the war that the European theater should receive top priority. Offensive operations against the Germans and Italians began when U.S. forces invaded North Africa in November 1942, and Sicily and Italy during the next year. Still, the main effort against Germany was put off until June 6, 1944, when Allied forces invaded the French beaches at Normandy. After tough going against determined German opposition, the invaders broke out across France and began approaching the German border. Edward Oxford's report, "Our Greatest Land Battle," describes what Americans came to call the "Battle of the Bulge" and its aftermath. After more months of fighting, with Germany caught between the western Allies and the Soviet armies advancing from the east, Adolf Hitler committed suicide and Germany finally surrendered on May 8, 1945. Prominent World War II historian Stephen E. Ambrose in " 'I Learn a Lot from the Veterans' " recalls how his understanding of what ordinary soldiers experienced was greatly enhanced by the letters he received from ex-GIs.

Meanwhile, American forces in the Pacific were steadily advancing toward the Japanese homeland. Capture of the Mariana Islands enabled the United States to mount massive air attacks against Japanese cities, and naval actions progressively strangled their war machine. Some historians have argued that President Harry S. Truman could have attained a Japanese surrender by the summer of 1945 if only he had assured them that they could retain their sacred emperor. That is incorrect. The Japanese will to resist still ran strong, as the bloody battles of Iwo Jima and Okinawa during the first half of 1945 had shown. "The Biggest Decision: Why We had to Drop the Atomic Bomb" shows that Truman used atomic weapons to end a bloody war that would have been far bloodier if an invasion had been necessary.

'Brother, Can You Spare a Dime?'

1930–1940: Making do and trying to forget reality during the Depression

By Henry Allen
Washington Post Staff Writer

It's not like you go out on your porch and see the Depression standing there like King Kong. Most neighborhoods, things look pretty normal, not that different from before the Crash. Paint peels on houses. Cars get old, break down. Nothing you'd notice right away. Kids play with their Buck Rogers ray guns. You go to the movies on Dish Night—you like the Fiesta Ware, very modernistic, red and blue.

Definitely, you read in the papers how in Chicago unemployment hit 50 percent, and men were fighting over a barrel of garbage; or in the Dust Bowl, farmers saying they'll lynch judges who foreclose on their property. That kind of thing. It's terrible.

But most places you don't see it. Roosevelt can say: "I see one-third of a nation ill-housed, ill-clad, ill-nourished." That leaves two-thirds where you don't see the hobo jungles, people lined up for government cheese.

You feel what isn't there: It's like on Sunday afternoon, the quiet. You don't hear carpenters driving nails, you don't hear rivet hammers going in the city.

Fewer cars in town, just the stoplights rocking in the wind. You don't hear as many whistles: factory, railroad. You don't hear as many babies crying. People are afraid to have them.

Down the block there's a man you don't see outside his house on workdays. He doesn't want the neighbors to know he's out of work again. Smoking cigarettes, looking out the window, waiting for "Amos 'n' Andy" to come on the radio.

He was a sales manager for a train wheel company, back when the railroads were buying 1,300 locomotives a year.

DOROTHEA LANGE/FARM SECURITY ADMINISTRATION COLLECTION; LIBRARY OF CONGRESS
Dorothea Lange's photograph of a migrant farm worker and her child has come to symbolize the wrenching poverty that characterized much of the decade.

UNITED PRESS INTERNATIONAL
In 1932, in the depths of the Depression, President Hoover called out troops to roust impoverished World War I veterans—"Bonus Marchers"—from their camp in Washington, D.C. Their burning shanties blackened the skies around the Capitol.

20. 'Brother, Can You Spare a Dime?'

In 1932, they don't buy any. The company lets him go.

He takes a job selling insurance. Insurance companies know you can sell policies to your family, your friends. When you can't sell any more, they let you go.

He sells vacuums, the encyclopedias, door to door. He ends up spending all day at the movies. He won't let his wife apply for relief. He's too proud. His son quits high school—he's out West building a national park for the Civilian Conservation Corps, $30 a month. He sends most of it home so his mother can get her teeth fixed. And put dimes in the chain letters she mails out.

People write songs about tramps—"Brother, Can You Spare a Dime?"—but you don't see them unless they come to your back door; people say they make a chalk mark on your fence if you're good for a handout. You've never found the mark but they keep coming. You wonder how they survive.

One guy's feet are coming out of his shoes but he's got a new tweed overcoat.

You say: "Glad to see you got a warm coat."

He says: "I got it raking leaves for an undertaker. They're good for clothes."

You see the Depression in the papers, the magazines and newsreels: heads getting busted during strikes, dust storms burying cows, Reds parading through Wall Street with their fists in the air, shouting "bread, bread," or Huey Long, the Louisiana Kingfish himself, flapping his arms and shouting about "every man a king," Roosevelt looking over plans for electric power dams in the Tennessee Valley, his cigarette holder pointing up—the columnists say "at a jaunty angle." And the lines: in front of soup kitchens, relief offices, banks that are failing. And cute stuff: Kids hang a sign that says "Depression" on a snowman and throw snowballs at it.

THEN YOU'RE LOOKING AT BLOOD and bullet holes from gangster shootouts, a girl drinking a glass of beer at the end of Prohibition, kids jitterbugging to Benny Goodman or Count Basie. Bathing beauties, bathing beauties, bathing beauties, and the glamour girls of cafe society—Brenda Diana Duff Frazier, the debutante of the year, smiling from her table at El Morocco or the Rainbow Room. No Depression there.

The Yankees win the pennant. Jesse Owens makes the Olympic team. Soldiers goose-step in front of Hitler or Mussolini or Stalin. Hemingway in the Spanish Civil War, glamorous in that manly way that took over from everybody wanting to look like boys in the 1920s, including the women.

In the new styles, women have waists and busts again. They aren't supposed to look bored anymore, either. You don't get a job, relief, whatever, looking bored. Hemlines go back down. People say hemlines go up and down with the stock market, but that's hooey. The idea is to look more mature. Women's hats, though—feathers, veils, flowers. You read how a woman in a New York tearoom put a bread basket on her head and nobody knew the difference.

From the Crash until Roosevelt took office in 1933, everybody tried to keep living the way they had been living. It didn't work. Things had to change. Now Fortune magazine says the Flaming Youth of the 1920s are gone and we've got "a generation that will not stick its neck out. It keeps its shirt on, its pants buttoned, its chin up, and its mouth shut."

If you're older, during those good years you felt like a self-made man, so now when you're cleaning out your desk, boarding up your store, you feel like a self-ruined man.

THE PREACHERS AND BUSINESSmen all have something to blame: moral breakdown, a natural cycle, the Wall Street short-sellers, the installment plan, high tariffs, low tariffs, the British, the Russians. That didn't use to be the American way, to blame anybody but yourself. Lot of things have changed.

Your father's job was to build towns, raise wheat. Your job is to buy things. A poster shows a guy with a lunch bucket and a paycheck, his wife smiling at him. The words say: "When You BUY an AUTOMOBILE You GIVE 3 MONTHS WORK to Someone Which Allows Him to BUY OTHER PRODUCTS."

If you ain't got the mazuma to spend, you don't count.

You hear a husband and wife arguing.

"Why don't you fix cars?" the wife asks. "Every time I go downtown I see a new garage, everybody's car is breaking down."

"I'm not a car mechanic. I'm a machinist," the husband says.

"It's money," she says.

"That's the sad part," he says. "Back when we got married, I had a trade. I'm a machinist. Then they bring in the efficiency experts with their clipboards, timing every move I make. They turn me from a machinist into a machine. I say, what the hell, it's still good money. Then they take away the money. What a mug I was to think we were on Easy Street. What have I got left?"

"You've got a wife and kids wearing cardboard in the bottoms of their shoes," she says.

"Take in a show," he says.

People think you get away from the Depression in the movies, but Hollywood knows there's hard times and unrest, and they don't just show it in the newsreels.

When Mickey Mouse first came along in "Steamboat Willie" he was a mean little pest, and now Walt Disney is making him the common man, a hero like the common man in the murals the government artists paint in post offices. The little guy as hero. That's a change, all right.

In the "Thin Man" movies, they make William Powell a pal with every working stiff in the city—he stops to gas with the iceman, the news butcher, the local pickpocket before he goes off to drink martinis someplace with white telephones and Myrna Loy sliding around in a bathrobe suitable for a coronation. Witty as hell. You walk out of the theater wanting to not give a damn like that.

She says: "I read you were shot five times in the tabloids."

He says: "It's not true. He didn't come near my tabloids."

Here's the power of the movies: You read that John Dillinger and his gang pretend to be a movie company on location in front of a bank in Sioux Falls, S.D. The whole city gawks while inside, the pretend actors clean out the bank.

The FBI guns Dillinger down outside a movie theater in Chicago. You hear the coroner sent part of his anatomy to the

Smithsonian Institution in Washington, it was that big.

YOU HEAR A LOT OF STORIES: you hear about a smart guy, out of work. He starts an employment agency and takes the first job he was supposed to fill.

The stories about stockbrokers jumping out windows on Black Tuesday, Oct. 29, 1929: the suicide rate was higher right before the Crash than after it, but nobody wants to hear it.

Everybody's brother-in-law knows a banker who works as a caddie at his old country club.

In 1931, Cameroon, in West Africa, sent New York City a check for $3.77 to help the starving. Immigrants are going back to Europe by the shipload. Makes you feel bad.

When Roosevelt closed all the banks in 1933, you hear about one lucky woman who overdrew her account the day before.

In Deming, N.M., the Southern Pacific yard dicks drive so many hobos off the trains, the town has to hire a constable to drive them back on. On the Grand Concourse in the Bronx they have a poorhouse for the rich, the Andrew Freedman home, a mansion, so when the rich lose their money they don't have to live like the poor.

Eleanor Roosevelt is out visiting the poor and she sees a boy hiding a pet rabbit. His sister says: "He thinks we are not going to eat it. But we are."

Babies go hungry while farmers in Iowa dump their milk trying to get the price up to where they can keep producing milk so babies won't go hungry.

Herbert Hoover himself believes that "many persons left their jobs for the more profitable one of selling apples."

The apple story is enough to make you think the Reds are right.

In 1930, right after the Crash, Washington State has a bumper crop of apples. Too many to sell. So instead of dumping them, they give them to vendors on credit.

Next thing, men are lined up in Wall Street, wearing homburgs and selling apples, 5 cents apiece. There are so many of them they start cutting prices on each other. At the same time, the growers get greedy—raise the prices and don't cull the rotten ones. Pretty soon, you can't make any money in the apple business, and it's all over.

The feeling is: damned if you do, damned if you don't. Like playing the Irish Sweepstakes. Lots of gambling now: bingo, punchboards, slot machines, the numbers.

SOME PEOPLE SAY COMMUNISM will save us. Guys in black hats and leather jackets at the union meetings. They know how to organize, they know what they think, but you wonder if they could sell apples any better than anybody else. People are scared of the Reds. A witness tells the House Un-American Activities Committee that out in Hollywood, Shirley Temple is "a stooge of the Reds" for sending money to the Spanish Loyalists. A little girl!

They say J. Edgar Hoover and the FBI will save us from the Reds, the Nazi spies, the gangsters. The kids love him, running around in their Junior G-Man badges.

They say Roosevelt will save us. He comes on the radio in the Fireside Chats, not like Father Coughlin yelling about Reds and Jews. Just talking. "My friends," he says. Like he knows you know he knows how you feel. He doesn't have it all figured out like the Reds or Huey Long. He'll try anything until the Supreme Court knocks it down. The problem is, things don't get much better. He said in 1932:

"The only thing we have to fear is fear itself." He's still right.

And science will save us. You go to the world's fairs in Chicago and New York and learn how technocrats will build things out of plastic and beryllium bronze, the World of Tomorrow. Diesel trains. Television.

No class struggle because science solved all the problems. You never have to sweat out a toothache. Modern management. All you need is brains, not courage. You wonder, though: Is that the American way?

What you know for sure is, whoever's running things right now, it isn't you.

First it was the trusts and the railroads that took control of your life, then Wall Street and advertising, and now it's Roosevelt's Brain Trust and the alphabet agencies—NRA, PWA, WPA, CCC, CWA. They prove everything with numbers and polls; 37 percent of housewives spend 22 percent more hours blah blah . . .

Everything's scientific. You don't just get married, you go to college and take a course in "modern marriage." Half the babies in the country are born in hospitals. A mother isn't supposed to feed her baby with her own milk. It doesn't have enough of the vitamins they've discovered now. Science turns into a fashion. White tile and stainless steel, waitresses wearing white uniforms. Progress.

ONE DAY THE OUT-OF-WORK salesman and his wife down the block are gone. Not a word of goodbye.

The machinist gets a job in an airplane factory, making bombers.

When your nephew comes to the breakfast table, he swings his leg over the back of the chair, like Clark Gable in "It Happened One Night." Or Mickey Rooney in the Andy Hardy movies with Judy Garland.

Men don't wear tops on their bathing suits anymore.

Girls wear saddle shoes and apron dresses. They drink Cokes in drugstores. The soda jerk thinks they all have a crush on him, his white paper hat cocked to one side.

If you want to show your social consciousness, you don't have a "cleaning woman" anymore, you have a "cleaning lady."

How is vaudeville going to stand up to movies and radio? What will Milton Berle do for a living?

Modern furniture gets crazier. You see a picture of a bedroom in Hollywood with these reading chairs only Ming the Merciless could be comfortable in, and a laminated wood bed you could put on a Mayan funeral barge, everything tapered—table legs, lamps, vases.

You hear stories that Roosevelt, the British and the Jews are trying to get us into a war.

Huey Long gets shot dead in Baton Rouge.

There's a feeling you hardly notice after a while—a shabby feeling, dust and phone wires, a cold spring wind, things exposed . . .

A Monumental Man

FDR's chiseled features defined an American epoch

By Gerald Parshall

Franklin Roosevelt made no small plans—except for his own commemoration. The first Roosevelt memorial, now all but forgotten, was installed outside the National Archives building in 1965. A marble slab about the size of Roosevelt's desk, it was scaled to its subject's wishes. The new Roosevelt memorial now being completed in Washington is scaled to its subject's significance: Some 4,500 tons of granite went into it. Designer Lawrence Halprin laid out a wall that meanders over 7.5 acres, forming four outdoor rooms, each devoted to one of FDR's terms in the White House and each open on one side to a stunning vista of the Tidal Basin. Waterfalls, reflecting pools, and sculptures are set along what is likely to become one of the most popular walks in the nation's capital. The entry building contains a photograph of FDR in his wheelchair and a replica of the chair itself. The memorial's time line includes these words: "1921, STRICKEN WITH POLIOMYELITIS—HE NEVER AGAIN WALKED UNAIDED." But because no statue depicts him in his wheelchair, the dedication ceremony on May 2 faces a threatened protest by the disabled. Controversy often surrounded Roosevelt in life; his spirit should feel right at home.

THE POWER OF HIS SMILE

Today, we carry the face of Franklin Roosevelt in our pockets and purses—it is stamped on more than 18 billion dimes. From 1933 to 1945, Americans carried it in their hearts. It was stamped on their consciousness, looking out from every newspaper and newsreel, FDR's smile as bright as the headlight on a steam locomotive. Roosevelt's portrait hung in bus stations, in barber shops, in kitchens, in parlors, in Dust Bowl shacks—and in Winston Churchill's bedchamber in wartime London. It was the face of hope and freedom for the masses. Even among the "economic royalists," the haters of "that man in the White House," the portrait could stir emotion—as a dartboard.

In 1911, when the 28-year-old Roosevelt was newly elected to the New York Senate, the *New York Times* found him "a young man with the finely chiseled face of a Roman patrician" who "could make a fortune on the stage and set the matinee girl's heart throbbing with subtle and happy emotion." Tammany Hall Democrats, however, weren't swooning. They noted the freshman's habit of tossing his head back and peering down his nose (on which he wore pince-nez like Theodore Roosevelt, a fifth cousin) and read in it a squire's disdain for grubby city boys. The quirk persisted but acquired a new meaning decades later, when FDR wrestled with unprecedented domestic and foreign crises. His upturned chin and eyes, along with his cigarette holder, itself tilted toward the heavens, became symbols of indomitable determination to triumph over adversity—his own and the country's.

It was, indeed, the face of a great actor, a living sculpture continuously reshaped by the artist. The knowing twinkle. The arched eyebrow. The eloquent grimace. Roosevelt was a master of misdirection. He could lie without blinking, disarm enemies with infectious bonhomie, and make a bore feel like the most fascinating fellow on Earth. Officials with rival agendas often came away from the Oval Office equally sure that they alone had the president's ear.

"Never let your left hand know what your right is doing," FDR once confided to a cabinet member. Idealism and duplicity fused behind his smile, buttressing one another like the two sides of a Roosevelt dime.

THE WARMTH OF HIS WORDS

He was one of the greatest orators of his time but suffered from stage fright. While he waited on the dais, Franklin Roosevelt fidgeted, shuffled the pages of his speech, chain-smoked, and doused the butterflies in his stomach with gulps of water. At last, they let him start—"My friends...." In a New York minute, his nervousness was gone and the audience under his spell. His voice—languid one moment, theatrical the next—dripped with Groton, Harvard, and centuries of blue blood. Yet no president has ever communicated better with ordinary people.

A Roosevelt speech sounded spontaneous, straight from the heart, effortless—effects that took much effort to achieve. Some speeches went through a dozen drafts, with speech writers laboring at the big table in the Cabinet Room until 3 a.m. Roosevelt then revised mercilessly—shortening sentences, substituting words with fewer syllables, polishing similes—until his own muscular style emerged. Sometimes, he wrote a speech entirely by himself. He used a yellow legal pad to draft his first inaugural address, which rang with one of the most effective buck-up lines in history: "The only thing we have to fear is fear itself." He dictated to his secretary most of the Pearl Harbor message he delivered to Congress. He edited himself, changing "a date which will live in world history" to "a date which will live in infamy."

Roosevelt held two press conferences a week right in the Oval Office. Relaxed and jocular, he gently decreed what could and could not be printed. He talked to reporters, John Dos Passos remembered, in a fatherly voice "like the

ATLANTA CHANCE—FRANKLIN D. ROOSEVELT LIBRARY
Revisionist. FDR rewrote his speeches until they sang.

voice of a principal in a first-rate boy's school." Likewise, Roosevelt's "fireside chats" on the radio reverberated with paternal intimacy. He had a flair for homely analogies, such as equating Lend-Lease aid to Britian with loaning your neighbor a garden hose to put out a house fire. Who wouldn't do that? Speaking into the microphone, he gestured and smiled as if the audience would somehow sense what it could not see. Millions shushed the children and turned up the radio. They ached for leadership and "Doctor New Deal"—soon to become "Doctor Win the War"—was making a house call.

THE SPLENDOR OF HIS STRIDE

At the 1936 Democratic National Convention, Franklin Roosevelt fell down as he moved across the podium to address the delegates. He was quickly pulled up again, his withered legs bruised but unbroken. No newspaper stories or radio reports mentioned this incident—and for good reason. It hadn't happened. America was in denial. Prejudice against "cripples" was widespread. The nation wanted no reminders that it was following a man who could not walk.

From the earliest days of the polio that ravaged his legs in 1921, denial had been Roosevelt's way of coping. He spoke of his infirmity with no one, not even with members of his family. For seven years, almost every day, he took his crutches, tried—and failed—to reach the end of his Hyde Park driveway. He could not walk. But how he ran. Campaigning animatedly from open cars and the rear platform of trains, he was elected governor of New York twice and president of the United States four times. No crutches were seen and no wheelchair. His steel leg braces were painted black to blend with his socks; he wore extra long trousers. The Secret Service built ramps all over Washington, D.C., to give his limousine close access to his destinations. FDR jerkily "walked" the final distance by holding on to one of his sons with his left arm and supporting his right side with a cane. Newsreel cameras stopped; press photographers took a breather. If an amateur was spotted attempting to get a picture, the Secret Service swiftly closed in and exposed the film.

"FDR's splendid deception," historian Hugh Gallagher dubbed the little conspiracy in his book of that title. It worked so well that most Americans never knew of Roosevelt's disability, or they repressed what they did know. Such was the national amnesia, cartoonists even drew him jumping. FDR dropped the ruse for only one group. Military amputee wards were filled with men brooding about what fate had done to their futures. A high official sometimes came calling. The severely wounded GIs recognized the visitor immediately—no face was more famous—and his arrival brought an exhilarating revelation. Down the aisles came the nemesis of Hitler and Hirohito, his wheelchair in full view and looking like a royal chariot.

THE MAINSPRING OF HIS MIND

When the British monarch visited America in 1939, Franklin Roosevelt greeted him with unaccustomed familiarity. He served him hot dogs at a Hyde Park picnic and addressed him not as "your majesty" but as "George." "Why don't my ministers talk to me as the president did tonight?" an enchanted George VI remarked to a member of his entourage. "I felt exactly as though a father were giving me his most careful and wise advice." It was Roosevelt's genius to treat kings like commoners and commoners like kings. And both loved him for it.

His monumental self-assurance was bred in the bone. His mother, Sara, had reared him, her only child, to believe he had a fixed place in the center of the cosmos like other Roosevelts. She—and the example set by cousin Theodore—imparted another formative lesson: Privileged people have a duty to do good. Noblesse oblige, Christianity, and the golden rule made up the moral core of the aristocrat who became both the Democrat of the century and the democrat of the century.

Critics called him a socialist and a "traitor to his class." History would call him the savior of capitalism, the pragmatist who saved free enterprise from very possibly disappearing into the abyss and taking democracy with it. It seemed evident to him that only government could curb or cushion the worst excesses of industrialism. But, at bottom, he was less a thinker than a doer. Luckily, like gardeners and governesses, intellectuals could be hired. Roosevelt hired a brain trust and pumped it for ideas to which he applied this test: Will it work? If one program belly-flopped, he cheerfully tried another. "A second-class intellect," Justice Oliver Wendell Holmes pegged him. "But a first-class temperament."

For all his amiability, FDR knew with Machiavelli that self-seekers abound this side of paradise. Navigating perilous domestic and foreign waters by dead reckoning, he often felt compelled to be a shameless schemer. He hid his intentions, manipulated people, set aides to contrary tasks—all to keep control of the game in trustworthy hands (his own). Charm and high purposes palliated the pure ether of his arrogance. Franklin Roosevelt was hip-deep in the muck of politics and power, but his eyes were always on the stars.

Eleanor Roosevelt

America's most influential First Lady blazed paths for women and led the battle for social justice everywhere

By Doris Kearns Goodwin

When Eleanor Roosevelt journeyed to New York City a week after her husband's funeral in April 1945, a cluster of reporters were waiting at the door of her Washington Square apartment. "The story is over," she said simply, assuming that her words and opinions would no longer be of interest once her husband was dead and she was no longer First Lady. She could not have been more mistaken. As the years have passed, Eleanor Roosevelt's influence and stature have continued to grow. Today she remains a powerful inspiration to leaders in both the civil rights and women's movements.

Eleanor shattered the ceremonial mold in which the role of the First Lady had traditionally been fashioned, and reshaped it around her own skills and her deep commitment to social reform. She gave a voice to people who did not have access to power. She was the first woman to speak in front of a national convention, to write a syndicated column, to earn money as a lecturer, to be a radio commentator and to hold regular press conferences.

The path to this unique position of power had not been easy. The only daughter of an alcoholic father and a beautiful but aloof mother who was openly disappointed by Eleanor's lack of a pretty face, Eleanor was plagued by insecurity and shyness. An early marriage to her handsome fifth cousin once removed, Franklin Roosevelt, increased her insecurity and took away her one source of confidence: her work in a New York City settlement house. "For 10 years, I was always just getting over having a baby or about to have another one," she later lamented, "so my occupations were considerably restricted."

> "The bottom dropped out of my own particular world. I faced myself, my surroundings, my world honestly for the first time."
>
> **ELEANOR ROOSEVELT,**
> **on discovering her husband's affair**

But 13 years after her marriage, and after bearing six children, Eleanor resumed the search for her identity. The voyage began with a shock: the discovery in 1918 of love letters revealing that Franklin was involved with Lucy Mercer. "The bottom dropped out of my own particular world," she later said. "I faced myself, my surroundings, my world, honestly for the first time." There was talk of divorce, but when Franklin promised never to see Lucy again, the marriage continued. For Eleanor a new path had opened, a possibility of standing apart from Franklin. No longer would she define herself solely in terms of his wants and needs. A new relationship was forged, on terms wholly different from the old.

She turned her energies to a variety of reformist organizations, joining a cir-

---

BORN Oct. 11, 1884, in New York City
1905 Marries distant cousin Franklin Delano Roosevelt
1918 Discovers F.D.R.'s affair with Lucy Mercer
1932 F.D.R., crippled by polio since 1921, is elected President. Eleanor becomes his eyes and ears.
1948 Helps secure passage of the U.N.'s Universal Declaration of Human Rights
1962 Dies in New York City on Nov. 7

POPPERFOTO—ARCHIVE PHOTOS
Eleanor, right, "never smiled" as a child

cle of postsuffrage feminists dedicated to the abolition of child labor, the establishment of a minimum wage and the passage of legislation to protect workers. In the process she discovered that she had talents—for public speaking, for organizing, for articulating social problems. She formed an extraordinary constellation of lifelong female friends, who helped to assuage an enduring sense of loneliness. When Franklin was paralyzed by polio in 1921, her political activism became an even more vital force. She became Franklin's eyes and ears," traveling the country gathering the grassroots knowledge he needed to understand the people he governed.

They made an exceptional team. She was more earnest, less devious, less patient, less fun, more uncompromisingly moral; he possessed the more trustworthy political talent, the more finely tuned sense of timing, the better feel for the citizenry, the smarter understanding of how to get things done. But they were linked by indissoluble bonds. Together they mobilized the American people to effect enduring changes in the political and social landscape of the nation.

Nowhere was Eleanor's influence greater than in civil rights. In her travels around the country, she developed a sophisticated understanding of race relations. When she first began inspecting New Deal programs in the South, she was stunned to find that blacks were being systematically discriminated against at every turn. Citing statistics to back up her story, she would interrupt her husband at any time, barging into his cocktail hour when he wanted only to relax, cross-examining him at dinner, handing him memos to read late at night. But her confrontational style compelled him to sign a series of Executive Orders barring discrimination in the administration of various New Deal projects. From that point on, African Americans' share in the New Deal work projects expanded, and Eleanor's independent legacy began to grow.

She understood, for instance, the importance of symbolism in fighting discrimination. In 1938, while attending the Southern Conference for Human Welfare in Birmingham, Ala., she refused to abide by a segregation ordinance that required her to sit in the white section of the auditorium, apart from her black friends. The following year, she publicly resigned from the Daughters of the American Revolution after it barred the black singer Marian Anderson from its auditorium. During World War II, Eleanor remained an uncompromising voice on civil rights, insisting that America could not fight racism abroad while tolerating it at home. Progress was slow, but her continuing intervention led to broadened opportunities for blacks in the factories and shipyards at home and in the armed forces overseas.

Eleanor's positions on civil rights were far in advance of her time: 10 years before the Supreme Court rejected the "separate but equal" doctrine, Eleanor argued that equal facilities were not enough: "The basic fact of segregation, which warps and twists the lives of our Negro population, [is] itself discriminatory."

There were other warps and twists that caught her eye. Long before the contemporary women's movement provided ideological arguments for women's rights, Eleanor instinctively challenged institutions that failed to provide equal opportunity for women. As First Lady, she held more than 300 press conferences that she cleverly restricted to women journalists, knowing that news organizations all over the country would be forced to hire their first female reporter in order to have access to the First Lady.

Through her speeches and her columns, she provided a powerful voice in the campaign to recruit women workers to the factories during the war. "If I were of debutante age, I would go into a factory, where I could learn a skill and be useful," Eleanor told young women, cautioning them against marrying too hastily before they had a chance to expand their horizons. She was instrumental in securing the first government funds ever allotted for the building of child-care centers. And when women workers were unceremoniously fired as the war came to an end, she fought to stem the tide. She argued on principle that everyone who wanted to work had a right to be productive, and she railed against the closing of the child-care centers as a shortsighted response to a fundamental social need. What the women workers needed, she said, was the courage to ask for their rights with a loud voice.

For her own part, she never let the intense criticism that she encountered silence her. "If I . . . worried about mudslinging, I would have been dead long ago." Yet she insisted that she was not a feminist. She did not believe, she maintained, that "women should be judged, when it comes to appointing them or electing them, purely because they are women." She wanted to see the country "get away from considering a man or woman from the point of view of religion, color or sex." But the story of her life—her insistence on her right to an identity of her own apart from her husband and her family, her constant struggle against depression and insecurity, her ability to turn her vulnerabilities into strengths—provides an enduring example of a feminist who transcended the dictates of her times to become one of the century's most powerful and effective advocates for social justice.

Doris Kearns Goodwin is a Pulitzer-prizewinning author, historian and political analyst

The Lone Dissenting Voice

A single vote forever established Representative Jeannette Rankin as a pacifist, and for the rest of her life she crusaded against the United States' involvement in all foreign wars.

By Glen Jeansonne

Four days after Republican Jeannette Rankin—the first woman elected to the House of Representatives—took her seat in Congress, she cast the first and most auspicious vote of her political career. Europe had been at war since August 1914, and on April 2, 1917, President Woodrow Wilson summoned a special session of Congress to call for the United States to join the Allies in their fight against Germany. Three days after Wilson's war message and one day after the Senate passed the war declaration, the House considered the resolution.

No one doubted that the resolution would pass—only the margin was questionable. During the debate, Rankin sat in silence, feeling enormous pressure to vote with the majority. Many of her suffragist supporters urged her to vote affirmatively. "The hardest part of the vote was that the suffragists were divided," she said later. "Many of my loved friends told me that I would ruin the suffrage movement if I voted against war." Nevertheless, she vowed to keep an open mind, listen to the arguments, and wait until the second roll call to vote. Her brother, Wellington, who had traveled from his home in Montana to be with his older sister, told Jeannette she would destroy her career if she voted against war.

Rankin passed on the first roll call, and Speaker Joseph Cannon, who assumed she would not vote at all, walked over to her seat. "Little woman, you cannot afford not to vote," he said. "You represent the womanhood of the country in the American Congress. I shall not advise you how to vote but you should vote one way or another—as your conscience dictates." There was silence in the chamber after Rankin's name was called a second time, and everyone turned to look at her. Rankin rose slowly and unsteadily clutching the chair in front of her. Softly yet emotionally she said, "I want to stand by my country, but I cannot vote for war." Her "nay" vote that followed was nearly inaudible in the noise and confusion that ensued. She had defied a 140-year House tradition by commenting on a vote during a roll call and defied the president by voting against war.

Jeannette Rankin was born on June 11, 1880, and grew up on the Montana frontier, the first of six children of pioneer parents. Eleven years earlier, her father, John, had emigrated from Canada in search of gold. Instead, he became a rancher and lumber merchant in Missoula. In 1878, Jeannette's mother, Olive Pickering, and her sister traveled by train from New Hampshire to live with an uncle in Missoula. Her sister soon returned to New Hampshire, declaring that, "Montana was no fit place to raise children," but Olive stayed and became the second schoolteacher in Montana Territory. She married John Rankin a year later.

The Rankins became one of the wealthiest families in Missoula, with a 1,480-acre ranch and an imposing home fitted with the first indoor plumbing in town. As a family, they were feisty, ambitious, and close-knit. Jeannette was creative and open-minded, but she could also be stubborn and opinionated. She disliked school and went to college only "because it was the thing to do." She was an undistinguished student at Montana State University—her most memorable accomplishment was a senior thesis she wrote about snail shells. She graduated from college in 1902 and became an elementary school teacher. Then she worked briefly as an apprentice dress-maker, and studied furniture design. In comparison, the Rankins' only son, Wellington, received a law degree from Harvard and became Montana's attorney general, associate justice of the state Supreme Court, and Republican national committeeman. He was also one of the state's most brilliant trial lawyers and richest citizens.

After John Rankin died of Rocky Mountain spotted fever in 1904, Jeannette helped her mother raise her siblings. Four years later she enrolled in a one-year course at the New York School of Philanthropy, a forerunner of Columbia University's School of Social Welfare. Her experiences there deepened her sense of the social injustices in America, and after earning her degree, Rankin returned to Missoula and tried to reform the whole town. Disheartened by the negative response there, she moved to Seattle, where she enrolled in sociology and economics courses at the University of Washington and joined the successful Washington state campaign for woman suffrage.

Rankin's own political career began after she returned to Missoula for the Christmas holiday in 1910. While at home she learned that a bill calling for a public vote on woman suffrage was to be brought before the Montana legislature the following February. Jeannette requested permission to speak before the state legislature, where she forcefully proposed that women be granted the right to vote. With Rankin's assistance and hard work, the women of Montana gained the vote in 1914. Two years later Jeannette decided to run for Congress after her brother agreed to finance and manage her campaign. One prominent Republican advised Wellington to "keep Jeannette from making a fool of herself." Wellington, however, believed that his sister could easily win the election—except for the governor, she was probably the best known person in the state. With Wellington's encouragement, Jeannette announced her candidacy in July 1916. Six men joined her in seeking the two Republican nominations, but she led the field.

Because both of Montana's House seats were at-large, Rankin had to mount a statewide effort. She campaigned in one-room schoolhouses, county fairs, ice cream socials, potluck dinners, and union halls. "I would go into a union hall when they were having a meeting and ask to be allowed to speak for five minutes when they had concluded their business," she recalled. "Sometimes I would have to wait for an hour until they had finished, sitting in a corner without opening my mouth."

She won the election by 7,567 votes and made national headlines. Reporters focused on her appearance—the color of her eyes, the shade of her hair. Rumors spread that the 37-year-old Montana native packed a six-shooter and trimmed her skirts with fur. They described her as a "red-headed cowgirl" (her hair was brown) and an "amazon" (she was 5 feet, 4 inches tall). Marriage proposals came in the mail, as did an offer of $5,000 to endorse a toothpaste.

On April 2, 1917, Jeannette arrived at the House of Representatives for her first session in Congress. Elderly John Evans, Montana's other representative, escorted her into the chamber, where Democrats as well as Republicans on the floor greeted her with a burst of applause. Ellen Maury Slayden, wife of a Texas congressman, was in the gallery that day and later wrote in her diary that Rankin "didn't look to right or left until she reached her seat... but before she could sit down she was surrounded by men shaking hands with her. I rejoiced to see that she met each one with a frank smile and shook hands cordially and unaffectedly. It would have been sickening if she had smirked or giggled or been coquettish."

During its first meeting in this special session of the 65th Congress, the House admitted new members and chose a speaker. The real business of the session did not begin until that evening when the Senate and House heard President Wilson call for war against Germany. Wellington had urged his sister to vote yes. "I knew she couldn't be elected again if she did vote against the war," he recalled. "I didn't want to see her destroy herself." According to Jeannette, however, "Never for one second could I face the idea that I would send young men to be killed for no other reason than to save my seat in Congress." When the votes were cast, 373 members voted in favor, 9 abstained, and 49 men joined Rankin in voting against war. It was Rankin's vote, however, that attracted the most attention.

As Wellington predicted, Jeannette's vote generated much ill will. The *New York Times* editorialized that it was "final proof of the feminine incapacity for straight reasoning." In Rankin's home state the Helena *Independent* called her "a dagger in the hands of the German propagandists, a dupe of the Kaiser, a member of the Hun army in the United States, and a crying schoolgirl." Newspapers reported that she had cried on the House floor, and while Rankin admitted to crying during the debate, she claimed to have composed herself by the time she voted. "I have more respect for a woman who cries before she votes upon whether or not we shall have war than [for] the man who goes to a saloon and takes three highballs in a similar situation," she said.

Rankin was far from inactive during the remainder of her term. Her work included sponsoring legislation to give women United States citizenship independent of their husbands and aide women with children whose husbands were fighting in World War I. She also called for equal job opportunities and pay for women in war industries, fought against a bill that gave the government the right to censor newspapers, and continued to work for a federal suffrage amendment.

Rankin did not run again in a statewide election. In 1917, Montana was divided into two congressional districts; Rankin's district was strongly Democratic. She felt committed, however, to seek reelection in 1918 and resolved to run for the Senate. Rankin narrowly lost the Republican primary and lost badly in the general election when she ran as a third-party candidate.

IN THE 1920s AND 30s RANKIN shifted her focus from feminism to pacifism. She worked as a lobbyist for the National Consumers League, the American wing of the Women's International League for Peace and Freedom, and the National Council for the Prevention of War. She retained her legal residence in Montana but established a second home in Georgia, where land was cheap and where she enjoyed the rural life. She spent much of her free time there growing vegetables and raising chickens.

Rankin lobbied for a constitutional amendment to outlaw war, supported strict neutrality legislation, and worked for passage of the Ludlow Amendment, which would have required a national referendum to declare war. She also created the Georgia Peace Society in an unsuccessful attempt to unseat Congressman Carl Vinson, a large-navy advocate. She grew to despise President Franklin D. Roosevelt, whom she considered an enemy of peace, and sided with his enemies, such as Huey P. Long and Father Charles E. Coughlin.

By 1940 war was once again enveloping Europe. Rankin, now 60, decided to run for Congress again to attract national attention for her peace doctrine. Although white-haired and somewhat slowed by age, she was still a formidable character. Her chief obstacle was her long absence from Montana, where she had spent only summer vacations. Her advantages were her influential connections and the widespread anti-war sentiment in Montana. Wellington was less enthusiastic than he had been in 1916 but agreed to fund his sister's effort.

Rankin began her campaign with a series of radio broadcasts advising Montanans to write to President Roosevelt and urge him to avoid war. Americans, she said, should defend their country instead of intervening abroad. Rankin believed that only an attack on the American mainland would justify a military response.

The feisty pacifist faced three male opponents in the Republican primary, including the incumbent, Jacob Thorkelson, an anti-British, anti-Semitic isolationist. She defeated Thorkelson by 1,000 votes, with the other candidates even farther back. In the general election she faced Democrat Jerry J. O'Connell of Butte, a former congressman who also opposed American involvement in the war, albeit less militantly than Rankin. After she defeated Butte by 9,264 votes, the *Christian Century* speculated, "One cannot but wonder whether she will be called upon to vote on the question of America's entrance into the war."

Rankin's arrival in Washington was a much more subdued affair than it had been after her first election. The representative from Montana began her second term by opposing the draft, military expenditures, the Lend-Lease bill to aid Britain, and the repeal of the neutrality legislation of the 1930s. Any illusions of peace that she harbored, however, were shattered on December 7, 1941, when Japanese planes attacked Pearl Harbor. The following day President Roosevelt delivered a brief war message to a joint session of Congress, and a war declaration against Japan was introduced in the Senate and the House simultaneously. The Senate passed it unanimously. In the House, Rankin attempted to have the matter referred to committee, which would have delayed the decision and given her more time to speak at length about the reasons for not going to war. Speaker Sam Rayburn, however, refused to recognize her, ignoring her repeated calls of "Mr. Speaker, I would like to be heard." Minority Leader Joseph Martin said the war effort must be bipartisan. "In the view of the developments of the past forty-eight hours, the president's request has my support," he said. "When the historic roll call is called, I hope there will not be a single dissenting vote."

There was one dissenting vote, however, and it was Rankin's. At the first roll call she spoke her "nay" in a firm, clear voice. She again violated protocol by adding, "As a woman I can't go to war, and I refuse to send anyone else." Her vote raised a chorus of hisses and boos from the floor and the galleries. When the roll call was over, the vote was 388 for war and 1 against it. Rankin retreated to the House cloakroom and then to a telephone booth to escape the crush of congressmen, spectators, photographers, and reporters. She dialed the Capitol police, who escorted her to her office. Rankin locked the door behind her, and a guard was posted outside for her protection.

The public reaction was similar to that following her 1917 vote. She was called a "skunk," a "traitor," and a "Nazi" although William Allen White wrote in the *Emporia Gazette,* "Probably 100 men in Congress would have liked to do what she did. Not one of them had the courage to do it. The *Gazette* entirely disagrees with the wisdom of her position. But Lord, it was a brave thing!" The Montana congresswoman stood alone in the House and ultimately in Montana, losing any chance for reelection in 1942.

She lived privately for the next 20 years, traveling extensively to South America, Europe, the Middle East, and India, where she became a follower of the philosophy of Mahatma Ghandi. She quietly opposed the Cold War and the United States' involvement in Korea. In 1967, however, Rankin lent her name to the "Jeannette Rankin Brigade," a group of pacifists who planned to protest the Vietnam War by demonstrating in Washington, D.C. On January 15, 1968, Rankin led several thousand women "brigade" members in a march to the Capitol. "No one can let up in this effort to bring about peace," Rankin declared. "We have to get it into our heads once and for all that we cannot settle disputes by eliminating human beings."

On Rankin's 90th birthday in 1970, members of Congress honored her with a champagne reception in the Rayburn House Office Building. One congressman called her "the original dove in Congress." Shortly before her death from a heart attack three years later, a reporter asked her whether she would do anything differently if she could relive her life. Rankin replied that she would not, with one exception: "I would have been nastier."

Glen Jeansonne is a professor of history at the University of Wisconsin-Milwaukee.

For more about women in politics, read "All Men and Women Are Created Equal," by Constance Rynder. You can find it starting March 1 [1999] on the world Wide Web at TheHistoryNet, http://www.thehistorynet.com.

Our Greatest Land Battle

BY EDWARD OXFORD Fifty years ago, amid the snow, blood, and death of Belgium's Ardennes forest, 600,000 American soldiers defeated a half-million Germans in the Battle of the Bulge—the largest engagement involving the U.S. army in World War II.

American soldiers manning an eighty-five-mile stretch of rugged, heavily wooded countryside along the Belgian-Luxembourg-German border were jolted awake in the predawn hours of December 16, 1944, by the thunder of mortar, rocket, and artillery fire. When the barrage finally ended, the Americans peered from their foxholes to see strange lights playing against the low-hanging clouds and reflecting onto the forest floor to reveal ghostly figures advancing among the trees. The bewildered GIs didn't know what to make of it.

The Americans were holding the northern sector of a five-hundred-mile line that extended across France and Belgium all the way from the Swiss border to the North Sea. During the six months since the Allied invasion of Normandy they had driven east in an effort to push the German Army across the Rhine and establish a foothold on the far side of the river. The Allies had been stopped short of their objective and suffered significant losses, especially in the bloody hard-fought offensive of the Hürtgen Forest, but they had inflicted an even higher toll on the enemy.

As the Americans paused just short of Germany's vaunted West Wall—also known as the Siegfried Line—to rest their battle-worn veterans and train newcomers, they did not suspect that the enemy was capable of anything but defensive action. For days, and in many cases weeks, more than eighty thousand soldiers of the 14th Cavalry Group, the 9th Armored Division, and four U.S. infantry divisions—the 4th, 28th, 99th, and 106th—had marked time along the mist-ridden battlefront.

Almost incredibly, spearheads of the "beaten" German Army were thrusting into U.S. lines.

During these pre-Christmas days, all seemed relatively secure. Film star Marlene Dietrich, heading a USO troupe, performed to the raucous applause of GIs. Numbers of men wangled three-day passes to Paris. One soldier wrote home: "As long as I stay where I am now I'll be safe."

But, in the half-light of that Saturday's dawn, the enemy soldiers advancing in the reflected glow of searchlights were very much alive and threatening. U.S. rifleman Bernard Macay saw "hundreds of Germans against the skyline as they came over the hill, right at us." American troops on the front lines opened up with rifle, machine-gun, and

NATIONAL ARCHIVES

mortar fire. Their first response, though earnest, was sporadic, uncoordinated, and confused. Almost incredibly spearheads of German Führer Adolf Hitler's "beaten" German Army were thrusting into U.S. lines.

The Battle of the Bulge, with fire and fury, had begun.

Somehow in the heart of Ardennes darkness, Hitler had discerned a glimmer of hope. Just as Allied commanders judged the rugged countryside unsuitable for an attack route into Germany so also did they disregard it as a likely approach for an enemy counteroffensive.

In the fifth year of devastating war, Hitler's "Thousand-Year" Third Reich was under siege. The Germans had fought hard, but Allied troops, quite like their leaders, felt a sense of momentum as they moved relentlessly through France and the Low Countries toward the Rhine. On the Eastern Front, Russian forces hammered the Germans with equal fury. By day and by night, air raids continued to turn the Fatherland's cities and factories into ruins. German ground forces had by this time suffered more than four million casualties, nearly half of them in the summer of 1944. Yet even an attempt on his life by his own officers in July had failed to break the Führer's determination to continue the war.

Refusing to listen to his military advisors, Hitler decided to draw upon the best of his remaining men and matériel in a do-or-die attempt to turn back the Allied onslaught. Under the cover of mist and snow, German forces would strike through a weak sector on the Allied front in the Ardennes, cross the Meuse River sixty miles to the West, and press on another sixty miles to capture the vital Channel port of Antwerp. They would, thereby, split the American and British forces—and their alliance as well—inflicting so many losses that, conceivably the Allies would sue for peace.

There was a grim, if fatalistic, logic to Hitler's plan. Unconditional surrender was unthinkable, and Germany could not survive by fighting a defensive war. The one route left was through the Ardennes. As a German adage put the choice: "Better an end in horror than a horror without end."

During the three months since Hitler revealed his scheme, the Germans east of the Ardennes had moved with remarkable stealth to ready thirty assault divisions. Although they fell short of that goal by two divisions, they had moved some 300,000 men, 1,900 artillery pieces, and nearly 1,000 tanks and armored vehicles into place. The operation was deceptively code-named "*Wacht am Rhein*" ("Watch on the Rhine").

Incredibly, the large-scale preparation went barely noticed by Allied intelligence. The Germans had begun to suspect that "Enigma," their code system, might be vulnerable to Allied codebreakers (which, throughout the war, it was). Hitler therefore directed that orders relating to the crucial Ardennes attack be sent by motorcycle rather than by radio. "Ultra," the Allied intelligence derived from cracking Enigma, dried up in that sector.

U.S. Army historian Hugh M. Cole has called the prelude to the Ardennes action "a gross failure by Allied ground and air intelligence.... The Allies had looked in a mirror for the enemy and seen there only the reflection of their own intentions." Bent upon attacking Germany they did not conceive that the enemy might strike back at them—much as the Germans, attacking at Stalingrad in 1942, had assumed that the Russians could not possibly attack *them*.

NATIONAL ARCHIVES

24. Our Greatest Land Battle

NATIONAL ARCHIVES

The top Allied commanders themselves accepted this analysis. Overconfidence, which led them to accept a paper-thin Ardennes line as a "legitimate risk," was to bring their forces to the brink of catastrophe.

Not until December 12, at Hitler's western command bunker north of Frankfurt, were his lower-echelon officers given the final details of the attack. The Fifth and Sixth SS Panzer Armies would make the main strike into Belgium, while the Seventh Army protected their southern flank. "This battle is to decide whether we shall live or die," the Führer exhorted his commanders: "I want all my soldiers to fight hard and without pity.... The enemy must be beaten—now or never!"

Hitler cannily scheduled the offensive for November to allow bad weather to set in, so as to cloak his ground attack from the view of Allied fighters and bombers. Logistical problems, however, necessitated delaying the assault until mid-December. As Hitler had hoped, at least for the first few days fog did keep the Allied planes grounded.

At 5:30 A.M. on December 16 the German barrage began. The firing continued for more than an hour, aiming for U.S. command posts, communications centers, and encampments. Soon, from out of the gloom, came the German foot-soldiers bathed in the eerie glow of searchlights. Thousands of GIs, many in combat for the first time, battled for their lives. Short of ammunition, without air support, and dazed by the devastating artillery fire, disciplined infantry assaults, and deadly tank attacks, some faltered. But the orders were to "hold fast." "In other words," wrote Sergeant Henry Giles in his diary "get killed but don't fall back."

In the north, the Sixth SS Panzer Army met unexpected trouble when the untried U.S. 99th Infantry Division offered stiff resistance, at a cost of more than two thousand casualties in the first four days of fighting. As the nearby 2nd Division deftly slipped battalions forward through the 99th to burrow into enemy forces, the two groups together formed an unbreakable barrier.

At the southern end of the German assault, the veteran U.S. 4th Infantry Division put up a fierce holding action at the village of Berdorf. Their steadfast refusal to budge held the enemy within two miles of their starting point and blocked their access to any of the main roads through the town.

At the center, however, the Fifth Panzer Army made penetrations with stealth and speed. On the thickly forested Schnee Eifel ridge, Panzer tank forces surrounded two regiments of the green 106th Division, subjecting them for three days to a numbing assault. Promised airdrops of supplies, the beleaguered units attempted to move out on December 18. But the relief drops never materialized. Nearly out of food, water, medical supplies, and ammunition, and facing vastly superior firepower, the regiments crumpled on December 19. In a kind of European "Bataan," seven to eight thousand men—the largest number of Americans ever captured in a single action—were taken prisoner by the Germans.

At his headquarters in Paris, Supreme Allied Commander General Dwight D. Eisenhower pondered the breakthrough. General Omar Bradley, whose command encompassed the Ardennes sector, first thought the assault to be a "spoiling attack" aimed at hindering the planned advance of the U.S. First and Third Armies in the region. Eisenhower, however, sensed major trouble: the massive attack had ominous momentum.

In this time of peril, Eisenhower held just about as much strategic power as Hitler himself did. He had full authority to put countermeasures into action at once. In a matter of days, he was to pour a quarter of a million men and thousands of tanks and artillery pieces into the Ardennes—a strike-back no other army in history has ever matched.

Concerned by the enormity of the German salient, Eisenhower imposed a news blackout on the battle action. It would be days before Americans on the home front found out what their sons, brothers, and husbands on the battlefront had learned firsthand: the Western Front's biggest ground battle had broken out in the Ardennes.

The Germans had driven a wedge between the First and Ninth U.S. Armies in the North and the Third Army under General George S. Patton in the South. Faced with that emergency, Eisenhower was forced to make the difficult decision to divide General Omar Bradley's command of these armies, giving charge of the First and Ninth Armies to British Field Marshal Bernard L. Montgomery and leaving Bradley in command of the Third. Among the American officers it was not a popular decision, but it had the added effect that Eisenhower had hoped for; it brought the British XXX Corps into the fray to back up the troops sent to block key bridges from the German advance.

Eisenhower's strategy overall was to hold the "shoulders" of the penetration—limiting the width of the breakthrough so that he could counterattack the flanks, hem in the Panzer columns so that they could not maneuver, and put a choke-hold on the breakthrough.

As the battle intensified, a dozen units were deployed to hold the northern edge of the salient.* In the very first hours, the 101st Airborne raced by truck through the night to reach Bastogne, a strategic crossroads town with seven paved roads radiating from its center, that lay directly in the path of the Fifth Panzer Army's advance. At the full tide of battle, thirty-two U.S. divisions would take part in the action.

By December 20, the Sixth Panzer Army had advanced only about five miles, but its First Panzer Division had driven forward

---

*These, ranging roughly east to west through the First Army sector commanded by General Courtney Hodges, would include: the 9th, 2nd, 99th, 1st, and 30th Infantry divisions; the 82nd Airborne; the 7th and 3rd Armored; the 75th, 84th, and 83rd Infantry; and the 2nd Armored. General George Patton's Third Army pressed up from the south. Here would be arrayed the 4th, 9th, and 5th Infantry divisions; the 10th Armored, the 80th, and 26th Infantry; the 6th, 4th, 9th, and 11th Armored; the 17th Airborne; and the 87th Infantry.

In one of the worst atrocities of the Western Front, SS troops murdered eighty-six American prisoners of war in a field near Malmédy.

---

twenty miles. The Fifth Panzer Army fared well, slashing more than fifteen miles ahead on a wide front and threatening the key crossroads town of Bastogne.

Though German advance forces quickly overran American outposts, with every new mile they found the going tougher. They fell behind their schedule, and—fatefully—their tanks began to run low on fuel.

GIs found themselves in a foot-by-foot fight for hills, villages, and woods. They struggled through mud and rain with their M-1 rifles slung on their shoulders; pockets stuffed with grenades, cigarettes, and candle stubs; sheets of toilet paper tucked inside their helmets. Some stuffed newspapers into their overcoats for warmth. Private Lester Atwell wrote: "Their chapped hands split open, their lips cracked, their feet froze. They had colds, frostbite, trench foot, pneumonia. After trudging miles through deep snow along they came, their faces pinched, astonished, mottled. The young looked old."

Driving captured jeeps, English-speaking German troops wearing U.S. Military Police armbands and GI field jackets and trousers over their uniforms began to infiltrate key road junctions. Many of these dissemblers were German-Americans who had lived in the United States before the war. They misdirected U.S. vehicles, turned signposts the wrong way and hung red ribbons to signify—falsely—that roads were mined.

Thousands of jumpy GIs played cat-and-mouse with one another as they tried to search out the roving saboteurs. At gunpoint, genuine MPs would ask American soldiers such questions as: "What's the capital of Illinois?" "Who are 'dem Bums'?" . . . "What's the name of Roosevelt's dog?" One U.S. general was put under guard when he mistakenly said the Chicago Cubs were an American League team.

Although their masquerade quickly came undone, the impostors managed to set off a scare throughout the American forces. Eighteen of those captured were executed by U.S. firing squads.

Hitler's hopes rode highest on SS Lieutenant Colonel Joachim Peiper, his handpicked choice to spearhead the Panzer drive through the American line. A believer in brutality, Peiper urged his commanders to "fight in the SS spirit."

On Sunday afternoon, December 17, in a field near Malmédy, SS troops under Peiper's command engaged in a particularly heinous episode of *blutraush*—killing frenzy. They had captured some 130 men of the U.S. 285th Field Artillery Observation Battalion and ordered them into rows, hands above their heads. According to later war-crimes testimony, SS soldiers moved among the prisoners, confiscating their rings, wallets, and cigarettes. A German officer then gave the command: "*Machen alles kaput!*" ("Kill them all!") German troops opened up with machine gun and pistol fire on the helpless Americans. Terrified GIs ran in all directions. Private James Mattera recalls: "SS soldiers came to men who were still alive and they shot them in the head." The executioners kicked some downed men in their faces, striking others with rifle butts. One man's eyes were gouged out.

Later that day, the unburied, bullet-ridden bodies of eighty-six soldiers were found in the bloodstained field. A few wounded but still living, survived by pretending to be dead. Forty or so others escaped into the woodlands.

The Malmédy Massacre undoubtedly strengthened the resolve of American soldiers—not just to stop the Germans but to beat them severely on the field of battle.* Gunners hammered at Peiper's

---

*This massacre was only one of many confirmed acts of brutality laid at Peiper's feet. All told, he was found responsible for ordering the murder of more than 350 American prisoners of war and 111 Belgian civilians along his line of march.

24. Our Greatest Land Battle

tanks. Engineers blew up bridges to thwart his advance. Major Paul J. Solis, commander of an armored infantry detachment sent to defend Stavelot, ignited thousands of gallons of fuel at a gasoline dump to form a barrier against him. By December 21, out of fuel, ammunition, and hope, Peiper ignominiously led eight hundred survivors of his original force of five thousand back toward Germany on foot.

Throughout the Ardennes, U.S. tanks and infantrymen did bitter battle against the more-heavily-armored German Mark IV, Panther, and Tiger tanks. "Our Sherman tanks would lie in wait, and hit those big tanks in the back, where their armor could be pierced," First Sergeant Bill Wagner recalls. "It was the only way to stop them. "In only three minutes, tank gunner Gerald Nelson knocked out three enemy tanks with three shots. Private Bernard Michin, firing a bazooka from only ten yards away hit and destroyed a Tiger; the blast left him blind for eight hours. In a dusk attack, a Sherman commanded by Lieutenant Charles Power set three Panthers afire. Sergeant Settimio Tiberio hunkered low when a Tiger tank rolled right over his foxhole and lived to tell of it.

Temperatures dipped below freezing, with intermittent snow, hanging mists, and ground fog. GIs went to sleep in overcoats and woke up encased in a film of ice. Water froze in canteens. C-rations became blocks of ice. Corporal Howard Peterson remembers: "To get out of the cold we crawled into a pigpen; soldiers and pigs—we all smelled the same." "It went down near zero one night," recalls infantryman Joseph Kiss. "By dawn I had half a foot of snow on top of me. We were dirty, wet, and tired. I saw some men cry. The Germans would yell at us to give up. But we never did." Sergeant Nat Youngblood tells of a twelve-year-old Belgian farm girl, scarved and bundled, plodding through snowdrifts to bring hot coffee to U.S. soldiers burrowed in foxholes. "I'll never forget her young face. 'Good morning,' she said to me. 'Coffee, sir?'"

For days, furious action centered around Bastogne. Here troopers of the 101st Airborne Division, along with soldiers from other units, formed an island of Americans in a sea of Germans. The 18,000 defenders fought in every direction at once, holding a sixteen-mile perimeter against more than twice their number. In relentless waves, German tanks and troops strove to smash into "the hole in the doughnut."

U.S. field guns dropped a "dam of fire" around the perimeter. Mud slowed and just about stopped the advancing tanks. As German infantry ran forward shouting, the Americans cut them down. The attackers kept on coming, climbing over bodies of their comrades before being killed themselves.

Midday on December 22, Brigadier General Anthony McAuliffe, commander of the besieged 101st, received an ultimatum to surrender or risk the annihilation of his troops. McAuliffe, who had earlier received word that part of Patton's Third Army was on their way to Bastogne, responded with his memorable, one-syllable reply: "Nuts!"

Hell-bent upon the rescue of Bastogne, tanks of the 4th Armored Division of Patton's Third Army went into high gear alongside infantry, punching up from the south. In their remarkable dash toward the besieged town, the Third Army moved farther and engaged more enemy divisions in less time then any other army in the history of the United States. As Patton had said to Eisenhower: "This time the German has stuck his hand in a meat grinder—and I've got hold of the handle."

"Hitler's weather," a blanket of fog and cloud, continued to cloak the battleground. Allied airpower, poised to strike, could but bide its time. Forlorn U.S. soldiers looked to the sky in vain.

Finally, at dawn on December 23, a cold front moved through, sweeping the clouds away. U.S. Army Air Force P-51 Mustangs, P-47 Thunderbolts, P-38 Lightnings, and B-26 Marauders, along with Royal Air Force Typhoons swarmed down on the Germans. The besieged troops at Bastogne received their first airdrop of badly needed supplies. At American-held Malmédy, however, a number of U.S. troops and Belgian civilians were killed when mistakenly bombed by the Ninth Air Force on three consecutive nights.

Come Christmas morning, with German forces closing in on Bastogne, paratroopers shook hands with one another in a farewell gesture. Hour after hour, enemy soldiers bore in upon them, full-circle. In one particularly dramatic showdown, beleaguered Americans knocked out eighteen German tanks and cut to ribbons waves of white-clad Panzer grenadiers. By nightfall, the paratroopers—with cooks and mechanics and clerks fighting alongside them—still held the rim. Their Christmas present came the next day. In the fast-fading afternoon light of the 26th, the first of Patton's tanks broke into Bastogne.

For Hitler, Bastogne became the crucial symbol—the place that *must* be taken. Even into the New Year, his Panzers hit Bastogne with as many as fifteen attacks a day—but could not break the ring. A German victory here was not to be.

The price, for both sides at Bastogne, was high. Some 7,000 Germans and 3,500 Americans were killed or wounded fighting for the village.

Spellbinding though the Bastogne action was, scores of bloody thrusts and ripostes—death-duels waged by tanks, artillery and foot-soldiers—were fought throughout the Ardennes woodlands. For the battle-worn "dogface," misery was the order of the day. "We would attack each pitch-black morning," says Corporal Mitchell Kaidy. "If we slept, it was sitting up—fitfully, shallowly, cradling our rifles and hand grenades like babies." Private First Class Thor Ronnigen remembers "dead Germans toppling into our foxholes." "There were shapes in the snow and we would fire and fire," recalls Private Charles Oxford, brother of the author of this article. "A shell-burst got me at one point. When they carried me out, my feet were frostbitten."

"The Germans came through after the moon had set," said Corporal William Fowler. "I fired my machine gun. I could hear them holler, begging for mercy when they were hit." At a roadblock, paratrooper Roger Carqueville stopped a hurrying jeep: "I stuck an M-1 at the driver's ear and asked him for the password. Turned out he was a chaplain.

I figured I wasn't going to make it through the scrap, so I asked him to hear my confession. Which he did, right in the middle of the road."

The battle map of the Ardennes action took on a whirlwind look—lines of advance and withdrawal, loops and counter-loops, swirls and twists as the contenders stalked, entrapped, and pounded one another. There was no pattern to it all—just ferocity in the mist.

German tank columns could push forward only as far as their fast-dwindling fuel sustained them. Their hope of "living off" captured fuel supplies, though sporadically realized, proved futile. The tide of advance, sector by sector, had begun to crest.

As of Christmas morning, German tanks had smashed to within sight of the Meuse River—the high-point of their advance, some sixty miles from their starting line. But the column ran short of fuel and hit a hardening wall of U.S. armor and infantry. This far, fate ruled—and no farther.

When the shock of American armor failed to produce breakthroughs, infantry men moved through deep snow on foot to get at enemy positions.

That day and the next, the Battle of the Bulge reached its climax. In and about Celles, the U.S. 2nd Armored Division caught the Second Panzer Division, out of fuel, dead in its tracks. American armor, artillery and infantry, strongly supported by fighter-bombers, ripped into the enemy. In "a great slaughter," they inflicted more than 2,000 casualties on the Germans, destroying 80 tanks, 450 other vehicles, and 80 assault guns caught on the road—losses fivefold those suffered by the Americans. The westernmost German spearhead had been decapitated.

Villages were taken, lost, retaken. In one night action, a single American artillery battalion fired eleven thousand rounds at enemy tanks. Two companies of 82nd Airborne paratroopers made a gallant, straight-ahead attack against German positions to take Cheneux. There, Corporal George Graves witnessed "bloody GI clothes. Dead bodies everywhere. Living troops hugging the ground."

The arrows of the Allied advance began to swing eastward. With clearing skies, U.S. fighter-bombers struck at enemy positions in more than five hundred sorties a day. German field commanders ordered gradual pullbacks. GIs drove through bitter enemy resistance, storms, and knee-deep snow to take back pieces of lost ground.

NATIONAL ARCHIVES

24. Our Greatest Land Battle

Headlines back home told of the turnaround: "First Army Drives Ahead in Sleet" ... "Third Army Gains" ... "Ice, Mud and Fog Slow Tanks" ... "Germans Battle Back" ... "Americans Cut Into Bulge" ... As the Germans had been fierce on the attack, so were they every bit as fierce in their withdrawal. Steadily collapsing the "Bulge" about themselves, they exacted heavy casualties for every foot of frozen earth.

Even in the face of disaster, many German troops remained loyal to the spirit of the *Fahneneid,* the ancient oath of the Teutonic knights that swore them to serve their leader to the death. A young SS Panzer commander had stated: "The snow must turn red with American blood. We will throw them from our homeland. It is a holy task."

Americans by the thousands found unceremonious death in the Ardennes. "I was a new replacement," recalls Private Harmon Horowitz. "One of the seasoned BAR guys said, 'Kid, stay close to me.' Two days later I saw him blown apart by a mortar shell." One soldier remembered a wounded GI, "perhaps twenty years old, with frightened eyes. The medic couldn't give him blood plasma; it was frozen. The soldier died in a barn." "Our squad had eight men," relates Private First Class Leslie Shellhase. "Within days, three had been killed—and five, counting me, had been wounded." Captain Frances Slanger, after working a string of eighteen-hour days as a nurse in a field hospital, got some time off. While she rested in her tent, an 88-millimeter shell burst overhead. She was buried in her green fatigues.

When the shock of American armor failed to produce breakthroughs, infantrymen moved through deep snow on foot, among wooded hills and steep defiles and along serpentine rivers, working past felled trees, mines, and anti-tank guns to get at enemy positions.

Hitler unleashed one last surprise. On January 1, 1945, almost a thousand German fighter planes swept in over the Western Front at treetop level. By midday they had struck twenty-seven Allied airbases in Belgium, France, and the Netherlands, destroying or damaging nearly three hundred planes. But in so

NATIONAL ARCHIVES

Fifty years ago, Theodore O. Simpson was a corporal with a "Pack 75 mm" battery in the 319 Glider Field Artillery Battalion of the 82nd Airborne Division. Simpson's vivid recollections of the Battle of the Bulge could fairly represent the memories [of] any of the 600,000 Americans who took part in that physically punishing and hard-fought campaign:

What I mainly remember are the still-shivering experiences of life in the "fridge" ... never knowing (nor particularly caring) where we were at any given moment, but rather, just swapping one set of woods, hills, mined valleys, for another.

Sleeping bags with frozen zippers. (Bad, when one has contracted diarrhea from small metal flakings that cracked away from inner walls of a canteen after being heated over the campfire to melt water inside.)

Changing fire zones and positions continuously. Guns always firing. Dropping with fatigue into trail pits dug for the howitzers and sleeping sounding despite middle-of-the-night "fire missions" when one's sleeping body was two feet from a barking cannon.

Mounds of bodies under a merciful wrapping of snow. Piles of O.D. body bags beside the morning chow line. Contorted positions of the frozen dead. Singing shrapnel headed earthward from just above our heads as larger artillery units, behind, experimented with new "posit fuzes."

Eyes burning with campfire smoke. Accumulating body dirt. No baths. Always the deep, penetrating cold. Snipers in the woods. Infrequent but blessed letters from home. One reassuring feeling: everyone was there—tanks, big guns, infantry, engineers, etc.

Death reminders in every direction. A frozen hand reaching from the snow. A ruptured helmet lying alone. A German wallet beside its former owner's mutilated body— spilling letters, pictures from home.

Tangled tanks and jeeps afire. Watching smoke bubble peacefully from a Belgian home on the hillside—and wondering why they were comfortably ensconced while we were out here trying to save their country.

Vicious artillery counter-battery attacks until one or the other contender was silent. Day after frozen day dragging by, with little comfort or hope.

Fifty years later, I still do no care much for snow, frozen woods, or unexplained mounds on the frosted white ground.

4 ❖ FROM THE GREAT DEPRESSION TO WORLD WAR II

NATIONAL ARCHIVES

Battle of the Ardennes has been the most decisive of the Second World War," stated Charles MacDonald, U.S. Army historian. "It was the most important feat of arms in the history of the United States Army."

British Prime Minister Sir Winston Churchill, addressing the House of Commons following the Battle of the Bulge, declared: "This is undoubtedly the greatest American battle of the war and will, I believe, be regarded as an ever-famous American victory."

The battle sealed Germany's fate. Casualties and prisoners exceeded 100,000 men—losses Germany could no longer make good.

The battle of the Ardennes lasted forty-three days and cost the United States nine times as many casualties as D-Day. Of 600,000 Americans who fought there, more than 80,000 became casualties: some 10,276 killed; 47,493 wounded; and 23,218 captured or missing. As well, U.S. forces lost about 700 tanks and tank destroyers and some 600 planes. British casualties totalled 1,400 men.

But the battle had sealed Germany's fate. Estimates of troop losses exceeded a staggering 100,000 men—with more than 10,000 killed, 50,000 wounded, and 40,000 captured—losses Germany could no longer make good. Some 800 tanks and assault guns were destroyed. And the Luftwaffe, in a near-death gasp, lost more than 800 aircraft, leaving Germany with virtually no air force.

The Ardennes campaign was a classic example of Hitler's willingness to expect the impossible—as though to will victory would be to win it. In so doing, he not only overestimated the strength of his own forces but also undervalued

doing, they lost about three hundred of their own planes, along with irreplaceable pilots.

By the second week of the new year, the issue had been decided. On January 16, patrols of the U.S. First and Third Armies linked up at Houffalize, closing off much of the Bulge. It would take another eight days to push the German troops back to their starting point. From blue skies on January 22, U.S. pilots devastated retreating German columns. By January 28, the last trace of the Bulge had disappeared.

Battle brought poignance. Captain Sally Zumaris-McKinney remembers "American soldiers shot to pieces, or frozen, or sick—just kids, some of them." Joining his battalion's mortician under cover of fire to recover bodies, Sergeant Edward Bergh came upon that of his best buddy. An infantryman relates: "One night we found shelter inside a church. It had been shattered by shellfire. It was quiet there. I prayed near the altar, then went to sleep before it."

A million men had been caught up in desperate fighting during a six-week period in forested, mountainous, frozen terrain of five hundred square miles. Out of it all emerged the memorable figure of the foot-slogging American GI—stoic, hard-eyed, and of abiding strength. He typified the whole array of U.S. soldiers—tankers, engineers, artillery men, drivers, clerks—who, each in his own way had fought the desperate fight. "The

24. Our Greatest Land Battle

the resolve of the American soldier.* The Germans, fierce though their determination was, failed to reach Antwerp; failed to destroy large pockets of trapped U.S. units; failed to get a single tank across the Meuse River. Thirty-two American and four British divisions had battled twenty-eight German divisions to a standstill, and then had driven them back into Germany.

Hitler's last, desperate gamble had, for a brief, astonishing time, seemed about to succeed. It did, in fact, upset the Allied timetable for the invasion of Germany—but at a crushing cost to his own manpower and armor. Soon the Allies would be at the Rhine.

The vast drama of the Ardennes ended, for Hitler's armies, in disillusion and disaster. "Rivers of men and machines flowed slowly toward the Fatherland," wrote historian John Toland. "Trucks, tanks and self-propelled guns rumbled east over icy roads and trails clogged with snow-drifts. Each refugee of the Battle of the Bulge brought home a story of doom, of overwhelming Allied might and of a terrible weapon forged in the Ardennes: the American fighting man."

Those who would seek Hitler's monument in those woods of death had but to look around them. Scattered upon the snow-mantled landscape rested shattered tanks, broken artillery pieces, charred vehicles. Corpses of German soldiers lay white and stiff, their weapons on the frozen earth about them.

As a German grenadier made his way out of a burning village, he scrawled on the side of a battered German scout car: *"Aus Der Traum." "The Dream is Over."*

New York writer Edward Oxford has contributed more than two dozen articles to American History. *His last contribution—on the World War II draft—appeared in the September/October [1994] issue.*

---

*Nearly a score of American soldiers, displaying valor beyond the call of duty in the Ardennes, were awarded the Medal of Honor.

"I learn a lot from the veterans"

Reminiscences of World War II's European Theater add up to considerably more than a bunch of good war stories

By Stephen E. Ambrose

In 1999 the author published his book Citizen Soldiers: The U.S. Army From the Normandy Beaches to the Bulge to the Surrender of Germany, June 7, 1944–May 7, 1945. *It quickly bounced onto bestseller lists across the country, and the reason this happened is suggested in the rich and moving correspondence it had the power to generate among its readers. Stephen Ambrose fashioned these letters into the essay that follows, which runs as an afterword in Touchstone's new paperbound edition of* Citizen Soldiers.

ONE OF THE NICEST THINGS ABOUT having a bestseller is the incoming mail. On this book it has been staggering and rewarding. One of my favorites came from Wallace Berger, who was "a scared, lonely 19-year-old replacement brought to the lines during the winter of 1944 with the 26th Division. . . . I felt again the cold, the fear of tree-bursts, the closeness with my foxhole buddy Pat Healy (we slept in each other's arms for warmth) and at times the sense that we would never get out of there alive.

"So thank you for writing a book about my war. I think that in a way it gave me a feeling of a certain kind of peacefulness, as if something has been put to rest by the telling."

In a handwritten letter, a former private, James Howley, recalled, "I am one of the soldiers you wrote about." He was drafted in 1943, trained in Texas, shipped over to Scotland in the spring of 1944, across the English Channel on D-day plus ten and assigned to the 9th Infantry Division. "I was trained as a wire man and sent over as a rifleman with no infantry training, then put on an antitank gun that I never had seen until then. My job became digging holes. We crossed the Rhine at night before the bridge collapsed and got a half track full of Schnapps—about eight or ten cases. For a few days we didn't care whether it rained or snowed. One of the guys we called 'mole' because he could always find a hole to jump into at the slightest sound. After we got that Schnapps he went out on a .50 caliber MG when a Jerry plane came over and fired up at it. The plane turned on him and in its strafing run killed him and a radio man."

The letters contain a fair amount of complaints, a principal one being that I left out this or that division, which is fair enough, but I can't do anything about it now, and anyway the book was not intended to be a comprehensive history. One veteran's criticism was that I made only a single mention of the National Guard. Guilty. My only excuse is that I just figured everyone knows that the 29th Division (242 days in combat, 204 percent turnover), which plays a major role in my account, was a National Guard division (the "Blue and Gray," from Virginia, Maryland, and Delaware) and one of the best outfits in the Army.

On a more positive note, a good number of veterans have written that the book caused them to reflect on what they had learned in the Army, especially responsibility. Private Berger concluded his letter, "I have known for a long time that my life was changed by that experience, and maybe I understand it a little better now."

Many veterans have written of how the Army made it possible for them to know far more about their fellow citizens. Cpl. William Schaufele described his experience. He turned eighteen on December 7, 1941. He was a student at

25. "I Learn a Lot from the Veterans"

Yale and managed to finish the year, then went into the 10th Armored Division and was in Bastogne for the Battle of the Bulge. He wrote: "One impression I took away from combat was that, in many, if not all, cases enlisted men knew better what to do in actual combat than their officers. Heterogeneity didn't seem to play a role. I served with people who had no high school education, worked at menial jobs, came from small rural villages or working-class neighborhoods, and many were better soldiers than I. Some were promoted to sergeant and busted two or three times in training, but, by the time we entered combat, they were back as tank commanders—and rightly so."

I get a lot of specific stories or anecdotes that are frustrating, because if I had known them, they would certainly have been in the book. Sometimes they confirm another guy's story. For example, a tale about a forward observer who saw a moving haystack and called in artillery fire on it prompted one of the gunners on the 105s that did the shooting to write. He said the gun crew thought it was all a joke, and for the remainder of the war and at postwar reunions they would get a laugh from remembering the time they shot at a moving haystack. Only to discover, fifty-three years later, there really was a target and they had knocked out a German tank.

Pvt. Jack Crawford provided another confirmation when he commented on a story about Ernest Hemingway's self-indulgent war "reporting." Crawford went ashore at Utah Beach on D-day plus twelve with the 4th Division. He fought in the hedgerows, at Mortain, and in the Hürtgen Forest, was wounded three times, and was awarded a battlefield commission. He went AWOL from a hospital to rejoin his outfit in the Hürtgen. When he arrived at Bradley's headquarters, in Spa, he went into a bar "and sitting there was Ernest Hemingway and Colonel Buck Lanham, C.O. of the 22nd Infantry, 4th Division. Lanham asked me to come over and I was very pleased to talk to Hemingway as I had read some of his books. As we drank and talked, I felt he was full of it and this really wasn't his war. He was telling

In many, if not all, cases, enlisted men knew better what to do in actual combat than their officers," one wrote.

tales of hijinks in Paris. I finally got pissed off and said he should come up to my battalion with me in the Hürtgen to see what the war was really like instead of sitting back thirty miles from the front lines. The Colonel jumped on me and said I was out of line, so I stood up, saluted the Colonel, said 'F—— you, Hemingway,' and walked out."

I've had dozens of letters from frontline veterans who say they never saw a colonel, much less a general, where they were. But I've also had a couple of GIs write to say that this colonel or that general made it to the front lines in their sector.

WYATT BARNES SAT DOWN TO write me a "two or three page letter, at most," but it ended up as a twelve-page single-spaced memoir, one of the best I've ever read. Some highlights: Barnes started off as an Army Specialized Training School student at Brooklyn College in mid-1943. Then it was off to Fort Polk, Louisiana, where "we were all miserable. Especially, we detested our new comrades, who were mostly from Appalachia and the deep South, with a few from Idaho and Montana. They were rural and spoke in funny accents; we despised their ignorant ways. In turn, they disparaged our elitism and urban mores. I flaunted my subscription to *The New York Times,* thus inviting their special loathing. In time we adjusted to them and they to us."

Barnes shipped over to England in August 1944, then on to France in mid-October and into the line with the 80th Division as a replacement. "Five of us were admitted to the 1st squad, 1st pla-

U.S. COAST GUARD

A soldier grabs a final smoke before the ramp drops on a Hollandia beach, 1944.

toon. We five knew each other slightly from our replacement trek, bonding among us came later."

In mid-December the 80th packed up and headed north, toward the southern shoulder of the Bulge, part of the 3d Army counterattack. "We were in $2^{1}/_{2}$ ton trucks for the trek north. This was a new torment in the bitter cold and interminable night. No rations. There were frequent stops because of the clogged roads, occasions we used for piss-calls. This task was an ordeal. Cramped and frozen, we eased ourselves off the back end into the furious wind and performed the needed function. The weather was utterly appalling."

On Christmas Day the 80th joined the 4th Armored for the final push to break through to Bastogne. "We formed a skirmish line. Not a word was spoken. Then we began to move, 8 or 10 feet separating the men. Soon the rounds started coming, their tiny sonic booms causing distinct snaps as they passed close by. A tracer round struck the frozen ground in front of me and described an arc over my head. Then, after about 100 yards, I felt the slug strike just below my right collar bone. After the impact, and this still seems incredible, I could actually feel the bullet piercing the tissues and organs within, clipping through each in sequence. Time, almost literally, must have stood still as my whole being concentrated on this devastating physical assault. The bullet exited down, just to the left of my right shoulder blade.

"I fell forward, and the instant I hit the ground I intoned 'two months' to myself. This was the million dollar wound! Two months would give me relief from the line and get me through the worst of winter." Actually, the wound was worse than Barnes thought; his right lung had been pierced. For him the war was over. Barnes recounted in some detail his evacuation from the snow-covered field back to a jeep, then to an aid station, then the 39th Evacuation Hospital, next Paris by train, and finally a flight to England to the 160th General Hospital near Cheltenham. He concluded, "Your tribute to the medical people in the ETO [European Theater of Operations] was richly deserved."

American Heritage printed the chapter on medics, nurses, and docs (my own favorite chapter, because lives are being saved, not destroyed) and got a big mail in response, nearly all of the writers telling this or that story about being saved by a medic and how wonderful the medics and nurses and doctors were. It almost breaks your heart to read some of them. We now have the letters in the Archives of the Eisenhower Center, available to scholars and visitors, and I hope someday someone does a book on U.S. Army medicine in World War II.

Pvt. Eldon McDermeit was an ATSP student who went to the front line with the 70th Infantry Division: "On our third night on the line, two of our guys were bayoneted in their foxholes. They had obviously been asleep. The next day all of the 70th Division infantry had to exchange our sleeping bags for two blankets. It was much harder to stay warm with blankets so we stayed awake. We seldom got hot meals on the front line. We ate K rations almost exclusively. Our first hot meal was after six weeks on the line."

I LEARN A LOT FROM THE VETERANS. Lt. Sidney Lowery was a field artillery liaison pilot. He said he and his friends flew the Piper Cubs without wearing parachutes, which would have been useless at the altitudes they flew anyway, and besides, "it was safer to stay in the Piper Cub when hit because of its aeronautical characteristics, which often enabled the pilot to make an emergency landing." Lowery added that "our greatest danger was friendly fire. Each of us was flying missions to direct fire by our own division artillery, but at the same time, and further back, Corps artillery were conducting their own missions, with larger caliber weapons, totally unaware of what we were doing. So as we were directing our own unit's fire while flying over the front line, we frequently felt a sort of 'whoosh' and a bump, as the Corps artillery shell passed by. I had more than one chum who was shot down by our own artillery."

The trench-foot mail has been heavy. The theme is summed up by one letter: "For five decades I've carried around a sense of shame at being evacuated for trenchfoot. The Army (but not the nurses and doctors) made me feel I had let down the side. Your account has helped me get over those bad feelings."

Pvt. Norman Redlich of the 100th Division remembered that "in late November, 1944, after spending another night in a cold wet foxhole, and after following as best I could the instructions to remove our boots at night and dry our socks, I awoke and found that I could no longer fit into my boots because my feet had swollen like balloons. Barely able to walk, I was removed to a field hospital and told that I would be back on the line in a matter of days. But the pain intensified, and my feet started to turn white, and then purple. The pain became so excruciating that I was given a shot of morphine. It was so bad that I could not place a sheet over my toes and had to sleep with the blankets and sheets turned back."

Redlich was shipped back to the States on the *Queen Elizabeth,* which had been converted into a hospital ship. He recalled that "virtually the entire contingent of passengers had trenchfoot, many of them with toes and legs amputated. I felt both lucky and guilty. In many respects, I still do."

Redlich's blunt honesty is typical of the GIs I've interviewed or corresponded with over the years. Shakespeare wrote that old men remember, with advantages, the deeds they did as warriors. With a few exceptions, I've always found the opposite. Many times in group interviews I've heard something like this exchange: "I'm no hero. He's the hero."

"No, not me. You want to hear about a real hero, let me tell you about so-and-so."

THE *AMERICAN HERITAGE* ARTICLE produced another story that has to be told. It comes from A. Bruce Campbell of the 11th Regiment, 5th Division, who wrote it up at the time and who described it as "probably the most remarkable piece of battlefield surgery in World War II."

November 10, 1944, the 5th Division was attacking at Metz. Pvt. Henry Roon of Company B, 2d Regiment, caught a mortar-shell fragment in his throat. He fell prostrate in the mud with "a perforating wound of the neck, with the wound exit over the tracheal area and a fracture of the trachea." Pvt. Duane N. Kinman, a nineteen-year-old medic with two years of high school education, finished binding up a chest wound and rushed over to help. "He saw Roon turning blue in the face, gasping and suffocating to death. Kinman whipped out his jackknife. Roon made protesting motions which Kinman overruled, saying, 'I don't like to do this, but it's the only way you're going to live.'

"Then, without wasting any more time in deliberation and with perfect presence of mind and recollection of two lectures given him a year previous in basic training, Kinman prepared to perform an operation which is delicate in the best of surgical conditions. He knew he had to open up the windpipe and he knew he had to have a tube or edge to insert to keep it open. He saw a fountain pen in Roon's pocket and seized that.

"With machine guns clattering all around, with mortar shells still landing, with a muddy field for an operating table, a gray sky for light, and his jackknife for a scalpel and without benefit of any anesthetic or drug, Kinman cut into Roon's throat, carefully avoiding the jugular, made a longitudinal one and a half inch incision in Roon's windpipe, cleanly and safely. Then he slipped the rounded end of Roon's fountain pen into the incision to keep the cut open and

25. "I Learn a Lot from the Veterans"

told Roon, 'Now keep that pen in your windpipe and you'll be okay.'"

Kinman helped Roon get to the rear and walk to an aid station. The battalion surgeon found nothing to improve upon. Two other tracheotomies performed by surgeons there the same day were unsuccessful.

Lt. Bryce Stevens, a combat engineer with the 87th Division, said the book "brought back memories of events, sights and even smells of that time and place that I hadn't thought of in a long time." One of those memories was of his first shower after three months of continuous combat: "The procedure was to strip off, put your dirty clothes (except for boots) in a pile, run buck-naked across duckboards to the next tent where the showers were. There they turned on the water long enough to get wet, then turned it off while you soaped up. The water then came on again to rinse off. Back to the dressing tent where clean clothes were issued. All this in freezing weather. I don't remember how we managed to get clothes that fit."

Richard Meier wrote that his uncle Gordon Meier was in the Losheimergraben railroad-station fight and Pvt. Herbert Meier, a German soldier quoted in the book who was also in that fight, was a cousin of his uncle. "It makes the Bulge almost like Gettysburg—cousins across the lines from each other."

Gordon Meier wrote: "I remember that railroad station very well. We came under artillery shelling. We got under the freight tracks (4 inches of concrete). The Germans came marching right down the railroad tracks. You could hear their steel-heeled boots. We killed lots of them. The shelling started again and we pulled back 500 yards. I remember the Germans had long overcoats and they would tuck them up around the waist so they could run easier. We got one young German officer for interrogation but he was dying. He had two pieces of bread with jelly on them."

Robert Kettler's father was in the 80th Division, wounded and captured near Nancy on September 22, 1944. He died in Stalag 4G on October 1. Kettler was four years old when the telegram came: "I still remember the emotional storm that swirled through our house that day. Standing by a blue chair where Mother sat weeping while family and friends gathered to console her in a ritual that was by then all too familiar, even in our small Indiana town, I knew that something monumental had happened to us." In 1995 Kettler and his daughter and his mother paid their first visit to his father's grave, in the American Cemetery and memorial near Liège, Belgium.

At the graveside, Kettler wrote, "I touched Mother's arm. 'It's a beautiful place,' I said."

"Yes, it is," she replied. "And I'm so grateful I could be here with you. But it's a long way from Shelbyville, Indiana."

As they drove away from the cemetery, Kettler continued, "we talked quietly in the car, our voices filled with relief and release. We had stood at my father's grave. Now we could go home."

I'M LEARNING ALL THE TIME. HERE'S one that I didn't know. In January 1945 Pvt. Richard Lockhart of the ill-fated 106th Division was a POW in Stalag IXB, Bad Orb, Germany. It was a smallish, primitive camp, housing several thousand Russian, Serbian, and French soldiers—all privates. There were no medical facilities, no sanitary services, no heat, and not much grass soup. When Lockhart and his fellow American POWs arrived, the guards held a roll call. They ordered all Jews to step forward. A dozen did. The guards separated them and sent them off to a slave-labor camp, over the vehement protests of Lockhart and others. Many of the Jewish POWs died. What prompted them to step forward? Lockhart wondered. He conjectured that it may have been an affirmation of their culture and religion, or it could have been out of naïveté, a sense that the U.S. Army uniform they were wearing would protect them.

I know one Jewish soldier who rightly feared capture, so when it was imminent, he switched dog tags with a dead buddy. It worked for him, but not for his folks, who got a telegram from the War Department telling them he had been killed in action.

My mentor, Dr. Harry T. Williams, taught me to let my characters speak for themselves. "They always say it better than you ever could," he insisted. The paragraph that follows proves his point. It was written by Lt. Charles Jordan, 9th Division.

"I have read of fearless people, I even had a runner for a short time who I think was pretty close to fearless (he got killed), but I was not fearless. My worst fear was of screwing up or showing my fear to those around me. A distant second was fear of death. In my earliest days this included the fear of being wounded but this rapidly transformed into a desire. The absolute worst period of fear came as we were organizing for an attack. We never knew what to expect or when to expect it, and the longer the wait the greater the fear. The fear of death came openly when I was lying in a ditch, or a hole, or on the ground and artillery or mortar shells were exploding around me. There was absolutely nothing positive to do about these situations except lay there and pray. Since the days when I lived with fear constantly, I have found that fear for yourself cannot hold a candle to the fear engendered by the serious illness of your wife and children. I'd rather be shot at every day of the week and all day Sunday than face that situation."

ONE OF THE BEST COMMENTS CAME in a beer-drinking bull session with some veterans. We were talking about what it all meant. I never caught the name of the man who gave us the following image, but I'll never forget what he said: "Imagine this. In the spring of 1945, around the world, the sight of a twelve-man squad of teenage boys, armed and in uniform, brought terror to people's hearts. Whether it was a Red Army squad in Berlin, Leipzig, or Warsaw, or a German squad in Holland, or a Japanese squad in Manila or Seoul or in China, that squad meant rape, pillage, looting, wanton destruction, senseless killing. But there was an exception: a squad of GIs, a sight that brought the biggest smiles you ever saw to people's lips, and joy to their hearts.

"Around the world this was true, even in Germany, even—after Septem-

The spirit of those GIs—we can do it—was the great gift of the New World to the Old World in the twentieth century.

ber 1945—in Japan. This was because GIs meant candy, cigarettes, C-rations, and freedom. America had sent the best of her young men around the world, not to conquer but to liberate, not to terrorize but to help. This was a great moment in our history."

Pfc. Royland Otter, of Madison, Indiana, takes a last look at France.

Another bright image came from a veteran who said that he felt he had done his part in helping change the twentieth century from one of darkness into one of light. I think that was the great achievement of the generation who fought World War II on the Allied side. As of 1945—the year in which more people were killed violently, more buildings destroyed, more homes burned than any other year in history—it was impossible to believe in human progress. World Wars I and II had made a mockery of the nineteenth-century idea of progress, the notion that things were getting better and would continue to do so. In 1945 one had to believe that the final outcome of the scientific and technological revolution that had inspired the idea of progress would be a world destroyed.

But slowly, surely, the spirit of those GIs handing out candy and helping bring democracy to their former enemies spread, and today it is the democracies—not the totalitarian states—that are on the march. Today one can again believe in progress, for things really are getting better. This is thanks to the GIs—along with the millions of others who helped liberate Germany and Japan from their evil rulers, then stood up to Stalin and his successors. That generation has done more to spread freedom—and prosperity—around the globe than any previous generation.

Sgt. Henry Halsted, who won a Bronze Star, participated after the war in an experimental program that brought together college-age German and American veterans in England, and a similar one in France. The idea was to teach through contact and example. In 1997 Halsted got a Christmas card from a German participant living in Munich: "I think often of our meetings and mutual ideals. Indeed, the 1948 program and everything connected with it was the most important, decisive event for me. Influenced my life deeply!"

A French participant wrote: "In 1950 France was in ruins. I saw only a world marked by war, by destruction, by the shadow of war, and by fear. I believed that it was not finished, that there would be a next war. I did not think it would be possible to build a life, to have a family. Then came the group of young Americans, attractive, idealistic, optimistic, protected, believing and acting as though anything was possible. It was a transforming experience for me."

That spirit—we can do it, we can rebuild Europe and hold back the Red Army and avoid World War III—was the great gift of the New World to the Old World in the twentieth century. America paid for that gift with the lives of some of her best young men. When I read the letters from the veterans, I'm almost always impressed by their brief accounts of what they did with their lives after the war. They had successful careers,

Veterans: Tell Us Your Story

ROBERT KETTLER GAVE HIS affecting account of his visit to his father's grave in the Summer 1996 edition of *Traces,* published by the Indiana Historical Society. I've received dozens of other articles, privately printed books, memoirs, and documents of all types, including company- or battalion-level oral histories gathered and printed by someone from the unit. This is wonderful. I'm delighted to be able to put them into the Archives at the Eisenhower Center at the University of New Orleans, where they will be open to future scholars and to descendants. I only wish they had been available when I wrote *Citizen Soldiers.*

The Eisenhower Center's address is 923 Magazine Street, New Orleans, LA 70130. Its director, Dr. Douglas Brinkley, continues actively to seek memoirs, documents, oral histories, and other material from veterans; although I'm retired, this is the project closest to my heart, and I urge all veterans to deposit copies of their material in the Archives. —S.E.A.

they were good citizens and family men, and many of them made great contributions to their society, their country, and the world. Then I think about those who didn't make it, especially all those junior officers and NCOs who got killed in such appalling numbers.

These men were natural leaders. They died one by one. Of each of them, I wonder, What life was cut off here? A genius? It is impossible to imagine what he might have invented; we do know that his loss was our loss. A budding politician? Where might he have led us? A builder? A teacher? A scholar? A novelist? I sometimes think the biggest price we pay for war is what might have been.

Stephen E. Ambrose's essay on the Medical Corps ran last November [1997].

The Biggest Decision: Why We Had to Drop the Atomic Bomb

Robert James Maddox

Robert James Maddox teaches American history at Pennsylvania State University. His Weapons for Victory: Hiroshima Fifty Years Later *is published by the University of Missouri Press (1995).*

On the morning of August 6, 1945, the American B-29 *Enola Gay* dropped an atomic bomb on the Japanese city of Hiroshima. Three days later another B-29, *Bock's Car*, released one over Nagasaki. Both caused enormous casualties and physical destruction. These two cataclysmic events have preyed upon the American conscience ever since. The furor over the Smithsonian Institution's *Enola Gay* exhibit and over the mushroom-cloud postage stamp last autumn are merely the most obvious examples. Harry S. Truman and other officials claimed that the bombs caused Japan to surrender, thereby avoiding a bloody invasion. Critics have accused them of at best failing to explore alternatives, at worst of using the bombs primarily to make the Soviet Union "more manageable" rather than to defeat a Japan they knew already was on the verge of capitulation.

By any rational calculation Japan was a beaten nation by the summer of 1945. Conventional bombing had reduced many of its cities to rubble, blockade had strangled its importation of vitally needed materials, and its navy had sustained such heavy losses as to be powerless to interfere with the invasion everyone knew was coming. By late June advancing American forces had completed the conquest of Okinawa, which lay only 350 miles from the southernmost Japanese home island of Kyushu. They now stood poised for the final onslaught.

Okinawa provided a preview of what an invasion of the home islands would entail. Rational calculations did not determine Japan's position.

Rational calculations did not determine Japan's position. Although a peace faction within the government wished to end the war—provided certain conditions were met—militants were prepared to fight on regardless of consequences. They claimed to welcome an invasion of the home islands, promising to inflict such hideous casualties that the United States would retreat from its announced policy of unconditional surrender. The militarists held effective power over the government and were capable of defying the emperor, as they had in the past, on the ground that his civilian advisers were misleading him.

Okinawa provided a preview of what invasion of the home islands would entail. Since April 1 the Japanese had fought with a ferocity that mocked any notion that their will to resist was eroding. They had inflicted nearly 50,000 casualties on the invaders, many resulting from the first large-scale use of kamikazes. They also had dispatched the superbattleship *Yamato* on a suicide mission to Okinawa, where, after attacking American ships offshore, it was to plunge ashore to become a huge, doomed steel fortress. *Yamato* was sunk shortly after leaving port, but its mission symbolized Japan's willingness to sacrifice everything in an apparently hopeless cause.

The Japanese could be expected to defend their sacred homeland with even greater fervor, and kamikazes flying at short range promised to be even more devastating than at Okinawa. The Japanese had more than 2,000,000 troops in the home islands, were training millions of irregulars, and for some time had been conserving aircraft that might have been used to protect Japanese cities against American bombers.

Reports from Tokyo indicated that Japan meant to fight the war to a finish. On June 8 an imperial conference adopted "The Fundamental Policy to Be Followed Henceforth in the Conduct of the War," which pledged to "prosecute the war to the bitter end in order to uphold the national polity, protect the imperial land, and accomplish the objectives for which we went to war." Truman had no reason to believe that the proclamation meant anything other than what it said.

Against this background, while fighting on Okinawa still continued, the President had his naval chief of staff, Adm. William D. Leahy, notify the Joint Chiefs of Staff (JCS) and the Secretaries of War and Navy that a meeting would be held at the White House on June 18. The night before the conference Truman wrote in his diary that "I have to decide Japanese strategy—shall we invade Japan proper or shall we bomb and blockade? That is my hardest decision to date. But I'll make it when I have all the facts."

Truman met with the chiefs at three-thirty in the afternoon. Present were Army Chief of Staff Gen. George C. Marshall, Army Air Force's Gen. Ira C. Eaker (sitting in for the Army Air Force's chief of staff, Henry H. Arnold, who was on an inspection tour of installations in the Pacific), Navy Chief of Staff Adm. Ernest J. King, Leahy (also a member of the JCS), Secretary of the Navy James Forrestal, Secretary of War Henry L. Stimson, and Assistant Secretary of War John J. McCloy. Truman opened the meeting, then asked Marshall for his views. Marshall was the dominant figure on the JCS. He was Truman's most trusted military adviser, as he had been President Franklin D. Roosevelt's.

Marshall reported that the chiefs, supported by the Pacific commanders Gen. Douglas MacArthur and Adm. Chester W. Nimitz, agreed that an invasion of Kyushu "appears to be the least costly worthwhile operation following Okinawa." Lodgment in Kyushu, he said, was necessary to make blockade and bombardment more effective and to serve as a staging area for the invasion of Japan's main island of Honshu. The chiefs recommended a target date of November 1 for the first phase, codenamed Olympic, because delay would give the Japanese more time to prepare and because bad weather might postpone the invasion "and hence the end of the war" for up to six months. Marshall said that in his opinion, Olympic was "the only course to pursue." The chiefs also proposed that Operation Cornet be launched against Honshu on March 1, 1946.

Leahy's memorandum calling the meeting had asked for casualty projections which that invasion might be expected to produce. Marshall stated that campaigns in the Pacific had been so diverse "it is considered wrong" to make total estimates. All he would say was that casualties during the first thirty days on Kyushu should not exceed those sustained in taking Luzon in the Philippines—31,000 men killed, wounded, or missing in action. "It is a grim fact," Marshall said, "that there is not an easy, bloodless way to victory in war." Leahy estimated a higher casualty rate similar to Okinawa, and King guessed somewhere in between.

King and Eaker, speaking for the Navy and the Army Air Forces respectively, endorsed Marshall's proposals. King said that he had become convinced that Kyushu was "the key to the success of any siege operations." He recommended that "we should do Kyushu now" and begin preparations for invading Honshu. Eaker "agreed completely" with Marshall. He said he had just received a message from Arnold also expressing "complete agreement." Air Force plans called for the use of forty groups of heavy bombers, which "could not be deployed without the use of airfields on Kyushu." Stimson and Forrestal concurred.

Truman summed up. He considered "the Kyushu plan all right from the military standpoint" and directed the chiefs to "go ahead with it." He said he "had hoped that there was a possibility of preventing an Okinawa from one end of Japan to the other," but "he was clear on the situation now" and was "quite sure" the chiefs should proceed with the plan. Just before the meeting adjourned, McCloy raised the possibility of avoiding an invasion by warning the Japanese that the United States would employ atomic weapons if there were no surrender. The ensuing discussion was inconclusive because the first test was a month away and no one could be sure the weapons would work.

In his memoirs Truman claimed that using atomic bombs prevented an invasion that would have cost 500,000 American lives. Other officials mentioned the same or even higher figures. Critics have assailed such statements as gross exaggerations designed to forestall scrutiny of Truman's real motives. They have given wide publicity to a report prepared by the Joint War Plans Committee (JWPC) for the chiefs' meeting with Truman. The committee estimated that the invasion of Kyushu, followed by that of Honshu, as the chiefs proposed, would cost approximately 40,000 dead, 150,000 wounded, and 3,500 missing in action for a total of 193,500 casualties.

That those responsible for a decision should exaggerate the consequences of alternatives is commonplace. Some who cite the JWPC report profess to see more sinister motives, insisting that such "low" casualty projections call into question the very idea that atomic bombs were used to avoid heavy losses. By discrediting that justification as a cover-up, they seek to bolster their contention that the bombs really were used to permit the employment of "atomic diplomacy" against the Soviet Union.

The notion that 193,500 anticipated casualties were too insignificant to have caused Truman to resort to atomic bombs might seem bizarre to anyone other than an academic, but let it pass. Those who have cited the JWPC report in countless op-ed pieces in newspapers and in magazine articles have created a myth by omitting key considerations: First, the report itself is studded with qualifications that casualties "are not subject to accurate estimate" and that the projection "is admittedly only an educated guess." Second, the figures never were conveyed to Truman. They were excised at high military echelons, which is why Marshall cited only estimates for the first thirty days on Kyushu. And indeed, subsequent Japanese troop buildups on Kyushu rendered the JWPC estimates totally irrelevant by the time the first atomic bomb was dropped.

26. Biggest Decision: Why We Had to Drop the Atom Bomb

Another myth that has attained wide attention is that at least several of Truman's top military advisers later informed him that using atomic bombs against Japan would be militarily unnecessary or immoral, or both. There is no persuasive evidence that any of them did so. None of the Joint Chiefs ever made such a claim, although one inventive author has tried to make it appear that Leahy did by braiding together several unrelated passages from the admiral's memoirs. Actually, two days after Hiroshima, Truman told aides that Leahy had "said up to the last that it wouldn't go off."

Neither MacArthur nor Nimitz ever communicated to Truman any change of mind about the need for invasion or expressed reservations about using the bombs. When first informed about their imminent use only days before Hiroshima, MacArthur responded with a lecture on the future of atomic warfare and even after Hiroshima strongly recommended that the invasion go forward. Nimitz, from whose jurisdiction the atomic strikes would be launched, was notified in early 1945. "This sounds fine," he told the courier, "but this is only February. Can't we get one sooner?" Nimitz later would join Air Force generals Carl D. Spaatz, Nathan Twining, and Curtis LeMay in recommending that a third bomb be dropped on Tokyo.

Only Dwight D. Eisenhower later claimed to have remonstrated against the use of the bomb. In his *Crusade in Europe*, published in 1948, he wrote that when Secretary Stimson informed him during the Potsdam Conference of plans to use the bomb, he replied that he hoped "we would never have to use such a thing against any enemy," because he did not want the United States to be the first to use such a weapon. He added, "My views were merely personal and immediate reactions; they were not based on any analysis of the subject."

Eisenhower's recollections grew more colorful as the years went on. A later account of his meeting with Stimson had it taking place at Ike's headquarters in Frankfurt on the very day news arrived of the successful atomic test in New Mexico. "We'd had a nice evening at headquarters in Germany," he remembered. Then, after dinner, "Stimson got this cable saying that the bomb had been perfected and was ready to be

---

Myth holds that several of Truman's top military advisers begged him not to use the bomb. In fact, there is no persuasive evidence that any of them did.

---

dropped. The cable was in code ... 'the lamb is born' or some damn thing like that." In this version Eisenhower claimed to have protested vehemently that "the Japanese were ready to surrender and it wasn't necessary to hit them with that awful thing." "Well," Eisenhower concluded, "the old gentleman got furious."

The best that can be said about Eisenhower's memory is that it had become flawed by the passage of time. Stimson was in Potsdam and Eisenhower in Frankfurt on July 16, when word came of the successful test. Aside from a brief conversation at a flag-raising ceremony in Berlin on July 20, the only other time they met was at Ike's headquarters on July 27. By then orders already had been sent to the Pacific to use the bombs if Japan had not yet surrendered. Notes made by one of Stimson's aides indicate that there was a discussion of atomic bombs, but there is no mention of any protest on Eisenhower's part. Even if there had been, two factors must be kept in mind. Eisenhower had commanded Allied forces in Europe, and his opinion on how close Japan was to surrender would have carried no special weight. More important, Stimson left for home immediately after the meeting and could not have personally conveyed Ike's sentiments to the President, who did not return to Washington until after Hiroshima.

On July 8 the Combined Intelligence Committee submitted to the American and British Combined Chiefs of Staff a report entitled "Estimate of the Enemy Situation." The committee predicted that as Japan's position continued to deteriorate, it might "make a serious effort to use the USSR [then a neutral] as a mediator in ending the war." Tokyo also would put out "intermittent peace feelers" to "weaken the determination of the United Nations to fight to the bitter end, or to create inter-allied dissension." While the Japanese people would be willing to make large concessions to end the war, "For a surrender to be acceptable to the Japanese army, it would be necessary for the military leaders to believe that it would not entail discrediting warrior tradition and that it would permit the ultimate resurgence of a military Japan."

Small wonder that American officials remained unimpressed when Japan proceeded to do exactly what the committee predicted. On July 12 Japanese Foreign Minister Shigenori Togo instructed Ambassador Naotaki Sato in Moscow to inform the Soviets that the emperor wished to send a personal envoy, Prince Fuminaro Konoye, in an attempt "to restore peace with all possible speed." Although he realized Konoye could not reach Moscow before the Soviet leader Joseph Stalin and Foreign Minister V. M. Molotov left to attend a Big Three meeting scheduled to begin in Potsdam on the fifteenth, Togo sought to have negotiations begin as soon as they returned.

American officials had long since been able to read Japanese diplomatic traffic through a process known as the MAGIC intercepts. Army intelligence (G-2) prepared for General Marshall its interpretation of Togo's message the next day. The report listed several possible constructions, the most probable being that the Japanese "governing clique" was making a coordinated effort to "stave off defeat" through Soviet intervention and an "appeal to war weariness in the United States." The report added that Undersecretary of State Joseph C. Grew, who had spent ten years in Japan as ambassador, "agrees with these conclusions."

Some have claimed that Togo's overture to the Soviet Union, together with attempts by some minor Japanese officials in Switzerland and other neutral countries to get peace talks started through the Office of Strategic Services (OSS), constituted clear evidence that the Japanese were near surrender. Their sole prerequisite was retention of their sacred emperor, whose unique cultural/religious status within the Japanese polity they would not compromise. If only the United States had extended assurances about the emperor, according to this view, much bloodshed and the atomic bombs would have been unnecessary.

A careful reading of the MAGIC intercepts of subsequent exchanges between Togo and Sato provides no evidence that retention of the emperor was the sole obstacle to peace. What they show instead is that the Japanese Foreign Office was trying to cut a deal through the Soviet Union that would have permitted Japan to retain its political system and its prewar empire intact. Even the most lenient American official could not have countenanced such a settlement.

Togo on July 17 informed Sato that "we are not asking the Russians' mediation in *anything like unconditional surrender* [emphasis added]." During the following weeks Sato pleaded with his superiors to abandon hope of Soviet intercession and to approach the United States directly to find out what peace terms would be offered. "There is ... no alternative but immediate unconditional surrender," he cabled on July 31, and he bluntly informed Togo that "your way of looking at things and the actual situation in the Eastern Area may be seen to be absolutely contradictory." The Foreign Ministry ignored his pleas and continued to seek Soviet help even after Hiroshima.

"Peace feelers" by Japanese officials abroad seemed no more promising from the American point of view. Although several of the consular personnel and military attachés engaged in these activities claimed important connections at home, none produced verification. Had the Japanese government sought only an assurance about the emperor, all it had to do was grant one of these men authority to begin talks through the OSS. Its failure to do so led American officials to assume that those involved were either well-meaning individuals acting alone or that they were being orchestrated by Tokyo. Grew characterized such "peace feelers" as "familiar weapons of psychological warfare" designed to "divide the Allies."

By late July the casualty projection of 31,000 that Marshall had given Truman at the June 18 strategy meeting had become meaningless.

Some American officials, such as Stimson and Grew, nonetheless wanted to signal the Japanese that they might retain the emperorship in the form of a constitutional monarchy. Such an assurance might remove the last stumbling block to surrender, if not when it was issued, then later. Only an imperial rescript would bring about an orderly surrender, they argued, without which Japanese forces would fight to the last man regardless of what the government in Tokyo did. Besides, the emperor could serve as a stabilizing factor during the transition to peacetime.

There were many arguments against an American initiative. Some opposed retaining such an undemocratic institution on principle and because they feared it might later serve as a rallying point for future militarism. Should that happen, as one assistant Secretary of State put it, "those lives already spent will have been sacrificed in vain, and lives will be lost again in the future." Japanese hard-liners were certain to exploit an overture as evidence that losses sustained at Okinawa had weakened American resolve and to argue that continued resistance would bring further concessions. Stalin, who earlier had told an American envoy that he favored abolishing the emperorship because the ineffectual Hirohito might be succeeded by "an energetic and vigorous figure who could cause trouble," was just as certain to interpret it as a treacherous effort to end the war before the Soviets could share in the spoils.

There were domestic considerations as well. Roosevelt had announced the unconditional surrender policy in early 1943, and it since had become a slogan of the war. He also had advocated that peoples everywhere should have the right to choose their own form of government, and Truman had publicly pledged to carry out his predecessor's legacies. For him to have formally *guaranteed* continuance of the emperorship, as opposed to merely accepting it on American terms pending free elections, as he later did, would have constituted a blatant repudiation of his own promises.

Nor was that all. Regardless of the emperor's actual role in Japanese aggression, which is still debated, much wartime propaganda had encouraged Americans to regard Hirohito as no less a war criminal than Adolf Hitler or Benito Mussolini. Although Truman said on several occasions that he had no objection to retaining the emperor, he understandably refused to make the first move. The ultimatum he issued from Potsdam on July 26 did not refer specifically to the emperorship. All it said was that occupation forces would be removed after "a peaceful and responsible" government had been established according to the "freely expressed will of the Japanese people." When the Japanese rejected the ultimatum rather than at last inquire whether they might retain the emperor, Truman permitted the plans for using the bombs to go forward.

Reliance on MAGIC intercepts and the "peace feelers" to gauge how near Japan was to surrender is misleading in any case. The army, not the Foreign Office, controlled the situation. Intercepts of Japanese military communications, designated ULTRA, provided no reason to believe the army was even considering surrender. Japanese Imperial Headquarters had correctly guessed that the next operation after Okinawa would be Kyushu and was making every effort to bolster its defenses there.

General Marshall reported on July 24 that there were "approximately 500,000 troops in Kyushu" and that more were on the way. ULTRA identified new units arriving almost daily. MacArthur's G-2 reported on July 29 that "this threatening development, if not checked, may grow to a point where we attack on a ratio of one (1) to one (1) which is not the recipe for victory." By the time the first atomic bomb fell, ULTRA indicated that there were 560,000 troops in southern Kyushu (the actual figure was closer to 900,000), and projections for November 1 placed the number at 680,000. A report, for medical purposes, of July 31 estimated that total battle and non-battle casualties might run as high as 394,859 *for the Kyushu operation alone*. This figure did not include those men expected to be killed outright, for obviously they would require no medical attention. Marshall regarded Japanese defenses as so formidable that even after Hiroshima he asked MacArthur to consider alternate landing sites and began contemplating the use of atomic bombs as tactical weapons to support the invasion.

The thirty-day casualty projection of 31,000 Marshall had given Truman at the June 18 strategy meeting had become meaningless. It had been based on the assumption that the Japanese had about 350,000 defenders in Kyushu and that naval and air interdiction would preclude significant reinforcement. But the Japanese buildup since that time meant that the defenders would have nearly twice the number of troops available by "X-day" than earlier assumed. The assertion that apprehensions about casualties are insufficient to explain Truman's use of the bombs, therefore, cannot be taken seriously. On the contrary, as Winston Churchill wrote after a conversation with him at Potsdam, Truman was tormented by "the terrible responsibilities that rested upon him in regard to the unlimited effusions of American blood."

Some historians have argued that while the first bomb *might* have been required to achieve Japanese surrender, dropping the second constituted a needless barbarism. The record shows otherwise. American officials believed more than one bomb would be necessary because they assumed Japanese hard-liners would minimize the first explosion or attempt to explain it away as some sort of natural catastrophe, precisely what they did. The Japanese minister of war, for instance, at first refused even to admit that the Hiroshima bomb was atomic. A few hours after Nagasaki he told the cabinet that "the Americans appeared to have one hundred atomic bombs... they could drop three per day. The next target might well be Tokyo."

Even after both bombs had fallen and Russia entered the war, Japanese militants insisted on such lenient peace terms that moderates knew there was no sense even transmitting them to the United States. Hirohito had to intervene personally on two occasions during the next few days to induce hard-liners to abandon their conditions and to accept the American stipulation that the emperor's authority "shall be subject to the Supreme Commander of the Allied Powers." That the militarists would have accepted such a settlement before the bombs is farfetched, to say the least.

Some writers have argued that the cumulative effects of battlefield defeats, conventional bombing, and naval blockade already had defeated Japan. Even without extending assurances about the emperor, all the United States had to do was wait. The most frequently cited basis for this contention is the *United States Strategic Bombing Survey*, published in 1946, which stated that Japan would have surrendered by November 1 "even if the atomic bombs had not been dropped, even if Russia had not entered the war, and even if no invasion had been planned or contemplated." Recent scholarship by the historian Robert P. Newman and others has demonstrated that the survey was "cooked" by those who prepared it to arrive at such a conclusion. No matter. This or any other document based on information available only after the war ended is irrelevant with regard to what Truman could have known at the time.

What often goes unremarked is that when the bombs were dropped, fighting was still going on in the Philippines, China, and elsewhere. Every day that the war continued thousands of prisoners of war had to live and die in abysmal conditions, and there were rumors that the Japanese intended to slaughter them if the homeland was invaded. Truman was Commander in Chief of the American armed forces, and he had a duty to the men under his command not shared by those sitting in moral judgment decades later. Available evidence points to the conclusion that he acted for the reason he said he did: to end a bloody war that would have become far bloodier had invasion proved necessary. One can only imagine what would have happened if tens of thousands of American boys had died or been wounded on Japanese soil and then it had become known that Truman had chosen not to use weapons that might have ended the war months sooner.

Unit 5

Unit Selections

27. **1948: The Presidential Election,** Michael D. Haydock
28. **Baseball's *Noble* Experiment,** William Kashatus
29. **The Split-Level Years, 1950–1960: Elvis, Howdy Doody Time, McDonald's, and the Rumblings of Rebellion,** Henry Allen
30. **Point of Order!** Thomas Doherty
31. **Martin Luther King's Half-Forgotten Dream,** Peter Ling
32. **The Spirit of '68,** John B. Judis
33. **Nixon's America,** Michael Barone
34. **Face-Off,** John Lewis Gaddis

Key Points to Consider

❖ How does one account for Harry S. Truman's victory in the presidential election of 1948 in view of the forces arrayed against him? To what extent was Thomas Dewey personally responsible for the outcome?

❖ How could what has become known as "McCarthyism" have emerged in the most powerful and prosperous country in the world? Discuss how the televised Army hearings contributed to McCarthy's downfall.

❖ Evaluate Martin Luther King's career. What does the author mean in his article by referring to King's "half-forgotten dream"?

❖ What was "The Spirit of '68?" Does John Judis make a convincing case for his claims about the impact of the 1960s on American culture?

❖ Discuss Richard Nixon's accomplishments as presented in "Nixon's America." Were they as important as the author claims? To what extent was Nixon merely responding to congressional and public sentiment?

 **Links**   www.dushkin.com/online/

21. **Coldwar0**
    http://ac.acusd.edu/history/20th/coldwar0.html
22. **The Federal Web Locator**
    http://www.infoctr.edu/fwl
23. **Federalism: Relationship between Local and National Governments**
    http://www.infidels.org/~nap/index.federalism.html
24. **The Gallup Organization**
    http://www.gallup.com
25. **STAT-USA**
    http://www.stat-usa.gov/stat-usa.html
26. **U.S. Department of State**
    http://www.state.gov

These sites are annotated on pages 4 and 5.

From the Cold War to 2000

President Franklin D. Roosevelt sought to build a working relationship with Soviet leader Josef Stalin throughout World War II. Roosevelt believed that the wartime collaboration had to continue if a lasting peace were to be achieved. At the Yalta Conference of February 1945, a series of agreements were made that FDR hoped would provide the basis for continued cooperation. Subsequent disputes over interpretation of these agreements, particularly with regard to Poland, raised doubts in Roosevelt's mind that Stalin was acting in good faith. Roosevelt died on April 12, 1945, and there is no doubt that he was moving toward a "tougher" position.

His successor, Harry S. Truman, assumed the presidency with little knowledge of Roosevelt's thinking. Truman attempted to carry out what he believed were Roosevelt's intentions: be firm with the Soviets, but continue to seek accommodation. After the Potsdam Conference of 1945, he left the talks believing that Stalin was a hard bargainer but one who could be trusted.

Events during the late summer and early autumn eroded Truman's hopes that the Soviets genuinely wanted to get along. Disputes over Poland and other Eastern European countries, the treatment of postwar Germany, and a host of other issues finally persuaded Truman that it was time to stop "babying" the Soviets. Increasingly hostile relations led to what became known as the "cold war," during which each side increasingly came to regard the other as an enemy rather than merely an adversary.

Meanwhile the United States had to cope with the problems of reconversion to a peacetime economy. Demobilization of the armed forces proved especially vexing as the public clamored to have servicemen and women, stationed virtually all over the world, brought home and discharged as quickly as possible. When the administration seemed to be moving too slowly, the threat "no boats, no votes" became popular. Race riots, labor strife, and inflation also marred the postwar period.

There was social ferment as well. Many blacks had served in the armed forces or worked in defense industries, presumably to win a war for freedom and justice. Yet they had encountered segregation in the military and unequal treatment in civilian jobs. Professional sports at that time was kept "lily white," an affront to the principles for which the war had been fought. In "Baseball's *Noble* Experiment," William Kashatus describes how Brooklyn Dodger president Branch Rickey maneuvered to break down the color line in baseball. Jackie Robinson, a former army officer, was chosen to be the test case as much for his mental toughness as for his physical skills. Robinson proved more than equal to the challenge. Despite the taunts of opponents, fans, and even some of his own teammates, he carved out a distinguished career and opened the doors for other black players.

"1948: The Presidential Election" analyzes Truman's presidential race against his heavily-favored opponent, Thomas Dewey. Beset by defections from both the right and left, Truman doggedly conducted an exhausting campaign. As opinion polls predicted a Dewey landslide virtually until election day, Truman's victory astonished practically everyone.

Relations with the Soviets continued to deteriorate. Perceived Soviet threats against Greece and Turkey led to promulgation of the "Truman Doctrine" in 1947, which placed the United States on the side of those nations threatened with overt aggression or internal subversion. That same year Secretary of State George C. Marshall sketched the outlines of what would become known as the "Marshall Plan," an even more ambitious effort to prevent economic chaos in Europe.

Domestically, the 1950s offered a mixed bag. Social critics denounced the conformity of those—many of whom well remembered the Great Depression—who plodded up the corporate ladder, purchased tract homes that all looked alike, or who had no greater ambition than to sit in front of their television sets every night. "The Split-Level Years, 1950–1960" provides a sketch of the decade that witnessed the emergence to stardom of Marilyn Monroe, Howdy Doody, and James Dean. There was a darker side. During the early 1950s many Americans believed that, as threatening as the Soviet Union was abroad, the real danger lay in subversion within the United States. Senator Joseph R. McCarthy claimed that all our basic institutions had been infiltrated by disloyal Americans and "fellow travelers" (those who were not Communists but who unwittingly aided their goals). "Point of Order!" tells how the televised hearings of McCarthy's accusations against the United States Army brought his demise.

Dwight D. Eisenhower was elected president in 1952. A truce ending the Korean war was hammered out the following year, but the cold war continued with a vengeance. Eisenhower and his secretary of state, John Foster Dulles, had come into office promising to "roll back the Iron Curtain" and to "free captive peoples." They did neither. More and more the entire globe was viewed as an arena of competition between the forces of communism and the free world.

Two essays in this unit deal with the turbulent 1960s. "Martin Luther King's Half-Forgotten Dream" places particular emphasis upon the last years of this inspiring civil rights leader's life. John B. Judis, in "The Spirit of '68," claims that during the 1960s the United States changed from a culture based on work, sacrifice, and deferred gratification to one that emphasized "consumption, lifestyle, and quality of life." He sees this passage as the result of what he calls "consumer capitalism."

Richard M. Nixon is best remembered for the Watergate scandals and for being the first president to resign from office in disgrace. Michael Barone's "Nixon's America" does not deny the man's transgressions but points out his important accomplishments. Nixon was responsible for a number of innovations in both foreign and domestic policies. The America we know today, Barone argues, has been shaped by Nixon's legacies.

Ronald Reagan campaigned for the presidency on the basis that government was not the solution to national ills but part of the problem. He also promised to "stand tall" against the Soviet Union in contrast to the perceived flabbiness of the Carter administration. The "Reagan Revolution" did bring about fairly radical changes in government structures and approaches and managed to run up the national debt to unprecedented amounts. During his second administration, against the advice of some of his hawkish advisers, Reagan did a near about-face with regard to the Soviets and helped to bring an end to the cold war. In "Face Off," John Lewis Gaddis provides a decade-by-decade account of the struggle and reminds us that it was not inevitable that it would end the way it did.

1948 The Presidential Election

The press and the polls agreed: Harry Truman was certain to lose. But instead of giving up, the president decided to "give 'em hell."

By Michael D. Haydock

FEW PEOPLE BELIEVED that President Harry S. Truman had a chance of winning the 1948 presidential election. The three great national polling organizations all predicted that Governor Thomas E. Dewey of New York, his Republican opponent, would win by a wide margin. The press was equally certain of a Dewey victory, for the odds against the incumbent seemed insurmountable. Truman's own party had split, with Democrat Strom Thurmond running in the South as a "Dixiecrat" and former vice president Henry Wallace running as the candidate of the newly formed Progressive Party. It was expected that Wallace would drain vitally needed liberal votes away from the president. Among Democratic politicians and his own campaign staff, it seemed that the only person who thought Truman could win was the candidate himself.

Of course, there were many who wondered how Harry Truman had ever made it into the White House in the first place. The son of a Missouri mule-trader-turned-farmer, Truman differed markedly from his predecessor, Franklin Delano Roosevelt. Truman, who had served as a captain of artillery in World War 1, was a failed businessman whose haberdashery in Kansas City had closed during a recession in 1922. While overseas, however, Truman had met Jim Pendergast, whose family was a Democratic political dynasty in Kansas City.

With the support of less-than-reputable political boss Tom Pendergast, Truman was elected eastern judge of Jackson County in 1922, and then, in 1934, United States senator. Though Truman himself was a man of impeccable personal honesty and political integrity, many in Washington looked down on him as the "Senator from Pendergast." Only during his second term in the Senate, when he headed a committee investigating the national defense program, did Truman gain a reputation for hard work and diligence and the respect of his fellow senators.

In 1944, Franklin Roosevelt picked Truman as his running mate to replace Vice President Henry Wallace, whose extreme liberal views were far out of alignment with those of Democratic party leaders. When Roosevelt died on April 12, 1945, Truman became president. It was not a job he had ever aspired to, and he confided in his diary and in letters to his family his doubts about his abilities.

By 1948, however, Harry Truman had grown into the job and was determined to seek a full term in his own right. He also sought vindication for the rebuff his party had suffered at the polls in the 1946 congressional elections, when the Republicans gained an overwhelming majority in both the House and the Senate.

The Republicans had selected Thomas Dewey in June on the third ballot at their convention in Philadelphia's Convention Hall. For his running mate, Dewey picked California governor Earl Warren. Roosevelt had defeated Dewey

27. 1948: The Presidential Election

in the 1944 election, but Truman's hopes looked slim. "Barring a political miracle, it was the kind of ticket that could not fail to sweep the Republican Party back into power," Time magazine proclaimed.

The Democratic convention opened on July 12 in the same Philadelphia hall the Republicans had used, but the mood in the building had darkened. The decorative flags and bunting had not been changed and now looked bedraggled and shop-worn. The Associated Press noted that "The Democrats act as though they have accepted an invitation to a funeral." Until a few days before the convention there had been an active movement to deny Truman the nomination. A diverse group of party leaders, headed by James Roosevelt, son of the former president, had pushed hard for General Dwight Eisenhower. The Eisenhower boom ended only when the general stated unequivocally that he would not accept the nomination if it was offered.

The Democrats were further fractured when a coalition of liberals led by Hubert Humphrey of Minnesota inserted a strong civil rights plank, modeled after Truman's own proposals to Congress, into the platform. Delegates from the conservative South, intent on maintaining segregation there, were adamantly opposed to the plank. Before the nominating process even began, Alabama's Handy Ellis announced that his state's presidential electors were "never to cast a vote for Harry Truman, and never to cast their vote for any candidate with a civil rights program such as adopted by the convention." Half of the Alabama delegation and the entire Mississippi contingent walked out. Two days later, disaffected southern Democrats met in Birmingham, Alabama, to nominate Governor Strom Thurmond of South Carolina for president. The new party officially called itself the States' Rights Democrats; the press dubbed them "Dixiecrats," and the name stuck. It appeared that Truman had lost the "Solid South"—a traditional Democratic stronghold. Meanwhile, on July 27, the Progressive Party nominated Henry Wallace for president.

Truman, who picked Senator Alben Barkley of Kentucky as his running mate, was undeterred by the defections from his party For his convention acceptance speech, the president used only an outline written in short, punchy sentences. He electrified the audience when he said, "Senator Barkley and I will win this election and make the Republicans like it—don't you forget it." It was the first time during the convention that anyone had spoken of actually winning. Truman then praised the higher wages, higher farm income, and greater benefits for Americans he claimed as Democratic accomplishments, and went on to condemn the Republican Congress. He spoke with scorn of the recently adopted Republican platform, contrasting the programs it contained with congressional inaction on similar programs he had proposed.

Truman roused the convention to a standing ovation when he announced his intention to call Congress back into special session to "ask them to pass the laws to halt rising prices, to meet the housing crisis—which they say they are for in their platform." When this special session did convene a few weeks later it accomplished little, as Truman expected, but it gave the president a campaign issue. The country's woes, he asserted, were the result of the "do-nothing" Republican Congress.

Truman excepted to run on issues. He had already begun running for reelection when he gave his State of the Union address on January 7, 1948, and continued with a cross-country trip a month before the Democratic convention. Officially he made the journey to accept an honorary degree from the University of California. Though he normally flew, this time Truman went by train, which allowed him to pass through 18 states and speak from the back platform at stops along the way.

Truman traveled in a special car, the *Ferdinand Magellan,* originally designed for President Roosevelt. It contained sleeping quarters, a galley and dining room, bath, and a walnut-paneled sitting room. Armor-plated and equipped with a special speaker system for addressing crowds, the *Magellan* served as Truman's traveling office throughout the campaign. The train also included a dining car converted into an office for staff, a special car for the Signal Corps to keep the president in touch with Washington, and another car for the press.

By the time Truman returned to Washington from this "nonpolitical" trip, he had covered 9,504 miles and made 73 speeches at stops in small towns and cities, in which he hammered away at "the do-nothing Congress." When Republican Senator Robert Taft complained in a speech about the spectacle of a president maligning Congress at every "whistle-stop" around the country, the Democratic campaign staff pounced on the remark. They telegraphed leaders in 35 communities in which the president had spoken and asked if they agreed with the senator's demeaning characterization of their towns. The response of the head of the Chamber of Commerce in Laramie, Wyoming, was typical: "Characteristically, Senator Taft is confused." A new term, "whistle-stop tour," entered the American political lexicon.

In contrast, Dewey decided to take a low-key approach and emphasize his own broad program statements rather than attack his opponent. He had reason to believe he could simply march down the high road into the White House. A Gallup poll published in early August gave the New York governor 48 percent of the vote, with only 37 percent going to Truman, and just 5 percent to Wallace. A few days later, a Roper poll estimated Truman's support at just 31.5 percent.

The science of opinion polling was still in its infancy, but already the public and political leaders had come to rely on it. Pioneered by George Gallup, the polls used "quota sampling"—the selection of a small, diverse group of people representing the entire public—to draw broad conclusions. In the 1934 congressional elections, Gallup's predictions were within one percentage point of the actual results. In 1936, he accurately predicted the outcome of the Roosevelt-Landon race, and by 1940, 118 newspapers were carrying Gallup's syndicated column, "America Speaks." People had faith in the accuracy of his predictions and those of his two chief rivals, the Roper and the Crosley Polls, which used similar methods. Meanwhile, older, less scientific gauges also favored Dewey: professional gamblers were offering odds of up to 30 to 1 against a Truman victory.

On the morning of September 17, Truman boarded the *Ferdinand Magellan* at Washington's Union Station for his first major tour of the campaign. Vice-presidential candidate Barkley exhorted him to "Mow 'em down, Harry!" Truman responded, "I'm going to give 'em hell." The tour took him cross-country to California, back through the Midwest and Northeast, and finally to his home in Missouri.

At his first major stop, the National Plowing Contest in Dexter, Iowa, the president delivered a hard, clear message. "This Republican Congress has already stuck a pitchfork in the farmer's back," he said. He pointed out that Congressional inaction in appropriating the funds for the construction of grain storage bins had forced many farmers to sell their crops at a loss, at prices below government minimums. "I'm not asking you to vote for me," Truman concluded. "Vote for your farms! Vote for the standard of living you have won under the Democratic administration."

Truman continued to attack the Republicans on the farm issue, among others, throughout the tour. The press noted that, while his audiences were large, they did not seem particularly enthusiastic. The reporters attributed the crowds to natural curiosity and reasoned that people wanted to see the president but were not necessarily interested in supporting him.

The press complained of the arrangements they had to endure on the Truman train. Their car had no speaker system, so reporters had to scramble out into the crowd to hear what Truman was saying, then hustle back on board before the train pulled out. Because the president spoke from outline notes, the reporters did not always receive copies of Truman's speeches ahead of time. The same apparently slipshod manner applied to the correspondents' living arrangements. They had no laundry facilities, and

On the Campaign Trail

As he headed back to Washington, D.C., by train following a round of Labor Day "whistle-stops," Harry Truman gave B&O Railroad supervisor Pete Cordic quite a thrill. Cordic had always been a firebrand of a Democrat but had soured on Truman when the president had threatened to take over the railroads during a strike two years earlier. Now, riding in the locomotive of the presidential special in the early morning hours of September 7, Cordic was told by Secret Service agents that the president wanted to ride up front.

Soon after, Cordic swung open the door of the locomotive to find the diminutive leader of the free world standing a few feet away on the end of the lead car, hanging onto his hat and bracing himself against the pitching and rolling of the train.

"I'm Harry Truman, What's your name, sir?" the president shouted.

"I'm Pete Cordic, Mr. President," Cordic boomed.

"Well, Pete," Truman laughed, "you'd better get me across here in one piece or we'll both be in trouble."

As concerned Secret Service men looked on, Cordic helped the president across the gap that separated the cars. "Pete, let's see what you've got here," Truman said eagerly.

Minutes later, Truman and his excited host stood in the train's cab, and Cordic asked the president if he would like to try his hand at the throttle. Truman grinned boyishly. "You aren't gonna let me run us all into the ditch, are you Pete?" Amid laughter, the engineer slid out of his seat, guided the president's food to the "dead man's" pedal, settled him into position, and replaced his fedora with an engineer's cap. "Now, Mr. President, you've got a couple of crossings to whistle for," Cordic said.

Truman leaned on the horn through Coraopolis along the misty Ohio River. Somehow, word of the president's excursion had spread, and photographers on the ground snapped pictures of the honorary engine man as he rolled along. "He really didn't do much running," Cordic said later," We kept a pretty good eye on things. But he looked like he was having a ... good time."

Too soon, it was over. Truman had to return to his car for breakfast. "Pete, you run a fine railroad," the smiling chief executive declared as he shook his delighted host's hand. "If you're ever in Washington, stop by the house."

Cordic's loyalty to Truman and the Democratic Party remained firm from then on. "He called me Pete y'know," he fondly remembered.

When the president's train rumbled into Richmond, Indiana, on the morning of October 12, Truman aide Clark Clifford stepped off in search of the latest issue of *Newsweek*. The magazine had announced that it would publish a poll of the nation's 50 leading political journalists on Truman's chances for election.

Climbed found a fresh stack of the still-wrapped magazines inside the railroad station and anxiously flipped through a copy. He was taken aback by the ominous headline: "Election Forecast: 50 Political Experts Predict a GOP Sweep." Clifford was not surprised that Dewey was favored, but the clean 50–0 vote shocked him. "It was very upsetting," he recalled, "because it was going to have a lot of impact on the electorate." He bought a copy and tucked it under his coat, hoping to prevent Truman from seeing it.

Back on the train, Clifford immediately encountered the president, who greeted him and asked, "Uh, what does it say?" Clifford feigned ignorance, but Truman persisted.

"Well," the president explained, "I saw you go into the station and you disappeared for a while and I think what you were doing was probably going in there to get a copy of the *Newsweek* magazine. And the way you're holding your left arm against your side, I think you may have a copy of that magazine under your coat."

Clifford sheepishly handed him the magazine. Truman looked it over quickly and said, "I know every one of those 50 fellows. Not one of them has enough sense to pound sand in a rathole."

That was it, Clifford remembered, amazed at his boss's confidence in victory. "He just tossed it off ... and went ahead as though it hadn't happened."

—Box Withers, adapted from his book *The President Travels By Train: Politics and Pullmans*, TLC Publishing, 1996.

when the train made an overnight stop they had to find their own hotel accommodations.

There were no such complaints about the Dewey "Victory Special," which pulled out of Albany, New York, on September 19. There were more than 90 reporters aboard—more than double the number that accompanied the president—and they usually received copies of the candidate's speeches a day in advance. The press car and both dining cars had loudspeakers, so writers did not even have to leave the train to hear Dewey speak. Campaign staff picked up and returned their laundry and arranged their hotel accommodations.

It was not just the mundane details of life aboard the Truman train that seemed disorganized. Funding was also a problem, with few people willing to contribute to what seemed a doomed campaign. The Truman tour came close to ending in Oklahoma City on September 28 when the railroad refused to move Truman's train out of the yards until overdue charges were paid. Only a hasty fund-raising campaign initiated by Oklahoma Governor Roy Turner allowed the president to roll on.

Although a second lengthy tour was planned for late October, Truman rested for only four days after returning to Washington before setting off on a series of short train journeys. On October 6 he began a three-day swing through the mid-Atlantic states, continuing to hammer the Republican-controlled Congress. The crowds he encountered were large; on the ride from Albany to Buffalo, between 5,000 and 10,000 people showed up at every stop. Invariably someone would shout, "Give 'em hell, Harry," and Truman would. The polls, and the reporters, continued to dismiss the crowds as gatherings of the naturally curious.

During a second short trip through the upper Midwest, Truman gave his aide George Elsey a state-by-state rundown of the electoral votes he expected to win. Truman predicted that he would receive 340 to Dewey's 108. He conceded that Thurmond would probably take 42 and that 37 were in doubt. Elsey had doubts as well—of the entire prediction—but he didn't tell the president.

Truman began his final swing through the country on October 24, still considered a certain loser. During this second tour, *Newsweek* published the election opinions of 50 highly respected political reporters. All 50 predicted Truman would lose. The president was unconcerned. (See "On The Campaign Trail.") Truman sensed what others could not— that the average voter was listening to him and believing in his message.

Still, many politicians avoided associating themselves with the Truman campaign for fear of damaging their own political futures. Frank J. Lausche, the Democratic candidate for governor in Ohio, was one. Lausche didn't want to jeopardize his bipartisan support by appearing on the campaign train as it passed through Ohio. Only with great reluctance did he eventually agree to get on board and ride a few miles to Dayton with the president. He was adamant that he would leave the train after that short ride.

What Lausche saw amazed him. There were 7,000 people at the first small-town stop. The crowd in Dayton spilled out of the station, blocking traffic in the streets. "Is this the way the crowds have always been?" he asked the president. "Yes, but this is smaller than we've had in most states," Truman responded. Lausche stayed on the Truman train all the way to Akron.

Toward the end of the campaign, some of the reporters on the Truman train began to sense the changing political winds, noting a particularly large crowd or noisy ovation as the president "gave 'em hell." While most maintained that Dewey would win by a wide margin, a few began to cautiously hedge on their earlier predictions. Even Dewey began to have doubts. With just two weeks left in the campaign, a Gallup poll showed that his lead was down to six points. On Dewey's instruction, his staff contacted 90 of the 96 Republican committee members around the country to ask their opinion on whether he should change his tactics. All but one counseled the governor that he was sure to win if he continued the type of campaign he had been running.

When the final campaign swings ended, both candidates predicted victory. No one believed Truman's prediction. The Gallup poll now had Dewey winning 49.5 percent of the vote to Truman's 44.5. The *New York Times* predicted that Dewey would take 29 states with a total of 345 electoral votes, to Truman's 11 states and 105 electoral votes. Strom Thurmond, it was expected, would carry four southern states. Elmo Roper had stopped taking polls in early September, based on his absolute confidence that Dewey would win and that further polling was unnecessary.

Not even Truman's closest associates shared the president's confidence. Clark Clifford, who had mapped most of the Truman campaign strategy, thought that Truman was gaining and might have been able to pull off a victory if the campaign had been a week or two longer.

On election eve, Truman spoke to the nation by radio from his home in Independence. "From the bottom of my heart I thank the people of the United States for their cordiality to me and their interest in the affairs of this great nation and of the world," he said. "I trust the people, because when they know the facts, they do the right thing."

On election day Thomas Dewey and his wife voted in a school on East 51st Street in New York City A nearby skyscraper was festooned with a sign that read, "Good luck, Mr. President." When he emerged from the booth, Dewey said, "Well, I know of two votes we got anyway.

Harry Truman, with wife Bess, and daughter Margaret, voted at 10:00 A.M. in Independence. They posed for photographers, and when asked about his chances, Truman responded, "It can't be anything but a victory." He said that he would probably go to bed early rather than sit up and listen to the results. He did exactly that. As reporters and cameramen conducted a sort of "death watch" around his house awaiting a statement from Truman conceding defeat, the president slipped away with a Secret Service detail and drove to the Elms Hotel in Excelsior Springs. After a ham sandwich and a glass of milk, Truman retired early.

Walter Cronkite was among the group of surprised press representatives who did not find out until the next morning that the president had not been home all night. During the night reporters had noticed the bathroom light in the Truman home turned on a few times, a sign that seemed to indicate Truman's presence. The press had apparently been hoodwinked. Cronkite later recalled, "After we had become good friends, the president's daughter, Margaret Truman, who was home that night, denied that the family had indulged in any such gambit, but I thought her denial was a little tentative."

At midnight, a Secret Service agent woke Truman and told him that he was 1.2 million votes ahead of Dewey but was still expected to lose. At 4:00 A.M. he was awakened again with news that his lead in the popular vote was now 2 million. Over the radio, NBC broadcaster H. V. Kaltenborn still forecasted his defeat. Truman rose, dressed, and hurried to Kansas City, knowing that his own prediction was coming true. Meanwhile, in New York City, Dewey's campaign manager was telling a large press contingent, "We're in there fighting. The returns are still coming in but it looks as if we won't know until morning."

When morning came, the results were clear. Thomas Dewey polled 21,991,291 votes, while Truman received 24,179,345. Henry Wallace cost Truman the electoral votes of New York, and Thurmond took Alabama, Louisiana, Mississippi, and South Carolina, but the president prevailed in the farm states of Iowa, Wisconsin, and Ohio, all of which had gone for Dewey in 1944. The Wallace vote in California was far below predictions, and the president carried that state as well. In all, Truman gathered 303 electoral votes. Dewey came up with 189, and Thurmond earned a total of 39 from the four states he carried and a single, renegade elector from Tennessee who refused to cast his ballot for Truman. After traveling 21,928 miles and making a total of 275 speeches, Harry Truman had engineered the most stunning upset victory in presidential election history.

At 11:14 on the morning after election day, Thomas Dewey—the man nearly every pollster, pundit, and politician in the country had believed was destined to be the next president—wired Harry Truman: "My heartiest congratulations to you on your election and every good wish for a successful administration."

Soon after the election, several newspapers dropped George Gallup's services. He and the other pollsters promised to determine how they could have been so wrong. They soon discovered that they had stopped polling far too early. Many voters had remained undecided until the very end—then they had cast their votes for the incumbent. After the 1948 race, pollsters adjusted their methods so that the people sampled were even more representative, and they continued to take polls right up to election day.

The press was mortified by its failure. Richard Strout, in the *New Republic,* described the election as a "personal humiliation" but added that it "gave a glowing and wonderful sense that the American people can't be ticketed by polls, know their own mind, and picked the rather unlikely but courageous figure of Truman to carry on its banner."

The president was willing to be magnanimous in victory. The day after his stunning win, Truman received a telegram from the *Washington Post* inviting him to attend a banquet at which the entire *Post* staff, dressed in sackcloth and ashes, would "eat crow" while the president, attired in white tie, would be served turkey. Truman wrote that, instead, "We should all get together now and make a country in which everybody can eat turkey whenever he pleases."

Michael D. Haydock is a freelance writer from Poughkeepsie, New York. His article about the sinking of the battleship Maine *appeared in the February 1998 issue of* American History.

For more on President Harry S. Truman, read "Shoot-out on Pennsylvania Avenue," by Elbert B. Smith. You can find it on the World Wide Web at TheHistoryNet, http://www.thehistorynet.com.

Baseball's *Noble* Experiment

When former Negro Leaguer Jackie Robinson took his place in the Brooklyn Dodgers' starting lineup on April 15, 1947, he initiated a major change not only in sports, but in American society as a whole.

by William Kashatus

On August 28, 1945, Jackie Robinson, the star shortstop of the Negro Leagues' Kansas City Monarchs, arrived at the executive offices of the Brooklyn Dodgers Baseball Club. Invited on the pretense that Branch Rickey, since 1942 a part owner of the club as well as its president and general manager, was seeking top black talent in order to create a Negro League team of his own, Robinson approached the meeting with great reluctance. Deep down he wanted to break the color barrier that existed in professional baseball, not discuss the possibility of playing for yet another all-black team. Little did he realize that Rickey shared his dream.

A shrewd, talkative man who had dedicated his life to baseball, the 64-year-old Rickey was secretly plotting a sweeping revolution within the national pastime. He believed that integration of the major leagues would be good for the country as well as for the game. Financial gain was only part of his motive—it was also a matter of moral principle. Rickey a devout Methodist, disdained the bigoted attitudes of the white baseball establishment.

Greeting Robinson with a vigorous handshake, Rickey wasted no time in revealing his true intentions. "The truth is," he confessed, "I'm interested in you as a candidate for the Brooklyn Dodgers. I think you can play in the major leagues. How do you feel about it?"

The young ball player was speechless. He had taught himself to be cynical toward all baseball-club owners, especially white ones, in order to prevent any personal disillusionment.

"What about it? You think you can play for Montreal?" demanded the stocky beetle-browed executive.

Robinson, awestruck, managed to say "yes." He knew that the Montreal Royals was the Dodgers' top minor-league team and that if he made good there, he had an excellent chance to crack the majors. "I just want to be treated fairly" he added. You will not be treated fairly!" Rickey snapped. " 'Nigger' will be a compliment!"

For the next three hours, Rickey interrogated the star shortstop. With great dramatic flair, he role-played every conceivable scenario that would confront the first player to break baseball's color barrier: first he was a bigoted sportswriter who only wrote lies about Robinson's performance; next he was a Southern hotel manager refusing room and board; then, a racist major leaguer looking for a fight; and after that a waiter throwing Robinson out of a "for whites only" diner. In every scenario, Rickey cursed Robinson and threatened him, verbally degrading him in every way imaginable. The Dodger general manager's performance was so convincing, Robinson later said, that "I found myself chain-gripping my fingers behind my back."

When he was through, Rickey told Robinson that he knew he was "a fine ballplayer. But what I need," he added, "is more than a great player. I need a man that will take abuse and insults for his race. And what I don't know is whether you have the guts!"

Robinson struggled to keep his temper. He was insulted by the implication that he was a coward. "Mr. Rickey," he retorted, "do you want a Negro who's afraid to fight back?"

"No!" Rickey barked, "I want a ballplayer with guts enough *not* to fight back. We can't *fight* our way through this. There's virtually nobody on our side. No owners, no umpires, virtually no newspapermen. And I'm afraid that many fans will be hostile too. They'll taunt you and goad you. They'll do anything to make you react. They'll try to provoke a race riot in the ball park."

In 1945, after a careful search for just the right man to do the job, Branch Rickey, president, general manager, and part owner of the Brooklyn Dodgers, bucked the long segregationist history of major-league baseball by signing Jack Roosevelt (Jackie) Robinson to play in the Dodger organization. At the time he signed with the Dodgers, Jackie was a shortstop with the Kansas City Monarchs of the Negro Leagues. During his ten seasons with the Dodgers, Robinson played under three managers—Burt Shotten, Chuck Dressen, and Walt Alston.

For the nearly one million African Americans who had served in the armed forces during World War II, the contradiction inherent in their fight against totalitarianism abroad while enduring segregation at home was insufferable. No longer willing to knuckle under to Jim Crow this young generation of black Americans was determined to secure full political and social equality. Many migrated to Northern cities, where they found better jobs, better schooling, and freedom from landlord control. Together with their white allies, these Northern blacks would lay the foundations of the momentous civil rights campaign of the 1950s and '60s. And Jackie Robinson became their hero.

To be sure, Robinson's challenge to baseball's whites-only policy was a formidable one. Blacks had been expelled from the major leagues when segregation was established by the 1896 Supreme Court ruling in *Plessy v. Ferguson.*** Racist attitudes were reinforced by the significant numbers of white Southerners who played in the majors, as well as by the extensive minor-league system that existed in the South. When blacks established their own Negro Leagues, white journalists, as well as historians, ignored them.

As he listened, Robinson became transfixed by the Dodger president. He felt his sincerity his deep, quiet strength, and his sense of moral justice. "We can only win," concluded Rickey, "if we can convince the world that I'm doing this because you're a great ballplayer and a fine gentleman. You will symbolize a crucial cause. One incident, just one incident, can set it back twenty years."

"Mr. Rickey," Robinson finally said, "I think I can play ball in Montreal. I think I can play ball in Brooklyn. . . . If you want to take this gamble, I will promise you there will be no incident."

The agreement was sealed by a handshake. Jackie Robinson and Branch Rickey had launched a noble experiment to integrate major-league baseball. Two years later, in 1947, when Robinson actually broke the color barrier, winning rookie-of-the-year honors with the Dodgers, he raised the hopes and expectations of millions of black Americans who believed that deeply rooted patterns of discrimination could be changed.

In 1945, segregation was the most distinguishing characteristic of American race relations. More than half of the nation's 15 million African Americans still lived in the South, amidst a society that sanctioned the principle of "equal but separate." A rigid system of state and local ordinances enforced strict separation of the races in schools, restaurants, movie theaters, and even restrooms. For blacks, these so-called "Jim Crow laws"* meant inferior public schools, health care, and public lodging, as well as discriminatory voter registration procedures that kept many of them disenfranchised.

---

* Originally used in connection with legislation enacted in Southern states during the nineteenth century to separate the races on public transportation, the term "Jim Crow law" eventually applied to all statutes that enforced segregation.

** The 1896 decision of the Supreme Court in *Plessy v. Ferguson* upheld a Louisiana law that required railroads in that state to provide "equal but separate accommodations for the white and colored races." It was this "equal but separate" doctrine that made the discriminatory practices of this century legal in the United States. The Court essentially reversed itself in its 1954 *Brown v. Board of Education of Topeka, Kansas* decision, effectively ending legal segregation.

28. Baseball's *Noble* Experiment

A versatile athlete, Robinson earned varsity letters in four sports, including track (above, left, while a student at the University of California at Los Angeles. As a lieutenant in the U.S. Army during World War II (above, right), Robinson faced a court-martial for refusing to move to the back of a military bus; he was acquitted and honorably discharged.

Despite the periodic efforts of some white club owners to circumvent the racist policies and sign exceptional Negro Leaguers, the majors continued to bar blacks through the end of World War II. Baseball Commissioner Judge Kenesaw Mountain Landis ensured the sport's segregationist policies by thwarting all efforts to sign blacks, while publicly stating that "There is no rule, formal or informal, or any understanding—unwritten, subterranean, or sub-anything—against the hiring of Negro players by the teams of organized baseball." Not until Landis died in 1944, however, did baseball open the door for integration.

The new commissioner, Albert "Happy" Chandler, was adamant in defending the "freedom of blacks," especially those who served in the war, to "make it in major league baseball." Chandler's support for integration earned for him the open hostility of the owners of 15 of the 16 major-league clubs, the exception being the Dodgers and Branch Rickey.

Publicly, Rickey never revealed his intentions of breaking the color barrier. Instead, he announced to the baseball world that he was going to organize a team to be known as the "Brown Dodgers" or the "Brown Bombers" as part of a new all-black "United States League." His scouts combed baseball leagues across the country, as well as in Cuba, Mexico, Puerto Rico, and Venezuela, for black prospects. What Rickey really wanted to find was a talented, college-educated ballplayer who would be able to contradict the popular myth of black ignorance. His search narrowed to Jack Roosevelt Robinson, then an infielder for the Kansas City Monarchs.

Born on January 31, 1919, in Cairo, Georgia, Jackie was the grandson of a slave and the fifth child of a sharecropper who deserted his family. Raised by his mother in a white, middle-class neighborhood in Pasadena, California, Jackie and his brothers and sister were verbally ridiculed and frequently pelted with rocks by local children. Rather than endure the humiliation, the boys formed a gang and began to return fire.

What saved the young Jackie from more serious trouble and even crime was his exceptional athletic ability. Robinson's high school career was distinguished by remarkable success in football, baseball, basketball, and track. His versatility earned him an athletic scholarship, first to Pasadena Junior College and later to the University of California at Los Angeles, where he earned varsity letters in four different sports and All American honors in football.

Drafted into the Army in the spring of 1942, Robinson applied to be admitted to Officers' Candidate School, but was denied admission because of his race. His application was eventually approved, however, thanks to the help of boxing champion Joe Louis, who was stationed with Jackie at Fort Riley, Kansas. Commissioned a second lieutenant, Robinson continued during the next few years to defy discriminatory practices within the military. When, in July 1944, he refused to move to the rear of a military bus at Fort Hood, Texas, Robinson was charged with insubordination and court-martialed. But the case against him was weak—the Army had recently issued orders against such segregation—and a good lawyer won his acquittal. Although he received an honorable discharge in November 1944, Robinson's time in the military had left him feeling vulnerable and uncertain about the future.

Shortly after his discharge, the Kansas City Monarchs, one of the most talented of baseball's Negro League teams, offered Robinson a contract for four hundred dollars a month. While with the Monarchs, Robinson established himself as a fine defensive shortstop with impressive base stealing and hitting abilities. But he hated barnstorming through the South, with its Jim Crow restaurants and hotels, and frequently allowed his temper to get the better of him.

Some teammates thought Jackie too impatient with the segregationist treatment of blacks. Others admired him for his determination to take a stand against racism. Yet Robinson never saw himself as a crusader for civil rights as much as an athlete who had grown disillusioned with his chosen career. "When I look back at what I had to go through," he recalled years later, "I can only marvel at the many black players who stuck it out for years in the Jim Crow leagues because they had nowhere to go. The black press, some liberal sportswriters and even a few politicians were banging away at those Jim Crow barriers in baseball, but I never expected the walls to come tumbling down in my lifetime. I began to wonder why I should dedicate my life to a career where the boundaries of progress were set by racial discrimination."

There were indications, however, that the tide was turning in favor of integration. On April 16, 1945, Robinson was invited along with two other Negro League stars—Marvin Williams of the Philadelphia Stars and the Cleveland Buckeyes' Sam Jethroe—to try-out for the Boston Red Sox. Manager Joe Cronin was especially impressed with the Monarchs' shortstop, but still passed on the opportunity to sign him. Nevertheless, the try out brought Robinson to the attention of Clyde Sukeforth, the chief scout of the Brooklyn Dodgers. Convinced of Robinson's exceptional playing ability and personal determination, Sukeforth set the stage for the memorable August meeting between Robinson and Rickey.

Robinson had no illusions about the purpose of his agreement with the Dodgers. He realized that Rickey's altruism was tempered by a profit motive, and yet he admired the moral courage of the Dodger president. "Mr. Rickey knew that achieving racial equality in baseball would be terribly difficult," Robinson remembered. "There would be deep resentment, determined opposition and perhaps even racial violence. But he was convinced that he was morally right and he shrewdly sensed that making the game a truly national one would have healthy financial results." Rickey was absolutely correct on both counts.

The Dodgers' October 23, 1945, announcement that Robinson had signed a contract for six hundred dollars a month* to play for their top minor-league club at Montreal was greeted with great hostility by baseball's white establishment. Rickey was accused of being "a carpetbagger who, under the guise of helping, is in truth using the Negro for his own self-interest." Criticism even came from the Negro League owners who feared, not without reason, that Robinson's signing would lead to declining fan interest in their clubs. The Monarchs were especially angered by the signing and went so far as to threaten a lawsuit against the Dodgers for tampering with a player who was already under contract.

By mid-November the criticism became so hostile that Rickey's own fam-

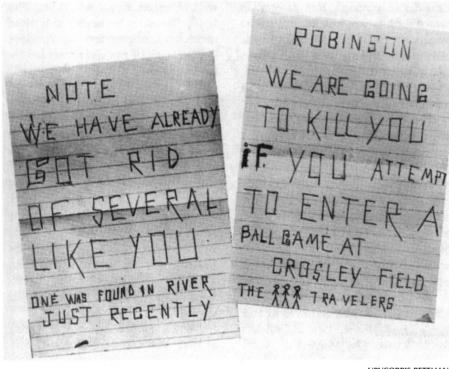

UPI/CORBIS-BETTMANN

Although many white fans eagerly sought Robinson's autograph, others did their best to make his life miserable by heckling, shouting insults, and making threats. Among the many pieces of hate mail Jackie received was a letter threatening his life if he played in Cincinnati's Crosley Field in May 1947; Robinson not only played, he hit a home run. At the end of the '47 season, J. G. Taylor Spink, publisher of *Sporting News*, presented Robinson with the magazine's award as "Rookie of the Year" in the National League.

---

* Robinson also received a bonus of $3,500.

28. Baseball's *Noble* Experiment

With Rachel's Support

When Jackie Robinson met with Branch Rickey in August 1945, the Dodgers' general manager asked him if he had a girlfriend, and was pleased when Jackie told him that he was engaged to be married. As he had made abundantly clear to Robinson that day, Rickey was aware that the first black player in the major leagues would face a terrible ordeal, and he clearly believed that he should not face it alone.

In her recent book, Jackie Robinson: An Intimate Portrait, Rachel Robinson writes that it was at the start of the '47 season that she and Jackie first realized "how important we were to black America and how much we symbolized its hunger for opportunity and its determination to make dreams long deferred possible." If Jackie failed to make the grade as a player, or if the pressures became so great that he decided to pull out of Rickey's "noble experiment," the hopes of all the nation's blacks would be done enormous, if not irreparable harm. It was a tremendous burden to have to bear, and it belonged not only to Jackie, but also to his family.

Rachel Isum had met her future husband in 1940 while they were both students at UCLA, where she earned a degree in nursing. Engaged in 1941, they endured long separations during World War II, and in 1945, as Jackie traveled with the Kansas City Monarchs. Finally, in February 1946—just before Jackie was due to report to Daytona Beach, Florida, to try to earn a place with the Montreal Royals—they were married.

Both Jackie and Rachel had known racial bigotry and discrimination in Southern California, where they grew up, but they realized that they would face something much more difficult in the institutionalized segregation of the 1940s South. During that first trip to Florida, they experienced repeated humiliations that were, according to Rachel, "merely a foreshadowing of trials to come." As the Royals played exhibition games in other Florida cities, Jackie got a taste of how many Americans viewed his presence in professional baseball.

Following spring training, Jackie joined the Royals in Montreal, where the couple found a much more receptive environment. Although Jackie still faced racism during road trips, the Robinsons' year in Canada was fondly remembered as a respite that helped them prepare for the real test that came when he moved on to the Dodgers in 1947.

As players and fans in cities around the National League tormented Jackie, Rachel was forced to sit "through name calling, jeers, and vicious baiting in a furious silence." For his part, the Dodgers' rookie infielder, who had promised Rickey that he would turn the other cheek, "found that the most powerful form of retaliation against prejudice was his excellent play." But after the '48 season, Robinson called off his deal with Rickey. He would no longer submit quietly to insults, discrimination, and abuses. Able at last to release some of the pent-up pressure and emotion, Robinson became a more confident player; in 1949, he won the National League batting championship with a .349 average and received a trophy ironically named for Kenesaw Mountain Landis, the man who tried to keep blacks out of baseball.

ily pleaded with him to abandon his crusade for fear that it would destroy his health. The Dodger president refused, speaking only of the excitement and competitive advantage that black players would bring to Brooklyn baseball, while downplaying the moral significance he attached to integration. "The greatest untapped reservoir of raw material in the history of the game is the black race," he contended. "The Negroes will make us winners for years to come and for that I will happily bear being called a 'bleeding heart' and a 'do-gooder' and all that humanitarian rot."

Robinson's first test came during the 1946 preseason, even before he debuted with the Montreal Royals. Rickey named Mississippian Clay Hopper, who had worked for him since 1929, to manage the Royals. There were reports, probably true, that Hopper begged Rickey to reconsider giving him this assignment. But Rickey's careful handling of Robinson's jump to the big leagues would seem to suggest that he believed that having a Southerner at the helm of the Montreal club would head off some dissension among the players and that he trusted Hopper to handle any situations that might arise.

Throughout the '46 season, Robinson endured racist remarks from fans and opposing players and humiliating treatment in the South. By season's end, the constant pressure and abuse had taken its toll—his hair began to gray, he suffered with chronic stomach trouble, and some thought he was on the brink of a nervous breakdown. Finding himself unable to eat or sleep, he went to a doctor, who concluded that he was suffering from stress. "You're not having a nervous breakdown," the physician told him. "You're under a lot of stress. Stay home and don't read any newspapers, and don't go to the ballpark for a week." Jackie, his wife Rachel remembered, stayed home for one day. The problem, she said, came from his not being able to fight back." It was, as Rickey had warned him, "the cross that you must bear."

Despite the tension and distractions, Robinson managed to hit for an impressive .349 average and led the Montreal Royals to victory over the Louisville Colonels in the Little World Series. After the final game in that championship series, grateful Royals fans hoisted Robinson onto their shoulders and carried him to the locker room. Hopper shook his shortstop's hand and said: "You're a real ballplayer and a gentleman. It's been wonderful having you on the team." Robinson had made his first convert.

Because Robinson's success with Montreal had been so impressive, Rickey assumed that all the Dodgers would demand his promotion to the majors for the 1947 season. "After all," he reasoned, "Robinson could mean a pennant, and ball players are not averse to cashing World Series checks."

To promote and protect his young black star, Rickey made some additional moves. First, in order to avoid Jim Crow restrictions, he held spring training in Havana, Cuba, instead of Florida. Next, he moved Robinson, an experienced shortstop and second baseman, to first base, where he would be spared physical contact with opposing players who might try to injure him deliberately.

Finally, Rickey scheduled a seven-game series between the Dodgers and the Royals in order to showcase Robinson's talent. "I want you to be a whirling demon against the Dodgers in this series," Rickey told Robinson. "You have to be so good that the Dodger players themselves are going to want you on their club.... I want you to hit that ball. I want you to get on base and run wild. Steal their pants off. Be the most conspicuous player on the field. The newspapermen from New York will send good stories back about you and help mold favorable public opinion."

Robinson more than obliged, batting .625 and stealing seven bases in the series. But instead of helping him, the performance served only to alienate him from his future teammates, many of whom were Southerners. Alabamian Dixie Walker drafted a petition stating that the players who signed would prefer to be traded than to play with a black teammate. While the team was playing exhibition games in Panama, Walker proceeded to gather signatures from Dodger teammates. Harold "Pee Wee" Reese, although a Kentuckian, refused to sign. It was a tremendously courageous act on his part because, as the team's shortstop, Reese had more to lose than any other Dodger. "If he can take my job," Reese insisted, "he's entitled to it."

When Dodger manager Leo Durocher learned of the petition, he was furious. He had asked Rickey to bring Robinson up to Brooklyn during the previous year's pennant drive. At a late-night team meeting, according to Harold Parrott, the Dodger road secretary, Durocher told Walker and the other petitioners that "I don't care if the guy is yellow or black, or if he has stripes like a zebra. I'm the manager of this team and I say he plays. What's more, I say he can make us all rich.... An' if any of you can't use the money, I'll see that you're traded."*

The rebellion squelched, Rickey announced on April 10, 1947, that Jackie Robinson had officially been signed to play first base for the Brooklyn Dodgers. The noble experiment was in full swing.

Of all the major-league cities, Brooklyn, with its ethnically diverse and racially mixed neighborhoods, was just the place to break the color barrier. Despite their reputation as "perennial losers"—since the franchise's establishment in 1883, no Brooklyn team had won a World Series—the Dodgers enjoyed an enduring love affair with their fans. This warm affinity was fostered, in part, by their cramped but colorful ballpark, Ebbets Field, located in the Flatbush section of Brooklyn. The double-decked grandstand stood only along the foul lines, allowing the fans a special intimacy with the players. "If you were in a box seat," said broadcaster Red Barber, "you were so close you were practically an infielder." Aside from the patchwork collection of local advertisements in left field; the large, black scoreboard in right; and the tone-deaf "Dodger Symphony Band" that roamed the grandstand, nothing came between the Dodgers and their die-hard fans.

When Robinson made his first appearance as a Dodger on April 15, 1947, more than 26,000 fans packed Ebbets Field; reportedly some 14,000 of those were African Americans. The afternoon was cold and rainy and Robinson went hitless. Nonetheless, the sight of a black man on a major-league diamond during a regular season game moved the crowd so deeply that they cheered the Dodgers on to a 5–3 victory over the Boston Braves. Every move the 28-year-old rookie made seemed to be greeted with the chant: "Jackie! Jackie! Jackie!" It seemed as if baseball had finally shed its three-quarters of a century of hypocrisy to become truly deserving of the title "national pastime."

When the Philadelphia Phillies arrived in Brooklyn a week later, however, all hopes that integration would come peaceably were shattered. In one of the lowest moments ever in baseball history the Phillies, led by their Southern manager, Ben Chapman, launched a tirade of racial epithets during the pregame batting practice. And the jeering did not let up throughout the entire three-game series.

Two weeks later, when the Dodgers traveled to the so-called "City of Brotherly Love," Chapman and his Phillies picked up where they had left off, warning the Dodger players that they would contract diseases if they touched Robinson and indulging in even more personal racial slurs. Robinson's less-than-stellar hitting in the series only added to the Phillies' contention that he did not belong in the majors and was a ploy to attract blacks to Dodger games and make more money for Rickey.

After the second game of the series, angry Dodger fans launched a full-scale

BASEBALL HALL OF FAME LIBRARY

By the 1948 season, Robinson was no longer the only black player in the majors. African Americans brought up by Rickey that year included catcher Roy Campanella, (above) who would be voted the National League's Most Valuable Player three times.

protest with the National League's president, Ford Frick, who responded by ordering Chapman and the Phillies to stop their verbal assault immediately. In fact, Chapman probably would have lost his job over the incident, if Robinson had not agreed to pose with him for a conciliatory newspaper photograph. Under duress, the Phillies' manager agreed to stand next to the Dodger rookie. "Ben extended his hand," Harold Parrott recalled, "smiling broadly as if they had been buddy-buddy for a lifetime. Robinson reached out and grasped it. The flicker of a smile crept across his face as the photographer snapped away getting several shots."

Years later Robinson admitted that the incessant abuse during those games with

---

* Walker, one of a handful of players who asked to be traded, eventually went to the Pittsburgh Pirates, but not until after the '47 season. Durocher, himself, was suspended from baseball before the '47 season and never had the opportunity to manage Robinson.

28. Baseball's *Noble* Experiment

After his baseball career ended, Robinson became even more deeply involved in the Civil Rights Movement, supporting the work of leaders such as Dr. Martin Luther King, Jr., (above). Jackie and his family took part in the 1963 March on Washington that featured King's stirring "I Have a Dream" speech.

the Phillies almost led him to the breaking point. As he described it: "For one wild and rage-crazed minute I thought, 'To hell with Mr. Rickey's noble experiment. It's clear that it won't succeed.... What a glorious, cleansing thing it would be to let go.' To hell with the image of the patient black freak I was supposed to create. I could throw down my bat, stride over to the Phillies dugout, grab one of those white sons of bitches and smash his teeth in with my despised black fist. Then I could walk away from it and I'd never become a sports star. But my son could tell his son some day what his daddy could have been if he hadn't been too much of a man."

The experience with the Phillies revealed the shocking severity of the racism that existed in baseball. At the same time, however, Robinson's tremendous restraint in the face of such ugly prejudice served to rally his teammates around him and the cause of integration. Eddie Stanky one of those who had signed the petition against Robinson joining the team, became so angered by the Phillies' relentless abuse that he challenged them to "yell at somebody who can answer back." Soon after, before a game in Cincinnati, the Reds' players taunted Pee Wee Reese about playing with a black teammate. The Dodger shortstop walked over to Robinson and, in a firm show of support, placed his arm around the first baseman's shoulders.

As the season unfolded, Dodger support for Robinson strengthened in response to the admirable way he handled all the adversity. Opposing pitchers threw at his head and ribs, while infielders would spit in his face if he was involved in a close play on the base paths. And the hate mail was unending. But through it all, Robinson persevered. He even managed to keep a sense of humor. Before one game in Cincinnati, when the Dodgers learned that their first baseman's life had been threatened, one teammate suggested that all the players wear Robinson's uniform number "42" on their backs to confuse the assailant. "Okay with me," responded the rookie. "Paint your faces black and run pigeon-toed too!"

Even the white baseball establishment began to embrace the Dodger infielder. In May of 1947, when Ford Frick learned of the St. Louis Cardinals' intention to instigate a league-wide strike by walking off the ball diamond in a scheduled game against the integrated Dodgers, he vowed to suspend the ringleaders if they carried out their plan. "... I don't care if I wreck the National League for five years," he declared. "This is the United States of America, and one citizen has as much right to play as another. The National League will go down the line with Robinson whatever the consequence." The conspiracy died on the spot.

When the season ended, the *Sporting News,* which had gone on record earlier as opposing the integration of baseball because "There is not a single Negro player with major league possibilities," named Robinson the National League's "Rookie of the Year" for his impressive performance that season—29 stolen bases, 12 home runs, 42 successful bunt hits, and a .297 batting average.

Those efforts helped the Dodgers to capture a pennant, and on September 23, jubilant Brooklyn fans cheered their first baseman with a "Jackie Robinson Day" at Ebbets Field. In addition to a new car and other gifts, Robinson received tributes for his contribution to racial equality. Song-and-dance man Bill "Bojangles" Robinson, one of the guest speakers, told the crowd: "I'm 69 years old but never thought I'd live to see the day when I'd stand face-to-face with Ty Cobb in Technicolor."

Jackie Robinson's death in October 1972 deeply affected African Americans and baseball fans across the country. As his funeral cortege made its way to his final resting place in Cypress Hills Cemetery in Brooklyn, the camera captured one mourner, shown in the foreground, offering Robinson a black-power salute.

The Dodgers forced the New York Yankees to a seventh and deciding game in the World Series. And when all was said and done, no amount of hate mail or verbal and psychological abuse could tarnish the indisputable fact that Jackie Robinson was an exceptional baseball player. He belonged in the major leagues.

Robinson's greatest accomplishment, however, was the inspiration that he provided for other African Americans, both in and out of baseball. Thousands of blacks came to watch him play, setting new attendance records in such cities as Chicago and Pittsburgh. Even in St. Louis, Cincinnati, and Philadelphia, where the opposing teams were the most hostile toward the Dodger rookie, black fans would arrive on chartered buses called "Jackie Robinson Specials," having traveled hundreds of miles just to see him play.

Ed Charles, a black youngster from the Deep South who went on to play in the major leagues himself, remembered the thrill of seeing his childhood hero for the first time. "I sat in the segregated section of the ball park and watched Jackie," he said. "And I finally believed what I read in the papers—that one of us had made it. When the game was over we kids followed Jackie to the train station. When the train pulled out, we ran down the tracks listening for the sounds as far as we could. And when we couldn't hear it any longer, we stopped and put our ears to the track so we could feel the vibrations of that train carrying Jackie Robinson. We wanted to be part of him as long as we could."

Indeed, Robinson had jolted the national consciousness in a profound way. Until 1947 all of baseball's heroes had been white men. Suddenly there was a black baseball star who could hit, bunt, steal, and field with the best of them. His style of play was nothing new in the Negro Leagues, but in the white majors, it was innovative and exciting. Robinson made things happen on the base paths. If he got on first, he stole second. If he could not steal third, he would distract the pitcher by dancing off second in order to advance. And then he would steal home. The name of the game was to score runs without a hit, something quite different from the "power hitting" strategy that had characterized major-league baseball. During the next decade, this new style of play would become known as "Dodger Baseball."

Before the '47 season was over, Branch Rickey had signed 16 additional Negro Leaguers, including catcher and future three-time "Most Valuable Player" Roy Campanella; pitcher Don Newcombe, who in 1956 would win 27 games; and second baseman Jim Gilham, like Robinson always a threat to steal a base. Together with Robinson and such white stars as Pee Wee Reese, Edwin "Duke" Snider, Gil Hodges, and Carl Erskine, these men would form the nucleus of a team that would capture six pennants and, at long last, in 1955, a world championship, before the Dodgers left Brooklyn for the West Coast at the end of the 1957 season. By 1959, every team in major-league baseball was integrated, one of every five players being of African-American descent.

When Rickey talked of trading Robinson to the New York Giants after the '56 season, the pioneering ballplayer chose to retire at the age of 38. His career totals, which included 1,518 hits, more than 200 stolen bases, and a lifetime batting average of .311, earned him a place in the National Baseball Hall of Fame in 1962, the first African American so honored. He continued to fight actively for civil rights long after his baseball career had ended, supporting Dr. Martin Luther King, Jr., and his call for the peaceful integration of American society.

Despite his tremendous accomplishments on and off the baseball field, Jackie Robinson, with characteristic humility never gave himself much credit. A year before his untimely death in 1972, he reflected on his struggle to break baseballs color barrier. "I was proud," Robinson admitted, "yet I was uneasy. Proud to be in the hurricane eye of a significant breakthrough and to be used to prove that a sport can't be called 'national' if blacks are barred from it But uneasy because I knew that I was still a black man in a white world. And so I continue to ask myself 'what have I really done for my people?' "

The answer was evident to everyone but him; for by appealing to the moral conscience of the nation, Jackie Robinson had given a young generation of blacks a chance at the "American Dream" and in the process taught many white Americans to respect others regardless of the color of their skin.

William Kashatus is a school teacher and freelance writer who lives in Philadelphia.

The Split-Level Years

1950–1960: Elvis, Howdy Doody time, McDonald's and the rumblings of rebellion

By Henry Allen
Washington Post Staff Writer

Smell it, smell it all, smell the sour cities you leave behind in bosomy cars that smell of dusty sunlight and thump over Eisenhower's concrete interstate highways whose joints ooze tar that smells like industrial licorice till you arrive in a suburb smelling of insecticide and freshly cut grass outside identical houses full of the scents of postwar America: baked air hovering over the TV set; the mucilage on stickers for your art-appreciation course—"Mona Lisa," "American Gothic" . . . ; the cozy stink of cigarette smoke freshened by Air-Wick deodorizer amid sweet pine paneling whose knots watch over you like the loving eyes of Disney forest creatures.

How sweet and new it all is, this incense of mid-century, this strange sense of coziness and infinite possibility at the same time.

Don't worry, Ike seems to say as he smiles and hits another tee shot. You light another Camel, knowing that "It's a psychological fact: pleasure helps your disposition: For more pure pleasure—have a CAMEL."

There's a cartoon fullness to things. Everybody is somebody. Everything is possible. Hence a cushiony give in the national psyche, a pleasant ache that feels like nostalgia dispensed by a spray can. You believe in the future, be it a perfect marriage, racial integration, commuting via your personal autogiro, Formica countertops, or a day coming soon when everybody will be sincere and mature. ("Sincerity" and "maturity" are major virtues.)

Ignore the viruses of dread that float through family rooms: the hydrogen bomb erupting from the South Pacific like a cancerous jellyfish the size of God; or the evil Sen. Joseph McCarthy and the evil Commies he never catches one of, not one, though he does manage to strew the land with damaged lives and the liberal tic of anti-anti-communism; or Sputnik, the first satellite, built by Russian slave labor, no doubt, while our top scientists were developing the Princess phone, 3-D movies and boomerang-shaped coffee tables.

Ignore Marilyn Monroe saying: What good is it being Marilyn Monroe? Why can't I just be an ordinary woman? . . . Oh, why do things have to work out so rotten? And ignore the Korean War, which is nothing but ugly except for the embroidered silk dragon jackets the soldiers bring back. Ignore the newspaper pictures of racists with faces like wet-combed hand-grenades, screaming at Martin Luther King's boycotters and schoolchildren who will overcome . . . people whose isolation and invisibility in this white society are incalculable. . . .

Progress will take care of everything.

Amid the Ford Country Squire station wagons and slate roofs, wealthier homeowners boast that neighborhood covenants still keep out Jews and Negroes. They offer you highballs and cigarettes. They show you black-and-white photographs of themselves waving from the rail of the Queen Elizabeth. They turn on lights till their houses blaze like cruise ships. What lonely darkness are they keeping off? Do they know their time has gone?

MEANWHILE, AMID THE TRACT housing and developments, the genius of William Levitt and Henry Kaiser creates the loneliness of growing up in your own bedroom, in your own house where the green grass grows all around. It takes some getting used to, but do you really want to go back to the apartment with three kids to a bedroom and Nana mumbling over the cabbage? You know your future is here. You wish you knew what it held.

"Children, your father's home!" Mom yells.

A father's Florsheim Imperials are heard. A Dobbs center-dent fedora is seen, with a jaunty trout-fly feather on the grosgrain band. Dad exudes the tired authority of cigarette smoke and Arrid underarm deodorant cream. His knuckles whiten on a Christmas-present attaché case.

"Can't you kids get up off your duffs and do something instead of sitting there watching . . ."

"Hey, Dad's home."

". . .'Howdy Doody,' a little children's show?"

"There's nothing else on, Dad."

Dad shouts over his shoulder: "Doris! You have any chores for these kids?"

"No, hon, everything's hunky-dory. You hungry?"

'Hell, yes, I'm hungry."

"Be dinner soon's I do the limas."

Sighing as if he has made a huge decision, Dad walks into the kitchen. He cracks ice for a drink. "The kids," he says. "It's like I'm not even here."

"Well, it's like I always am," she says. "They're scared of you, but they take me for granted."

"Make you a drink?"

"Not too big, now."

His face struggles toward some home truth, but doesn't find it. "Au, Doris," he says. "Turn off the stove and let's go to the Roma for veal scaloppine. Please. Just the two of us."

"I have to drop Tommy at Boy Scouts, and then Kitty Kennard is doing her slide show at L'Esprit Francais. Forgive me?"

Doris and Tom Sr. are only trying to live by what their parents taught them—manliness, graciousness, a day's work, good posture—and pass it on to their children. The problem is, they don't quite believe it themselves, anymore, but they have to teach their kids something.

Should they really confess their emptiness and bad faith instead? Should the children feel betrayed by parents who are only trying to do the best they know how?

HOW SQUALID. LETS LEAVE ALL this behind. It's a symptom, not a cause, a failure where success is what you see on "Ozzie & Harriet" and all the other shows about breakfast-nook families where no one is taken for granted and everyone says hello.

Hi, Rick. Hi, Pop. Hi, Dave. Good morning, Mom.

Dad's a bit of a bumbler, and what won't those darn kids think of next! Nevertheless, perfection is attainable. How smug one feels to know this. How inadequate one feels to know one hasn't attained it yet, oneself, but one can put on a long-playing record of the perfect Ella Fitzgerald singing the Jerome Kern songbook perfectly.

Some of the young folks seem to have a hard time adjusting.

If I could have just one day when I wasn't all confused. . . . If I felt I belonged someplace.
—James Dean as the anguished son in "Rebel Without a Cause"

Be part of progress like everybody else—the everybody you see on television and in Life magazine. Here's the equation: If you're just like everybody, then you're somebody.

The way to be somebody is to buy something that makes you like everybody else who's bought the same thing—Ford owners reading their Ford Times, Parliament smokers joined in aromatic sophistication. Remember: Consumption is a moral good. Madison Avenue admen are cultural heroes, with cool slang like 'Let's run it up the flagpole and see who salutes."

Look at all the college kids stuffing themselves into phone booths and Volkswagens. And a lovely girl whose picture appears in Life next to the comment: "She has forgotten all about emancipation and equality. To belong is her happiness." And Mary Ann Cuff, a regular among the teen dancers who appear on Dick Clark's "American Bandstand": "What it is we all want is to get married and live on the same street in new houses. We'll call it Bandstand Avenue."

Ignore the hipsters and intellectuals sneering at Bandstand Avenue, and at the triumphalism of tailfins, Time magazine and pointy bras whose tips sort of crinkle under sweaters. Fun can be made of bomb shelters stocked with Franco-American canned spaghetti and Reader's Digest Condensed Books.

J.D. Salinger can appeal to adolescent self-righteousness by railing against phonies in "The Catcher in the Rye." Scorn can be heaped on Ray Kroc, who runs those new McDonald's drive-ins; he writes a memo: "We cannot trust some people who are non-conformist. The organization cannot trust the individual, the individual must trust the organization."

And certainly critics can make a living by attacking the men in the gray flannel suits, the organization men, the lonely crowd of ulcer-proud hidden persuaders bringing us ads where women in crinoline-fluffed shirtwaists invite us to buy into the carefree new patio-perfect world of hyper-power Torqueflite Cyclamatic Teletouch Whatever that gives you more pleasure. (Repeat thru fade-out: MORE PLEASURE! MORE PLEASURE! MORE PLEASURE!)

WHICH DOES NOT MEAN SEX, boys and girls. Sex is for Europeans, people in movies (off-screen) and juvenile delinquents. White people believe that colored people have sex lives of unimaginable ecstasy and variety. Italian kids drive surly Mercurys to the Jersey Shore, spread blankets and neck in Ace-combed 1953 look-at-me majesty beneath the outraged stares of moms in bathing suits with little skirts. . . . prefiguring the erotic insolence of Elvis, Marilyn, James Dean, and the secret subtext of Annette on "The Mickey Mouse Club."

Otherwise, sex, the lonely vandal, is safe in the stewardship of middle-class women who manage the courtship rituals of dating, going steady, pinning and engagement, and aren't very interested in sex anyway, according to the Kinsey Report on Women. Life magazine sums it up: "Woman is the placid gender, the female guppy swimming all unconcerned and wishing she could get a few minutes off to herself, while the male guppy pursues her with his unrelenting courtship. . . . Half or more of all women . . . seldom dream or daydream about sex;

they consider the human body to be, if anything, rather repulsive."

Maybe men make cracks about women's driving and spending, and they want dinner served on time, but Life has learned that the unrelenting guppy is becoming "the new American domesticated male" who is "baby tender, dishwasher, cook, repairman.... Some even go to baby-care classes, learn to wrap a neat diaper and to bubble Junior deftly. With father available as sitter, wives can have their hair done, shop, go to club meetings." Lawn mowing gives him "a sense of power and a gadget to tinker with."

What happened to the red-blooded, can-do, all-American male? And female?

Well, sexed women and powerful men are a threat. We don't need them now. Passion has been replaced by love, adventure by fun. If you want sex, watch Elvis Presley on "The Ed Sullivan Show," even if Ed refuses to show the King below the waist. Or go to a movie with Marilyn Monroe or Ava Gardner. If you want male brooding and rage, go see Marlon Brando or Montgomery Clift, the prince of loneliness. The great thing about the '50s is that rebels can fling their grenades of anger and irony into the cafes of the conformists, safe in the knowledge that they can't really change anything. The '50s are an irresistible force still in search of an immovable object.

So pay no attention to that slouching bohemian with sunglasses black as telephones and a tremor induced by his benzedrine inhaler. He says he wants to get back to Europe, "where they really know how to live, where they don't have these hang-ups."

"Europe?" asks the astonished corporate executive who helped liberate Europe from the Nazis only a decade or so ago. "You can't even drink the water in Europe."

"You drink wine, man," says the bohemian. "You drink wine."

Don't worry about snooty intellectuals, either. For a moment, a Columbia University professor named Charles Van Doren is a national celebrity on a big-money TV quiz show called "Twenty-One." He appears on the cover of Time. He seems to be the answer to the old American question: "If you're so smart, why aren't you rich?"

Then it turns out the producers are slipping him the answers to keep him on the show. Van Doren is disgraced, treated like a traitor for lying on television. Well, intellectuals. It just goes to show you. They're all homos or Commies anyway.

And don't worry about the alienation of the modern jazz that lures college boys to the big city for a taste of hip, and the self-loathing notion that "white cats don't swing."

DON'T WORRY ABOUT ROCK-and-roll, which sounds like a national anthem for the republic of vandalism and anarchy, which it is. Rock may drive the young folk to drugs and groin-thrusting madness, it may cause riots in the streets and insurrection in the schools, which it does—but it can't last, it's just a fad.

Ignore the sly joke of Frankie Lymon and the Teenagers singing "No, no, no, no, no, I'm not a juvenile delinquent" to suburban kids who actually think JDs are cool in their rumbles fought with bicycle chains and switchblade knives. So cool that Leonard Bernstein, Mr. Music Appreciation Class himself, will write "West Side Story," a musical that puts romantic love and gang wars together in a climactic switchblade duel.

Forget about civil rights workers heading south, where they're known as "Northern agitators." And the revival of pinko folk singers like Pete Seeger and the Weavers. And marijuana in Harvard Square. And Hugh Hefner proposing in Playboy magazine that we should think of sex as fun, like a game of picnic badminton where nobody tries too hard to win.

"There's a place for us," the cast sings at the end of "West Side Story," to reassure us that, despite the tragedy of Tony and Maria, the promise of progress is intact. "Someday, somewhere, we'll find a new way of living."

There are no VA mortgages for veterans of gang wars, but America will find a way to get them into little Cape Cod starter homes sooner than you think. Haircuts, briefcases, Peter Pan blouses, Formica, Bisquick and pole lamps while the whole family sits in front of the television to sing along with Mitch:

I'm looking over a four-leaf clover...
How could it be otherwise?

Point of Order!

The 1954 lawsuit brought against the US Army by Joseph McCarthy marked a turning point in public attitude towards the 'Red Scare' Senator. **Thomas Doherty** *tells how television played a crucial role in his demise.*

No political figure of the modern world was ever looked at so thoroughly as Joseph McCarthy was between April and June 1954. (Emile de Antonio).

Since his death in 1957, the shadow cast by Joseph R. McCarthy has grown in length and deepened in darkness. According to the *National Standards for United States History: Exploring the American Experience,* a volume published in 1992 by the National Center of History in the Schools, a dominant part of the American experience revolves around him. McCarthyism warranted nineteen separate references while such lesser lights in American history—Robert E. Lee, Thomas Edison, the Wright Brothers—failed to garner a single notation.

Historical lustre of that degree of magnitude is conferred mainly by television. No less than the post-war creation of the national security state, the other great beast born of the Cold War, it was television that propelled the career and instigated the destruction of Joseph McCarthy. Between February 1950, when 'the junior senator from Wisconsin' launched his first charges of Communist subversion in the State Department, and December 1954, when the Senate voted to condemn his actions, the medium and the man were locked in a symbiotic relationship—in televised press conferences and congressional hearings, in live appearances on interview shows such as *Meet the Press* and *American Forum of the Air,* and on Edward R. Murrow's *See It Now,* the pioneering news magazine that in late 1953 began firing the first shots from the small screen at what had already become known as 'McCarthyism'.

Yet it was the Army-McCarthy hearings that forged the permanent link between McCarthy and television. Broadcast from April 22nd to June 17th, 1954, the hearings were the first nationally televised congressional inquiry and a landmark in the commingling of television and American politics. Though the Kefauver Crime Committee hearings of March 1951 can claim priority as a congressional TV show, and subsequent political spectacles (the Watergate hearings, the Iran Contra hearings, the Thomas-Hill hearings) would rivet the attention of later generations of American televiewers, for sheer theatricality and narrative force the Army-McCarthy hearings remain the genre prototype—not least because the constitutional drama has been kept alive in memory through a pathbreaking compilation film, Emile de Antonio's *Point of Order!* (1963).

Ostensibly, the Army-McCarthy hearings convened to investigate a convoluted series of charges levelled by McCarthy at the United States Army and vice versa. In November 1953, a consultant on McCarthy's staff named G. David Schine was drafted into the Army. Even before Schine's formal induction, Roy M. Cohn, McCarthy's chief counsel, had waged a personal campaign to pressure military officials, from the Secretary of the Army down to Schine's company commander, into giving Schine special privileges. In fact, military men at the highest levels devoted an extraordinary amount of time and attention to Schine, whom newspapers dubbed 'the most famous private in the US Army'. When on March 11th, 1954, the Army issued a detailed chronology documenting Cohn's improper intrusions into Schine's military career, McCarthy responded by claiming the Army was holding Schine 'hostage' to deter his committee from exposing Communists within the military ranks. To resolve the dispute, the Senate Permanent Subcommittee on Investigations, of which McCarthy was chairman, voted to investigate the matter and to allow live television coverage of the hearings. McCarthy relinquished his chairmanship to Karl Mundt (R-SD) to become, with Cohn, contestant and witness in a widely anticipated live television drama.

Initially, all four networks were expected to carry the hearings live, 'gavel to gavel'. ABC and DuMont announced commitments early, but a calmer look at the bottom line caused NBC and CBS to balk at the costs of this public service programming. With an eye to its profitable daytime soap opera line-up, CBS opted to forego coverage before the hearings began, leaving NBC, ABC, and DuMont formally committed to broadcast the hearings live. At the end of the second day of hearings, however, after a tedious afternoon session, NBC bailed out. Henceforth NBC, like CBS, transmitted nightly round-ups edited from kinescopes of the daytime ABC coverage. CBS broadcast from 11.30pm to 12.15am, so NBC counter-programmed its recaps from 11.15pm to midnight. Angling for a way to raise the profile of

30. Point of Order!

his third string news division, ABC president Robert E. Kintner stuck with his decision to broadcast the entire event live, jettisoning the network's daytime programming for continuous coverage.

Throughout the thirty-six days of hearings, 188 hours of airtime were given over to broadcasts originating from Senate Caucus Room 310. Directed by twenty-five-year-old Ed Sherer from a remote truck outside the building, the network 'feed' came courtesy of the facilities of ABC's Washington DC affiliate, WMAL-TV. Though most local stations across the nation followed the policy of their network affiliates, a few broke ranks with home office policy: CBS affiliates taking the ABC feed, for example, or an ABC affiliate staying with its regular programming. Thus, some major markets in the United States (Los Angeles for one) were deprived of live coverage when none of the local stations took the ABC feed.

In televisual terms, the hearings pitted a boorish Joseph McCarthy and a bleary-eyed Roy Cohn against a coolly avuncular Joseph N. Welch of the Boston law firm of Hale & Dorr, whom the Army had hired as its special counsel. Welch's calm patrician manner served as an appealing contrast to Cohn's unctuous posturing and McCarthy's rude outbursts (the senator's nasal interjection 'point of order!' became a national catchphrase). Senators, military men and obscure staffers blossomed into household names and faces, among them chain-smoking committee counsel Ray H. Jenkins, mild-mannered Secretary of the Army Robert T. Stevens and, visible backscreen as if awaiting his cue to walk on to the stage of history, a young lawyer for the committee Democrats named Robert F. Kennedy. Along with an often partisan gallery in the packed, smoke-filled hearing room, an audience of some 20 million Americans watched the complicated testimony, a crossfire of mutual recriminations over monitored telephone conversations, doctored photographs and fabricated memoranda.

The afternoon of June 9th, 1954, brought the emotional climax of the hearings. Ignoring a pre-hearing agreement between Welch and Cohn not to bring up the matter, McCarthy insinuated that Fred Fischer, a young lawyer at Hale & Dorr, harboured Communist sympathies because of his past membership of an alleged Communist front organisation, the Lawyers Guild. Welch responded with a righteous outburst that hit all the hot buttons:

> Until this moment, Senator, I think I never gauged your cruelty or recklessness.... Let us not assassinate this lad further, Senator. Have you no sense of decency, sir, at long last? Have you left no sense of decency?

When McCarthy tried to strike back, Welch cut him off and demanded the chairman 'call the next witness'. Pausing just a beat, the hushed gallery erupted in applause. The uncomprehending McCarthy, shot dead on live TV, turned to Cohn and stammered, 'What happened?'

What happened was that television, whose coverage of McCarthy's news conferences and addresses to the nation had earlier lent him legitimacy and power, had now become the forum for his downfall. Some viewers, then and since, have suspected Welch's seemingly spontaneous outburst was actually rehearsed, that the rhythms of his address scanned a little too poetically to be unscripted ('It is true he is still with Hale & Dorr/It is true that he will continue to be with Hale & Dorr/It is, I regret to say, equally true that he will bear a scar needlessly inflicted by you.') Nevertheless, prolonged exposure to McCarthy's odious character and ill-mannered interruptions was a textbook demonstration of how a hot personality wilted under the glare of a cool medium. Towards the close of the hearings, Senator Stuart Symington underscored the lesson in media politics during a sharp exchange with McCarthy: 'The American people have had a look at you for six weeks. You are not fooling anyone'. That December the Senate voted to condemn, though not formally censure, McCarthy for 'conduct contrary to senatorial traditions' thereby effectively neutering him. At the time of his death in 1957, the once feared demagogue was a sad alcoholic, ignored by the press.

The televisual resurrection of Joseph McCarthy was not long in coming, however. In 1963 film-maker Emile de Antonio edited the Army-McCarthy hearings into *Point of Order!*, the definitive record of America's first great made-for-TV political spectacle and a landmark experiment in documentary form. With *Point of Order!*, film historian Jay Leyda's dictum that 'films beget films' was expanded to embrace a new moving-image technology: 'television begets films'. It showed that the history recorded and mediated by television, once deemed disposable, could present a priceless picture of the past.

De Antonio culled the film from the original kinescopes (or 'kinnies') stored in the CBS News Archives. Ironically, in accord with William S. Paley's vision of CBS News as the *New York Times* of television, the only network to opt out of any gavel-to-gavel coverage was the only one to save the complete footage. However, such was the network's trepidation over potential right-wing assaults that CBS specified it was to be a 'secret partner' in its contract with de Antonio. Only after the film received a warm reception from the public did CBS publicly admit to its participation in the project.

For over two years de Antonio and producer Daniel Talbot screened and edited the footage, winnowing down 188 hours to twelve hours, then to three hours, and finally to ninety-seven minutes. The 16mm footage was then blown up to 35mm for theatrical exhibitions. Early on the director made two crucial decisions about the shape of the film: first, it would be comprised purely of kinescopes, with no supplementary stock footage or 'expert testimonies'. Except for the fifty-nine-second voice-over preceding the film and written crawls introducing sequences, no narration or subtitles interrupt the pure flow of the footage. More controversially, de Antonio decided not to follow chronological order but to structure the film dramatically. The 'actual hearings were 188 formless hours ending with a whimper', he observed in 1964. 'Film moves freely through all the material to make its points'. Producer Daniel Talbot concurred with the 'charactological position' taken toward the material. Besides, both men wanted to present 'a good show'. Thus, unlike the hearings, which concluded on June 17th, with McCarthy droning on about his (largely fabricated) war record, *Point of Order!* climaxes with the Welch-McCarthy show-down. Then, as a kind of coda, the film concludes with a scene of the senators walking out of the hearing room as McCarthy rambles on, attacking his harshest senatorial opponent on the committee, 'Sanctimonious Stu' Symington.

After advance screenings at the New York Film Festival, *Point of Order!* premiered on January 14th, 1964, at the Beekman Theater in New York. The original press release billed it as the 'most controversial of motion pictures', but a decade after McCarthy's moments in the limelight the senator was no longer all that controversial. *Point of Order!* underscored an emergent cultural consensus about the sinister impact of the senator and nightmare quality of the era he lent his name to. The generally apolitical trade paper *Variety* praised the film for spotlighting an 'era when panic and fraud very nearly overwhelmed this nation's constitutional heritage'. Even before *Point of Order!*, John Frankenheimer's conspiracy thriller *The Manchurian Candidate* (1962) had prominently featured a fictional senator who was a ripe incarnation of McCarthy: an unscrupulous, television-dependent, anti-Communist demagogue.

Though the question of McCarthy's character seemed settled, the nature of *Point of Order!* was harder to pinpoint. So original in conception and unprecedented in form was the film that some critics did not quite know how to take it. The Museum of Modern Art's programme notes suggested that *Point of Order!* might not even be strictly defined as a film. Likewise, the laudatory review in *Variety* also noted that 'in a film of this kind, it's difficult to know where the praise should go'. Certainly the young Ed Sherer who directed the hearings for WMAL-TV was responsible for one of the most dramatic moments replayed in *Point of Order!*: during the Welch-McCarthy face-off, the film intercuts reaction shots that show a squirming, sweating Roy Cohn, who unlike McCarthy, was aware that the senator was playing right into Welch's hands.

Both on television in the 1950s and on film in the 1960s, the Army-McCarthy hearings were a media milestone not only because of the inherent significance of the event but because television coverage itself was crucial to the meaning and unfolding of events. The hearings marked the first nationwide transmission of the ritual of the American constitution, a democratic drama radiating out not in broadsheets, pronouncements, telegrams, newsreels or radio, but sound and image, beheld in the privacy of the home. Moreover, unlike many historic television moments from the 1950s, the hearings have remained alive in popular memory due to *Point of Order!*, America's first small-screen political spectacle.

FOR FURTHER READING:

Edwin R. Bailey, *Joe McCarthy and the Press* (Pantheon Books, 1981); William Bragg Ewald, Jr, *Who Killed Joe McCarthy?* (Simon and Schuster, 1983); R.D. Heldenfels, *Television's Greatest Year: 1954* (Continuum Publishing Company, 1994); Thomas Rosteck, *See It Now Confronts McCarthyism: Television Documentary and the Politics of Representation* (University of Alabama Press, 1995); Michael Straight, *Trial by Television* (Beacon Press, 1954).

Thomas Doherty is Associate Professor of American Studies and Chair of the Film Studies Program at Brandeis University, Massachusetts.

Martin Luther King's Half-Forgotten Dream

Peter Ling *argues that, by adulating King for his work in the Civil Rights campaigns, we have misrepresented the complexity of those struggles and ignored some of the equally challenging campaigns of his last years.*

Martin Luther King is the only African-American honoured by a national public holiday. Thirty years after his assassination in Memphis, Tennessee, the Martin Luther King remembered on such occasions is overwhelmingly the orator of 1963 who mesmerised a nation from the steps of the Lincoln Memorial with the declaration 'I Have a Dream'. One of the first national events broadcast live and in full, the March on Washington has provided sound-bites that have been used again and again. Alongside the images of President Kennedy's assassination in the same year, the King speech has become far more of an icon than a simple historical document.

In recent years, however, historians have become unhappy with the distorting effect of the King legacy. The first sign of this discomfort, which reflects the misgivings of veterans of the Civil Rights movement, was the insistence that the movement was far more than Martin Luther King, Jr and that its achievements should not be ascribed to one man, however charismatic. More recently, this criticism has been enlarged by those scholars who have focused on the local struggles within which King was an occasional and sometimes marginal player. This has been particularly the case in studies of civil rights activism in Mississippi and Louisiana. For specialist historians, the television montage of the movement, which has King in the lead role of a thirteen- or fourteen-year epic from 1954–55 to 1968, because of its emphasis on the 'war reports' from Montgomery in 1955–56 to the Selma-to-Montgomery march of 1965, fails to capture vital aspects of what made the movement possible and successful.

As recently as 1995, Charles Payne in his award-winning account of the movement in Mississippi could argue persuasively that 'The issues that were invisible to the media and to the current generation of Black activists are still almost as invisible to scholars'. The King-centric popular literature, which scholars like Payne find especially culpable, is guilty not only of neglecting other actors in the civil rights struggle but of emphasising the first ten years of King's public ministry over the years that followed. There is a need to explore in more detail King's later campaigns from 1966 to 1968.

Looked at closely, King's successful national role was episodic and short-lived. The media did catapult the young preacher into the global spotlight in 1956 as the Montgomery Bus Boycott intensified. But, as the best scholar of King's Southern Christian Leadership Conference, Adam Fairclough, admits, the organisation's early years from 1957 to 1959 were 'fallow years'. A near fatal attack on King himself by a deranged black woman is commonly overlooked as one of the reasons why he had failed to develop a leadership programme by 1960. Yet there is some merit in the gripes of the Student Non-violent Coordinating Committee (SNCC) veterans that it was their initiatives in the form of the sit-ins of 1960, the Freedom Ride to Mississippi in 1961, and the voter registration attempts in the Magnolia state that did more to shape the movement than did any action of the Southern Christian Leadership Conference. By 1962, for some hard-core activists, King seemed more a media figure than a true leader, getting headlines and donations largely for talk rather than actions.

It is worth noting the time span of just over six years between the settlement of the Montgomery Bus Boycott in December 1956 and the dramatic Birmingham campaign of April–May 1963 to underline the brevity of King's period of critical national influence that followed. This peaked in August 1965 with the passage of the Voting Rights Act and fell away steadily during 1966 with the setbacks of his Chicago campaign and the media's interest in the new protest slogan of 'Black Power'. Even if one stretches King's influence at the national level to February 1967, when his public denunciation of US involvement in Vietnam permanently closed the doors of President Johnson's Oval Office to him, his most powerful period was shorter than a single presidential term and considerably shorter than the public career that preceded it.

At the outset of his period of significant influence King had written the 'Letter from Birmingham Jail' in which he explained why he had led the protest campaign in Alabama's largest city. He explained his strategy of non-violent direct action as being organised 'to create such a crisis and foster such a tension that a community which has constantly refused to negotiate is forced to confront the issue'. Such a creative tension was necessary to compel change since 'freedom is never voluntarily given up by the oppressor'. Much of the Letter was devoted to explaining the importance of protest to a white moderate audience alarmed by the spectre of social disorder. Such people had to understand the difference between laws that guaranteed justice and a legal system that preserved order. It was the inaction of people of so-called good will, King argued, rather than the activities of racial extremists that sustained segregation and racial discrimination. This emphasis on the political significance of the guilty bystander became even more central to King's thinking in the years after 1966 when he addressed the economics of racism and militarism.

It is misleading to portray the Civil Rights movement as exclusively a southern struggle intent on ending desegregation and disenfranchisement in the South. In the early 1960s national leaders like the trade unionist A. Philip Randolph and black figures within northern radical circles recognised dangerous trends in employment, education and housing discrimination. The famous March on Washington was officially a march for jobs and freedom and, in addition to crowds attracted to the fiery separatist rhetoric of Malcolm X, there were major protest campaigns in Boston, Chicago and other northern cities well before 28 blacks died in the Watts disturbances in August 1965. Nonetheless, King was as ill-prepared to launch an effective assault on ghetto problems in 1966 as he had been to orchestrate an attack on legal segregation in the South in 1957. But, given his belief that a failure to act against a social evil made one complicit in its perpetuation, he had no choice but to offer a programme, especially when it appeared that other sources of non-violent leadership, notably SNCC and the Congress of Racial Equality, were no longer committed to non-violence.

Chronology

1955 December 5th: King as head of the Montgomery Improvement Association leads bus boycott.

1956 December 21st: boycott ends after the city's bus segregation is declared illegal.

1957 February: Southern Christian Leadership Conference (SCLC) is founded with King as president.

1958 September 20th: King is stabbed in the chest at a book-signing in Harlem.

1960 February: Beginning in Greensboro, North Carolina, lunch counter sit-ins spread across the South. April: Student Non-violent Coordinating Committee (SNCC) established at an SCLC sponsored conference.

1961 January: John F. Kennedy is inaugurated as president.
May–June: Freedom Rides are begun by Congress of Racial Equality (CORE) and continued by SNCC. SNCC begins voter registration in hard-core districts in Mississippi.

1962 Unsuccessful campaign in Albany, Georgia.

1963 April–May: King leads demonstration in Birmingham, Alabama. While imprisoned he writes 'Letter from the Birmingham Jail'. TV cameras show police brutality.
August 28th: King delivers 'I Have a Dream' speech at March on Washington.
November 22nd: President Kennedy is assassinated in Dallas, Texas.

1964 June–September: The Freedom Summer voter registration project in Mississippi.
July 2nd: The Civil Rights Act outlawing segregation becomes law.
August 7th: Gulf of Tonkin resolutions allow US troop escalation in Vietnam.
December 10th: King receives the Nobel Peace Prize.

1965 January–March: Escalating protests over right to vote in Selma, Alabama.
February 21st: Malcolm X is assassinated.
March 15th: President Johnson calls for voting rights legislation.
August 6th: Johnson signs the Voting Rights Act.
August 11th–16th: Violent disorder in the Watts district of Los Angeles.

1966 Troop numbers in Vietnam escalate from 184,000 to 385,000.
January–August: SCLC campaign in Chicago.
June: New SNCC chairman Stokely Carmichael popularises the slogan 'Black Power' during a mass march through Mississippi. King expresses misgivings.
July: CORE endorses 'Black Power'; NAACP condemns it.
December: SNCC votes to exclude white members.

1967 February: King denounces US involvement in Vietnam.
April 4th: King preaches against Vietnam at Riverside church, New York. He next participates in a huge anti-war demonstration—larger than the 1963 March.
July: Major ghetto disturbances in Newark, Detroit and elsewhere.
August: King attends Chicago conference on a 'New Politics', but is heckled and booed.
November: Carl Stokes elected as first black mayor of Cleveland.
December: Marion Wright proposes interracial anti-poverty campaign in Washington.

1968 January 31st: Tet offensive shakes US hopes of victory in Vietnam.
February: King is warned that plans for the 'Poor People's Campaign' are faltering.
March 18th: King agrees to lead a march by striking Memphis sanitation workers. After this is marred by violence, he feels compelled to return to lead a non-violent march.
April 4th: King is assassinated while standing on the balcony at the Lorraine Motel in Memphis.
May–June: Ralph Abernathy leads the Poor People's Campaign in Washington.

By the same token, while King recognised that speaking out against the Johnson administration's policy in Vietnam would attract enormous criticism, he could not remain silent without giving sustenance to a gross evil. Biographers report how he was deeply shaken by pictures of Vietnamese casualties of the intensified bombing campaign and decided that in conscience he had to speak out. At New York City's Riverside Church on April 4th, 1967, King denounced his own country as 'the greatest purveyor of violence in the world today'. Linking the deepening crisis in America's ghettos with the escalating military expenditures in Vietnam, he warned the bombs that were dropped in Vietnam would explode at home. 'The security we profess to seek in foreign adventures,' he warned the crowds at an anti-war rally at the United Nations building later that month, 'we will lose in our decaying cities'. Giving credence to this warning, major civil disturbances in Newark, Detroit and other cities that summer resulted in massive destruction of property, injuries and deaths.

In this desperate context, King agreed to attend the National Conference for a New Politics in Chicago in August 1967, which was supposed to provide a programme for radical social change. Previously derided by militants for maintaining links with the political establishment, King indicated that SCLC planned to end its affiliation with the Democratic Party. Speaking in a manner not heard from a national African-American figure since anti-Communist attacks silenced the socialist educator W.E.B. Du Bois and the singer Paul Robeson in the early 1950s, King denounced capitalism and urged a guaranteed minimum income. The West, he added, should not oppose but should support Third World revolutions. Deaf to King's radicalism, many in the audience of New Left activists and Black Power militants jeered or walked away. Rejected by the self-declared revolutionaries, and alienated from the Cold War liberals who dominated the Democratic Party, King searched for a new strategy. His public standing was so dubious that black electoral candidates like Carl Stokes, who was elected mayor of Cleveland in 1967, preferred to downplay King's role in their campaigns.

King had never been a master strategist. Others had launched the Montgomery Bus Boycott, the Birmingham and Selma movement, and some of his young lieutenants, notably former sit-in student James Bevel, were more adept tactically. It was Bevel who had recognised the value of recruiting children to march in Birmingham and who urged the use of 'coercive' non-violence to prevent the existing social order from conducting 'business as usual'. Predictably, therefore, the idea for the Poor People's Campaign (to pressurise the federal government to withdraw from war in Vietnam and to intensify instead the War on Poverty), although built logically on the philosophy of non-violent direct action enunciated in the 'Letter from Birmingham Jail', was the brainchild of Marion Wright, a black lawyer with strong ties to the Mississippi movement. Ironically, the plan to have the nation's poor converge on Washington for a campaign of non-violent direct action was also far more similar to A. Philip Randolph's original March on Washington movement of 1941 (which protested at African-Americans being excluded from defence employment) than was the 1963 event that had confirmed King's pre-eminence as a race leader. Like the earlier set piece campaigns of SCLC, it would seek to induce sufficient creative tension to compel Congressional action. As King told a BBC correspondent only a week before his assassination in 1968, 'We're going to escalate non-violence and seek to make it as dramatic, as attention-getting, as anything we did in Birmingham or Selma, without destroying life or property in the process.'

In the event, King did not live to see the Poor People's Campaign and its failure can at least partly be attributed to the organisational confusion that followed his sudden death.

However, the campaign marked a significant departure from his previous campaigns. Unlike Birmingham or Selma or even Chicago, it did not seek to build on existing local protest activities in their home bases but to take local movements onto the national stage by moving them to the capital. In doing so, SCLC organisers underestimated the resources needed to sustain such a transplanted community. When the campaign occurred, Resurrection City, as the Poor People encampment was called, absorbed much of SCLC's energy.

Whereas earlier campaigns had tried to use the leverage of a federal political system to bring national power to bear against local state and city power, the Poor People's Campaign targeted the Federal Government in the expectation that the disruption of normal practice and the pressure from a sympathetic public audience would revise the Congressional agenda and re-shape policy. The peculiar status of the District of Columbia as the creature of Congress facilitated this focus on the Federal Government, but complicated public perceptions. Non-violent demonstrators were no longer confronting authorities in somebody else's community but in every American's capital city. In previous campaigns, the tension between national embarrassment and local resentment had tended to favour peaceful demonstrators but in 1968, in a context of increasing insecurity and conservatism, they operated mainly against the movement.

The Poor People's Campaign also repeated the same tactical errors that had helped to frustrate the Chicago campaign of 1966 in that it had too many targets. By concentrating on the right to vote in Selma, the SCLC had dramatised the need for federal voting rights legislation. It was unrealistic to suppose that a militant Poor People's Movement could be organised in nine months so as to command sufficient resources to compel the Federal Government to reverse established policy in many different areas. To those who argue that King might have provided sounder guidance in this respect than did his successor, Ralph Abernathy, one can respond that the last year of King's life was characterised by an escalation of his goals rather than a shrewd selection of immediate aims. His decision to go to the aid of the striking Memphis sanitation workers in March 1968 was symptomatic of this tendency. In 1966 the SCLC had struggled to manage the difficulties of handling many local groups in Chicago, yet in 1968, at a the factionalism within the [movement] had intensified, it proposed [to be] an even more diverse coalition.

So, what does a focus on the 1966–68 period rather than the 1963–65 period of King's career reveal about him? One argument would be that it provides a vantage point from which to see the weaknesses within his leadership. In essence, he repeated mistakes. He needed to learn more about the ghetto before he could attack it, just as he had needed to know more about the rural Deep South before he could organise effective campaigns there. He needed to adapt his repertoire of non-violent tactics, which had relied heavily on the cumulative and interactive impact of economic pressure and media censure, to a new terrain and new objectives. Despite the pressures from unfulfilled expectations and worsening economic and political indicators, King needed to have more realistic tactical objectives. As he himself told a press conference in 1967, he needed a victory, even a limited one, to retain credibility in the context of rival calls for separatism.

The ultimate charge in such a critique is one of *hubris*. King believed that he was the only one who could address the ghetto crisis non-violently and, with equal fervour, he believed that the Nobel Prize and his own Christian ministry had made him an anointed international champion for peace. This led him to dissipate his own and SCLC's energies outside of the South and the immediate needs of African-Americans in that region. At a time when effective implementation of the Civil Rights Act of 1964 and the Voting Rights Act of 1965 provided the potential for a genuine political reconstruction, SCLC continued to devote much of its depleted resources to Chicago and King himself was prepared to sacrifice his access to the President by his pronouncements on foreign policy.

The criticisms against King seem largely to boil down to a condemnation of the philosophy of non-violent direct action. Consistent with his axiom that 'Injustice anywhere is a threat to justice everywhere', King believed that he had to provide an alternative to urban conflagration as a means of signalling the plight of inner-city dwellers. Similarly, being convinced that evil was sustained more by the inaction of others than by the deeds of the wicked, he felt unable to stay silent while the United States pursued a foreign policy that entailed wanton warfare against a people who had not attacked the United States. Rather than lamenting the failure of King to mobilise enough support to end the war in Vietnam or to shift government priorities back to the issues of social and economic justice, it seems more useful to reflect on the accuracy of his analysis.

Was he wrong to stress that uneven distribution of wealth was crucial to the persistence of racial inequality? At a time when indices suggest that the gulf between rich and poor, black and white, is widening in the United States, one would have to accept his diagnosis. If the South that emerged after the Voting Rights Act did not fulfil the hopes of those who dreamed of a more egalitarian and more tolerant America, was this not due more to the failure to re-educate white southerners than to a failure of African-American leadership? Similarly, if King's calls for America to make the elimination of poverty its priority failed to prevent the impoverishment of the unskilled working classes since the 1960s, surely this was due to a lack of moral commitment not from King, but from so many of his contemporaries? Thirty years after his death, King's concept of the guilty bystander still points us to the injustices that we support by our inaction. We each make history—by the causes we pursue, but much more commonly by the many times we stand aside.

FOR FURTHER READING:

Charles Payne, *I've Got the Light of Freedom: The Organizing Tradition and the Mississippi Freedom Struggle* (University of California, 1995); Adam Fairclough, *To Redeem the Soul of America: The Southern Christian Leadership Conference and Martin Luther King, Jr* (University of Georgia Press, 1987); James M. Washington, ed., *A Testament of Hope: The Essential Writings and Speeches of Martin Luther King, Jr* (Harper Collins, 1986); David J. Garrow, *Bearing the Cross: Martin Luther King, Jr. and the Southern Christian Leadership Conference* (Jonathan Cape, 1986); Taylor Branch, *Parting the Waters: America in the King Years, 1954–1963* (Touchstone, 1989); Robert Cook, *Sweet Land of Liberty? The African-American Struggle for Civil Rights in the Twentieth Century* (Longman, 1998).

Peter Ling is Senior Lecturer in American Studies at the University of Nottingham and is currently writing a book on political education in the Civil Rights movement.

What really caused the Sixties.

The Spirit of '68

By John B. Judis

This year Bob Dylan's album *Time Out of Mind* won the Grammy for best popular record, and teenagers in my local video store were waiting in line to rent *Don't Look Back,* D.A. Pennebaker's 1967 documentary about the irreverent Dylan. The National Organization for Women, the Consumer Federation of America, the Environmental Defense Fund, and other organizations from the Sixties are still influential in American politics. On the other hand, a host of grumpy social critics and cultural commissars, from Robert Bork and William Bennett to John Leo and Hilton Kramer, have continued to make a career out of denouncing that climactic period of American politics and culture. According to these critics, the "Vietnam syndrome" ruined our foreign policy, and the spirit of permissiveness and "anything goes" corrupted our schools and youth and destroyed the nuclear family. "The revolt was against the entire American culture," Bork declared recently.

Why all the fuss? As a political era—one characterized by utopian social experiments, political upheaval, and dramatic reform—the Sixties ended sometime during Richard Nixon's presidency. But the era left an indelible mark on the decades that followed. It vastly expanded the scope of what citizens expect from their government—from clean air and water to safe workplaces, reliable products, and medical coverage in their old age. It also signaled a change in what Americans wanted out of their lives. During the Sixties, Americans began to worry about the "quality of life" and about their "lifestyle" rather than simply about "making a living." The Sixties unleashed conflicts within these new areas of concern—over affirmative action, abortion, homosexuality, drugs, rock lyrics, air pollution, endangered species, toxic waste dumps, and automobile safety. And the era raised questions about the purpose of America and its foreign policy that are still being debated. The Sixties have preoccupied late-twentieth-century America almost as much as the Civil War preoccupied late-nineteenth- century America.

The difficulty in understanding the Sixties lies partly in the sheer diversity of people, events, and institutions that defined it—from John Kennedy's New Frontier to the Weatherman "Days of Rage," from the Black Panther Party to the Ford Foundation, from Betty Friedan and Ralph Nader to Barry Goldwater and George Wallace. Many of the books and articles that purport to be about the Sixties focus on one aspect of the era to the exclusion of the others. Todd Gitlin's excellent book, for instance, has only a passing reference to Nader and to the Sierra Club's David Brower but multiple references to Carl Oglesby, Huey Newton, and Staughton Lynd.

The nature of the Sixties has also been clouded by conservative jeremiads. Much of what disturbs the critics of the Sixties—from the spread of pornography to the denigration of the work ethic—was not the product of radical agitators but of tectonic shifts in American capitalism. Many of those who complain most vociferously about the Sixties' counterculture, such as House Speaker Newt Gingrich, are themselves products of the period. They no longer carry signs, as Gingrich once did, proclaiming the right of campus magazines to publish nude pictures, but, even as they denounce the Sixties, they echo the decade's themes and vocabulary in articulating their own political objectives. Unable to come to terms with their own past, they sow confusion about one of the most important periods in our history.

Like most periods described by the name of a decade, the Sixties don't strictly conform to their allotted time span. You could make a good case that the Sixties began in December 1955, when Rosa Parks refused to give up her seat in a segregated Montgomery, Alabama, bus, and only ended in 1973 or 1974, when the New Left lost its fervor. You could also make a case for dividing the Sixties into two periods. The first period—running from 1955 to 1965—spans the rise of the Southern civil rights movement and of Martin Luther King, the founding of Students for a Democratic Society (SDS) in 1960, the passage of the civil rights bills and Medicare, and the initiation of the War on Poverty. The second period begins with the escalation of the war and the ghetto riots and goes through the rise of the black power and militant antiwar movements, the growth of the counterculture, the rapid development of environmental, consumer, and women's movements, and the major legislative achievements of Nixon's first term.

On the most visible level—the level at which most books about the period

---

This article draws from JOHN B. JUDIS's book on twentieth-century American politics, *The Paradox of American Democracy* (Pantheon Books, 2000).

have dwelled—there is a pronounced shift in mood during the escalation of the war and the onset of the riots in the mid-'60s. The antiwar and black movements became violent and apocalyptic, and the country itself seemed on the verge of disintegration. But the sharp difference in tone between the two periods obscures important continuities. Most of the major movements that began in the Sixties—the consumer and environmental movements, the modern women's movement—started in the early years of the decade. And the roots of the counterculture go back well into the 1950s, if not before. These movements, as well as the counterculture, took root in Europe, too. In the United States, the simultaneous presence of massive antiwar demonstrations, riots, and demands for black power merely lent those movements and the counterculture a frenzy and an urgency that they might otherwise not have possessed.

The first period of the Sixties looks exactly like a belated continuation of the Progressive era and the New Deal. Just as in earlier periods of reform, political change was precipitated by an economic downturn. Successive recessions in 1958 and 1960 helped Democrats increase their margin in Congress and helped put Kennedy in the White House. In 1964, Johnson, benefiting from a buoyant economy and an impolitic opponent, Barry Goldwater, identified with Southern segregationists and with a trigger-happy foreign policy, won a landslide victory, and liberal Democrats gained control of Congress for the first time since 1936.

Just as before, reform was aided by an alliance of popular movements, elite organizations, and pragmatic business leaders. By the early '60s, the Southern civil rights movement enjoyed enormous support in the North, financial backing from the Ford Foundation and the Rockefeller Brothers Fund, and editorial support from the major media. Business leaders, encouraged by prosperity after having endured four recessions in a decade, accepted Johnson and the administration's major legislative initiatives with equanimity. They didn't oppose Medicare (only the American Medical Association lobbied against it), and they actively backed the Great Society and War on Poverty programs, which they saw, correctly, as creating demand for new private investment. When Johnson appointed a National Commission on Technology, Automation, and Economic Progress, the nation's most powerful businessmen joined labor and civil rights leaders in recommending a guaranteed annual income and a massive job-training program.

The spirit of the early '60s—epitomized in Johnson's vision of the Great Society—was one of heady, liberal optimism. Many of the key leaders of the period, including Martin Luther King Jr., George McGovern, Hubert Humphrey, and Walter Mondale, were raised on the Protestant Social Gospel's millennial faith in the creation of a Kingdom of God in America. The political-economic premise of this optimism, enunciated in Galbraith's *The Affluent Society* and in Michael Harrington's *The Other America*, was that American industry, which was becoming highly automated, was capable of producing great abundance, but archaic political and economic arrangements were preventing many Americans from enjoying its fruits. The goal of such programs as Medicare and the War on Poverty was to allow the poor, the aged, and the disadvantaged to share in this abundance.

This first phase of the Sixties was also marked by signs of a looming redefinition of politics that would differentiate it from early reform epochs. During the Progressive era and the New Deal, politics pivoted primarily on conflicts among different sectors of business and between business and labor. The great battles of the first five decades of the twentieth century had been over the trusts, the tariff, the banking system, the abolition of child labor, and government regulation of collective bargaining. No legislative struggle attracted so many lobbyists, was fought as fiercely, and had as much impact on presidential politics as the Taft-Hartley labor bill in 1947.

In the early '60s, new issues that didn't fit easily within this pattern began to emerge. Americans became concerned not merely with obtaining lower prices for goods but with government overseeing the safety, reliability, and quality of goods. President Kennedy announced a consumer bill of rights" in 1962. That same year, over the strong objection of the clothing industry, Congress passed landmark legislation requiring flame-resistant fabrics in children's clothing. In 1964, Assistant Secretary of Labor Daniel P. Moynihan hired a young Harvard Law graduate, Ralph Nader, to research auto safety. Two years later, amidst the furor created by Nader's work, Congress passed the National Traffic and Motor Vehicle Safety Act.

In the early '60s, Americans also became concerned about the environment—not merely as a source of renewable resources or as a wildlife preserve but as the natural setting for human life. In 1962, Rachel Carson's *Silent Spring* became a best-seller. Congress passed its first Clean Air Act in 1963 and its first Clean Water Act in 1965. During the early '60s, American women also began to stir as a political force in their own right. In 1963, Betty Friedan published *The Feminine Mystique*, and, three years later, she and other feminists formed the National Organization for Women. While the older women's movement had focused on suffrage, the new movement reached into the workplace and the home and even into the private lives of men and women.

The new concerns about work, consumption, and personal life were part of a fundamental change in American culture that began to manifest itself clearly in the early '60s. During the nineteenth and early twentieth centuries, Americans had still adhered to the Protestant work ethic introduced by seventeenth-century English emigrants to America and memorialized in Benjamin Franklin's *Autobiography*. They viewed idleness and leisure as sinful and saw life and work as unpleasant prerequisites to a heavenly reward. By the early '60s, Americans had begun to abandon this harsh view for an ethic of the good life. They wanted to discover a "lifestyle" that suited them. They worried about the "quality of life," including the kinds of foods they ate, the clothes they wore, and the cars they drove.

This change was not the work of sinful agitators but reflected deep-seated changes that had taken place in American capitalism over the century. In the nineteenth century and early twentieth century, economic growth, and the growth of the working class itself, was driven by the expansion of steel, railroads, machine tools, and other "capital goods" industries. Workers' consumption was held down in order to free up funds that could be used to invest in these new capital goods. To prevent recurrent economic crises, American industrialists were always on the lookout—in China, among other places—for new outlets for investment in railroads and other capital goods. But, as the historian Martin J. Sklar has demonstrated, sometime around the 1920s, the dynamic of economic growth changed. The growth of capital goods industries became, ironically, a threat to prosperity.

It happened because American industry, like American agriculture, became too successful for its own good. The introduction of electricity and the assembly line made the modern factory so productive that it could now increase its output without increasing its overall number of employees. During the '20s, manufacturing output grew 64 percent, but the number of workers in capital goods industries fell by twelve percent. Expanding the production of capital goods no longer required the sacrifice of workers' consumption. By the same token, it imperiled prosperity by encouraging the production of more goods than those producing them—the workers—could purchase and consume.

During the '20s, Edward Filene and other far-seeing businessmen understood that the fulcrum of the economy had shifted from production to consumption and that, to avoid depressions, employers would have to pay higher wages and induce their workers, through advertising, to spend money on consumer goods. Filene advocated a different kind of "industrial democracy" centered on workers' freedom to consume. After World War II, businesses adopted Filene's ethic and his strategy. They paid higher wages and devoted growing parts of their budgets to advertising, which was aimed at convincing Americans to spend rather than to save. Advertising budgets doubled between 1951 and 1962. Businesses and banks also introduced the installment plan and consumer loans and, later, credit cards as inducements to buy rather than to save.

In search of profit, businesses also invaded the family and home. They sold leisure and entertainment on a massive scale; they produced not merely clothes but fashion; they processed exotic foods and established fast-food chains; they sold physical and psychological health; they filled the home with appliances and gadgets. They convinced Americans that they should care about more than just having food on the table, a house to live in, and clothes on their backs. They encouraged the idea that Americans could remake themselves—that they could create their own "look," their own personality. They encouraged the idea that sex was not merely a means to procreate but a source of pleasure and visual excitement.

The origins of the counterculture lay at the interstices of this new American culture of leisure and consumption that business helped to promote. The counterculture was a product of the new culture at the same time as it represented a critique of and a counter to it. It rejected Filene's suggestion that workers seek their freedom entirely in consumption rather than work. It held out for meaningful work, but not as defined by the nineteenth or early twentieth centuries. In 1960, when Paul Goodman, writing in *Growing' Up Absurd,* complained that "there are not enough worthy jobs in our economy for average boys and adolescents to grow up toward," he was not complaining about the lack of jobs at General Motors or on Wall Street.

The counterculture also rejected TV dinners and cars with tail fins that the advertisers urged Americans to buy, but it did so on behalf of more discriminating standards of its own. The critique of consumerism—articulated in the '50s by Vance Packard's *The Waste Makers* and *The Hidden Persuaders*—led directly to the formation of the modern consumer and environmental movements. And the rejection of sex symbols and stereotypes did not lead to a celebration of abstinence but to a wider exploration into sexual pleasure and to a reevaluation of homosexuality and heterosexuality. In the early '60s, all these concerns became the subjects not merely of books and small artistic cults, but of political manifestos and platforms and embryonic social movements.

The movements initially took root among college students and recent college graduates. Students who entered college in 1960 had been born after the Depression—they had been, in the words of SDS's Port Huron Statement, "bred in at least modest comfort." Living in a time of unprecedented prosperity, they could afford not to worry about whether they would be able to get a job. They were raised to think about the "quality of life" rather than the iron law of wages, even to scorn some elements of what was then called "materialism." By 1960, they had become a major social group, capable on their own of disrupting society and upsetting its politics.

The New Left movements of the early '60s attacked the new economy, but they, too, implicitly used the new standards and ideals it had fostered. SDS's Port Huron Statement condemned the "idolatrous worship of things" but called for "finding a meaning in life that is personally authentic"—a formulation that would have made no sense to an industrial worker in 1909. In Berkeley, the Free Speech Movement of 1964—aimed at reclaiming the rights of students to distribute political literature on campus—gave way the next year to the Filthy Speech Movement, aimed at defending students against literary and sexual censorship. Over the next decade, these two movements—political and cultural—would develop in tandem.

The second period of the Sixties began with the Watts riot and Lyndon Johnson's escalation of the Vietnam War in 1965. These events signified and helped to precipitate a darker, more frenzied and violent period of protest. By escalating the war, Johnson broke a campaign promise not to send "our American boys to do the fighting for Asian boys." The war's escalation also threw into question the purpose of American foreign policy. Students who entered college in the Sixties had been imbued with the idea that America's mission was to create a democratic world after its own image. But, in Vietnam, the United States was backing a corrupt dictatorship, which, at our urging, had ignored the 1954 Geneva agreements to hold elections in Vietnam. The seeming contradiction between U.S. intervention and American ideals, Johnson's dishonesty and betrayal, and the rising list of casualties on both sides of the war inspired a growing rage against Johnson and the government. The antiwar movement split into a moderate wing that sought a negotiated withdrawal and a violent pro-North Vietnamese wing that threatened to bring the war home." As the conviction grew that U.S. intervention was not an unfortunate blunder but reflected the priorities of American capitalism and its power elite, antiwar militants began to see the United States itself as the enemy. SDS, the leading student organization, imagined itself by 1969 to be the vanguard of a violent revolution *against* the United States.

The first ghetto riots took place in the summer of 1964 and then grew in size and strength over the next three summers. In the Watts riot of 1965, 1,072 people were injured, 34 were killed, 977 buildings were damaged, and 4,000 people were arrested. In July 1967, there were 103 disorders, including five full-scale riots. In Detroit, 43 people were killed, and 7,200 were arrested. 700 buildings were burned, and 412 were totally destroyed. The riots were spontaneous. but the) were invariably triggered by black perceptions of unequal treatment, particularly at the hands of white police officers.

At the same time that the riots began, Martin Luther King Jr. attempted to take the civil rights movement northward to Chicago. Contrary to the fantasies of his current conservative admirers, King never saw political and civil equality as ends in themselves but as part of a longer struggle for full social and economic equality. King wanted to desegregate housing in the North (which was the key to de facto school segregation), improve city services for blacks, and gain higher wages and better jobs for blacks. He failed abysmally in Chicago. The combination of the ghetto riots and King's failure contributed to the radicalization of the black movement. By 1968, when King was assassinated in Memphis while trying to support striking black garbage-men, many in the black movement had turned toward insurrectionary violence. It saw the Northern ghettos as Third World colonies that had to be liberated from their white imperialist oppressors.

Both the radical antiwar and the black power movements espoused what they called "revolutionary politics." They saw themselves in the tradition of Marx, Lenin, Mao, Fanon, Castro, and even Stalin, but, by the late '60s, they had become unwitting participants in a much older American tradition of Protestant millennialism. As historian William G. McLoughlin argued in *Revivals, Awakenings and Reform,* the Sixties were part of a religious revival comparable to the great awakenings of the mid-eighteenth and early nineteenth centuries. At such times, the seeming discord between ideal and reality has inspired intense self-examination, the proliferation of new sects and schisms, and alternating visions of doom and salvation. While the first phase of the Sixties saw the revival of the post-millennial Protestant Social Gospel—the view that the world would end after the millennium—the second phase saw "pre-millennial" visions of the apocalypse and Armageddon occurring before the millennium.

The emergence of this pre-millennial vision was provoked by the war's escalation and the combination of rage and guilt (guilt at complicity in the slaughter of seeming innocents) that it inspired; the repeated visions of violence and destruction in Vietnam and in American cities, which reinforced an image of change as conflagration; the assassinations of John and Robert Kennedy and of Martin Luther King, Jr., and Malcolm X; the Republican advances in 1966 and Nixon's election in November 1968, which discouraged New Left activists who had believed they could achieve majority support for their revolutionary aspirations; and the apparent success of the North Vietnamese in the war and the onset of China's Cultural Revolution, which suggested that revolution in the United States would occur only after a global revolution against American imperialism had succeeded.

The New Left of the late '60s dreamed not of America's salvation but of its destruction. If socialism or the "good life" were to come to the United States, it would be only after Armageddon—after a victorious armed struggle that would lay waste to the United States. The Panthers referred to the United States as "Babylon." When the Weatherman group took over SDS in 1969, it changed the name of SDS's newspaper, *New Left Notes,* to *Fire.* The new revolutionaries steeled themselves for a life of sacrifice and eventually death in the service of world revolution. Huey Newton, the cofounder of the Panther Party, described its program as "revolutionary suicide." Hal Jacobs, a Weatherman sympathizer, wrote in the movement magazine *Leviathan:* "Perhaps the best we can hope for is that in the course of the struggle we can develop human social relations among ourselves, while being engulfed by death and destruction."

The vision of Weatherman or the Panthers perfectly matched that of the Millerites—the precursors of today's Seventh Day Adventists. They were preparing themselves to be saved in the face of an imminent Armageddon. Even their organization resembled that of earlier Christian sects. The Weatherman group abandoned any pretense of building a mass movement. Instead, it sought to establish "revolutionary Marxist-Leninist-Maoist collective formations" that, through "criticism—self-criticism," would convert its members to true revolutionaries. Under Weatherman leadership, SDS, which at one point boasted 100,000 members, dwindled to several hundred aspiring visible saints.

During the late '60s, many of the people in the New Left, myself included, got caught up in the debate over class struggle, imperialism, racism, and revolution as if it were a genuine discussion based on reasonable, if debatable, assessments of world conditions. But others sensed that something was deeply wrong. In his 1968 campaign as the Democratic antiwar candidate, Eugene McCarthy continually frustrated his own followers by counseling calm and "reasoned judgment." Said McCarthy, "It is not a time for storming the walls, but for beginning a long march." Paul Goodman, whose writings had inspired the New Left, realized by 1969 that the political movement had turned unworldly even while it pretended to speak of world revolution:

> If we start from the premise that the young are in a religious crisis, that they doubt there is really a nature of things and they are sure there is no world for themselves, many details of their present behavior become clearer. Alienation is a powerful motivation, of unrest, fantasy and feckless action. It can lead . . . to religious innovation, new sacraments to give life meaning. But it is a poor basis for politics, including revolutionary politics.

At the time, however, these voices were largely ignored. The question wasn't whether it made any sense at all to talk of revolution, but when the revolution would come and who would be on what side of the barricades.

This turn toward violence and revolutionary fantasy alienated many Americans and led to the rise of Ronald Reagan in California and George Wallace's surprising showing in the 1968 presidential election. That year, Richard Nixon ran a subtle "law and order" campaign to exploit the unpopularity of the antiwar and black protesters. Yet these movements still wielded enormous influence over the nation's political and legislative agenda. By the early '70s, they had helped force the Nixon administration to withdraw from Vietnam and had provoked Congress and the administration into pouring money into cities and adopting a strategy of affirmative action in hiring and federal contracts. During Nixon's first term, spending on Johnson's Great Society programs and on welfare and Food Stamps dramatically increased, while spending on the military went down.

There were two reasons for the movements' remarkable success. First, the movements were large and unruly enough to pose a constant threat of disruption. The major riots stopped by 1969, but the threat of riots persisted—both in actual fact and in the rhetoric and behavior of the black activists. In the summer of 1970 alone, city officials reported that black and Chicano militants made over 500 attacks on police, resulting in the deaths of 20 policemen. The antiwar movement also became increasingly violent. During the fall semester in 1970, 140 bombings occurred; at Rutgers, classes had to be vacated 175 times because of bomb threats.

Second, these movements had either the support or sympathy of policy elites. Some members of the foreign policy elite, acting partly out of conviction and partly out of fear of further disruption, favored immediate negotiation with the North Vietnamese and later unilateral withdrawal from Vietnam. By 1968, these included *The New York Times* editorial board and prominent members of the Council on Foreign Relations. Foundations and policy groups responded to the antiwar movement and to the riots and the black power movement the same way elite organizations in the early 1900s had responded to the threat of socialist revolution. They sought to tame the militants by helping them achieve their more reasonable objectives.

The Ford Foundation, the wealthiest and most powerful of all the foundations, with assets four times that of the Rockefeller Foundation, was particularly important. In 1966, Henry Ford and foundation board chairman John McCloy desirous that the foundation play a more active role in national affairs, brought in former Kennedy national security adviser McGeorge Bundy as the new president. Bundy threw the foundation into the struggle for racial equality. He helped new groups get off the ground, including La Raza and the Mexican-American Legal Defense Fund. But he also embroiled the foundation in controversy. Money that Ford gave to the Congress of Racial Equality in Cleveland went to funding a voter registration drive that helped elect Democrat Carl Stokes as Cleveland's first black mayor—in seeming violation of the foundation's nonpartisan status. In New York, Bundy sold New York City Mayor John Lindsay on a plan for community control of schools that put local blacks in charge of their own schools, which ended up pitting the city's blacks against the predominantly Jewish teachers' union.

While the late '60s are remembered mainly for the violent antiwar and black power movements, their most enduring legacy was the establishment of the environmental, consumer, and women's movements. By the early '70s, the National Organization for Women had 200 local chapters and had been joined in effort by the National Women's Political Caucus, the National Association for the Repeal of Abortion Laws, and hundreds of small local and national women's organizations. The movement enjoyed remarkable success. In 1972, the year Ms. magazine was founded, Congress approved the Equal Rights Amendment to the Constitution, strengthened and broadened the scope of the Equal Employment Opportunity Commission, and included a provision in the new Higher Education Act ensuring equal treatment of men and women.

The consumer and environmental movements enjoyed equally spectacular success. Organizations like the Sierra Club, Wilderness Society, and the Audubon Society expanded their purview and quadrupled their membership from 1960 to 1969. They were also joined by new groups, including Environmental Action, the Environmental Defense Fund, and Friends of the Earth. The Consumer Federation of America, a coalition of 140 state and local groups, was founded in 1967, and Consumers Union, which had published a magazine since 1936, moved its office to Washington in 1969. These groups got the Nixon administration and Congress to adopt a raft of reforms from establishing the Environmental Protection Agency and the Consumer Product Safety Commission to major amendments to the Clean Air and Clean Water acts.

The key individual behind these movements was Nader. He used his fame and income from *Unsafe at Any Speed*—his best-selling book about auto safety—and his successful battle with General Motors to help build a consumer movement. Nader started hiring young lawyers called "Nader's Raiders" in 1968 and founded his first campus-based Public Interest Research Group in 1970. By the mid-'70s, he had founded eight new organizations, including the Center for Responsive Law, Congress Watch, and the Health Research Group, which played an important role in getting Congress to pass a mass of new legislation, including the Wholesome Poultry Products Act, the Natural Gas Pipeline Safety Act, and the Occupational Safety and Health Act.

If Nader was the key individual, the key institution was once more the Ford Foundation. The foundation stepped in when the Audubon Society, worried about its own contributors, balked at funding the Environmental Defense Fund, the first public interest law firm designed to force business and government to comply with the new environmental laws. Ford also gave generous grants to the Sierra Club Legal Defense Fund and to the Los Angeles-based Center for Law in the Public Interest. By 1972, Ford was providing 86 percent of the grants to groups practicing consumer and environmental public interest law.

Unlike the later antiwar and civil rights movements, the environmental and consumer movements enjoyed enormous popular support. Republican and Democratic politicians vied to sponsor environmental and consumer legislation. In 1970, Nixon and Edmund Muskie, who was planning to run for president in 1972, got into a bidding war for the movements support, with each championing successively tougher revisions to the Clean Air Act. Businesses might have fought environmental and consumer legislation, but, in these years, they were restrained by a combination of complacency and defensiveness. From February 1961 to September 1969, the United States enjoyed the longest consecutive boom on record. The economy grew by 4.5 percent a year, compared to 3.2 percent in the '50s. Secure in their standing, only 50 corporations had registered lobbyists stationed in Washington in the early '60s.

In the mid-'60s, as the country's mood darkened, the public's opinion of business began to fall precipitously, but, as David Vogel recounts in *Fluctuating Fortunes,* business's initial response was to stress corporate social responsibility and to accommodate the demands of the consumer and environmental movements. While the auto and tobacco companies took umbrage at regulations targeted at them, business as a whole thought it could adapt the new environmental and consumer legislation to its own ends just as it had done earlier with the Interstate Commerce Commission and the Federal Trade Commission. A Fortune survey in February 1970 found 53 percent of Fortune 500 executives in favor of a national regulatory agency and 57 percent believing that the federal government should "step up regulatory activities." In a spirit of social responsibility, 85 percent of the executives thought that the environment should be protected even if that meant "reducing profits."

In the second phase of the Sixties, the counterculture spread from Berkeley, Madison, Ann Arbor, and Cambridge to almost every high school and college in America. Teenagers from pampered suburban homes who had never read Allen Ginsberg or Nelson Algren nevertheless denounced the "rat race" and the "neon wilderness." In extensive polls and interviews conducted from 1968 to 1974, Daniel Yankelovich saw steadily growing "acceptance of sexual freedom," rejection of "materialism," opposition to the laws against marijuana, and questioning of "such traditional American views as putting duty before pleasure [and] saving money regularly."

Like the other movements of the Sixties, the counterculture had its theorists, and its own millennial vision, which propounded a utopian version of consumer capitalism. Sociologist Theodore Roszak, ecologist Murray Bookchin, Yale Law School professor Charles Reich, and other post-millennialists foresaw a transformation in human nature and human arrangements that would subordinate work to play and science to art. The instrument of change would not be a political movement but the change in consciousness that had already begun among college students. Reich saw the essence of change in the new "freedom of choosing a lifestyle." Work would become an "erotic experience, or a play experience."

Reich attributed the new counterculture to capitalism—what he called the "machine." As capitalism became capable of producing more goods than it could sell, it was forced to devise ways to expand people's needs and wants. It had to transform people themselves, moving them from the work ethic of "Consciousness II" to the lifestyle ethic of "Consciousness III," where a human being could "develop the aesthetic and spiritual side of his nature."

Reich, Roszak, and other spokesmen for the counterculture did not exalt idleness but artistic expression. They didn't promote pornography but eroticism. Most of what their current critics like Bork and Kramer lay at their door was attributable to consumer capitalism rather than the counterculture. And, while much of their vision of the future appears daffy, they—in contrast to their latter-day critics—realized that America had turned a corner. What they didn't understand was exactly where it was headed.

As a political era, the Sixties came to a close around 1973. In January 1973, Nixon signed a peace accord with North Vietnam, which not only put an end to the antiwar movement but, in doing so, removed a major source of political mobilization and energy. In 1969, the booming war economy also began a six-year slowdown. This slowdown, aggravated by the energy crisis of 1973, put a damper on the counterculture. Students became focused on preparing for jobs and careers rather than discovering the meaning of life.

The downturn of the early '70s, combined with a wave of strikes that began in 1969 and with growing competition from Japan and Western Europe, made American business leaders lose their tolerance for new government intervention. They began to push hard to limit new consumer and environmental regulations. They began hiring lobbyists and establishing corporate offices in Washington and funding policy groups and think tanks, and by the mid-'70s, many business leaders were beginning to look fondly upon Republican conservatives who combined their opposition to the social movements of the Sixties with support for business's agenda of "deregulation." By 1978, these two groups were setting the nation's political and legislative agenda, even with Democrats in control of the White House and Congress.

What, then, is the legacy of the Sixties? It endures, for one thing, in Bill Clinton's passionate commitment to racial reconciliation and in Al Gore's ardent environmentalism. It also could be found in Clinton's mistaken belief after November 1992 that he could fashion a "new beginning," including a wildly ambitious health care plan. But the era also endures ironically in its most bitter opponents—Gingrich, Dick Armey, Phil Gramm, and many of the leaders of the religious right. Gingrich and Armey's fantastic belief that they had led a "revolution" in November 1994 was straight out of the late '60s. So, too, is Gingrich's futurism and his insistence that Americans should have the highest "range of choices of lifestyle." Within the religious right, Weatherman has been reincarnated as Operation Rescue, and the communards of the Sixties have become the home-schoolers of the 1990s.

The Sixties clearly bequeathed political conflicts that continue to seethe but also made lasting contributions that cannot easily be undone. Medicare and the environmental and consumer legislation of Nixon's first term have withstood furious attacks from conservatives and business. While the issues of urban poverty and decay that King addressed in the last years of his life remain unsettled, the premises of the Civil Rights Act of 1964 and the Voting Rights Act of 1965 are no longer open to question.

The Sixties enlarged the scope of politics by adding new issues and constituencies to the traditional mix created by business and labor, and they changed the way politics was conducted. A proliferation of new movements, interests, and interest groups—some of them funded door-to-door and others through the mail—shifted the struggle to change the country from the halls of Congress to the media and even to time streets. By the 1980s, business lobbyists were employing "grassroots" techniques developed by shaggy protesters from the Sixties.

Perhaps most important of all, America passed irreversibly during the Sixties from a culture of toil, sacrifice, saving, and abstinence to a culture of consumption, lifestyle, and quality of life The agent of this change was not the counterculture but consumer capitalism, to which the counterculture, like the religious right, is a reaction. This new stage of capitalism has opened to the average American possibilities of education, leisure, and personal fulfillment that had been reserved in the past for the upper classes. It has also, of course, exalted consumption over production, razed redwoods, turned shorelines into boardwalks, flooded cyberspace with spain, used sex to sell detergents, and helped to transform many American teenagers into television zombies. If our cultural commissars would understand this distinction between the culture of capitalism and the counterculture, perhaps they would waste less of our time blaming the radicals of the Sixties for all of today's problems and turn their attention to the real causes.

Nixon's America

He still personifies the evil politician. But his effect on the country was more complicated—and more positive

By Michael Barone

Just before noon on Aug. 9, 1974, 25 years ago, Richard Nixon walked across the South Lawn of the White House and climbed the steps to the presidential helicopter. When he reached the top, he turned, raised his right arm in a sweeping gesture, and awkwardly waved goodbye. Then, just minutes before his resignation as president became effective, he stepped into the helicopter for the first leg of his journey to exile in San Clemente, Calif. He was lifted over the White House, the gleaming Washington Monument, and Jefferson Memorial—symbols of America's enduring greatness. But aboard Air Force One for the final time, Nixon quickly closed his eyes as he set off across a country that was deeply troubled—and not just by the drawn-out Watergate crisis that had caused him to resign. Nixon's America was plagued by an economy in recession and a dollar weakened by inflation. It was a country just recently freed from fighting the Vietnam War overseas and still fighting over the consequences of that war at home. It was a country in which crime and welfare rolls had tripled over a decade; in which trust in major institutions and confidence in the future had fallen sharply. When Richard Nixon first entered public life, as a candidate for Congress in 1946, America seemed on top of the world: victorious in war, poised for an economic burst, and enjoying that kind of social cohesion and cultural unity most nations could only envy. When he left public office 28 years later, America seemed weak and uncertain abroad, with a sputtering economy and deep social divisions at home.

But if Nixon left office a president repudiated by most Americans, he was also a president of major achievements who in many ways shaped the America of today. For a new generation—62 percent of Americans today were under voting age or not yet born when Nixon left office—he is mostly caricatured as the malevolent politician (Oliver Stone's film *Nixon*) or lampooned as the embodiment of a clueless age (the recent satire *Dick*). Nixon's legacy runs far beyond the political reforms spawned by Watergate. To an extent few people appreciate, we still live in Richard Nixon's America.

An extreme record. How did Nixon shape America? For a long while, it's been hard to reach an honest verdict. Nixon aroused strong feelings, especially among his opponents, whose visceral dislike for the man often warped their vision, but also among his supporters, who were uncomfortable with many of his achievements. Americans are used to classifying their presidents as heroes or goats. On one side we have the Mount Rushmore pantheon—George Washington, Thomas Jefferson, Abraham Lincoln, Theodore Roosevelt—plus Franklin Roosevelt, great presidents who positively shaped America. On the other side, we have presidents dismissed (in some cases unfairly) as failures—Franklin Pierce, James Buchanan, Warren Harding. It takes considerable straining to fit Nixon into either group. As president he had both great policy achievements—the opening to China is usually the first to spring to mind—and great failures—he is the only American president forced to resign. His adversaries called him "Tricky Dick"; his supporters cherished him for the hatred he aroused in the East Coast elite. Both groups had such a psychological stake in their views that they overlooked and distorted much of what he did.

Today, a quarter century after he left office and five years after he died, a more temperate assessment can be made. Richard Nixon was the most enduring politician of post-World War II America. He was a national political figure from August 1948, when he charged Alger Hiss with having been a Communist spy, until August 1974, when he resigned. No president since John Quincy Adams has been such a prominent national politician for so long. No other American has served longer in national office, and only one other, Franklin Roosevelt, was nominated for national office by a major party five times.

Nixon came to public office just as postwar America was taking shape, and he rose rapidly—from small-town lawyer to vice president in just six years—by following, and helping to establish, the rules of postwar politics. But by the time he became president, in 1969, Nixon sensed that—amid the riots and tumult of the late 1960s—the old policies were failing. He responded with new initiatives, from engagement with China to racial quotas and preferences, many of which endure to this day.

A calmer country. Nixon could plausibly argue that the country was stronger when he left the White House than when he entered. The riots in black ghettos and uprisings on college campuses that were so common in the late 1960s had disappeared by 1974. The

From *U.S. News & World Report*, September 20, 1999, pp. 20-27. © 1999 by U.S. News & World Report. Reprinted by permission.

war in Vietnam, which the Johnson administration found impossible to win and impossible to end, seemed to be over, with America's allies at least tenuously in power in South Vietnam. The United States had made a successful opening to China and had signed arms-control treaties with the Soviet Union. The recession of 1973–74, while painful, was not as deep as the 1930s Depression. But not all of his policies endured. In some cases he assumed, wrongly, that policies that had worked in the early postwar period would work in the 1970s: The prime example is wage and price controls. And he failed to understand until it was too late that American presidents would be held, by the press and the public, to higher ethical and moral standards than in the past. In retrospect, neither his enemies nor his admirers got Nixon right.

In September 1945, Richard Nixon, awaiting discharge from the Navy after uneventful duty in the South Pacific, got a letter from a banker back home in Whittier, Calif., a small Quaker town amid farm fields 15 miles southeast of Los Angeles. The banker asked if he "would like to be a candidate for Congress on the Republican ticket in 1946." The answer was a quick yes. Nixon had worked his way through Whittier College and graduated from Duke law school near the top of his class but failed to get a job in a New York firm or with the FBI. Now, at 32, Nixon faced the prospect of practicing law in Whittier for maybe $2,000 a year. No wonder he jumped into the race, raising money from Republican businessmen and meticulously researching the record of 10-year Democratic incumbent Jerry Voorhis. In a debate, Nixon flummoxed Voorhis by charging that he was supported by pro-Communist unions and that his voting record resembled that of pro-Communist New York Rep. Vito Marcantonio. Smears, his enemies said, then and later. But the charges were accurate, and Nixon was careful to say that Voorhis himself was not pro-Communist. But more important than Nixon's attacks was the demographic transformation of the Los Angeles basin, which was filling up with veterans and war-industry workers who were tired of wartime price controls, high taxes, and militant labor strikes. Opinion all over the nation shifted to Republicans in 1946, and Nixon won with 56 percent of the vote.

Nixon entered Congress as a promising member of the majority party, with a seat across the table on the Education and Labor Committee from a freshman Democrat named John F. Kennedy. Even in an aggressive Republican Congress—it passed bills cutting taxes, ending price controls, and reducing the power of labor unions—the freshman Nixon stood out and quickly became a national figure. He had agreed to take a seat on the House Un-American Activities Committee, known for its investigations of Communists, and in August 1948, after listening carefully to charges by Whittaker Chambers and responses from Alger Hiss, a former high State Department official, he charged that Hiss was a Communist. Although Hiss was convicted of perjury, the incident became a flashpoint of American cold war politics—and earned Nixon the eternal enmity of the country's liberal establishment. Many believed that the patrician Hiss, with his elite education and credentials, had been framed, and they lumped Nixon together with others who did make false charges of Communist activity. It wasn't until after Nixon left office that his charge was fully vindicated: Hiss was clearly recognizable as the spy "Ales" in the Soviet Venona papers made public over the last few years.

Political phenom. By 1950, Nixon had vaulted to a Senate seat, and when Dwight Eisenhower was nominated as the Republican presidential candidate two years later, he never seriously considered anyone else as his running mate. At 39, Nixon became the youngest vice president in 92 years.

It was during Eisenhower's two terms that Nixon developed a mastery of foreign and domestic policy. In his early 40s he conversed with Winston Churchill and Charles de Gaulle. He behaved with appropriate restraint during Eisenhower's illnesses in 1955 and 1956. He was calm when under attack by crowds in Venezuela in 1958 and bested Nikita Khrushchev in the kitchen debate in Moscow in 1959. And despite the scorn of liberals, he was popular with voters. When he ran to succeed Eisenhower in 1960, his loss to John Kennedy was by one of the narrowest percentages in history. Many Republicans urged him to challenge an election they thought was stolen, but he refused, on the grounds that it might undermine the American political system.

Suddenly the most accomplished postwar politician was a private citizen. In 1962 Nixon ran for governor of California and lost to incumbent Democrat Pat Brown; voters seemed to sense that he cared little about the job but just wanted a steppingstone back to the presidency. They were right. By 1968, one of the nation's most tumultuous years, he had put together a new campaign team and won a narrow majority at the Republican National Convention. While Nixon was out of office, the postwar consensus had unraveled. Southern whites had resisted, sometimes violently, the end of legal segregation. Blacks in Northern cities rioted in 1964, 1965, 1967, and 1968. College students were protesting the Vietnam War and using marijuana and harder drugs as never before. Lyndon Johnson's Great Society programs, far from mollifying their intended beneficiaries, seemed to produce more disorder. The nation seemed to be splintering into hostile groups. In February, Americans were shocked by the Viet Cong's Tet offensive; in March, Lyndon Johnson, after only narrowly defeating Eugene McCarthy in the New Hampshire primary, withdrew from the race; in April, Martin Luther King Jr. was murdered in Memphis, and riots followed in many cities; in June, Robert Kennedy was murdered in Los Angeles the night after winning the Democratic primary; in August, the Democratic convention was marred by clashes between antiwar demonstrators and Chicago police.

A healer. Through all this, Nixon campaigned in a conciliatory tone, with almost none of the sharp attacks so common in his early career. He gave a dignified speech at the convention and avoided the harsh rhetoric of Alabama Gov. George Wallace, who was running as an independent.

He said he would work to end the Vietnam War, without specifying exactly

SO CLOSE. Campaigning against John Kennedy in 1960, here in Illinois, Nixon lost by one of the narrowest margins in history.

how; at the end of the campaign he cited the sign held up by a teenage girl as his train stopped at Deshler, Ohio: "Bring us together." In his bestseller *The Selling of the President,* Joe McGinniss accused Nixon of running a manipulative media campaign. But his media dollars were spent on nonincendiary political ads and on live broadcasts showing him spontaneously answering substantive questions posed by supporters. His early lead narrowed, but he held on to beat Hubert Humphrey.

Nixon's heroes were Churchill and de Gaulle. As he wrote in his 1982 book, *Leaders,* both also "had a 'wilderness' period. The insights and wisdom they gained during that period, and the strength they developed in fighting back from it, were key elements in the greatness they demonstrated." Like Churchill in 1940 and de Gaulle in 1958, Nixon was called on to lead a nation in serious trouble; he took office under more difficult circumstances than any president but Lincoln and Franklin Roosevelt. The postwar consensus was in tatters, and no one could be sure what would take its place. The elite was moving left, embracing the rhetoric of the college protesters and the complaints of black rioters. The voters were moving right, demanding the restoration of law and order, the repeal of poverty and welfare programs, and peace with victory in Vietnam.

Nixon responded by reaching out to his political adversaries. Like Churchill and de Gaulle, he sought to form a national government, including eminent men outside his wing of the Republican Party. As his chief foreign policy adviser, he appointed Henry Kissinger, Harvard professor and longtime adviser to Nixon's rival, Nelson Rockefeller. As his chief domestic policy adviser he appointed Daniel Patrick Moynihan, Harvard professor and proud appointee of John Kennedy and Lyndon Johnson. Both were men of strong intellect and extraordinary originality, and would back policies very far from those of conventional Republicans; neither had known or admired Nixon before he asked them to join his administration. He ignored almost entirely the governors, lawyers, and businessmen he appointed to his cabinet, and, with the important exception of Defense Secretary Melvin Laird, his administration included almost none of the small-town Republicans who had long been his political base.

Like de Gaulle, Nixon sought to close the growing gap between the elites and ordinary people. Typically, he tailored his policies to left-leaning opinion leaders while crafting his rhetoric to propitiate the right-leaning "silent majority." De Gaulle, brought to power by French citizens eager to retain Algeria, instead ended the French presence there and withdrew. Nixon, supported by many who wanted a more aggressive strategy to hold Vietnam, liquidated the American military effort there, though he left the South Vietnamese with a government that had at least a chance for survival.

Yet Nixon's Vietnam policy did not achieve the consensus he desired. Liberals in the Northeast cities and universities and Democrats in Congress, who had meekly acquiesced in every escalation of American involvement by Kennedy and Johnson, now bellowed with outrage that Nixon was withdrawing too slowly. They charged that he was starting a new war when he sent troops into Cambodia to attack North Vietnamese forces in May 1970.

Democrats murmured quiet approval in 1969 when protesters tried to shut the government down during the Moratorium on Washington. Campus demonstrations continued, especially after the "incursion" (Nixon's word) into Cambodia and the fatal shooting of four Kent State University students by Ohio national guardsmen in May 1970.

The China coup. If Nixon failed to salve his critics, he also risked disillusioning many longtime supporters. Back in 1967, long before he conferred with Henry Kissinger, he published an article in *Foreign Affairs* suggesting the opening of diplomatic relations between the United States and mainland China. He wanted to use China to check its former ally, the Soviet Union, and to make the Soviets more amenable to arms control agreements with the United States. In July 1971, he sent Kissinger on a secret mission to China; in February 1972, while Democrats Edmund Muskie and George McGovern were fighting it out in the snows of New Hampshire, Nixon was in China, accompanied by an awed press corps, meeting with Zhou Enlai and Mao Zedong.

On domestic policy he also talked right and moved left. As historian Joan Hoff writes in *Nixon Reconsidered,* he "exceeded the accomplishments of the New Deal and the Great Society in the area of civil rights, social-welfare spending, domestic and international economic restructuring, urban parks, government reorganization, land-use initiatives, revenue sharing, draft reform, pension reform, and spending for the arts and humanities." He embraced many of the goals of the new environmental movement and institutionalized it by creating the Environmental Protection Agency. He transformed American Indian policy from one seeking assimilation to one seeking tribal preservation. Nixon created the Occupational Safety and Health Administration and supported the National Endowment for the Arts. He instituted racial quotas and preferences through his Labor Department's "Philadelphia Plan"—favorite targets of conservative Republicans ever since. In 1970 Nixon pushed hard for Moynihan's Family Assistance Plan, which would have provided a guaranteed annual income for welfare recipients; it was defeated, amazingly enough, by liberals who argued that it was not generous enough.

Nixon never showed the flair for economics that he did for foreign policy. By 1971 Moynihan had returned to Harvard, and Nixon's favorite domestic adviser became John Connally, the former Texas governor injured in the shooting of John Kennedy in 1963 and, though still a Democrat, secretary of the treasury. In August 1971, when inflation had risen to 3.6 percent, Nixon was persuaded by Connally to end the promise made at Bretton Woods to convert dollars to gold and to order wage and price controls. These were astonishing reversals. Bretton Woods maintained price stability in the postwar era, and Nixon had loathed price controls since the 1940s. Inflation in 1971 was not anywhere near a historic high, and the Vietnam War was winding down. But Nixon seemed in thrall to the forceful and confident Connally, whom he would have nominated as vice president to succeed Spiro Agnew in October 1973 if there had been enough votes to confirm him in Congress.

Cynically eyeing the upcoming election, he persuaded the Democratic Congress to increase domestic spending and, in early 1972, cut a deal with House Ways and Means Committee Chairman Wilbur Mills to increase Social Security payments and to index them to inflation. The increases would be reflected in checks delivered Oct. 3, 1972. Previous Social Security increases had been kept down by Mills's firm control of legislation and the desire of presidents to balance the budget. But Mills, perhaps affected by alcoholism, was running a quixotic presidential campaign: This was a bidding war between two candidates desperate for popularity. The federal budget deficits of the 1980s, often blamed on Ronald Reagan's tax cuts and defense spending increases, could just as easily be blamed on Nixon's and Mills's Social Security increases.

The burglary. Nixon entered the 1972 campaign with no certainty that he would win, let alone carry 49 states. In a May 1972 poll, Nixon led the dovish George McGovern by only 48 to 41 percent. But two weeks later Nixon ordered the bombing of Haiphong harbor, and Soviet leader Leonid Brezhnev appeared with him at a summit and agreed to an arms control agreement: It seemed likely the American military involvement in Vietnam was ending and that the Soviets would sign an arms control agreement. By mid-June 1972—precisely the time of the Watergate burglary—Nixon had jumped ahead in the polls and was on his way to his landslide victory.

But it would not be a Republican Party victory. For 1972 Nixon abandoned his 1970 goal of electing a Republican Congress and urged Democrats to split their tickets and vote for him. Much of the money spent by the Committee to Re-elect the President went for ads that featured John Connally arguing that other Democrats should join him in voting for Nixon. No great efforts were made to recruit or elect Republican candidates. Opportunities to elect Republicans in the South, which Nixon carried by more than 2 to 1, were mostly missed, a failing that became important when Southern Democrats abandoned Nixon over Watergate.

Nixon did not understand how the old rules of postwar politics were changing. For years, the press and the public had overlooked the seamy and corrupt tactics of political leaders. The press showed little interest, as Nixon complained later, in vote fraud in Chicago and elsewhere, in Franklin Roosevelt's misuse of the Internal Revenue Service and the FBI, in Robert and John Kennedy's wiretapping of Martin Luther King, in FDR's lunches with his former mistress, or in JFK's constant womanizing. From the Depression through the postwar years, the press felt an obligation to strengthen the public's confidence in the nation's great institutions and leaders.

Paranoid atmosphere. But during the Vietnam War and the turbulence of the 1960s that sense of obligation withered. The press—particularly young reporters—felt an obligation to expose the faults and misdeeds of national institutions and leaders. Nixon's illegal conduct began in response to another illegal act—Daniel Ellsberg's leaking of the Pentagon Papers to the *New York Times,* the *Washington Post,* and other papers. Nixon could have done nothing in response: The documents illustrated the feckless Vietnam policy of the previous administration. But he chose to regard their publication as a breach of national security and sent the Justice Department to court to plead, unsuccessfully, to stop the papers from printing them. He also caused junior staffers to burglarize the safe of Ellsberg's psychiatrist. The daffiness of this enterprise was a sign that Nixon had become unhinged by the virulent opposition of elite liberals who were labeling as a war crime his deescalation—U.S. troop strength was falling by then—of a war their party's president had, with little or no protest from most of them, constantly escalated. This paranoid atmosphere helps to explain why G. Gordon Liddy, in a campaign meeting in Attorney General John Mitchell's office, was not immediately ejected from the room when he proposed the burglary of the Democratic National Committee headquarters in the Watergate office building. The purpose of this crime has never become clear, and there is no evidence that Nixon knew anything about it until sometime after the June 17 break-in.

Nixon quickly decided not to confess that his campaign organization had been behind the burglary and moved to use the CIA to conceal the crime—the obstruction of justice for which the House was ready to impeach him in August 1974. In fact, the crimes might have been concealed but for the maximum sentences handed down to the burglars by Judge John Sirica, the detailed incriminatory testimony of former White House counsel John Dean, and the audiotapes of White House meetings made (and never erased) by Nixon himself. Nixon could argue that other presidents had taped White House meetings and had used irregular, if not criminal, tactics to get back at political enemies. But the public was holding him to a higher standard than previous presidents, and he failed to recognize that attitudes had shifted.

Nixon's political situation was further undermined by a worsening economy. The measures he used to produce a boom in the election year of 1972 were causing a bust in 1973. Wage and price controls were not sustainable. When they were applied to oil after the Organization of Petroleum Exporting Countries' price increases in 1973, they produced gas lines and shortages. By 1974, the nation was beset by both inflation and recession.

Nixon's policies lasted for a generation or longer—a more lasting legacy than any postwar president between Truman and Reagan. His opening to China has set the course for China policy to this day, even though the collapse of communism reduced the need to use China as a counterweight to Russia. His policy of seeking détente and disarmament deals with the Soviet Union continued up through the Reagan years. His Social Security increases permanently ratcheted up benefits and kept old people out of poverty but in a way that is unsustainable into the next century. His environmental, job safety, and Indian policies have been mostly followed by later administrations, with impressive reductions in pollution but at a cost probably larger than necessary. Racial quotas and preferences are firmly embedded as a controversial feature of American society.

Today we are visibly a different nation from the postwar America that elected Nixon to Congress or from the changing America of his days in the White House. The large institutions—big government, big business, big labor—that dominated America in 1946 had by 1969 grown frayed and weakened. Nixon tried to reform government, but often in ways more suited to the waning postwar consensus than to the changing times. Not until the 1980s and 1990s did lower taxes, the less constricted market forces, and privatization allow small businesses to challenge lumbering dinosaurs. In foreign policy, Nixon made it possible for America to co-exist with the Communist powers that seemed fated to become more powerful over time. Not until the 1980s and 1990s did it become apparent that Communist systems were dysfunctional, with the Soviet empire falling apart and China embracing capitalist reforms.

Nixon shared the view, common as he came to office, that market capitalism and political democracy were on the defensive; even as he championed these causes, he like almost everyone else underrated their suppleness and staying power. But he did see, intermittently and with exceptions, that the postwar consensus was fraying and tattered, and that the country needed a new course. This strangely solitary man, so politically knowledgeable yet never a graceful campaigner, so gifted with historical vision yet given to astonishing lapses of judgment, was a president who tried to remake government institutions and policies to fit the new and emerging America. If he did not entirely succeed, he deserves respectful attention for the effort he made. Postwar America did not move gracefully into the quite different America we know today, but its movement was shaped in many ways by Richard Nixon and it cannot be imagined without him.

Face-Off

East-West tension defined the Cold War, but its legacy is the victory of hope over fear

By John Lewis Gaddis

The Cold War began to end 10 years ago, not with any great decision grandly proclaimed but with a hapless official spokesman fumbling his lines. On Nov. 9, 1989, Gunter Schabowski, Berlin district secretary for the ruling East German Communist Party, was *supposed* to announce a decision by his bosses to allow a limited and controlled flow of East Germans through the Berlin Wall, to take effect the next day. This concession would, they hoped, relieve the pressures on the German Democratic Republic that had been mounting throughout the summer and fall, as Mikhail Gorbachev made it increasingly clear that the Soviet Union would no longer prop up its fellow Marxist-Leninist regimes in Eastern Europe. Schabowski slipped up on a detail, however, telling a televised press conference that the new rules were to take effect "immediately, without delay."

Within hours, excited East Berliners had overwhelmed the border guards, forced open the crossing points, and surged into West Berlin, forbidden territory for as long as most of them could remember. Soon they were dancing on top of the wall, chipping away at it with hammers and crowbars, and then quite literally toppling it with bulldozers and backhoes. The very symbol of a continent divided for almost half a century—indeed of a world so divided—came tumbling down, almost overnight.

Nobody on either side had anticipated this: The wall had seemed as permanent a fixture of the Berlin landscape as the Cold War had appeared to be within the post-World War II international system. That such a forbidding structure proved so fragile surprised everyone. But even then, few who witnessed the wall's collapse would have guessed what was soon to come: that the division of Germany would disappear within a year, or that in just over two years the Soviet Union itself would cease to exist.

Today we take for granted what astonished us then: We assume, far more easily than we should, that the process that began with the opening of the Berlin Wall and ended with the Soviet Union's essentially peaceful breakup could *only* have happened in the way that it did. History works like that: Our view of the past is so much clearer than our vision of the future that we tend to forget that the past once had a future, and that it was just as opaque to those who lived through it as our own future is for us today. My college students were between 8 and 11 years old when the Berlin Wall came down. They've known only a pitifully weak Russia that cannot keep its borders secure, its military intact, its economy afloat, or its prime ministers in office. How, they wonder, could such a country have ever caused Americans and their allies to fear for their future?

I suggest, as an answer, a short time-machine trip. Set the dial first for November 1989, the anniversary we're commemorating, to get a sense of the unexpectedness of what happened and of the euphoria it produced. Then go back in 10-year intervals from that event. A very different picture emerges.

November 1979: Jimmy Carter is in his third year as president of the United States, and the mood is anything but euphoric. The American Embassy staff has just been taken hostage in Tehran, following the overthrow of a longtime friend, the shah of Iran. In Nicaragua, the Sandinistas have deposed the Somoza regime, an even older ally. The Soviet Union under Leonid Brezhnev has deployed a new generation of SS-20 missiles aimed at European targets and is openly encouraging Marxist revolutions in what Carter's national-security adviser, Zbigniew Brzezinski, has called an "arc of crisis" running from Southern Africa to Southeast Asia. The Russians are on the verge of invading Afghanistan and are threatening to crack down on Poland, where the Solidarity trade union movement is only beginning to test its capacity for resistance. Still reeling from defeat in Vietnam, the disruptions of Watergate, and a continuing energy crisis, Americans are confronting the prospect of double-digit inflation and unemployment. Détente is dying, if not dead, and a highly visible Committee on the Present Danger has been insisting that if nothing is done to reverse these trends, the credibility of the United States as a superpower will not survive. Ronald Reagan has announced his intention to run for the

The East-West Divide

The Cold War dominated politics for 40 years

■ **MARCH 1946.** Former British Prime Minister Winston Churchill warns the world, during a speech in Fulton, Mo., that an "iron curtain" is descending across Europe.

■ **APRIL 1948.** Start of Marshall Plan, a U.S.-sponsored economic program to aid 16 European nations ravaged by World War II.

■ **JUNE 1948.** Soviet troops block all road, rail, and water traffic between West Berlin and the West. U.S., Britain, and France airlift 2.3 million tons of food and supplies to the city for 15 months.

■ **APRIL 1949.** North Atlantic Treaty Organization (NATO) sets up common defense alliance to counter-weigh Soviet forces in Eastern Europe.

■ **AUGUST 1949.** Soviet Union tests its first atomic bomb.

■ **OCTOBER 1949.** China turns Communist under Mao Zedong's leadership.

■ **JUNE 1950.** North Korean troops invade South Korea. U.S. and 16 other United Nations countries fight alongside South Korea until July 1953 armistice.

■ **JUNE 1953.** Soviet troops quell anti-Communist revolts in East Germany.

■ **MAY 1955.** Warsaw Pact signed by Soviet Union and seven Eastern European countries to ensure unified command against NATO.

■ **NOVEMBER 1956.** Soviet tanks crush national rebellion against communism in Hungary. Thousands flee to the West.

■ **MAY 1960.** American U-2 reconnaissance plane shot down over Sverdlovsk, Russia. Pilot Francis Gary Powers survives and in August is sentenced to 10 years' confinement in U.S.S.R. In 1962 Powers is exchanged for Soviet spy Rudolf Abel.

■ **APRIL 1961.** U.S.-sponsored invasion of Cuba by 1,500 Cuban exiles opposed to Fidel Castro fails at Bay of Pigs. Between 1962 and 1965, Cuba releases captured prisoners in exchange for $53 million worth of food and medicine.

■ **APRIL 1961.** Soviet cosmonaut Yuri Gagarin gains worldwide fame as first man to travel in space aboard the Vostok 1 spacecraft.

■ **AUGUST 1961.** East Germany erects Berlin Wall to stem increasing flight of its citizens to the West.

■ **OCTOBER 1962.** President John Kennedy orders naval blockade of Cuba to prevent Soviet shipments of nuclear missiles. Threat of nuclear war recedes when Soviet Premier Nikita Khrushchev halts work on launch sites and removes missiles already in Cuba.

■ **AUGUST 1963.** Nuclear Test-Ban Treaty prohibits nuclear-weapons tests in the atmosphere, underwater, and in space.

■ **AUGUST 1964.** Congress authorizes expansion of U.S. involvement in Vietnam after North Vietnamese torpedo boats attack two American destroyers.

■ **AUGUST 1968.** Troops from the Soviet Union, East Germany, Poland, Hungary, and Bulgaria invade Czechoslovakia to prevent political reforms.

■ **FEBRUARY 1972.** President Richard Nixon reopens severed ties with China during 10-day official visit.

■ **MAY 1972.** SALT I agreements curtail Soviet and U.S. nuclear-arms race by limiting antiballistic missile systems.

■ **APRIL 1975.** Vietnam War ends as Communist North Vietnamese forces occupy Saigon without resistance.

■ **DECEMBER 1979.** Soviet Army invades Afghanistan on Christmas Day. Soviets suffer 60,000 casualties in nine-year war against Afghan guerrillas.

■ **SEPTEMBER 1980.** Independent trade union, Solidarity, founded in Poland under Lech Walesa.

■ **MARCH 1985.** Mikhail Gorbachev launches economic and political restructuring program dubbed "perestroika."

■ **NOVEMBER 1989** Fall of Berlin Wall. East German government opens the country's borders with West Germany.

■ **OCTOBER 1990.** East and West Germany reunify under NATO auspices and with Soviet approval.

■ **DECEMBER 1991.** Soviet reformer Gorbachev resigns from office. The Soviet Union collapses, ending 74 years of Soviet communism.

---

presidency, precisely with a view to restoring it.

November 1969: The United States is mired in an unwinnable war in Southeast Asia. Although Richard Nixon's new administration has promised gradually to withdraw American troops, some 500,000 remain in Vietnam—most disillusioned about their mission, many demoralized and on drugs, and some even challenging the authority of their officers. The Air Force is secretly bombing enemy sanctuaries in Cambodia, while at home antiwar protests have mounted to such an extent that Nixon has had to ask the "silent majority" of Americans to help him avoid national humiliation. The Soviet Union has overtaken the United States in the production and deployment of intercontinental ballistic missiles, thereby ending an American

> **Flashpoints.** *East Berlin, 1953: Workers clash with riot police. Prague, 1968: Soviet tanks crush Czechoslovakia's hopes for reform.*

superiority in strategic weaponry that had prevailed since the beginning of the Cold War. In striking contrast to the Americans' failure in Vietnam, the Soviet Union has crushed Alexander Dubcek's reform movement in Czechoslovakia and has threatened to respond similarly to such experiments elsewhere. China, still in the throes of Chairman Mao Zedong's Great Cultural Revolution, is preparing for nuclear war—not with the United States, as one might have expected, but with its erstwhile ideological ally. How would the Americans react, a Soviet diplomat has discreetly inquired in Washington, if the Russians were to launch a pre-emptive strike against the Chinese?

November 1959: Soviet space achievements—the first ICBM, the first artificial Earth satellite—have caused a crisis of confidence in the United States, where an aging Dwight Eisenhower is presiding over a country seriously worried about its apparent inferiority in science and technology. The Soviet leader is the ebulliently bumptious Nikita Khrushchev, who is claiming to be turning out rockets "like sausages," capable of devastating any point on the face of the Earth. He has challenged the exposed position of the United States and its allies in West Berlin, has exploited growing anti-American sentiment in the Middle East, and has just returned from a highly publicized visit to the United States, where he repeated his frequent prediction that America's grandchildren would live under communism. Just to the south, a young guerrilla fighter and occasional baseball player named Fidel Castro has come to power in Cuba—with the result that the former playground for American gangsters and vacationers already seems well along the path that Khrushchev has laid out.

November 1949: Joseph Stalin is alive and in command inside the Kremlin, while Harry S. Truman is president of the United States. The Soviet Union has consolidated its post-World War II sphere of influence in Eastern Europe, forcing the United States to respond with the Truman Doctrine, the Marshall Plan, and most recently the North Atlantic Treaty Organization—an unprecedented peacetime commitment to the defense of an increasingly desperate Western Europe. The Russians have just exploded their first atomic bomb, several years earlier than expected, and Truman is under pressure to respond by building thermonuclear weapons with a thousand times the destructive power of the device the Americans had dropped, only four years before, on Hiroshima. Mao has proclaimed the People's Republic of China and will soon depart for Moscow to forge a Sino-Soviet alliance, thereby confirming communist control over most of the Eurasian continent. Allegations of espionage within the United States are creating an atmosphere of near hysteria, which Sen. Joseph McCarthy will soon exploit and which his critics will name for him. Meanwhile, George Orwell has published *1984,* a profoundly pessimistic vision of survival in an apparently endless Cold War.

What this brief trip through time suggests is that for anyone living in November of 1949, 1959, 1969, or 1979, the Cold War's outcome would not have been at all clear. If anything, it looked as though the Soviet Union and its allies might win: There was a remarkable gap between what people *thought* was hap-

Confrontation. *The Soviet Union closed all land routes from the West to Berlin in 1948. Britain and the United States responded with a massive airlift.*

pening and what we now know to have happened. Fears outweighed hopes for so long that when the latter actually prevailed it was a completely unexpected development.

It's now the historians' task to explain this triumph of hopes over fears. It helps to have partial access to Soviet, Eastern European, and Chinese archives. Before the Cold War ended, the American public had more than enough information from Western sources to expose the shortcomings of the United States and its allies, but historians could only hint at those that may have existed on the other side. We now know much more, and what emerges is a pattern of brutality, shortsightedness, inefficiency, vulnerability, and mistrust within the Marxist-Leninist world that dates back to the earliest days of the Cold War.

Just as important, though, is our knowledge of how the Cold War turned out. The view from inside any historical event is bound to be limited—and the Cold War was an unusually protracted event. We have a better sense now of where it's going to fit within the long sweep of history. And we can see, more clearly, why so much of what the West feared never came to pass.

A list of such fears, for an American at the end of 1949, might well have included the following: that, as Orwell's novel suggested, authoritarianism could be the wave of the future; that, as the Marshall Plan and NATO implied, Europe was in danger of becoming a Soviet sphere of influence; that, as Mao's victory seemed to indicate, international communism was a coordinated, monolithic movement; that, as the Soviet atomic bomb appeared to show, a new and far more devastating world war

34. Face-Off

loomed on the horizon; that, as the spy cases revealed, the nation's most closely held secrets were transparent to the enemy. Today, half a century later, we can see how each of these fears became hopes, and then accomplishments, and then the means by which the West prevailed in the Cold War.

■ **Authoritarianism.** It was not at all unreasonable in 1949 to have feared the eventual triumph of authoritarianism: Democracy and capitalism had hardly enhanced their reputation during the 1930s, and the United States and Great Britain had defeated Nazi Germany in World War II only by collaborating with Stalin's Soviet Union. There were plenty of people who, during those difficult years of Depression and war, saw at least a short-term denial of liberties as a necessary evil and found a certain allure in a vision of socialism they hoped would overcome the shortcomings of capitalism. But as postwar economic recovery proceeded, it began to reward lateral rather than hierarchical forms of organization: Only the decentralized, largely spontaneous market system could make the millions of decisions required each day if the supply and demand of goods and services was to be kept in balance. And with freedoms so obviously suppressed in the authoritarian East even as they flourished in the democratic West, it became increasingly hard to see how coercion could ever lead to equity. It was no coincidence, then, that as the Cold War neared its end, democracies were replacing, rather than succumbing to, dictatorships. Or that the first modern examples of what Marx understood a proletarian revolution to be—a spontaneous mass movement led by workers and intellectuals, aimed at achieving liberty and justice—occurred only in Eastern Europe in 1989 and in the Soviet Union in 1991.

■ **Spheres of influence.** We can now see, as a consequence, that the spheres of influence the United States and the Soviet Union maintained in Europe were always asymmetrical: The first existed by invitation, the second by imposition. Stalin may well have expected the Europeans to welcome him as a liberator at the end of World War II, but when that did not happen—largely because his regime's reputation preceded its armies—he could establish his authority only by imposing it. But that caused the Europeans beyond his reach to invite the Americans to remain as a counterweight. Europe was divided, as a result, but there was dissimilarity in the division: Washington's sphere of influence arose by consent; Moscow's by denying it. That distinction made all the difference in how the Cold War came out, because it allowed the NATO countries to legitimize the American presence through free elections that repeatedly ratified it. No such opportunities existed within the Warsaw Pact: hence the ease with which it fell apart in 1989–90 when the only glue that had kept it together—Moscow's determination to use force—itself dissolved.

■ **International communism.** The consolidation of Soviet authority in Eastern Europe, together with Mao's victory in China, caused many Americans in 1949 to worry that the Kremlin commanded not only the traditional resources of a great state but also the subversive capabilities of a purposefully expansionist ideology. If Marxism-Leninism continued to advance as it had since the end of World War II, then the Western democracies could find themselves surrounded by hostile communist states. What happened instead, though, was that as communists took over states, the states took over the communists. Quarrels over how to align a common ideology with dissimilar national interests led first the Yugoslavs, and then the Chinese, and then the Poles, Hungarians, and Czechs, to challenge Moscow's authority. By the 1970s the American diplomat W. Averell Harriman could point out, with total accuracy, that it was the *Soviet Union* that now found itself surrounded by hostile communist states. And by the end of the 1980s, so little was left of the international communist movement that it was difficult to remember why the West had ever feared it in the first place.

■ **The bomb.** The Soviet atomic bomb also alarmed the West in 1949, but its effect over the long run was to make war with the United States not more likely but less so. The single most important characteristic of the Cold War—

Setting the Record Straight

Archives slowly yielding their secrets

There is much we still don't know—and may never know—about the Cold War. But once-secret documents are providing a glimpse into key events and showing that some of what we do know—or think we know—is wrong. Among the findings:

■ Moscow secretly deployed 100 nuclear warheads in Cuba during the 1962 missile crisis, making the era's most dangerous standoff even scarier in retrospect.

■ President Eisenhower in 1957 gave U.S. military commanders *advance* permission to use nuclear weapons if they were in danger of being overwhelmed by a Soviet attack and could not reach him.

East-bloc archives have provided the most important new revelations, showing that communism wasn't a monolith:

■ Stalin reluctantly approved North Korea's June 1950 attack on the South (Kim Il Sung pestered him with 48 telegrams), believing the United States would not respond militarily. Stalin may have been motivated more by intramural competition with Mao Zedong, newly victorious in China, than by the global struggle with the United States. U.S. officials thought the attack was a Soviet foray that had to be met head on, a misjudgement that led to America's re-armament and eventual involvement in Vietnam.

In many other instances, Moscow's clients called the tune (or tried to), says Christian Ostermann, director of the Woodrow Wilson Center's Cold War International History Project:

■ East German leader Walter Ulbricht was the driving force behind the Berlin Wall, not a hesistant Soviet Premier Nikita Khrushchev.

■ Former Polish leader Wojciech Jaruzelski has long maintained he imposed martial law in 1981 to forestall a Soviet invasion. A Soviet general's diary indicates the opposite: Jaruzelski pleaded fruitlessly for Moscow to intervene, fearing he could not handle the challenge posed by Solidarity alone.

But the communist threat was no chimera:

The U.S. Venona code-breaking project and KGB archives belatedly removed any doubt that dozens of Moscow spies penetrated the U.S. government and the scientific community. While not every U.S. communist in the '30s and '40s was a spy, the U.S. party actively helped the Soviet Union. But Joe McCarthy isn't vindicated. By the time he began sounding off on the issue, Moscow had already cut ties to U.S. Communists. "What is vindicated is the much broader and more general... anticommunism of the postwar period," says historian John Haynes.

Also vindicated: fears about KGB dirty tricks. *The Sword and the Shield,* a new book based on secret KGB archives, details how Moscow tried to smear U.S. leaders ranging from Martin Luther King Jr. to President Reagan, obsessed over famous Soviet dissidents and planned sabotage in America and Europe.

—*Warren P. Strobel*

---

the reason we attach the adjective to the noun—is that it went on for so long with such high levels of tension without ever producing a direct military clash between its major antagonists. The obvious explanation is nuclear weapons, which expanded the potential arena of military conflict to such an extent that the superpowers had no way of fighting each other with any assurance of keeping their own territories insulated from the resulting violence. Since wars had mostly arisen, in the past, over the *protection* of territory, this was a fundamental change in the way nations thought about, and used, military force. The Cold War may well be remembered as the point at which the costs of hot wars, at least among the great powers, became too exorbitant, the benefits too problematic, and the issues that had always before provoked such wars too insignificant. The fact that the Soviet Union collapsed with its military power intact is as eloquent an indication as one might want of such power's ultimate irrelevance.

■ **Espionage.** Even the spies look less sinister now than they did in 1949, despite the fact that we now know there were more of them than anyone then suspected. For the Cold War also changed our thinking about secrecy. Whereas the idea in the past had been to *conceal* information from enemies, a paradoxical side effect of ICBMs was the reconnaissance satellite, from which very little could be concealed. The Americans and the Russians soon saw the benefits of this new technology and agreed tacitly to tolerate it: Neither side made any effort to shoot down such spies in space, as a well-known spy in the sky, U-2 pilot Francis Gary Powers, had been shot down over the Soviet Union in 1960. The strategic arms limitation agreements of the 1970s could hardly have worked without overhead surveillance. But if transparency made sense when it came to the arms race, might it have at earlier stages of the Cold War? We know little, as yet, about how Stalin used the information his spies provided. There is reason to suspect, though, that on balance it reassured him by minimizing the possibility of surprise, just as reconnaissance satellites did for a subsequent generation of Cold War leaders. If that is the case, then some future historian may well revise what we think of the spies as well, finding that even in those deep fears there was some hope.

The world has spent the past half-century having its worst fears not confirmed. That is a big difference from the way in which it spent the first half of this century, when the opposite happened. No one could have anticipated, in 1900, that the next five decades would see unprecedented violence, including two world wars, a nearly successful effort to wipe out an entire people, and the invention of the most lethal form of military technology in human history.

But it is equally the case that few people at the beginning of 1950 could have imagined that the five decades to follow would witness great-power peace—that, although the world was hardly free from violence and injustice during the second half of the 20th century, the record was decidedly preferable to that of the first half. Fears did become hopes, although it took us a while to begin to realize what was happening. With the dancing feet, and then the hammers and crowbars, and then the bulldozers and backhoes at the Berlin Wall, however, a certain amount of progress in human affairs became difficult to deny.

John Lewis Gaddis is Robert A. Lovett professor of history at Yale University. His most recent book is We Now Know: Rethinking Cold War History.

United at last.
Doing what was for more than 40 years unthinkable, East Berliners used crowbars and sledgehammers to tear down the wall on Nov. 9, 1989.

Unit 6

Unit Selections

35. **The Near-Myth of Our Failing Schools,** Peter Schrag
36. **Divided We Sprawl,** Bruce Katz and Jennifer Bradley
37. **A Politics for Generation X,** Ted Halstead

Key Points to Consider

❖ Analyze the article on our "failing schools." Is the author persuasive in rejecting crosscultural and historical comparisons of performance as invalid?

❖ Discuss ways in which integration of cities with their surrounding suburbs may be achieved. What forces will oppose such integration?

❖ Contrast the goals and aspirations of young adults today with those of their parents and grandparents. What are the likely changes these new attitudes will bring about?

Links www.dushkin.com/online/

27. **American Studies Web**
    http://www.georgetown.edu/crossroads/asw/
28. **National Center for Policy Analysis**
    http://www.public-policy.org/~ncpa/pd/pdindex.html
29. **The National Network for Immigrant and Refugee Rights (NNIRR)**
    http://www.nnirr.org
30. **STANDARDS: An International Journal of Multicultural Studies**
    http://www.colorado.edu/journals/standards
31. **Supreme Court/Legal Information Institute**
    http://supct.law.cornell.edu/supct/index.html

These sites are annotated on pages 4 and 5.

New Directions for American History

The collapse of the Soviet Union and the end of the cold war was welcomed by those who feared a great power confrontation might mean all-out nuclear conflict. At the same time, these events deprived American foreign policy of a unifying theme. The "peace dividend" that some had hoped for never materialized, and conflicts around the world presented American policymakers with a bewildering variety of choices. At home the United States entered a period of unprecedented prosperity that continues to this writing. Serious social and economic problems remain, however, and whether they will be overcome in the forseeable future is uncertain. This unit provides a sampling of essays on some of the issues that must be confronted.

Many Americans fear that our educational system is failing to prepare our young people adequately for a new age. The news media periodically trumpet some study showing how badly American students perform in reading and mathematics compared with their counterparts in other nations. Individuals and groups often use these alarming statistics to promote some agenda with regard to American education. Peter Schrag, in "The Near-Myth of Our Failing Schools," shows how crosscultural and historical comparisons of performance can be misleading. Without minimizing what is wrong with our schools, Schrag argues that they are not doing as badly as many people think. "The dumbest thing we could do," he concludes, "is to scrap what we're doing right."

The United States is becoming a suburban nation. Many cities are rapidly losing population to the suburbs because of high crime rates, steep taxes, and poor schools. This exodus has the effect of depriving the cities of the tax base they so desperately need, thereby aggravating urban problems. "Divided We Sprawl" deplores the tendency to treat cities and suburbs as separate entities, and offers a number of recommendations to help integrate them into larger communities.

Young adults today differ in many respects from their parents and grandparents with regard to their allegiance to political parties, their concept of "patriotism, and a host of other matters. "A Politics for Generation X" examines these differences, and speculates on whether their attitudes and goals will prevail in the future.

The Near-Myth of Our Failing Schools

Ideologically inspired lamentations about the parlous state of American education mask the much more complex truth

by Peter Schrag

In the spring of 1991, as warnings accumulated that America's second-rate schools were dooming the nation to permanent failure in the global economy, systems analysts at Sandia National Laboratories, a federal institution of generally impeccable reputation, compiled a lengthy report showing that the picture in American education was far more complex—and in many respects a great deal less gloomy—than the rhetoric of alarm allowed. But for two years the report—a collection of tables and statistics on everything from dropout rates and SAT scores to college degrees awarded in engineering and other technical fields—was buried by the Department of Energy, which had commissioned it. The document, said James Watkins, George Bush's Secretary of Energy, was "dead wrong," and would be regarded as "a call for complacency at a time when just the opposite is required." It had a small underground circulation, but even after the Clinton

---

Peter Schrag writes frequently on education and politics. He is the author of Paradise Lost: The California Experience and the American Future.

Good news undermines the sense of crisis essential both to liberal demands for more money and to conservative arguments for vouchers and other radical solutions.

Administration finally released it, in 1993, neither the Sandia data nor similar findings from other sources got much attention. Mixed reports don't make for good headlines, and qualified good news undermines the sense of crisis essential both to liberal demands for more money and to conservative arguments that only vouchers and other radical solutions will do. Good news, even qualified good news, runs counter to the conventional wisdom and undermines almost everybody's agenda of reform.

It was always thus: in the late 1950s, after the launching of *Sputnik*; in the early 1980s, after publication of the federal report *A Nation at Risk*, which warned that the failures of the nation's schools were about to undermine America's ability to compete economically; in 1989, when President George Bush and the nation's governors initiated what came to be called Goals 2000, pledging to make this country the world leader in education by the year 2000; in 1993, when President Bill Clinton and a Democratic Congress followed that up with legislation to develop voluntary national standards in English, history, science, and other fields; and in 1995–1996, when that same effort collapsed in controversy and dispute over the standards that were produced.

Now, as President Clinton is calling yet again for higher school standards, and for a program of national testing in reading and math, the same assumptions of crisis and failure that have fueled every other recent reform debate are being invoked. The debate is driven once again by our favorite myths: that there was once a golden age, an era when schools maintained rigorous academic standards, when all children learned, when few dropped out and most graduated on time; that sometime in the past generation or so (most commonly pegged to the 1960s) the system began to fall apart under a siege of social promotion, grade inflation, and progressive mush that is leaving America helpless against superior foreign education; and that the large amounts of new money that have gone to the schools in the past generation have largely been wasted. House Speaker Newt Gingrich and the University of California regent Ward Connerly, who spearheaded California's drive against race-based affirmative action, wrote in a recent *New York Times* op-ed piece,

> The education bureaucracy won't concede that, despite spending trillions of dollars on education over the past 30 years, American children are further behind today. It doesn't want to admit that the S.A.T. scores of African-American children, which average 100 points less than the scores of white children, are the direct result of the current [Great Society] policies.

In some places, circumstances, and contexts, some of those criticisms are correct. Many schools are academically flabby, mindless, and laced with an anti-intellectualism sometimes bordering on outright sabotage; some are wastelands of crime, drugs, and despair; many are afflicted by multicultural fashion and politically correct clichés. Some are run by arrogant, rigid bureaucracies or crippled by unions that make it impossible to move any teacher with seniority, let alone fire the bad ones, and classrooms are often without a regular teacher for the first month of school while the seniority system slowly determines who may be assigned where. Many schools don't demand nearly as much as they should. But many others suffer from few of those things, and without a more realistic sense of what is going on—a better understanding of the myths—the country will never get beyond the horror stories and ideological set pieces that seem endlessly to dominate the education debate.

MISLEADING STATISTICS AND COMPARISONS

Among the Sandia findings, many of them corroborated by other studies, are the following: High school completion rates—now roughly 90 percent—and college graduation rates are the highest in history. One in four adult Americans has at least a bachelor's degree—the highest percentage in the world (and the percentage keeps getting higher). A larger percentage of twenty-two-year-olds receive degrees in math, science, or engineering in the United States than in any of the nation's major economic competitors. Although SAT verbal scores declined over the years 1975 to 1990, the decline occurred chiefly because a larger percentage of lower-ranking students (those from the bottom half of their school classes) began taking the test. If the same population that took the SATs in 1975 had taken them this year, the average score would be significantly higher than it was then—and higher than it was in 1990.

Because of reforms instituted in the 1980s, more American high school students than ever before are taking four years of English and at least three years of math and science. Far more are taking and passing Advanced Placement examinations (198,000 in 1978 and 535,000 in 1996). More teachers, for all the flaws in our teacher training-and-reward system, are subject to tough standards for certification and promotion.

To be sure, as the Sandia report recognized, on tests like the Third International Mathematics and Science Study and other international comparisons of academic achievement American students continue to score lower than their peers in Singapore, Taiwan, Japan, Korea, and elsewhere. Whereas parents of high-achieving students in Japan or China worry that their children are not doing well enough and ought to work still harder, among parents of American students who are scoring far less well on the same tests "satisfaction with . . . students' achievement and education remains high and standards remain low," according to a team led by the University of Michigan psychologist Harold W. Stevenson. "Innate ability [not diligence or high expectations] continues to be emphasized by Americans as a basis for achievement." Stevenson's collaborator James Stigler, of the University of California at Los Angeles, has found an academic intensity in Japanese classes that is almost unthinkable in this country. Many American universities, including even as selective an institution as the University of California, continue to provide remedial courses to their freshmen; a quarter of the students entering UCLA are required to take what used to be called bonehead English, and nearly a third of those entering the University of California system as a whole are.

But as Iris Rotberg, a professor at George Washington University, points out, cross-cultural comparisons of academic achievement are tough to make. Many countries begin specialized education at age fourteen or even earlier, which means that some students have already left school and many others have begun cramming for (in the words of the Sandia report) the "life determining tests . . . that specify their eventual position in the workforce." Many lower-achieving students in Great Britain and other countries have by age seventeen already been tracked into job-training programs or have simply left school and thus are not included in the test samples, making comparisons meaningless. (For example, England and Wales rank near the bottom in international math comparisons of eighth-grade students; in comparisons of twelfth-graders, only six percent of whom in England take math, they rank near the top.) Intense competition in places like Singapore and Japan for good university slots and other rewards that will have consequences for a lifetime must wonderfully concentrate the mind.

The late Albert Shanker, for many years the president of the American Federation of Teachers, argued persuasively that the fierce competition in other countries is hardly an excuse for a U.S. system in which academic success or failure has so few consequences—for either teachers or students—and in which so little fosters intense academic effort. Even the best American students, he argued, do not perform as well as their peers elsewhere. Questions that all college-bound nineteen-year-olds in France or Great Britain are expected to answer would be impossible for most graduating seniors here. But the debate ought to make the complexity and ambiguities of the larger issue obvious enough. Which is better for the student—

to have the discipline that intense competition for relatively few college openings brings, or to have ample opportunity?

MISLEADING HISTORICAL COMPARISONS

What is true of cross-cultural comparisons is even more emphatically true of historical ones. Precisely when was the golden age of American education that the conventional wisdom assumes existed? Was it in the early years of this century, when, as the education historian Colin Greer pointed out years ago, "All minority groups, white as well as black, with the exceptions of the English, Scots, Germans, and Scandinavians, were negatively portrayed" in American textbooks; when "Jews, Italians, Chinese and blacks were mean, criminal, immoral, drunken, sly, lazy, and stupid in varying degrees"? Was it in the 1920s, when most students never went beyond the eighth grade, when large numbers of children, especially in the South, never went to school at all from April to November, and when no one had ever heard of any such concept as the dropout rate? Was it in the 1930s and 1940s, when even the more enlightened medical schools had strict quotas for Jews and blacks, and the others systematically excluded them, as did a great many other educational institutions as well? Was it in the 1950s, when the historian Arthur Bestor published *Educational Wastelands: The Retreat From Learning in Our Public Schools* (reissued, significantly, in a new edition in 1985), when Rudolf Flesch's *Why Johnny Can't Read* was long a best seller, and when the schools were thought to be failing because, with the launching of *Sputnik*, the Russians had beaten us into space? Was it in 1963, when Admiral Hyman Rickover published *American Education, a National Failure?*

Consider our contemporary why-Johnny-can't-read arguments. In 1987 Chester Finn and Diane Ravitch, two of the country's most thoughtful conservative school critics, published a set of statistics and related data about what American students don't know about their own history and literature. The book title took the form of a question, *What Do Our 17-Year-Olds Know?*, and the answer was unequivocal. "If there were such a thing as a national report card," Finn and Ravitch wrote, "then we would have to say that this nationally representative sample of 11th-grade students earns failing marks in both subjects." But as at least some parents have noticed, and as Gerald Bracey, a prolific debunker of schools-are-failing stories, reported in the journal *Phi Delta Kappan* in March of 1995, students may in fact know more than their parents and grandparents do. In any case, Bracey showed, such complaints are hardly new. In 1943 *The New York Times*, citing findings by the historian Allan Nevins, reported its shock at discovering that

> a large majority of [college] students showed that they had virtually no knowledge of elementary aspects of American history [and] could not identify such names as Abraham Lincoln, Thomas Jefferson, Andrew Jackson, or Theodore Roosevelt.... Some students believed that George Washington was president during the War of 1812.... St. Louis was placed on the Pacific Ocean, Lake Huron, Lake Erie, the Atlantic Ocean, Ohio River, and almost every place else.

Similarly, the college students described Walt Whitman as a missionary, a pioneer, a colonizer, an unpatriotic writer, a humorist, an English poet, and (not surprising in the days of Paul Whiteman) a band leader. Plus ça change . . .

Chester Finn and like-minded people point to scores on the National Assessment of Educational Progress (NAEP), widely considered to be among the most reliable measures of academic achievement, to show how little progress has been made from the late 1970s to the present, despite the orgy of curricular reforms and the growing amounts of money that have been appropriated for K–12 schools in most states over the past decade. But rarely do these people point to the changing demographics of the American school—the growing proportion of students whose native language is something other than English (now more than 25 percent in California, and nearly half in Los Angeles), and the growing proportion of students from poor or one-parent families. A Rand analysis of the same NAEP scores, issued in December of 1994, shows that although overall scores for students aged thirteen and seventeen didn't rise much from 1970 to 1990, scores for all ethnic subgroups were up (three percentage points for whites, eleven points for Hispanics, nineteen points for blacks). And although one reason for that change was that the parents were better educated (in 1970, 38 percent of mothers had not finished high school; in 1990 the figure was 17 percent), Rand's researchers concluded that the gains for blacks and Hispanics were larger than any change in family characteristics could explain. Whether the gains were a direct effect or a second-generation effect of the parents' better schooling, public investment, contrary to the conservative critics, had made a difference.

CONTRADICTORY OBJECTIVES

That the same charges now being directed at the schools were leveled a half century ago is hardly reason to ignore them, but it does say something about those myths. Editorials in *The Wall Street Journal*, a newspaper long devoted to the cause of school vouchers, often complain that Americans spend more per pupil in their public schools than the French or the Germans and get less in return. But what goes unmentioned is that the French and the Germans spend more on health and child care, public transportation, and related social services (not counted in their school spending, though it often is part of ours), and that theirs are for the most part still monocultural societies with less social pathology. Nor is it generally recognized that most of the growth in American school spending in the past three decades has gone for special education for the ballooning numbers of students officially considered handicapped or disabled, a designation that hardly existed in the years immediately after the Second World War. The Sandia report estimates that from 1960 to 1988 constant-dollar spending for "regular" students increased by 39 percent per pupil while spending for all students increased by roughly 150 percent. The difference is almost entirely accounted for by special education, which, as the report points out, can have little impact on average performance on national standardized tests. (Among unfunded federal mandates special education, which diverts huge sums from the regular classroom, is certainly one of the most costly.)

Another myth is that Americans really do want schools with high academic standards, and would get them if the education establishment didn't stand in their way.

None of this is meant to deny the system's enormous problems and failures—crime, drugs, arteriosclerotic bureaucracies, self-serving unions, decaying facilities, vocational-education programs a half century out of date—or to suggest that all our students are doing splendidly. Despite the glories of a higher-education system that, even after the sharp tuition increases and the cutbacks in public funding of the past few years, is still the world's most accessible and abundant, Albert Shanker was right: as long as so few real rewards are given for distinction and so few real penalties exacted for failure, the educational process will tend to remain lackadaisical and inefficient. The question is whether Americans will ever tolerate anything more demanding. Equally important, the schools are so riven with contradictory objectives—merit versus inclusion, for example—and so loaded down with extraneous social mandates for everything from drug education and AIDS counseling to diversity training and social awareness (often imposed by the same politicians who complain about school failure) that it's a wonder anyone learns anything. But flat generalizations about crisis and failure, the superiority of foreign schools, or the glorious past will do nothing to solve the problems.

WHO WANTS RIGOR?

Which brings us to yet another myth: that Americans—and parents in particular—really do want schools with high academic standards, and would get them if the education establishment didn't stand in their way. In *Inside American Education* (1993) Thomas Sowell, of the Hoover Institution, listed the usual complaints, from the travesties of sex education and the overemphasis on school sports to the pressure for political correctness in curricula. But if he had ever been to a school-board meeting where someone proposed making it harder for students with bad grades to play football, he'd know that it's not only educationists who foist this stuff on the system. Ross Perot's first great public campaign—for tougher school standards in Texas—wasn't against teachers but against ordinary folks all across Texas. The censors and the enemies of high standards come as often from outside the system as from inside. They may be religious fundamentalists fighting the teaching of evolution or demanding equal time for creationism in science programs, or complaining about witches and secular humanism in reading textbooks and dirty words in novels. They may be gays complaining that Michelangelo and Tchaikovsky are not identified in the history books as homosexual, or black self-esteemers blocking the adoption of updated history texts because they're short on the civilizations of Africa (even though the older texts don't mention them at all). They may be civil-rights groups demanding that *The Adventures of Huckleberry Finn* be taken out of the syllabus because it contains the word "nigger," or opposing tougher standards because they fear that more poor children will fail. Clinton's new proposal for national testing is already under assault from groups that include the Mexican American Legal Defense and Educational Fund and FairTest on the left, and the Christian Coalition and Phyllis Schlafly's Eagle Forum on the right. (The right, Chester Finn has said, doesn't like anything with the word "national" in it; the left doesn't like anything with the word "testing.") In addition, groups all across the spectrum have fought over the content and requirements of every form of educational testing, asserting that the SAT is biased against minorities and women, that the (now defunct) California CLAS test was too intrusive into the personal lives of students and their families and didn't focus enough on the basics, that yet another test simply demands too much. And then there are the age-old fights (in and outside the schools) about phonics versus whole language, math facts versus constructivism, progressivism versus drill-and-kill. Of course the school establishment is not an innocent in these things, but it is hardly the only culprit. Virtually every national poll shows that although only a fifth of Americans rate the nation's public schools very highly, some 70 percent of us think that the schools our own children attend are doing just fine—a phenomenon that Finn calls "retail complacency." We could be wrong on either count, or on both, but things are obviously not quite as simple as the rhetoric of failure suggests. Anti-intellectualism is as American as apple pie.

THE WEAK ECONOMIC ARGUMENT

There was a time when American schools were known for their successes: the children of immigrants who made it to City College or Columbia or Harvard and went on to have professional careers. Dropouts and failures simply vanished into the large market for unskilled labor. Now the schools tend to be known for their failures: dropouts, kids who bring guns to school, students who score lower than their counterparts abroad. We forget that we are trying to take children from an unprecedented array of ethnic and cultural backgrounds, many of them speaking little or no English, and educate them all to a level of sophistication never imagined for so large a proportion of any population.

A few years ago our presumed failure to do that was blamed for what was regarded as the nation's slipping competitiveness against the Germans and the

Japanese, but now that the business pages—and the front pages, too—are celebrating a triumphant economic recovery, no one credits the schools. The old litany simply continues. In 1995, at yet another "national summit" in Washington on "world-class education for all America's children," business people blithely reiterated that American students were being insufficiently educated for the global economy in which they will have to survive. All assumed that if young people were well enough educated, great jobs would await them; none seemed concerned that since 1979, according to the Bureau of Labor Statistics, real wages have declined for all men except those with more education than four years of college. The business people did not mention that increasing numbers of college graduates were doing jobs that required no college training at all—that, as *Phi Delta Kappan* reported a couple of years ago, the number of college-educated door-to-door salesmen, for example, grew from 57,000 in 1983 to 75,000 in 1990, and the number of bus drivers with bachelor's degrees rose from 99,000 to 166,000. The job market for college graduates has surely improved with the economic recovery, but the boom will not last forever either.

In 1995, when the University of Illinois surveyed its 1994 graduates about whether their college training was being put to good use, nearly 40 percent said they regarded themselves as overqualified. In the early 1990s Sam Ginn, the chairman of Pacific Telesis, went around California talking about how his company had given seventh-grade reading tests to 6,400 applicants for operator positions and only 2,700 had passed. He didn't point out that the jobs paid less than $7.00 an hour, or that since the company had only 700 jobs to offer, there were almost four qualified applicants for every available slot. For such problems a lot of fixes are needed, many of them only remotely connected with the schools.

The Stanford University educationist Larry Cuban may well have been right when he said, "The myth of better schools as the engine for a leaner, stronger economy was a scam from the very beginning." Yet even if he wasn't, economic recovery has changed the basis for argument. It's hard to read without embarrassment a statement like the one from *A Nation at Risk* about how the country must reform its educational system "if only to keep and improve on the slim competitive edge that we still retain in world markets." But the obsolescence of the economic rationale hardly weakens the case for better schools and higher standards, particularly in the inner cities, from which a disproportionate number of the nation's school failures have always come. On the contrary, it returns our attention to the broader case for good public education—the desirability of a liberally educated community, Thomas Jefferson's argument about the importance of an enlightened citizenry, the desperate need to end our cycles of poverty and to apply resources accordingly. But those objectives require a far more realistic appreciation of what we have done in our educational system in the past, what we are doing now, and what we think we want to do. Despite the problems encountered by Goals 2000 and Clinton's national-standards effort, the trend of the past few years—surely a healthy one—has been to find ways to set broad goals and standards, and to free local schools and teachers to accomplish them in their own ways. But those things can be done only if we can see the results without ideological blinders, if the tests and assessments we use really measure what we want to know, and if we have the confidence to support the schools that this society needs. A growing number of people, in the name of world-class standards, would abandon, through vouchers, privatization, and other means, the idea of the common school altogether. Before we do that, we'd better be sure that things are really as bad as we assume. The dumbest thing we could do is scrap what we're doing right.

Divided We Sprawl

A call for the reinvention of the American city and suburb that would exploit the infrastructure of the one and mitigate the "frantic privacy" of the other

By Bruce Katz and Jennifer Bradley

Bruce Katz is a senior fellow at the Brookings Institution and the director of its Center on Urban and Metropolitan Policy. Jennifer Bradley is a senior analyst at the Brookings Institution's Center on Urban and Metropolitan Policy.

BY many accounts Baltimore is a comeback city. It has a beautiful piece of calculated nostalgia in the Camden Yards baseball stadium, which draws tens of thousands of visitors throughout the spring and summer. It has a lively waterfront district, the Inner Harbor, with charming shops and hot snacks for sale every hundred yards or so. But although it may function well as a kind of urban theme park (and there are plenty of cities that would love to achieve that distinction), as a city it is struggling. For twenty years Baltimore has hemorrhaged residents: more than 140,000 have left since 1980. Meanwhile, the surrounding suburbs have steadily grown. The population of Howard County, a thirty-minute drive from the city, has doubled since 1980, from 118,600 to 236,000. The people who have stayed in Baltimore are some of the neediest in the area. The city has 13 percent of Maryland's population but 56 percent of its welfare caseload. Only about a quarter of the students who enroll in a public high school in the city graduate in four years.

And Baltimore is not unique. The image of America's cities has improved greatly over the past few years, thanks to shiny new downtowns dotted with vast convention centers, luxury hotels, and impressive office towers, but these acres of concrete and faux marble hide a reality that is in many cases grim. St. Louis, Cleveland, Philadelphia, and Washington, D.C., lost population throughout the 1990s. These cities are also losing their status as the most powerful economies in their regions. Washington started the 1990s with a respectable 33 percent of the area's jobs. Seven years later it had only 24 percent. The rate of population growth in the nation's suburbs was more than twice that in central cities—9.6 percent versus 4.2 percent—from 1990 to 1997. In just one year—1996—2.7 million people left a central city for a suburb. A paltry 800,000 made the opposite move. In the major urbanized areas of Ohio 90 percent of the new jobs created from 1994 to 1997 were in the suburbs. Ohio's seven largest cities had a net gain of only 19,510 jobs from 1994 to 1997; their suburbs gained 186,000. The 1990s have been the decade of decentralization for people and jobs in the United States.

Not even cities that are growing—southern and western boom cities—are keeping pace with their suburbs. Denver has gained about 31,000 people in the 1990s (after having lost residents during the 1980s), but the counties that make up the Denver metropolitan area have gained 284,000 people—about nine times as many. In Atlanta and Houston central-city growth is far outmatched by growth in outlying counties. And these cities, too, are losing their share of the jobs in their respective regions. In 1980, 40 percent of the jobs in the Atlanta region were in the city itself; by 1996 only 24 percent were.

Meanwhile, the poor have been left behind in the cities. Urban poverty rates are twice as high as suburban poverty rates, and the implementation of welfare reform appears to be a special problem for cities. Although welfare caseloads are shrinking in most cities, in general they are not shrinking as quickly as they are in the states and in the nation as a whole. Often cities have a disproportionate share of their states' welfare recipients. Philadelphia County, for example, is home to 12 percent of all Pennsylvanians but 47 percent of all Pennsylvanians on welfare. Orleans Parish, in which the city of New Orleans is located, has 11 percent of Louisiana's population but 29 percent of its welfare recipients. This hardly adds up to an urban renaissance.

Cities—both the lucky, booming ones and the disfavored, depleted ones—are losing ground for two reasons. First, they push out people who have choices. Urban crime rates have fallen, but they are still generally higher than suburban rates. Some urban school systems are improving, but in most of the nation's twenty biggest urban school districts fewer than half of high school freshmen graduate after four years. City mayors have cut taxes, but urban tax rates (and insurance rates, too) are often higher than suburban ones. Second, suburbs pull people in. This is not a secret. What is less well known—in fact, is just beginning to be understood—is how federal, state, and local policies on spending, taxes, and regulation boost the allure of the suburbs and put the cities at a systematic, relentless disadvantage. People are not exactly duped into living in detached houses amid lush lawns, peaceful streets, and good schools. Still, it is undeniable that government policies make suburbs somewhat more attractive and affordable than they might otherwise be, and make cities less so.

Federal mortgage-interest and property-tax deductions give people a subtle incentive to buy bigger houses on bigger lots, which almost by definition are found in the suburbs. States also spend more money building new roads—which make new housing developments and strip malls not only accessible but financially feasible—than they do repairing existing roads. Environmental regulations make building offices and factories on abandoned urban industrial sites complicated and time-consuming, and thus render untouched suburban land particularly appealing.

The policies that made it easier for people to flee the cities and move to the suburbs are causing problems for suburbanites, too.

Together these policies have set the rules of the development game. They send a clear signal to employers, householders, builders, and political leaders: build out on open, un-urbanized, in some cases untouched land, and bypass older areas. These policies were never imagined as a coherent whole. No individual or committee or agency wrote the rules of development as such. No one stopped to consider how these rules, taken together, would affect the places where people live and work. The rules are simply the implacable results of seemingly disparate policies, each with unintended consequences.

When the policies that made it easier for people to flee the cities and move to the suburbs hurt only urban neighborhoods, the people who chose or had to stay behind suffered. Now, however, these policies, together with the problems of decay and decline in the cities and rapid suburban development, are causing problems for suburbanites, too—most notoriously the problem known as sprawl.

Thus much of the unhappiness of the cities is also the unhappiness of the suburbs. The familiar image of a beleaguered urban core surrounded by suburban prosperity is giving way to something more realistic and powerful: metropolitan areas in which urban and suburban communities lose out as a result of voracious growth in undeveloped areas and slower growth or absolute decline in older places. The idea that cities and suburbs are related, rather than antithetical, and make up a single social and economic reality, is called metropolitanism.

METROPOLITANISM describes not only where but also in some sense how Americans live—and it does this in a way that the city-suburb dichotomy does not. People work in one municipality, live in another, go to church or the doctor's office or the movies in yet another, and all these different places are somehow interdependent. Newspaper city desks have been replaced by the staffs of metro sections. Labor and housing markets are area-wide. Morning traffic reports describe pileups and traffic jams that stretch across a metropolitan area. Opera companies and baseball teams pull people from throughout a region. Air or water pollution affects an entire region, because pollutants, carbon monoxide, and runoff recognize no city or suburban or county boundaries. The way people talk about where they live reflects a subconscious recognition of metropolitan realities. Strangers on airplanes say to each other, "I'm from the Washington [or Houston or Los Angeles or Chicago or Detroit] area." They know that where they live makes sense only in relation to other places nearby, and to the big city in the middle. Metropolitanism is a way of talking and thinking about all these connections.

The aging of the U.S. population will soon make it clear that suburban sprawl is of no benefit to people who cannot drive.

The old city-versus-suburb view is outdated and untenable. We can no longer talk about "the suburbs" as an undifferentiated band of prosperous, safe, and white communities. There are two kinds of suburbs: those that are declining and those that are growing. Declining suburbs, which are usually older and frequently either adjacent to the city or clustered in one unfortunate corner of the metropolitan area, are starting to look more and more like central cities: they have crumbling tax bases, increasing numbers of poor children in their schools, deserted commercial districts, and fewer and fewer jobs. For such suburbs to distance themselves from cities makes about as much sense as two drowning people trying to strangle each other.

Growing suburbs are gaining, sort of. They are choking on development, and in many cases local governments cannot keep providing the services that residents need or demand. Loudoun County, a boom suburb in northern Virginia, epitomizes this kind of place. The county school board predicts that it will have to build twenty-three new schools by 2005 to accommodate new students. In February of this year the board proposed that the next six new schools be basic boxes for learning, with low ceilings, small classrooms, and few windows. "We cannot ask the voters to keep voting for these enormous bonds," a county official told *The Washington Post* earlier this year, referring to a $47.7 million bond issue in 1998 for the construction of three new schools. "Nor can we continue to raise taxes every single year to pay for school construction." Predictably, parents complained about the cutbacks in amenities—after all, they had moved there for the schools. "I just think they have to maintain their standards," a disgruntled parent told *The Washington Post*. But these suburbs cannot maintain their standards. There are simply too many new people who need too much new, expensive infrastructure yesterday—not just schools but also sewer and water lines, libraries, fire stations, and roads.

Whether they moved to these places for rural tranquillity, lovely views, and open space, or for good schools, or for the chance to buy a nice house, or just because they wanted to get away from urban hassles, residents of growing suburbs sense that frantic, unchecked growth is undermining what they value and want to keep. The old paradigm of cities and suburbs as opposites, or partisans in a pitched battle, doesn't explain the relationship between these gaining suburbs and their declining older cousins a few exits back on the highway.

Suburbs are not the enemies of cities, and cities are not the enemies of suburbs. That is the first principle of metropolitanism. Cities and suburbs have a common enemy—namely, sprawl. The cycle described above, of draining the center while flooding the edges, is familiar to almost anyone who has driven from one edge of a metropolitan area to another. It is endlessly repeatable, at least potentially: the center just gets bigger, and the edges move out. Metropolitanism is a way of thinking that might break this cycle.

Alas, the city-suburb dichotomy is alive and well in law and in policy. The result is a tangle of regulations and programs that are excellent at throwing growth out to the edges of metropolitan areas and ineffectual at bringing it back to or sustaining it in the metropolitan core. One reason the problem of growth has not been solved is that the city-versus-suburb analysis doesn't properly describe it. The metropolitan reality requires different kinds of policies—ones that take connections and the varying impact of growth into account.

THE metropolitanist policy agenda has four basic elements: changing the rules of the development game, pooling resources, giving people access to all parts of a metropolitan area, and reforming governance. These are interlocking aspects of how to create good places to live; they are closely related and can be hard to distinguish. To understand the cascade of consequences that policies can have, consider the policy chain reaction that would begin if the rules of the development game were changed to fit the metropolitanist paradigm. Those rules are mainly the policies that guide transportation investments, land use, and governance decisions, all of which are themselves entangled. Start at one end of the knot: transportation. Major highways, built by federal and state dollars, act as magnets for new development. This has been clear ever since the 1950s, when the interstate-highway system made the suburbs widely accessible and hugely popular. A metropolitanist viewpoint recognizes that these highways will probably pull lots of investment and resources away from the metropolitan core. New development, spawned by highways, will necessitate expensive state-funded infrastructure, such as sewer systems, water pipes, and new side roads. Meanwhile, existing roads, pipes, and sewers, which already cost taxpayers plenty of money, are either not used to the fullest or starved of funds for repair.

A metropolitanist transportation pol'stead direct federal transportation dollars to public transit, which draws development toward rail stations rather than smearing it along a highway, or to repairing existing roads rather than building new ones. That is what Governor Parris Glendening, of Maryland, and Governor Christine Todd Whitman, of New Jersey, have proposed for their states, and what elected officials are working on or have accomplished in the metropolitan areas of Boston, Chattanooga, and Portland, Oregon. New businesses and housing developments will be steered toward where people already live and public investments have already been made.

At this point land use comes into play. "Land-use planning" may sound a little soporific, but it is simply a brake on chaos. It allows communities to prepare for growth in a way that avoids gridlock and preserves public resources. It connects the basic places of life: where people work, where they live, where they play, drop off their dry cleaning, check out a library book, buy a box of cereal. A metropolitanist land-use scheme would preserve open spaces and create parks and other public areas, thereby taking big parcels of suburban land off the development market. Where, then, would all the new development go? An enormous amount of vacant land already exists inside the boundaries of metropolitan areas, which generally have developed in leapfrog fashion, with big gaps between one subdivision or strip mall and the next. Parks and open spaces will not fill all those gaps, which could support development—as could the abandoned urban properties known as brownfields.

Land-use decisions can affect how as well as where things are built. Zoning policies can call for transit-oriented development—clusters of shops, apartment buildings, and offices around bus or rail stops, so that people will drive a little less. They can require or at least encourage varied housing near office buildings and supermalls, so that everyone who works there, from the receptionist to the escalator repairer to the middle manager to the chief financial officer, can live near his or her workplace.

Pooling resources is the second element of a metropolitanist agenda. In most metropolitan areas a new office complex or amusement park or shopping mall tends to confer benefits on a single jurisdiction by adding to its property-tax coffers. Meanwhile, neighboring communities are stuck with some of the burdens of development, such as additional traffic and pollution and the loss of open space. Pooling resources—specifically, a portion of the extra tax revenue from development—means that development's benefits, like its burdens, are spread around. The Twin Cities area has a tax-base-sharing scheme whereby 40 percent of the increase in commercial and industrial property-tax revenues since 1971 is pooled and then distributed so that communities without substantial business development are not overwhelmed by needs and starved of resources. In other parts of the country regional jurisdictions have agreed to tax themselves to support cultural and sports facilities; this makes sense, because the entire region benefits from those facilities.

The third element of a metropolitanist agenda is giving everyone in the metropolitan area access to all its opportunities. Access is easy for people with decent incomes and decent cars. They can live where they wish, and they can get from their houses to their jobs without enduring extraordinary hassles. Poor people do not have this kind of mobility.

There are three ways to solve the access problem: make it easier for urban workers to get to suburban jobs; provide affordable housing (through new construction or vouchers) throughout a metropolitan region; or generate jobs in the metropolitan core or at least near public-transportation routes. State and federal governments are now implementing programs that help people to overcome core-to-edge transportation problems, and through housing vouchers are giving low-income people more choices in the metropolitan housing market. Across the country churches and nonprofit organizations are running jitney services and private bus lines to get people to work. A group of Chicago business leaders has called on major employers to weigh affordable-housing options and access to public transit in their business location and expansion decisions. Businesses and nonprofit groups are also trying to bring jobs and people closer together. Housing vouchers administered by nonprofit organizations with a metropolitan scope allow low-income families to move into job-rich municipalities. The nonprofits counsel families about their options and develop relationships with landlords. In the Atlanta region BellSouth will soon consolidate seventy-five dispersed offices, where 13,000 people have worked, into three centers within the Atlanta beltway, all of which are easily accessible by mass transit. After studying where employees lived, the company picked locations that would be of roughly equal convenience for commuters from the fast-growing northern suburbs and from the less-affluent southern suburbs.

Free association is hard to come by in decentralized environments. Sprawl can create a cultural agoraphobia, depleting public life.

The final element of the metropolitanist agenda has to do with governance. Whereas markets and—more important—lives operate in a metropolitan context, our governmental structures clearly do not. They hew to boundaries more suited to an eighteenth-century township than to a twenty-first-century metropolis. Chicago's metropolitan area, for example, encompasses 113 townships and 270 municipalities. This fragmentation works against sustainable metropolitan areas and facilitates segregation by race, class, and ethnicity. Welfare-to-work programs are hindered when public transportation stops at the city-suburban border, for example. Issues that cross jurisdictional borders—transportation, air quality, affordable housing—need cross-jurisdictional solutions and entities that bring together representatives from all the places, small and large, within a metropolitan area to design and implement these solutions. Some such entities already exist: In every urban region in the country a metropolitan planning organization coordinates the local distribution of a chunk of federal transportation funds. Oregon and Minnesota have established metropolitan governments for their largest urban areas, Portland and the Twin Cities. But informal metropolitan governance, in which local governments coordinate their policies and actions, is possible and efficacious. Also, it's necessary.

METROPOLITANISM is a genuinely different view of the American landscape, and politicians from both parties are beginning to think that a majority of voters might find something to like in it. Like Governor Glendening and Governor Whitman, Governor Thomas Ridge, of Pennsylvania, has laid out land-use objectives for his state that include linking new development to existing infrastructure and encouraging metropolitan cooperation. Governor Roy Barnes, of Georgia, has proposed a strong metropolitanist transportation authority for Atlanta, and in March the state legislature approved it. Governors and state legislators are central to the metropolitanist agenda, because states control an important array of tax, land-use, governance, transportation, workforce, and welfare issues.

Vice President Al Gore clearly recognizes the political potential of this issue and is trying to establish it as one of his signature issues. "We're starting to see that the lives of suburbs and cities are not at odds with one another but closely intertwined," he said in a speech last year. "No one in a suburb wants to live on the margins of a dying city. No one in the city wants to be trapped by surrounding rings of parking lots instead of thriving, livable suburban communities. And no one wants to do away with the open spaces and farmland that give food, beauty, and balance to our post-industrial, speeded-up lives." For more than a year Gore has been talking about America's growing "according to its values," and has even implied that development is not always welcome.

Of course, the idea of cities and suburbs coming together to solve common problems has been around for decades. No one ever before thought of using it to propel a presidential campaign, because the idea of metropolitanism had yet to prove its appeal, in referenda or in elections or in state legislatures. This is no longer the case.

These ideas are only just beginning to penetrate a recalcitrant real-estate-

The image of a beleaguered urban core amid suburban prosperity is giving way to something more complex.

development industry, however. Christopher Leinberger is a managing director of one of the nation's largest real-estate advisory and valuation firms and a partner in a new urbanist consulting company. He has thought a lot about how the industry works, and he has concluded that sprawl is extremely attractive to the industry, because the kind of development it involves is simple and standardized—so standardized that it is sometimes hard to tell from the highway whether one is in Minneapolis or Dallas or Charlotte. These cookie-cutter projects are easy to finance, easy to build, and easy to manage. Builders like the predictability of sprawl. They know how much a big parking lot is worth, but they aren't sure how to value amenities in older communities, such as density, walkability, and an interesting streetscape. More or less the same can be said of big retail chains. For example, they often overlook the fact that although people in core neighborhoods may have low incomes, they are densely concentrated, which works out to a significant amount of purchasing power. Developers and retailers will have to be willing to think differently if development is to come back to the core. There are encouraging signs. Magic Johnson Theaters, Rite Aid pharmacies, and Pathmark supermarkets are all recognizing that the people left in core communities need places to earn money and to spend it; each of these companies has opened outlets in central cities in recent years. The National Association of Homebuilders has joined with Gore, the U.S. Conference of Mayors, and the U.S. Department of Housing and Urban Development to encourage the development of a million new owner-occupied homes.

Of course, for the politicians' plans to work and the developers' projects to take off, urban core communities will have to win people over. Unless these places have good schools, safe streets, and efficient governments, people will not move from the edge back toward the center. Some mayors have realized this and are trying to make their cities better places to live. Richard Daley, of Chicago, and Stephen Goldsmith, of Indianapolis, are finding innovative ways to address issues that have bedeviled cities for decades: schools, crime, public services, and taxes. It is hard and often unpleasant work; it means privatizing some services, eliminating others, and ending wasteful patronage. But cities must be ready to take advantage of the opportunities that metropolitanist policies offer them.

ACADEMICS, architects, and bohemians may decry the soullessness of sprawl, but people seem to like it. Why put up such a fight to save dying places, whether they are called cities or older suburbs or metropolitan cores? After all, as people who see no harm in sprawl like to point out, Americans are living on a scant five percent of the land in this country. Why not just keep sprawling?

There are several reasons to defend not cities against suburbs but centeredness against decentralization, metropolitanism against sprawl. One reason to encourage development in metropolitan cores is a familiar one: the people who live there are among the poorest in their regions—indeed, in the country—and they need these opportunities and this investment. It is not fashionable to talk about having a moral obligation to poor people, but that doesn't mean that the obligation has disappeared. John Norquist, the mayor of Milwaukee, is fond of saying "You can't build a city on pity"; but disinvestment and the resulting lack of good schools, good jobs, and good transportation options is also impractical. The U.S. economy needs workers, and there are people in the metropolitan cores who are not getting into the work force. The need for workers will only increase as the average age of the population rises. By 2021 almost 20 percent of the American people will be over sixty-five, as compared with about 12.7 percent today. Whatever Social Security and Medicare reforms are enacted, these elderly people will need an abundance of payroll-tax-paying workers to support them.

The aging of the U.S. population will soon make it clear that sprawl is of no benefit to people who cannot drive. For a seventy-five-year-old without a car, sprawl can be uncomfortably close to house arrest. But metropolitan core communities where public transportation is available and distances are shorter between homes, pharmacies, doctors' offices, and libraries are navigable for older people in a way that settlements on the metropolitan fringe are not. Apartment buildings for the elderly are being built in the suburbs, with a variety of services under one roof, and vans to get people from here to there. But there should be choices for elderly men and women who do not want to be segregated from neighborhoods where babies and teenagers and middle-aged people also live.

Unlimited suburban development does not satisfy everyone. Metropolitanism will probably provide a greater range of choices, for the elderly and for everyone else. Policies that strengthen the metropolitan core lead to safer, more viable urban neighborhoods for people who prize the density and diversity of city life. These policies can reinvigorate older suburbs, with their advantages of sidewalks and public transit and a functioning Main Street. And, of course, they allow for brand-new, sizable single-family houses with yards.

It is also possible to argue against sprawl because of a commitment to community. Throughout this essay we have used the word "community" interchangeably with "township," "suburb," "municipality," "jurisdiction," "city," and "place." But "community" also designates a feeling, an ideal—as in "a sense of community," which many people worry that they have lost and would like to re-create. And they are trying to re-create it. Newspaper dispatches from the suburbs of Detroit and Washington, D.C., report that developers are trying to build what people left behind in older places: town centers, with wide sidewalks and big storefronts, where a person can perhaps run into a friend or an interesting stranger and have a place to hang out in public. In a 1998 essay titled "The City as a Site for Free Association," the political philosopher Alan Ryan writes, "If people are to be self-governing, they must associate with each other in natural and unforced ways from which their political association can spring." By "political association" Ryan means involvement in public life and public decision-making. The underlying assumption of a democracy is that this involvement is a wonderful thing. Yet it is unclear whether the new town centers can generate the unforced interactions that make municipalities feel like communities. For all the good intentions of the developers who build them and the government officials who support them, they are not natural centers. They are places where people are invited to go and be social or civic-minded, but, as Ryan says, "Telling people to go to such and such a café in order to promote political cohesion and political activity is like telling people to be happy; there are many things they can do that will make them happy, but aiming directly at being happy is not one of them."

These town centers are actually some of the few places where suburban people might mingle with crowds and see people who are not like themselves. They are, along with shopping malls, the public spaces of sprawl. Free association, in the sense of unexpected, unplanned encounters that draw us out of ourselves, is hard to come by in decentralized environments. Driving alone or with family members or close friends from one destination to another leaves little opportunity for spontaneity. Sprawl can create a kind of cultural agoraphobia that depletes public life.

Certainly, the outer edges of metropolitan areas are not the only places that are finding public life difficult to sustain. The most depleted neighborhoods of metropolitan cores, with their forlorn "community centers," dingy streets, and empty sidewalks, are not fertile ground for free association either. And yet the architecture and layout of these places are at least supposed to facilitate interaction. Moreover, Ryan writes, there are still "galleries and concert halls, city parks, monuments, and other such places" in our urban cores for

> communities to come together, group by group and interest by interest.... To the degree that this is irreplaceable by seeing and hearing it all on television or on the stereo system, it encourages people to understand themselves as members of one society, engaged in a multitude of competing but also cooperative projects. A society that does not understand this about the basis of its cultural resources is a society in danger of losing them. At present, we seem to be such a society.

Suburbs are not new. They have been in existence in the United States since the nineteenth century. But hypersuburbanization, decentralization, and sprawl are new—less than two generations old. Americans are now discovering how hard it is to live without a center. In a typical attempt to move simultaneously in opposite directions, they are moving out but also trying to come back. This is not merely nostalgia for some dimly remembered era of civility and good cheer. People are honestly trying to balance the frantic privacy of the suburbs with some kind of spontaneous public life. By now it seems clear that continued sprawl will make this public life very hard to achieve—at the edges of metropolitan areas, where there are no places to gather, and at the cores of metropolitan areas, where the gathering places are unsafe or abandoned. Is this really a good trade for a big back yard?

A Politics for Generation X

Today's young adults may be the most politically disengaged in American history. The author explains why, and puts forth a new political agenda that just might galvanize his generation

by Ted Halstead

EVERETT Carll Ladd, a political scientist, once remarked, "Social analysis and commentary has many shortcomings, but few of its chapters are as persistently wrong-headed as those on the generations and generational change. This literature abounds with hyperbole and unsubstantiated leaps from available data." Many of the media's grand pronouncements about America's post–Baby Boom generation—alternatively called Generation X, Baby Busters, and twentysomethings—would seem to illustrate this point.

The 1990s opened with a frenzy of negative stereotyping of the roughly 50 million Americans born from 1965 to 1978: they were slackers, cynics, whiners, drifters, malcontents. A *Washington Post* headline captured the patronizing attitude that Baby Boomers apparently hold toward their successors: "THE BORING TWENTIES: GROW UP, CRYBABIES." Then books and articles began to recast young Americans as ambitious, savvy, independent, pragmatic, and self-sufficient. For instance, *Time* magazine described a 1997 article titled "Great Xpectations" this way: "Slackers? Hardly. The so-called Generation X turns out to be full of go-getters who are just doing it—but their way."

Stereotyping aside, some disquieting facts jump out regarding the political practices and political orientation of young Americans. A wide sampling of surveys indicates that Xers are less politically or civically engaged, exhibit less social trust or confidence in government, have a weaker allegiance to their country or to either political party, and are more materialistic than their predecessors. Why are so many young people opting out of conventional politics, and what does this mean for the future of American democracy? Might it be that today's political establishment is simply not addressing what matters to the nation's young? And if so, what is their political agenda?

THE DISENGAGED GENERATION

ALTHOUGH political and civic engagement began to decrease among those at the tail end of the Baby Boom, Xers appear to have enshrined political apathy as a way of life. In measurements of conventional political participation the youngest voting-age Americans stand out owing to their unprecedented levels of absenteeism. This political disengagement cannot be explained away as merely the habits of youth, because today's young are markedly less engaged than were their counterparts in earlier generations.

Voting rates are arrestingly low among post-Boomers. In the 1994 midterm elections, for instance, fewer than one in five eligible Xers showed up at the polls. As recently as 1972 half those aged eighteen to twenty-four voted; in 1996, a presidential-election year, only 32 percent did. Such anemic participation can be seen in all forms of traditional political activity: Xers are considerably less likely than previous generations of young Americans to call or write elected officials, attend candidates' rallies, or work on political campaigns. What is more, a number of studies reveal that their general knowledge about public affairs is uniquely low.

The most recent birth cohort to reach voting age is also rejecting conventional partisan demarcations: the distinction between Democrats and Republicans, which has defined American politics for more than a century, doesn't resonate much with the young, who tend to see more similarities than differences between the two parties. Even those young adults who are actively engaged in national politics see partisan boundaries

From The Atlantic Monthly, August 1999, pp. 33-42. © 1999 by Ted Halstead. Reprinted by permission.

blurring into irrelevance. Gary Ruskin, an Xer who directs the Congressional Accountability Project, a public-policy group in Washington, D.C., puts it this way: "Republicans and Democrats have become one and the same—they are both corrupt at the core and behave like children who are more interested in fighting with each other than in getting anything accomplished."

Surveys suggest that no more than a third of young adults identify with either political party, and only a quarter vote a straight party ticket. Xers are the group least likely to favor maintaining the current two-party system, and the most likely to favor candidates who are running as independents. Indeed, 44 percent of those aged eighteen to twenty-nine identify themselves as independents. Not surprisingly, young adults gave the strongest support to Ross Perot in 1992 and to Jesse Ventura in 1998.

More fundamental, Xers have internalized core beliefs and characteristics that bode ill for the future of American democracy. This generation is more likely to describe itself as having a negative attitude toward America, and as placing little importance on citizenship and national identity, than its predecessors. And Xers exhibit a more materialistic and individualistic streak than did their parents at a similar age. Moreover, there is a general decline in social trust among the young, whether that is trust in their fellow citizens, in established institutions, or in elected officials. These tendencies are, of course, related: heightened individualism and materialism, as Alexis de Tocqueville pointed out, tend to isolate people from one another, weakening the communal bonds that give meaning and force to notions of national identity and the common good.

EXPLANATION X

MANY explanations have been advanced for the political apathy of Generation X, but none seems to tell the entire story. One theory holds that television, which the average child now watches for forty hours a week, is to blame for the cynicism and lack of civic education among the young. Another is that growing up during the Reagan and Bush presidencies, when government-bashing was the norm, led many Xers to internalize a negative attitude toward politics and the public sector. A third theory blames the breakdown of the traditional family, in which much of a child's civic sensitivity and partisan orientation is said to develop. And, of course, the incessant scandals in contemporary politics deserve some blame for driving young people into political hiding. Each of these theories undoubtedly holds some truth, but a simpler and more straightforward explanation is possible—namely, that young Americans are reacting in a perfectly rational manner to their circumstances, at least as they perceive them.

As they enter adulthood, this explanation goes, Xers are facing a particularly acute economic insecurity, which leads them to turn inward and pursue material well-being above all else. They see the outlines of very real problems ahead—fiscal, social, and environmental. But in the nation's political system they perceive no leadership on the issues that concern them; rather, they see self-serving politicians who continually indenture themselves to the highest bidders. So Xers have decided, for now, to tune out. After all, they ask, what's the point?

To be sure, today's young have a great deal to be thankful for. Xers have been blessed to come of age in a time of peace and relative material prosperity—itself a significant historical aberration. And the positive legacy they are inheriting goes much deeper: Generation X enjoys the fruits of the civil-rights, women's-rights, and environmental-conservation battles waged by its parents. Finally, who could deny that today's young are benefiting from significant leaps in technology, science, and medicine? But for all these new opportunities, the world being passed on to young Americans is also weighed down by truly bedeviling problems. Prevailing ideologies have proved incapable of accommodating this seeming contradiction.

Ever since the pioneering work on generational theory by the German sociologist Karl Mannheim, in the 1920s, political generations have been thought to arise from the critical events that affect young people when they are most malleable. "Early impressions," Mannheim wrote, "tend to coalesce into a *natural view* of the world." At the very heart of the Xer world view is a deep-seated economic insecurity. In contrast to Baby Boomers, most of whom came of age during the period of unparalleled upward mobility that followed the Second World War, Xers grew up in a time of falling wages, shrinking benefits, and growing economic inequality.

Since 1973, while the earnings of older Americans have mostly stagnated, real median weekly earnings for men aged twenty to thirty-four have fallen by almost a third. In fact, Xers may well be the first generation whose lifetime earnings will be less than their parents'. Already they have the weakest middle class of any generation born in this century.

Falling wages and rising inequality have affected all young Americans, regardless of educational achievement. During the said-to-be economically strong years 1989–1995 earnings for recent college graduates fell by nearly 10 percent—representing the first time that a generation of graduates has earned less than the previous one. And circumstances are far worse for the roughly 67 percent of Xers aged twenty-five to thirty-four who don't have a college degree. In 1997 recent male high school graduates earned 28 percent less (in dollars adjusted for inflation) than did the comparable group in 1973, and recent female high school graduates earned 18 percent less. When politicians and the media continually extol the economy's performance, many Xers just scratch their heads in disbelief.

The economic hardship facing today's young cannot be overstated: America's rate of children in poverty—the highest in the developed world—rose by 37 percent from 1970 to 1995. During the same period the old notions of lifetime employment and guaranteed benefits gave way to the new realities of sudden downsizing and contingent, or

37. Politics for Generation X

Xers appear to be calling for a synthesis that unites components thought to be mutually exclusive. Like conservatives, they favor fiscal restraint. Like liberals, they want to help the little guy.

temporary, employment. Forty-four million Americans lack basic health insurance today, and Xers—many of whom are part of the contingent work force—are the least insured of all. To compound these problems, many Xers received a poor education in failing public schools, which left them especially ill-prepared to compete in an ever more demanding marketplace.

A LEGACY OF DEBT

BESIDES struggling against downward economic mobility, Generation X is inheriting a daunting array of fiscal, social, and environmental debts. Although most media reports focus on the national debt and the likely future insolvency of Social Security, the real problem is actually much broader. When they envision their future, Xers don't just see a government drifting toward the political equivalent of Chapter 11; they also see a crippled social structure, a dwindling middle class, and a despoiled natural habitat.

Despite bipartisan fanfare about balancing the federal budget, the fiscal outlook remains quite bleak for young adults—and for reasons seldom discussed. Long before Social Security and Medicare go insolvent under the burden of Boomer retirement, entitlement payments will have crowded out the public investments that are essential to ensuring a promising future. Government spending on infrastructure, education, and research has already lessened over the past twenty-five years, from 24 percent to 14 percent of the federal budget, and the downward squeeze will only worsen. In other words, Xers will be forced to pay ever higher taxes for ever fewer government services.

Financially most frightening, however, are the nation's skyrocketing levels of personal debt and international debt. With all the focus on balancing the federal budget, not enough attention has been paid to the fact that American families, and Xers in particular, are increasingly unable to balance their own books. Xers carry more personal debt than did any other generation at their age in our nation's history; in fact, a full 60 percent of Xers carry credit-card balances from month to month. In addition, those who attend college face the dual burden of soaring tuition bills and shrinking federal education grants. From 1977 to 1997 the median student-loan debt has climbed from $2,000 to $15,000. The combination of lower wages and overleveraged lifestyles is doubly worrisome to a generation that wonders if it will ever collect Social Security.

Then there is America's ballooning international debt. For the past two decades the nation as a whole has consumed more than it has produced, and has borrowed from abroad to cover the difference—nearly $2 trillion by the end of this decade, or more than a fifth of the total annual output of the U.S. economy. In the short life-span to date of most Xers, America has gone from being the world's largest creditor to being its largest debtor. At some point in the future, especially as interest on our international debt accumulates, investors in other countries will become reluctant to keep bankrolling us. When they do, we will have no choice but to tighten our belts by cutting both investment and consumption. In other words, just as Xers start entering their prime earning years, with their own array of debts and demographic adversities awaiting them, they may well find themselves having to pay off the international debt that Boomers accumulated in the 1980s and 1990s.

Despite the penumbra of long-term debt, the U.S. economy remains the envy of the world; U.S. social conditions, however, are certainly not. America has some of the worst rates of child poverty, infant mortality, teen suicide, crime, family breakup, homelessness, and functional illiteracy in the developed world. In addition, many of our inner cities have turned into islands of despair, a frightening number of our public schools are dangerous, and almost two million of our residents are behind bars.

Many Xers sense that the basic fabric of American society is somehow fraying. Traditional civic participation, community cohesion, and civility are in decline, and not just among the young. The long-held belief in the value of hard work is under assault, as many Americans work longer hours for less pay, watch the gap between rich and poor grow ever wider, and see their benefits cut by corporations with little allegiance to people or place. The result is a fundamental loss of trust: between citizens and elected officials, between employees and employers, and, ultimately, between individuals and their neighbors. Yet trust and civility are the pillars on which any well-functioning democracy and free-market economy depend.

Finally, Xers face large environmental debts that stem from the use and abuse of our natural resources. Well over half of the world's major fisheries are severely depleted or overfished; loss of species and habitat continues at an unprecedented rate, with some 50,000 plant and animal species disappearing each year; freshwater tables across the globe, including parts of America, are falling precipitously; each year America alone loses more than a million acres of productive farmland to sprawl; and emissions of carbon dioxide and other greenhouse gases continue to rise, threatening to raise global temperatures by two to six degrees within the next century.

Global warming is a revealing case study from the perspective of Generation X. There is nearly unanimous scientific agreement on the problem, and a consensus among economists that the nation could reduce its greenhouse-gas emissions without harming its economy. In addition, there is ample evidence—ranging from temperature increases to abnormally frequent weather disturbances to icebergs breaking off from the poles—to warrant deep concern. Yet our political establishment has resigned itself to virtual inaction. Why act now, politicians appear to reason, when we can just pass the problem on to our kids?

How, Xers have every right to ask, can one generation justify permanently drawing down the financial, social, and natural capital of another?

But whining will do no good. The only way for Xers to reverse their sad situation—and to realize the promise of the economic opportunities and technological innovations of the next century—is by entering the political arena that they have every reason to loathe. After all, collective problems require collective solutions. Xers cannot reasonably expect the political establishment to address, let alone fix, the sobering problems they are to inherit unless they start participating in the nation's political process, and learn to flex their generational muscle. Whether or not they do so will depend on two more immediate questions: Does this generation share a set of political beliefs? And if so, how might these translate into a political agenda?

"BALANCED-BUDGET POPULISM"

THREE quarters of Generation X agree with the statement "Our generation has an important voice, but no one seems to hear it." Whatever this voice may be, it does not fit comfortably within existing partisan camps. "The old left-right paradigm is not working anymore," according to the novelist Douglas Coupland, who coined the term "Generation X." Neil Howe and William Strauss, who have written extensively on generational issues, have argued in these pages that from the Generation X perspective "America's greatest need these days is to clear out the underbrush of name-calling and ideology so that simple things can work again." If Xers have any ideology, it is surely pragmatism.

In an attempt to be more specific Coupland has claimed, "Coming down the pipe are an extraordinarily large number of fiscal conservatives who are socially left." The underlying assumption here is that the Xer political world view stems simplistically from a combination of the 1960s social revolution and the 1980s economic revolution. This kind of thinking has led some to describe young adults as a generation of libertarians, who basically want government out of their bedrooms and out of their pocketbooks. As it turns out, however, the political views of most Xers are more complex and more interesting than that.

To say that Xers are fiscal conservatives is to miss half the economic story; the other and equally powerful force at play can best be described as economic populism. In fact, the Xer consensus represents a novel hybrid of two distinct currents of economic thought that have rarely combined in the history of American politics. It might well be called "balanced-budget populism."

On the one hand, many Xers are worried about the debts being loaded onto their future, and therefore support fiscal prudence, balanced budgets, and a pay-as-you-go philosophy. On the other hand, Xers are more concerned than other generations about rising income inequality, and are the most likely to support government intervention to reverse it. The majority believe that the state should do more to help Americans get ahead.

What makes the Generation X economic agenda so surprising is that its two main components have thus far proved to be mutually exclusive in contemporary politics. Fiscal conservatism, widely viewed as the economic philosophy of the Republican right, has generally been accompanied by calls for lower taxes, smaller government, and reduced assistance to the neediest. Meanwhile, concern about the distribution of wealth and helping low-income workers, customarily a pillar of the Democratic left, has been associated with notions of tax-and-spend liberalism and big government. Xers appear to be calling for a new economic synthesis. Like conservatives, they favor fiscal restraint—but unlike the conservative leadership in Congress, only 15 percent believe that America should use any budget surplus to cut taxes. Like Democrats, they want to help the little guy—but unlike traditional Democrats, they are unwilling to do it by running deficits.

The Generation X social synthesis is no more conventional. Although the young are presumed to be more tolerant and socially permissive than their elders, today's young are returning to religion, have family-oriented aspirations, and are proving to be unsupportive of some traditional liberal programs, among them affirmative action. There are numerous indications that Xers—many of whom grew up without a formal religion—are actively searching for a moral compass to guide their lives, and a recent poll suggests that the highest priority for the majority of young adults is building a strong and close-knit family.

Wade Clark Roof, a professor of religion and society at the University of California at Santa Barbara, who studies the religious life of Generation X, says, "It is too early to predict whether today's young adults will form lasting commitments to particular religious denominations or institutions, but it is quite clear that there is a renewed level of interest in religion and spirituality among the post–Baby Boom generation. Many, in fact, have embarked upon a spiritual quest." As if they were spiritual consumers, young adults are shopping around among a wide range of religious traditions. In the process they are finding new ways to incorporate religion into their daily lives: for instance, church socials are rapidly becoming the new singles scene for Xers who want to combine their devotional and romantic ambitions. A clear majority of older Americans believe that a more active involvement of religious groups in politics is a bad idea, but Xers are divided on the issue.

This revival of spiritual and family-oriented aspirations represents a partial repudiation of the moral relativism that took hold in the 1960s and has since become a mainstay of American pop culture. In essence, many Xers are struggling to find a new values consensus that lies somewhere between the secular permissiveness of the left and the cultural intolerance of the right.

When it comes to race relations, Xers are particularly difficult to categorize. They are the cohort most likely to say that the civil-rights movement has not gone far enough. Yet, like Americans of all ages, they register a high level of opposition to job- and education-related affirmative-action programs. The American National Election Survey has reported that 68 percent of Xers oppose affirmative action at colleges. This seeming paradox can be explained in part by the fact that most Xers—though genuinely concerned about improving race relations—are among the first to have felt the actual (or perceived) bite of the affirmative-action programs that their parents and grandparents put into place.

Improving public education is one of the highest policy priorities for Xers. In fact, when asked what should be done with any future budget surplus, nearly half favor increased education spending. They seem to understand that knowledge will be the key to success in the information- and service-based economy of the twenty-first century. Their strong emphasis on education betokens a larger belief in the importance of investing in the future. Rather than maintaining the social-welfare state, the Xer philosophy would favor the creation of a social-investment state.

Although Xers have forsaken conventional political participation en masse, it would be a mistake to assume, as many do, that they are wholly apolitical. There is considerable evidence to suggest that volunteerism and unconventional forms of political participation have increased among young adults. Local voluntary activities, demonstrations, and boycotts all seem to be on the rise within their ranks. Heather McLeod, a Generation X co-founder of *Who Cares* magazine, has provided the following explanation: "We can *see* the impact when we volunteer. We know the difference is real." The implication, of course, is that the conventional political system has become so ineffectual and unresponsive that young people can make a positive difference only by circumventing it.

Xers may be poorly informed when it comes to public affairs, but they know enough to believe that our political system is badly in need of reform. At a very basic level they recognize that the political system is rigged against their interests. For one thing, Xers continually see a large gap between the issues they care most about and the ones that politicians choose to address. For another, they understand that Democrats and Republicans, despite an appearance of perpetual partisan infighting, collude to favor upper-income constituencies and to prevent a range of issues (including campaign-finance reform) from being acted on. Seeing themselves as the "fix-it" generation, Xers long for leaders who will talk straight and advocate the shared sacrifices necessary to correct the long-term problems that preoccupy them most. But today's elected officials are far too deeply trapped in a politics of short-term convenience to deliver anything of the sort. Not surprisingly, then, Xers are eager to do away with the two-party system. They register particularly strong support for third parties, for campaign-finance reform, and for various forms of direct democracy.

The final core belief that helps to define the political views of today's young adults is their commitment to environmental conservation. Thanks to the advent of environmental education and the spread of environmental activism, Xers grew up experiencing recycling as second nature; many actually went home and lobbied their parents to get with the program. In fact, the environment is one of the rare public-policy arenas in which Xers are fairly aware. Many have incorporated their environmental values into their lifestyles and career choices. For instance, a 1997 *Harvard Business Review* article titled "Tomorrow's Leaders: The World According to Generation X" revealed that most current MBA students believed that corporations have a clear-cut responsibility to be environment-friendly in their practices. This generation does not believe that a trade-off is necessary between a strong economy and a healthy environment.

Fiscal prudence, economic populism, social investment, campaign reform, shared sacrifice, and environmental conservation—this constellation of beliefs transcends the existing left-right spectrum. It should be immediately apparent that this generation's voice is not represented by any of the established leaders or factions in the political mainstream. And Xers seem to recognize as much— 61 percent agree with the statement "Politicians and political leaders have failed my generation." So how would American politics change if the voice of Generation X were suddenly heard?

A NEW POLITICAL AGENDA

DESPITE its feeble rates of political participation, Generation X has already—if unwittingly—exerted an influence on the substance of our politics. This may seem counterintuitive, but who would deny that young Americans were a major force in pushing the balanced-budget cause to the fore? In part this is owing to the large number of Xer votes cast in 1992 for Ross Perot, the candidate who staked much of his campaign on balancing the federal books. Though Perot lost, his pet issue gained momentum as candidates from both parties scrambled to win over Reform Party voters, and the young ones in particular. Recognizing that Generation X makes up a large and particularly unpredictable voting bloc, candidates from across the spectrum have gone out of their way to woo the youth vote, usually by paying lip service to some of young people's more obvious concerns, including, most recently, Social Security reform. Over time, however, Xer support for issues such as balancing the budget and saving Social Security will turn out to be only part of a much broader agenda, one that could come to challenge the status quo on everything from taxes to social policy to political reform.

For years the nation's tax debate has revolved around the question of how much to tax, with the left arguing for more and the right for less. In keeping with the concept of balanced-budget populism, the Xer economic agenda would start with the assumption that the government's share of national income should remain roughly constant. It would focus instead on a far more profound set of questions: What should be taxed? Who should be taxed? What should we invest in? and Who should get the benefits? Over the past several decades the tax burden has crept further and further down the income and age ladder, with the benefits going increasingly to the elderly and the well-to-do—the government now spends nine times as much on each elderly person as it does on each child. If Xers had their way, the collection of taxes would become more progressive and the distribution of benefits more widespread.

One would never know it from partisan skirmishes over income-tax cuts, but the payroll tax actually constitutes the largest tax burden borne by 70 percent of working families and by a full 90 percent of working Americans under age thirty. It is also the most regressive of all taxes, because it kicks in from the first dollar earned, falls exclusively on wages, and is capped at $72,600. An appealing solution to this problem would be to replace payroll taxes with pollution taxes, thereby boosting wages, promoting jobs, and cleaning up the environment, all without raising the deficit. Taxing waste instead of work is precisely the kind of innovative and pragmatic proposal that could help to galvanize the members of Generation X, who have been put to sleep by the current tax debate.

Sooner or later Xers will figure out that America could raise trillions of dollars in new public revenues by charging fair market value for the use of common assets—the oil and coal in the ground, the trees in our national forests, the airwaves and the electromagnetic spectrum—and the rights to pollute our air. We currently subsidize the use of these resources in a number of ways, creating a huge windfall for a small number of industries and a significant loss for all other Americans. The idea of reversing this trend by charging fair market value for the use of common assets and returning the proceeds directly to each American citizen plays to a number of Xer political views—it is populist, equitable, libertarian, and pro-environment all at once.

The populist economic leanings of young adults will also lead them to rethink various other elements of the social contract between citizens, government, and business. For one thing, ending corporate welfare would appeal to a generation weaned on the principle of self-sufficiency. The hidden welfare state, composed of corporate subsidies and tax loopholes that overwhelmingly benefit the well-to-do, has grown several times as large as the hotly debated social-welfare state that benefits the disadvantaged through means-tested programs. Yet today's politicians are too much indebted to the beneficiaries of this governmental largesse to do anything about it. Here, then, may be the key to keeping the budget balanced while funding the social investments that are so important to Xers: all of the money raised or saved by charging for the use of common assets, ending corporate welfare, and closing unproductive tax loopholes could be used to make a topnotch education affordable and accessible to all and, just as important, to make every American child a "trust-fund" baby from birth.

Making economic incentives more progressive and redirecting budgetary priorities is only one part of an Xer economic agenda. Today's young adults, more than any other group at a comparable age, are concerned about their economic outlook and their ability to balance the conflicting demands of work and family. If such problems worsen as a result of economic globalization, then the populism of Generation X, which up to this point has been relatively mild, may suddenly become more pronounced. For instance, the 2030 Center, an advocacy group concerned about the economic well-being of Generation X, is launching a campaign to promote a contingent workers' bill of rights, which calls on employers to provide health care and other benefits to more of their workers.

Even as they were being told that education is the key to a promising future, many Xers were learning the hard way how bad our urban schools have become, and how inequitable is the access to a high-quality education. Neither party is providing a palatable solution: Republicans are all but writing off public schools by emphasizing vouchers that favor private schools, and Democrats are perpetuating many of the worst public-school problems by refusing to challenge the teachers' unions. There are no simple solutions to the predicament, but an obvious starting point would be to sever the traditional link between public-school funding and local property taxes, which only exacerbates existing socioeconomic inequalities. (Several states have already begun moving in this direction.) Another significant improvement would be to increase the skill level of our public-school teachers by imposing stricter standards and offering more-competitive salaries.

Xers would support enacting new policies to advance racial integration

> *Balanced-budget populism, social investment, and other elements of the Xer agenda could resonate with Americans of all ages—and help to create the nation's next majoritarian coalition.*

and civil rights in America—policies that avoid the divisiveness and unintended consequences of race-based affirmative action. Although such policies made sense when they were introduced, many Xers believe, race is no longer the determining factor in who gets ahead. In the twenty-first century poor black Americans will have more in common with poor white Americans than they will with upper-middle-class blacks. If the goal is to help those most in need, it would make a lot more sense to pursue class-based affirmative-action programs. Doing so would enable all those at the bottom—regardless of race—to get the help they need, in a way that promoted national unity and racial integration. Another promising alternative to race-based affirmative action is the Texas Ten Percent Plan, whereby all students graduating in the top tenth of their high school classes—whether in inner-city schools or in elite private ones—are automatically accepted into the state's public universities.

Fundamental campaign and political reform is the sine qua non of a Generation X political agenda. Like most Americans, Xers would like to see bold steps taken to get money out of politics. But persuading America's young that their individual votes matter is likely to require reforms far more radical than any currently under consideration.

Until recently most political-reform movements in the United States were based on the assumption that the problem was not the two-party system itself but rather its corruption by special interests and incumbency (hence the proposed cures of campaign-finance reform and term limits). But neither the reduction of private campaign contributions nor the implementation of term limits for elected officials will alter what seems to alienate Xers most of all: the political duopoly of Democrats and Republicans. The rules of today's two-party system actively discourage a third or a fourth party. Consequently, there is growing interest among the young in replacing our archaic electoral process (itself a remnant from eighteenth-century England) with a modern multiparty system. With three or four parties contesting many races, politics might become exciting enough to draw in disenchanted Xers who believe, correctly, that in most elections today their votes do not count.

As the vanguard of the digital age, Xers will also be inclined to support experiments with electronic democracy. For instance, one Xer has launched an effort to make information about the sources of campaign contributions immediately available to the public and the media over the Internet. But the full potential of digital democracy runs much deeper. Already groups are experimenting with electronic town-hall meetings and various forms of deliberative democracy, in which individuals are provided with a full range of information on a particular issue and can register their opinions with the push of a button. It is not hard to imagine a day when citizens will be able to register and vote online, and to monitor the performance of their elected officials with electronic scorecards.

The introduction of electronic communication within corporate America has helped to flatten organizational hierarchies, boost information flows, increase decision-making speed, and, most of all, empower workers. It is at least conceivable that the introduction of electronic forms of democracy could serve to re-engage a generation that has been alienated by today's money-, spin-, and celebrity-dominated politics. And if Xers do eventually enter the fray, their agenda will transform America's political landscape.

THE FUTURE OF AMERICAN POLITICS

REPUBLICANS and Democrats will be tempted to dismiss the Xer agenda, because it threatens their electoral coalitions and the politics of short-term convenience. But both parties will do so at their peril, because many of the issues that Xers care most about are already rising to the political surface.

A glimpse of the future may come, strangely enough, in the election of Jesse Ventura as governor of Minnesota. Much of Ventura's support came from young adults, who took advantage of Minnesota's same-day registration law and stormed the polls, helping to create a record turnout. This suggests that if a political candidate can somehow capture the passion of young adults, they will do their part. Ventura offered young Minnesotans something refreshing: a clear alternative to Democrats and Republicans, and a willingness to take on the status quo. But Jesse Ventura is no figurehead for Xers; he is just an early beneficiary of their pent-up political frustration.

As the Xer political agenda starts to take hold, it will further strain existing loyalties. On the Republican side, the odd-bedfellow coalition of social conservatives and economic libertarians that has defined the party for the past two decades is coming apart as a result of the Clinton impeachment saga, whose most lasting legacy may be that it dealt a coup de grace to the political aspirations of the religious right. The Democratic coalition is just as fragile, particularly since it has been losing its base of working-class white men, and the potential retreat of the religious right may deprive Democrats of an obvious opponent against which to rally. As these de-alignments unfold, major shifts in the makeup and core agendas of both parties become almost inevitable.

The stability of today's political consensus is also contingent on the promise of an economy that continues to expand. Take that away, and the props of the status quo—a balanced budget and the novelty of a budgetary surplus, a booming stock market and stable price structures, low unemployment and rising wages, falling welfare rolls and crime rates, and the illusion of a painless fix to Social Security—all topple at once. No business cycle lasts forever, and the global economic crisis of 1998 should come as a warning of what may lie ahead. The prospect of a significant recession leaves the future of American politics wide open.

Turning points in our nation's political history, occasioned by the collapse of an existing civic and political consensus, have usually been accompanied by rampant individualism, weakened institutions, and heightened levels of political alienation. On these scores Xers are playing out their historic role remarkably well. But such periods of civic unrest have also stimulated new political agendas, which eventually force one or both parties to remake themselves around new priorities and coalitions. Could the Generation X political agenda serve as the basis of America's next political consensus?

Balanced-budget populism, social investment, no-nonsense pragmatism, and shared sacrifice could resonate quite strongly with Americans of all ages—particularly the increasing number who are fed up with conventional politics. What is more, the Xer synthesis of a middle-class economic agenda with a moderate social one could remake the powerful alliance between progressives and populists that dominated national politics (and brought widespread upward mobility) from the 1930s to 1960s, when it was ripped apart by the cultural upheaval of the Baby Boom. In practical terms this new politics—based on fiscal prudence, economic populism, family-friendly morality, social investment, campaign reform, environmental conservation, and technological innovation—could eventually take hold in either of the major parties, both of which are now searching for a coherent agenda and a lasting voter base. For Democrats it could mark a return to the party's New Deal roots, and for Republicans it could give substance to heretofore vague calls for a "compassionate conservatism."

Since this new politics could speak to many of those who are alienated by the current political order, Xers and older Americans alike, it could give birth to our nation's next majoritarian coalition. Such a coalition could do a great deal to reinvigorate our nation's democracy, benefit the majority of its citizens, and restore legitimacy to our political system.

When history books are written at the end of the twenty-first century, it is unlikely that the post–Baby Boom generation will still be referred to as a nondescript "X." One way or another, this generation will be judged and labeled by its legacy. Today's young adults will be remembered either as a late-blooming generation that ultimately helped to revive American democracy by coalescing around a bold new political program and bringing the rest of the nation along with them, or as another silent generation that stood by as our democracy and society suffered a slow decline.

The great question of twenty-first-century politics is whether a critical mass of Xers will eventually recognize the broader potential of their agenda, and outgrow their aversion to politics.

Ted Halstead is the president of the New America Foundation, in Washington, D.C.

Index

A

abduction, of Aimee Semple McPherson, 108–113
access, to all opportunities, for metropolitan area, 198
Affluent Society, The (Galbraith), 172
African American regulars, 21–26
African Methodist Episcopal (AME) Church, 83, 84
Aguinaldo y Famy, Don Emilio, 70, 72, 73, 74
Amalgamated Association of Iron and Steel Workers (ASISW), 57, 58, 59, 60, 62
Ambrose, Stephen E., 16, 136–140
American Century 1900–1910, 77–79
American politics, future of, 207–208
American Railway Union, 65
anti-imperialists, 71, 75
Apache Indians, 23, 24, 25
Ardennes forest, Belgium, 127–135
Army, African Americans and, 21–26
Army-McCarthy hearings, 164–166
Asian War, 69–76
atomic bomb, 141–145, 186
authoritarianism, 185

B

balanced-budget populism, 204–205, 208
baseball, integration of, 153–160
"Battle Cry of Freedom," 67
Battle of the Bulge, 127–135, 137
Bean, Judge Roy, 50–56
Belgium, 127–135
Big Four, 33, 34
Big Three, 143
birth control: legalization of, 97–98; racism and, 98
Birth of a Nation, 8
Black Georgia in the Progressive Era, 1900–1920 (Dittmer), 83
"Black Power," 167, 168
blacks, 14; American society and, 8; Army and, 21–26, 44; equal citizenship for, 9; organizations, 11; progressive movement and, 82–85; suffrage and, 9, 11; supremacy, 8, 10, women, 86
"Bolo War," 69
Bowers, Claude G., 8, 9, 11
Bradley, Omar, 129, 130
Brandeis, Louis D., 94, 95
Brooklyn Dodgers, 153–160
Brown v. Board of Education, 83
Bryan, William Jennings, 63, 65, 66, 67, 68, 71, 91, 94
buffalo soldiers, 21–26, 44
Bureau of Labor Statistics, 194
Bush, George, 92, 190, 202

C

campaign trail, of Harry Truman, 150
Carlisle Indian Industrial School, 42–49
Carnegie, Andrew, 57, 58, 59, 61, 71
Carnegie Steel Company, 57–62
Carpenter, Louis H., 21
carpetbaggers, 8, 10
Cheyenne Indians, 16, 17, 18, 19
child labor, 86; abolition of, 123
China, 181; feelings against, 33–34
Churchill, Winston, 179, 180
cities, American, 195–200
civil rights, 122; movement, 167–170; Reconstruction and, 13
Civil Rights Act of 1964, 177
Civil War, 8, 63
Clean Air Act, 172, 175, 176
Clean Water Act, 172, 175
Cleveland, Grover, 64, 71
Clinton, Bill, 26, 171, 190, 193, 194
Coal & Iron Police, 28, 29, 31
Cohn, Roy M., 164, 165, 166
cold war, 92, 183–187
Confederacy, defeat of, 8
Constitution, of 1879, 34
Consumer Federation of America, 171
contraception, Margaret Sanger and, 97
corruption: in New York, 14; during Reconstruction, 8
cotton, 12; production of, 11
Crazy Horse, 15–20
Credit Mobilier scandal, 10
Crocker, Charles, 33, 34
Crook, George, 16, 17, 18, 19, 20
cross-cultural comparisons, of academic achievement, 191, 192
Crusade in Europe (Eisenhower), 143
Custer, Elizabeth, 22
Custer, George Armstrong, 15–20, 21–22

D

Dallek, Robert, 91–96
de Antonio, Emile, 164–166
de Gaulle, Charles, 179, 180
Debs, Eugene V., 65, 94
debt, 203–204
Democratic Party, 63, 64, 65, 66, 68, 91, 169; ascendancy of, 10
Depression, 64, 65, 116–118
Dewey, George, 69, 71, 72
Dewey, Thomas E., 148, 149, 150, 151
Doherty, Thomas, 164–166
"do-nothing" Republican Congress, 149
Dormer, "Big Pat," 28
Du Bois, W. E. B., 9, 14, 83, 84–85

E

East-West conflict, 183–187
economic rebuilding, Reconstruction and, 13
education, 190–194; modern approach to, for Native Americans, 48; Reconstruction and, 13
Eisenhower Center, memoirs of veterans in, 138
Eisenhower, Dwight D., 129, 130, 143, 149, 184
elitism, 92
Environmental Protection Agency, 175, 181
Equal Rights Amendment, 175
espionage, 187
Exclusion Act of 1882, 34
experimental debt, 203

F

Fair Labor Standards Act of 1938, 87
family life, autonomy of, 11
Federal Reserve Act, 95
female progressive activism, 86
Fifteenth Amendment, 9, 10, 82
Filene, Edward, 173
Finn, Chester, 192, 193
first lady, Eleanor Roosevelt as America's most influential, 122–123
fiscal debt, 203
Ford, Henry, 175
foreign wars, 124–126
Foursquare Gospel, 110
Fourteen Points, 96
Fourteenth Amendment, 9, 10
Franklin, Mollie Parker, 84
free silver, 65, 67, 68
Free Speech Movement, 173
Freedman's Bureau, 10
freedmen, 8, 13; autonomy of family life and, 11; political power of, 10; Reconstruction and, 10; white-controlled churches and, 11
Freedom Ride, 167, 168
Frick, Henry Clay, 58, 59, 60
fugitives, Molly Maquire, 31

G

Gallup, George, 149, 151, 152
General Federation of Women's Clubs (GFWC), 86, 87
Generation X, politics for, 201–208
Georgia Peace Society, 125–126
Geronimo Campaign of 1885–1886, 26
Gingrich, Newt, 171, 191
Goals 2000, 190, 194
Gone with the Wind, 8
Gorbachev, Mikhail, 183
Gore, Al, 177, 198, 199
Gowen, Franklin Benjamin, 29, 20, 32
Grant, Ulysses S., 44
Great Cultural Revolution, 184
Greene, James K., 13
guerrilla warfare, 72–74

H

Harding, Florence, 104–107
Harding, Warren, 104–107
Hearst, William Randolph, 70
Hemingway, Ernest, 137
Hitler, Adolf, 128, 129, 131, 134, 135
Homestead strike of 1892, 64
Hope, Lugenia Burns, 84, 89
Hiroshima, bombing of, 141, 143, 145
Humphrey, Hubert, 149

I

"I Have a Dream" (King), 167
idealism, 92
idealists, 9

imperialists, 71
industrial democracy, 173
industrializing economy, 12
international communism, 186
Irish, in northern cities, 14

J

Jacobins, 8
Japanese cities, atomic bomb in, 141–145
Jefferson, Thomas, 68
"Jim Crow" laws, 154, 156, 157
Johnson, Andrew, 8,9
Johnson, Lyndon Baines, 91–96
Judge Roy Bean Country (Skiles), 55
Justice Department, 105, 106, 107
Justice of the Peace of Precinct No. 6, 52

K

Kehoe, John Jack, 28, 29, 31, 32
Kerrigan, James "Powder Keg," 29, 32
Kettler, Robert, 140
King, Martin Luther, 167–170, 171
Kohl, David R., 69–76
Ku Klux Klan, 10, 103

L

labour-capital relations, 64
Lady Windermere's Fan (Wilde), 54
laissez-faire, 11, 64
land-use scheme, 197, 198
law, Judge Roy Bean and, 51, 53, 55
League of Nations, 91, 95–96
Lend-Lease aid, 120, 126
"Letter from Birmingham Jail" (King), 168, 169
Life for World Peace, A (Nordholt), 91
Lincoln, Abraham, 8, 9; America of, 12
Ling, Peter, 167–170
Little Big Man (Berger), 20
Little Bighorn, 15–20; Battle of, 18–19
Lochner decision, 87
Lodge, Henry Cabot, 71
Ludlow Amendment, 125

M

MacArthur, Arthur, 75
MAGIC intercepts, 143, 144
Malcolm X, 168
Malmedy Massacre, 130
March on Washington movement, 169
Marshall Plan, 185
Marxist International Association of Workingmen, 34
Mather, Sarah, 42, 45
McCarthy, Joseph, 164–166
McCarthyism, 164
McClellan, George B., 29–30
McKenna, James, 27, 28, 29, 31
McKinley, William, 63, 65, 66, 67, 68, 69, 71
McLuckie, John, 59, 60, 61, 62
McPherson, Aimee Semple, 108–113
Means, Gaston, 106, 107

Merritt, Wesley, 69, 72
metropolitanism, 196–199
minimum wage, establishment of, 123
mining, 12
Molly Maguires, 27–32, 59
monetarization, of silver, 65
monopolizing credit, 11
Montgomery Bus Boycott, 167, 169
Morrow, Albert B., 24, 25
Moynihan, Daniel Patrick, 180, 181
Muller v. Oregon, 87

N

Nagasaki, bombing of, 141
National Association for the Advancement of Colored People, 83, 86
National Baseball Hall of Fame, 160
National Child Labor Committee, 86
National Consumers League (NCL), 86, 87, 125
National Detective Agency. *See* Pinkerton's National Detective Force
National Organization for Women, 171, 172, 175
Negro League, 153, 155, 156
Negro Wall Street, 99, 100, 101
Nevedon-Morton, Cynthia, 84
New Deal, 88, 172; programs, 123
New Freedom, 94, 95
New Left activists, 169, 171, 173, 174, 175
new synthesis, emergence of, 82–85
Nineteenth Amendment, 89
Nixon, Richard, 178–182, 184
noble experiment, to integrate major-league baseball, 153–160
North Atlantic Treaty Organization, 185, 186
Northern capitalists, 8, 9

O

Occupational Safety and Health Administration, 181
O'Donnell, Hugh, 57, 61
Office of Strategic Services (OSS), 144
"Old Line" Whig Unionists, 10
Origins of the New South, 1877–1913 (Woodward), 82
Other America, The (Harrington), 172
Oxford, Edward, 127–135

P

pacifism, 125
Parks, Rosa, 171
Parrish, Mary E. Jones, 101–102
Payne, Charles, 167
peace feelers, 143, 144
Pennsylvania: Carlisle Indian Industrial School in, 42–49; violent crimes in, 27–32
People's Party, 65
Philippine Insurrection, 69
Philippine-American War of 1892–1902, 69–76
Pinkerton, Allan, 29, 30, 31

Pinkerton's National Detective Force, 29, 30, 57–62
Planned Parenthood Federation of America, 97
"Plenty Kill," 42, 48
Plessy v. Ferguson, 82, 154
political agenda, 205–207
Pollock v. Farmers' Loan and Trust Company, 65
pooling resources, 197–198
Poor People's Campaign, 169
populist economic leanings, of young adults, 206
Populist Party, 65, 66
Potter, John, 58
Powell, Colin, 26
Pratt, Richard Henry, 42–49
presidential election: of 1896, 63–68; of 1948, 148–152
Progressive Era, 82–85, 86–90
Progressive Party, 148, 149
protective labor legislation, campaign for, 87
Pulitzer, Joseph, 70
Pullman, George M., 65

Q

"quota sampling," 149

R

race war, in Tulsa, Oklahoma, 99
racial domination, 13
racism, 71
Radical Reconstruction, 10, 11; corruption in, 13; ouster of planter class and, 13; uniqueness to United States, 113. *See also* Reconstruction
Radical Republicans, 8, 9
Radicals, 8, 12; in Congress, 9
rail workers strike, 34
railroad, national network, 12
Randolph, A. Philip, 168, 169
Rankin, Jeannette, 124–126
Ransom, Reverdy, 83
Ravitch, Diane, 192
Reagan, Ronald, 202
reconcentrado camps, 71
Reconstruction, 8–14, 63. *See also* Radical Reconstruction
revisionists, 10, 11, 12
Red Cloud, 15
"Red Scare," 164–166
Redlich, Norman, 138
reformist organizations, 122–123
Reich, Charles, 176
"reign of terror," 27
religious fundamentalism, 110
Reno, Marcus, 18, 19
Republican Party, 63, 64, 65, 96
retail complacency, 193
"revolutionary politics," 174
Rickey, Branch, 153–160
riot commission resolution, 100
riots, in Tulsa, Oklahoma, 99–103
Robinson, Jackie, 153–160
Robinson, Rachel, 157

Roosevelt, Eleanor, 122–123
Roosevelt, Franklin Delano, 91–96, 119–121, 126, 148
Roosevelt, Theodore, 71, 77, 78, 91, 94
Ross, Don, 100, 102, 013
Rushkin, Gary, 202
Ryan, Alan, 200

S

Salinger, J. D., 162
Sandia National Laboratories, 190, 191
Sanger, Margaret, 97–98
SAT scores, 190, 191
scalawags, 8, 10
scandal, in the oval office, 104–107
Schaufele, William, 136–137
school systems, 190–194
Schurz, Carl, 46
Schuylkill County, Pennsylvania, coal mining in, 27
Scott, Anne Firor, 84
Scott, Thomas, 61
"search and destroy" missions, 75
Second Seminole War, 75
secret society, Molly Maguires as, 27–32
Selling of the President, The (McGinniss), 180
Seventh Day Adventists, 174
Shanker, Albert, 191, 193
Shapp, Milton J., 30, 32
Sheppard-Towner Maternity and Infancy Act, 88
Sherman Silver Purchase Act of 1890, 65
Siegfried Line, 127
Simpson, Theodore O., 133
Sioux Indians, 15, 16, 17, 18, 19, 26
Sitting Bull, 15, 16, 19
Sixties, 171–177; conflicts of, 171
Skiles, Jack, 53, 55
Sklar, Martin J., 173
slavery, abolition of, 121
"silent majority," 181, 184
Silent Spring (Carson), 172
Smith, Jess, 105, 160, 107
Snowden, George R., 60
Social Christianity, 83
social debt, 203
"social history," 11
Social Security Act in 1935, 88
Son of the Morning Star (Connell), 16, 17
South Carolina, 13; black majority in state legislature, 10; black office holders in, 12; Negro rule, in, 14
South, economy in, 9
Southern Christian Leadership Conference (SCLC), 168, 169, 170
Southern states, readmission of, to the Union, 8
Soviet atomic bomb, 186
Spanish-American War, 70, 71

Spotted Tail, 15
sprawl, urban, 195–200
SS Panzer Armies, 129, 130
Stalin, Joseph, 143, 185
Starr, Ellen Gates, 88
steel industry, 12
Stevens, Thaddeus, 9
Stevenson, Harold W., 191
"strategic hamlets," 75
Student Nonviolent Coordinating Committee (SNCC), 167, 168
suburbs, 195–200
suffrage, universal, 13–14
Sumner, Charles, 9, 37

T

Taft, William Howard, 75, 88, 84
Tammany Hall Democrats, 119
Tariff Act of 1894, 65
tariff, 64, 65, 66, 94
taxes, 13
Teapot Dome, 104, 105, 106
television, 164–166
Teller, Henry Moore, 65, 66
tenant farms, 11
tent revivalism, 110
Terrell, Mary Church, 84
Terry, Alfred, 16, 20
Texas Ten Percent Plan, 207
Third International Mathematics and Science Study, 191
"Thousand-Year" Third Reich, 128
Thurmond, Strom, 148, 149, 151
Tocqueville, Alexis de, 14
Toland, John, 135
"total immersion philosophy, for civilizing Indians," 48
totalitarianism, 154
trade unions, as beneficial to labor and capital, 58
Truman, Harry S., 91, 141, 143, 148–152, 185
Tulsa, Oklahoma, 99–103
Turner, Elizabeth Hayes, 84
Twain, Mark, 71

U

ULTRA intercept, 144, 145
Underwood, Oscar W., 94
Underwood Tariff, 95
unionization, 87
United Mine Workers of America, 32
United States Army: lawsuit against, 164–166; in World War II, 127–135
United States Department of Labor, 88
Unk, Arthur S., 93

V

Versailles Treaty, 95–96
Veterans Bureau, 105, 106, 107
veterans, war stories, 136–140

Victorio, chief of Warm Springs Apaches, 24, 25, 26
Viele, Charles, 25, 26
Vietnam syndrome, 171
violent crimes, 27–32
Voorhis, Jerry, 179
Voting Rights Act of 1965, 89, 167, 168, 169, 177

W

Wallace, Henry, 148, 152
War on Poverty, initiation of, 171
Waring, Mary, 84
Warsaw Pact, 186
Washington, Booker T., 83
Watergate burglary, 181
Watts riot, 173, 174
Weinstein, Edwin A., 96
Wells-Barnett, Ida, 84, 89
Wensyel, James W., 69–76
Wheaton, Lloyd, 75
Wheeler, Ed, 103
Whiskey Ring, 10
"white" education, 42
white Republicanism, in Tennessee and North Carolina, 10
white supremacy, 8
White, William Allen, 126
Wickham, J. T., 73
Wiggans Patch incident, 31
Wilde, Oscar, 54
Wilson, Woodrow, 91–96
Woman of Valor: Margaret Sanger and the Birth Control Movement in America (Chesler), 98
women: liberation of, 97–98; progressivism and, 86–90; reformers, 84; right to vote and, 125
Women's International League for Peace and Freedom, 125
women's movement, 122
Woodward, C. Vann, 82
Woolworth: Corporation, 35; Frank Winfield, 35–39
Workingmen's Benevolent Association, 27
Workingmen's Party of California (WPC), 34
World War II, 91; European theater of, 136–140
Wright, Henry, 23, 24

X

xenophobia, 33

Y

Yankelovich, Daniel, 176
Yost, Benjamin, 28, 29

Z

Zedong, Mao, 184, 185, 186

Test Your Knowledge Form

We encourage you to photocopy and use this page as a tool to assess how the articles in **Annual Editions** expand on the information in your textbook. By reflecting on the articles you will gain enhanced text information. You can also access this useful form on a product's book support Web site at **http://www.dushkin.com/online/.**

NAME: DATE:

TITLE AND NUMBER OF ARTICLE:

BRIEFLY STATE THE MAIN IDEA OF THIS ARTICLE:

LIST THREE IMPORTANT FACTS THAT THE AUTHOR USES TO SUPPORT THE MAIN IDEA:

WHAT INFORMATION OR IDEAS DISCUSSED IN THIS ARTICLE ARE ALSO DISCUSSED IN YOUR TEXTBOOK OR OTHER READINGS THAT YOU HAVE DONE? LIST THE TEXTBOOK CHAPTERS AND PAGE NUMBERS:

LIST ANY EXAMPLES OF BIAS OR FAULTY REASONING THAT YOU FOUND IN THE ARTICLE:

LIST ANY NEW TERMS/CONCEPTS THAT WERE DISCUSSED IN THE ARTICLE, AND WRITE A SHORT DEFINITION:

ANNUAL EDITIONS revisions depend on two major opinion sources: one is our Advisory Board, listed in the front of this volume, which works with us in scanning the thousands of articles published in the public press each year; the other is you—the person actually using the book. Please help us and the users of the next edition by completing the prepaid article rating form on this page and returning it to us. Thank you for your help!

ANNUAL EDITIONS: American History, Volume II, 16th Edition

ARTICLE RATING FORM

Here is an opportunity for you to have direct input into the next revision of this volume. We would like you to rate each of the 37 articles listed below, using the following scale:

1. **Excellent: should definitely be retained**
2. **Above average: should probably be retained**
3. **Below average: should probably be deleted**
4. **Poor: should definitely be deleted**

Your ratings will play a vital part in the next revision. So please mail this prepaid form to us just as soon as you complete it. Thanks for your help!

We Want Your Advice

RATING	ARTICLE
	1. The New View of Reconstruction
	2. A Road They Did Not Know
	3. Buffalo Soldiers
	4. Undermining the Molly Maguires
	5. 'The Chinese Must Go'
	6. The Nickel & Dime Empire
	7. Captain Pratt's School
	8. "Hang 'em First, Try 'em Later"
	9. "If You Men Don't Withdraw, We Will Mow Every One of You Down"
	10. Electing the President, 1896
	11. Our First Southeast Asian War
	12. The American Century, 1900–1910: How It Felt When Everything Seemed Possible
	13. Blacks and the Progressive Movement: Emergence of a New Synthesis
	14. The Ambiguous Legacies of Women's Progressivism
	15. Woodrow Wilson, Politician
	16. Margaret Sanger
	17. Unearthing a Riot
	18. Scandal in the Oval Office

RATING	ARTICLE
	19. The Abduction of Aimee
	20. 'Brother, Can You Spare a Dime?'
	21. A Monumental Man
	22. Eleanor Roosevelt
	23. The Lone Dissenting Voice
	24. Our Greatest Land Battle
	25. "I Learn a Lot from the Veterans"
	26. The Biggest Decision: Why We Had to Drop the Atomic Bomb
	27. 1948: The Presidential Election
	28. Baseball's *Noble* Experiment
	29. The Split-Level Years, 1950–1960: Elvis, Howdy Doody Time, McDonald's and the Rumblings of Rebellion
	30. Point of Order!
	31. Martin Luther King's Half-Forgotten Dream
	32. The Spirit of '68
	33. Nixon's America
	34. Face-Off
	35. The Near-Myth of Our Failing Schools
	36. Divided We Sprawl
	37. A Politics for Generation X

(Continued on next page)

ANNUAL EDITIONS: AMERICAN HISTORY, Volume II, 16th Edition

NO POSTAGE
NECESSARY
IF MAILED
IN THE
UNITED STATES

BUSINESS REPLY MAIL
FIRST-CLASS MAIL PERMIT NO. 84 GUILFORD CT

POSTAGE WILL BE PAID BY ADDRESSEE

**McGraw-Hill/Dushkin
530 Old Whitfield Street
Guilford, CT 06437-9989**

ABOUT YOU

Name _____ Date _____

Are you a teacher? ☐   A student? ☐
Your school's name _____

Department _____

Address _____ City _____ State ____ Zip ____

School telephone # _____

YOUR COMMENTS ARE IMPORTANT TO US!

Please fill in the following information:
For which course did you use this book?
_____

Did you use a text with this *ANNUAL EDITION*? ☐ yes ☐ no
What was the title of the text?
_____

What are your general reactions to the *Annual Editions* concept?
_____

Have you read any particular articles recently that you think should be included in the next edition?
_____

Are there any articles you feel should be replaced in the next edition? Why?
_____

Are there any World Wide Web sites you feel should be included in the next edition? Please annotate.
_____

May we contact you for editorial input? ☐ yes ☐ no
May we quote your comments? ☐ yes ☐ no